ART AND AGENCY

ART AND AGENCY

An Anthropological Theory

Alfred Gell

CLARENDON PRESS · OXFORD

OXFORD

UNIVERSITY PRESS

Great Clarendon Street, Oxford OX2 6DP
United Kingdom

Oxford University Press is a department of the University of Oxford.
It furthers the University's objective of excellence in research, scholarship,
and education by publishing worldwide. Oxford is a registered trade mark of
Oxford University Press in the UK and in certain other countries

© Alfred Gell 1998

The moral rights of the author have been asserted

Reprinted 2013

British Library Cataloguing in Publication Data
Data available

Library of Congress Cataloging in Publication Data
Data available

ISBN 978-0-19-828014-9

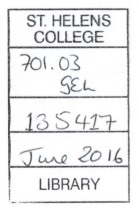

To Simeran
with love

FOREWORD

Nicholas Thomas

Alfred Gell, who died in January 1997, was widely regarded as one of the most brilliant social anthropologists of his generation. His writing and thought were rigorously analytical, yet often also playful and provocative; he was equally deft in engaging the most general issues of social theory, and the most intricate elements of rituals, practices, and artefacts. These capacities are exemplified in this book, which may amount to the most radical rethinking of the anthropology of art since that field of inquiry emerged. The book certainly combines a good deal of abstract model-making with remarkably insightful discussions of particular art objects and art styles.

Yet, despite it being written in a lucid and direct way, it is not necessarily an easy book to grasp. It does need to be acknowledged here that, had the author lived longer, he would certainly have done further work; he indeed left notes toward revisions that he did not have the time to carry out. What we have is the full draft of a book, most of which was written over a period of only a month, not an absolutely refined version. It should be added, though, that Alfred Gell's essays and books did, for the most part, emerge well formed; he wrote with great intensity, but preferred to write when his ideas were clearly worked out, from start to finish. The book can therefore be said to approximate an intended final form, but it does lack polishing, and there are certainly forceful passages that would have been qualified, points that would have added or elaborated, and sections that would have been better integrated with the whole, had Gell had the opportunity.

What the book lacks, in particular, is a preface or introduction proper, that concisely foreshadows its overall argument. While I hesitate to summarize another scholar's book, and am frankly unsure of my capacity to do justice to the various dimensions of a complex and involved argument, I believe that this is what this foreword should attempt, in order to make the arguments that follow more accessible, particularly to readers unfamiliar with Alfred Gell's other work. This book builds on a number of essays, and anthropologists who have read 'The Technology of Enchantment and the Enchantment of Technology' (1992*b*), 'Vogel's Net: Traps as Artworks and Artworks as Traps' (1996), or Gell's study of Polynesian tattooing, *Wrapping in Images* (1993), will anticipate the directions that it takes.

The essay on 'The Technology of Enchantment', in particular, foreshadows some of the larger arguments here. In that paper, Gell provocatively claimed that the anthropology of art had got virtually nowhere thus far, because it had failed to dissociate itself from projects of aesthetic appreciation, that are to art as theology is to religion. He argued that if the discipline was instead to adopt the position analogous to that of the sociology of religion, it needed a method-ological philistinism equivalent to sociology's methodological atheism. This required disowning the 'art cult' to which anthropologists, as cultured middle-class intellectuals, generally subscribe. This was not, however, to advocate a demystifying sociological analysis that would identify the role of art in sus-taining class cultures, or in legitimizing dominant ideologies: Gell suggested that approaches of this kind failed to engage with art objects themselves, with their specificity and efficacy. More particularly, he was relatively uninterested in the questions raised by art world institutions, believing instead that the anthropology of art should address the workings of art in general.

   He proposed that it was possible to address questions of the efficacy of the art object, without succumbing to the fascination and aura of those objects, by taking art as a special form of technology, and especially by regarding art objects as devices 'for securing the acquiescence of individuals in the net-work of intentionalities in which they are enmeshed' (1992*b*: 43). For example, brilliantly involuted and captivating forms such as those of Trobriand prow-boards (of the Massim region, Papua New Guinea) work a kind of psycholo-gical warfare, in a situation of competitive exchange. These boards confront the hosts of exchange partners, ideally dazzle them, beguile them, and confuse them, leading them to surrender their valuables—anthropology's famous kula shells—for less than their value. The claim here is not reductive, however: it is not suggested that in some sense the object *by itself* does this, or would do it, independently of a field of expectations and understandings, which in this case envelope the artefact with magical prowess, which is known to have entered into its making. Technology is enchanting because it is enchanted, because it is the outcome of some process of barely comprehensible virtuosity, that exemplifies an ideal of magical efficacy that people struggle to realize in other domains.

   There was a minor inconsistency in the 1992 article, in the sense that it seemed to be assumed that the anthropology of art remained the study of 'primitive' art (Gell rejected the euphemistic term 'non-Western' on the grounds that this included high Oriental art and other traditions, which clearly possessed an entirely different social location to the canonical tribal art forms). However, the examples he proceeded to use, in pointing to the 'halo effect of technical difficulty' and other aspects of the art objects, included the paintings of the American illusionist J. F. Peto, and Picasso. The implication that his theory might in fact be a theory of the workings of all art, rather than that supposedly characteristic of particular populations, is a premiss of the present book.

   The first chapters amount to a dramatic elaboration of the arguments of the 1992 essay. Gell begins by deferring to the desirability, in broader cultural and political terms, of acknowledging the distinctness of non-Western aesthetic systems, but asserts that this cannot constitute an 'anthropological' theory, on the grounds that anthropological theories are essentially concerned with social relations, over the time-frame of biographies. As he acknowledges, this definitional orientation may be contentious, but it arguably provides a productive departure point for this particular inquiry. There are two linked arguments for a shift away from cross-cultural aesthetics. The first is that many canonical pieces of tribal art, such as the Asmat shields of south-west New Guinea, are plainly not intended to elicit 'aesthetic' appreciation in the conventional sense—they rather had a part to play in the deadly psychological warfare of headhunting, that was so fundamental to Asmat sociality before pacification. The second is a categorical rejection of the linguistic analogies that have been mobilized by so many semiotic and symbolic theories of art. And this is perhaps the sense in which this book is most radical. For many scholars, and indeed in much common-sense thinking about art, it is axiomatic that art is a matter of meaning and communication. This book suggests that it is instead about *doing*.

'Doing' is theorized as agency, as a process involving indexes and effects; the anthropology of art is constructed as a theory of agency, or of the mediation of agency by indexes, understood simply as material entities which motivate inferences, responses or interpretations. Indexes stand in a variety of relations to prototypes, artists, and recipients. Prototypes are the things that indices may represent or stand for, such as the person depicted in a portrait—though things may be 'represented' non-mimetically, and non-visually. Recipients are those whom indexes are taken to effect, or who may, in some cases, be effective themselves via the index (a view of a country estate commissioned by the landowner may be a vehicle of the recipient's self-celebrating agency, more than that of the artist. Artists are those who are considered to be immediately causally responsible for the existence and characteristics of index, but as we have just noted, they may be vehicles of the agency of others, not the self-subsistent, creative agents of Western commonsense ideas and art-world theory. In this respect, it is worth noting that despite the notable differences between the style and orientation of this book, and the Melanesianist deconstructionism of Marilyn Strathern (1988; see also Wagner 1992), Gell could be seen to fully embrace Strathern's notion of the 'partible' or 'distributed' person, and indeed to make explicit the ways in which it follows from this concept that actions and their effects are similarly not discrete expressions of individual will, but rather the outcomes of mediated practices in which agents and patients are implicated in complex ways. On the one hand the agency of the artist is rarely self-sufficient; on the other the index is not simply a 'product' or end-point of action, but rather a distributed extension of an agent. The chilling example of one of Pol Pot's soldiers, who distributes elements of his own efficacy in the form of landmines, is one of the many unexpected, yet apt instances that gives what would otherwise be an intractable, abstract exposition of these terms, some concreteness.

The theory receives more sustained exemplification in Chapters 6 and 7, which address forms of 'decorative' and 'representational' art respectively. The first discusses apotropaic patterns, involuted designs intended to entrance and ward off dangerous spirits; with examples such as the Asmat shield, these perhaps manifest most obviously one of the book's larger theses, namely that art objects mediate a technology to achieve certain ends, notably to enmesh patients in relations and intentionalities sought or prescribed by agents. Lest this appear a reductive approach to art, one that takes objects essentially as vehicles of strategies, it is important to emphasize that the formal complexity, and indeed the technical virtuosity, exhibited in works of art is not incidental to the argument but absolutely central to it. It is crucial to the theory, in fact, that indexes display 'a certain cognitive indecipherability', that they tantalize, they frustrate the viewer unable to recognize at once 'wholes and parts, continuity and discontinuity, synchrony and succession'. Even though this book engages in little sustained cognitive theorizing, it is notable at this point and elsewhere that cognitive observations animate Gell's argument, to a degree that has become unusual in anthropology.

The long chapter which follows ranges widely over idolatry, sorcery, ritual, and personhood, and incidentally displays Gell's grasp of a bewildering range of south Asian and Polynesian source material, but is fully consistent with the claims of the previous sections. Idols are indeed of special relevance for the book, because they stand for an agent or patient (in the case of sorcery), for persons or deities, in manifest and powerful ways. They are indices that may be animated in a variety of ways, that enable transactions in lethal effect, fertility, auspiciousness, and the like. The particular forms of agency and intention at issue here, and the process of consecration, are explored in detail. The larger point is that there are multiple implications of agency in objects, 'an inseparable transition' between them and actual human agents. Once appreciated as indexes of agency, iconic objects in particular can occupy positions in the networks of human social agency that are almost equivalent to the positions of humans themselves.

Up to this point, Gell's theorizing and exemplification have focused upon the work of particular objects or indexes in particular actions, on specific processes rather than entire repertoires of artworks. He concludes Chapter 7 by acknowledging that there are many vital respects in which artworks do not appear as singular entities, but rather as ensembles. The remainder of the book appears to take a sharp turn away from the paradigm of the agent and index that has received such concerted attention thus far. It tackles the question of familial relations among artworks, and seems to shift back to conventional ground, in engaging with the concept of style. Yet this discussion, which proceeds via a rich formal analysis of the extraordinary corpus of Marquesan art documented by the German ethnologist Karl von den Steinen, is in the end consistent with what comes before.

Gell is again concerned to avoid linguistic models such as 'a grammar of style' and instead seeks rather to identify axes of coherence through a strictly formal analysis of generative relations among motifs. The bulk of the chapter consists of a richly visual analysis of these relations. The point that Janus figures (which are almost pervasive in Oceanic art) indexed invulnerability had already been made in *Wrapping in Images*; it was not simply that the figure could see in all directions, but that the face was itself an expression of power, and, in sculptural form, was canonically the face of a deity rather than a human. One of the central claims of *Wrapping in Images* was that eastern Polynesian tattooing was a technology that reinforced the body, and in the highly competitive, unstable, and violent societies of the Marquesas, it is not unexpected to find that tattooing entailed the multiplication of the body's faces. These themes are highly salient to Gell's discussion of Marquesan forms such as the famous *u'u* clubs, described here as 'the ultimate double-double tiki', but the chapter goes well beyond the earlier discussions of the arts of empowerment in these societies. The real object, in this case, is the diagnosis of the formal principles that give Marquesan art its singularity, and these are identified, not at the level of appearance, but through the types of transformations that link Marquesan artworks.

At the most abstract level, the principles that govern these transformations can be connected to the cultural milieu. Gell suggests that the most basic principle to be detected in the Marquesan corpus is a principle of 'least difference': 'the forms taken by motifs and figures are the ones involving the least modification of neighbouring motifs consistent with the establishment of a distinction between them.' This trend can in turn, he claims, be connected with the most basic feature of identity-formation in Marquesan society, which was characterized by acute status competition; this was not simply a matter of political jockeying, but rather a ritually saturated process of inter-individual contact and commensality. Personal integrity was continually threatened by dispersal and de-differentiation; many Marquesan artefacts amounted, individually, to devices that wrapped the body and protected particular orifices, or the body as a whole in situations of crisis; in the ensemble as a whole, the principle of least difference resonated with a preoccupation with a continually prejudiced effort of differentiation, of differentiation in the midst of dissolution. 'There was an elective affinity between a *modus operandi* in the artefactual domain, which generated motifs from other motifs by interpolating minuscule variations, and a *modus operandi* in the social realm which created "differences" arbitrarily against a background of fusional sameness.'

It is worth underlining the distinction between this effort and that of Allan Hanson, which Gell finds, in an opening section of the chapter, to be worthy but misconceived. Whereas Hanson attempted to identify one-to-one correspondences between formal properties in Maori art (such as disrupted symmetry) and properties of Maori culture (competitive reciprocity), Gell points out that the stylistic elements that are singled out are universal, or at least commonly encountered, and cannot therefore be determined by singular features of Maori culture. Although the 'elective affinity' that he seeks to identify between Marquesan style and culture could be seen to be similar to the relation of recapitulation that Hanson postulated between Maori aesthetic form and culture, for Gell the affinities will emerge not at the level of characteristic relations in particular bodies of material but at that of 'relations between relations'; at the level, in other words, of meta-properties that demonstrably render that style peculiar to itself.

The final chapter makes a further, equally ambitious step, on to ground that has often been unsatisfactorily traversed, the problem that has been conventionally posed in terms of what collective counterparts individual minds and consciousnesses possess. Gell's approach to the issue may be fresh and rewarding precisely because it does not start from the usual departure points, but rather builds on several preceding arguments—'inner' and 'outer', internal and external, have already been shown to be relatively rather than absolutely contrasted. Inspired by Peer Gynt's onion, by Strathern's fractal conception of personhood, and by the extraordinary exemplification of fractal and distributed personhood in Polynesian and especially Marquesan art, Gell evokes the notion of a 'distributed mind' through an argument that 'the structures of art history demonstrate an externalized and collectivized cognitive process.' The famous Malangan of New Ireland and the Kula transactions of the Massim region of Papua New Guinea are invoked to advance this argument, demonstrating, with the support of the work of Nancy Munn in particular, that the Kula operator 'is a spatio-temporally extended person'. At this point two of the book's key themes, that of the distributed mind, and that of efficacious agency—upon which so much emphasis is placed in the opening sections of the book—are drawn together. Efficacy is founded on a comprehensive internal model of the outside field. One becomes a great Kula operator, in other words, by modelling a working simulacrum, a dynamic space-time map, of the play and history of Kula in the world. Internal mental process and external transactions in objectified personhood are (ideally) fused. Mind, therefore, can exist objectively as well as subjectively, as a pattern of transactable objects.

Gell does not conclude with this large claim, but proceeds to vindicate the concept of the distributed mind through the more familiar instance of the individual (canonically Western) artist's work, turning also to engage with questions of continuity over time, and foreshadowing the concluding discussion of questions of tradition. His key terms here are 'protention' and 'retention', which advert to the ways artworks at once anticipate future works and hark back to others. His key example is the *œuvre* of Duchamp, and particularly the very striking notion of 'the network of stoppages' which inspired not only Gell's understanding of the issue, but the diagrammatic form in which he presents it. The final section of the book reverts to the collective register, arguing that a similar pattern of protentions and retentions can be identified in the history of Maori meeting houses, therefore understanding this historical corpus as 'a distributed object structurally isomorphous to consciousness as a temporal process'. There are many incidental accomplishments of this discussion, such as the demonstration of the extent to which 'fractal personhood', a concept fashioned and largely isolated within Melanesianist anthropology, possesses great salience beyond it.

This is a demanding book. The range of the examples that are discussed in detail is quite breath-taking, as is the ensemble of big conceptual questions that are tackled. It will inevitably be contentious: many anthropologists of art have exhibited great virtuosity in semiotic interpretations, and will no doubt remain unpersuaded that an approach which eschews linguistic analogies and concepts can represent an advance on their own. Regional specialists, such as Polynesianists, may be taken aback by the unexpected character of Gell's way of seeing. Yet the fertility of his provocation cannot be questioned. His specific claims concerning Oceanic and other materials give specialists a chance to move beyond the interpretations, too often bland interpretations, that have assumed the status of received wisdom; while the unprecedented effort to theorize fundamental questions of personhood and cognition from the vantage point of a theory of art may be as destabilizing and suggestive for the former as for the latter. Friends and colleagues remain painfully conscious of our lost opportunities to debate the issues further with Alfred in person; yet he has left us with a distributed element of his own personhood, an index of his own creative virtuosity, a gift.

ACKNOWLEDGEMENTS

This book chronicles a momentous and sad time for the many people who loved and admired Alfred, and a cataclysmic one for me and my son Rohan, and for Alfred's parents. Alfred began the final chapter directly upon receiving confirmation of an incurable condition; in the weeks that followed he devoted considerable time towards giving clear instructions concerning its posthumous publication. He had absolute confidence in Peter Momtchiloff of Oxford University Press, with whom he had previously liaised. It gives me pleasure to record that this confidence was amply justified in the months following Alfred's death just three days after the posting of the manuscript. With the exception of two illustrations pertaining to Chapter 8 the book appears in the form in which Alfred left it. It amounts to a first draft written during an intense three-week period over the Easter vacation of 1996. Alfred intended to draw with his own hand many of the photographic illustrations and had begun to make notes towards the revision of the manuscript shortly before he was taken ill. Blessed with implacable contentment and good humour, he was pleased and grateful for being granted time enough in which to squeeze completion of a book on art—the subject that truly gripped and delighted him—and was satisfied with the final product.

It must be made clear that the people listed herein were collaborators whose commitment to ensuring the book's smooth publication, while different in nature from mine, arose out of a direct personal involvement with Alfred. Stephen and Christine Hugh-Jones had been at school with Alfred. Stephen devoted many hours of his time to scanning the illustrations so that the manuscript could be sent to the publishers while Alfred was alive. He combined this with keeping a watchful, solicitous eye over Rohan and, in common with Christine, with providing Alfred with an openly affectionate companionship during his last weeks. Alfred, never at a loss to respond verbally, was significantly silent when it came to his notice that Stephen was putting in so much work. Nicholas Thomas and Alfred had enjoyed a mutually stimulating intellectual partnership that evolved into a close friendship over many years: it would be fair to say that he has taken as active a role as mine in all matters relating to the publication process. Chris Pinney gave constant moral and intellectual support and Michael O'Hanlon arranged for permissions in relation to the illustrations held at the British Museum. Other friends of Alfred's and mine, namely Don Gardner, Carrie Humphrey, Eric Hirsch, Marilyn Strathern, Suzanne Küchler, and Howard Morphy, attended to various queries that came up in the course of publication. Susan Gell, Alfred's mother, and Trudi Binns redrew some of the illustrations from rough sketches of Alfred's.

On grounds different from those for the people mentioned above, I would like to thank those who responded to my requests for help: Anita Hurley, Don Manning, Paul Caldwell, Aidan Baker, Alison Deeprose, and Madhu Khanna. The following institutions generously waived normal reproduction charges: The British Museum, London; Musée de l'Homme, Paris; Haddon Museum, Cambridge; Naprstek Museum of Asian, African and American Culture, Prague; Rijksmuseum voor Volkenkunde, Leiden; and Germanisches National-museum, Nuremberg. And finally, I wish to record a personal debt I owe to Robert Ritter of Oxford University Press. As the person in charge of produ-cing a complicated book, Robert has impressed me by his constant sensitivity, patience, and warmth towards me.

SIMERAN GELL

Cambridge, 1998

CONTENTS

LIST OF FIGURES

TABLE

Asmat shield. *Source*: Rijk Museum voor Volkenkunde (RMV 1854–446)

1

The Problem Defined: The Need for an Anthropology of Art

1.1. *Can there be an Anthropological Theory of Visual Art?*

An 'anthropological theory of visual art' probably suggests a theory dealing with the art production in the colonial and post-colonial societies anthropologists typically study, plus the so-called 'Primitive' art—now usually called 'ethnographic' art—in museum collections. The 'anthropological theory of art' equals the 'theory of art' applied to 'anthropological' art. But this is not what I have in mind. The art of the colonial and post-colonial margins, inasmuch as it is 'art', can be approached via any, or all, of the existing 'theories of art', in so far as these approaches are useful ones. Critics, philosophers, and aestheticians have been busy for a long time; 'theories of art' constitute a vast and well-established field. Those whose profession it is to describe and understand the art of Picasso and Brancusi can write about masks from Africa as 'art', and indeed need to do so because of the very salient art-historical relationships between the art of Africa and twentieth-century Western art. There is no sense in developing one 'theory of art' for our own art, and another, distinctively different theory, for the art of those cultures who happened, once upon a time, to fall under the sway of colonialism. If Western (aesthetic) theories of art apply to 'our' art, then they apply to everybody's art, and should be so applied.

Sally Price (1989) has rightly complained about the essentialization and concomitant ghettoization of so-called 'Primitive' art. She argues that this art deserves to be evaluated by Western spectators according to the same critical standards we apply to our own art. Art from non-Western cultures is not essentially different from our own, in that it is produced by individual, talented, imaginative artists, who ought to be accorded the same degree of recognition as Western artists, rather than being viewed either as 'instinctive' children of nature, spontaneously expressing their primitive urges, or, alternatively, as slavish exponents of some rigid 'tribal' style. Like other contemporary writers on the subject of ethnographic arts (Coote 1992, 1996; Morphy 1994, 1996), Price believes that each culture has a culture-specific aesthetic, and the task of the anthropology of art is to define the characteristics of each culture's inherent aesthetic, so that the aesthetic contributions of particular non-Western artists can be evaluated correctly, that is, in relation to their culturally specific aesthetic intentions. Here is her credo:

The crux of the problem, as I understand it, is that the appreciation of Primitive Art has nearly always been phrased in terms of a fallacious choice: one option is to let the aesthetically discriminating eye be our guide on the basis of some undefined concept of universal beauty. The other is to bury ourselves in 'tribal lore' to discover the utilitarian or ritual function of the objects in question. These two routes are generally viewed as competitive and incompatible . . . I would propose the possibility of a third conceptualization that sits somewhere between the two extremes . . . It requires the acceptance of two tenets that do not as yet enjoy widespread acceptance among educated members of Western societies.

—One tenet is that the 'eye' of even the most naturally gifted connoisseur is not naked, but views art through the lense of a Western cultural education.

—The second is that many Primitives (including both artists and critics) are also endowed with a discriminating 'eye'—similarly fitted with an optical device that reflects their own cultural education.

In the framework of these two tenets, anthropological contextualization represents, not a tedious elaboration of exotic customs that competes with true 'aesthetic experience,' but rather a means to expand the aesthetic experience beyond our own narrowly culture-bound line of vision. Having accepted works of Primitive Art as worthy of representation alongside the works of our own societies' most distinguished artists . . . our next task is to acknowledge the existence and legitimacy of the aesthetic frameworks within which they were produced.   (Price 1989: 92–3)

This view is perfectly consistent with the close relationship between art history and the theory of art in the West. There is an obvious analogy between 'culture-specific aesthetics' and 'period-specific aesthetics'. Art theorists such as Baxendall (1972) have shown that the reception of the art of particular periods in the history of Western art was dependent on how the art was 'seen' at the time, and that 'ways of seeing' change over time. To appreciate the art of a particular period we should try to recapture the 'way of seeing' which artists of the period implicitly assumed their public would bring to their work. One of the art historian's tasks is to assist in this process by adducing the historical context. The anthropology of art, one might quite reasonably conclude, has an approximately similar objective, except that it is the 'way of seeing' of a cultural system, rather than a historical period, which has to be elucidated.

I have no objection to Price's suggestions so far as increasing the recognition afforded to non-Western art and artists is concerned. Indeed what well-intentioned person could object to such a programme, except possibly the 'connoisseurs', who derive a reactionary satisfaction from imagining that the producers of the 'primitive art' they like to collect are primeval savages, barely descended from the trees. These idiots can be dismissed out of hand.

All the same, I do not think that the elucidation of *non-western aesthetic systems* constitutes an 'anthropology' of art. Firstly, such a programme is exclusively cultural, rather than social. Anthropology, from my point of view, is a social science discipline, not a humanity. The distinction is, I admit, elusive, but it does imply that the 'anthropology of art' focuses on the social context of art production, circulation, and reception, rather than the evaluation of particular works of art, which, to my mind, is the function of a critic. It may be interesting to know why, for example, the Yoruba evaluate one carving as aesthetically superior to another (R. F. Thompson 1973), but that does not tell us much about why the Yoruba carve to begin with. The presence of large numbers of carvings, carvers, and critics of carvings in Yorubaland at a certain period in time is a social fact whose explanation does not lie in the domain of indigenous aesthetics. Similarly, our aesthetic preferences cannot by themselves account for the existence of the objects which we assemble in museums and regard aesthetically. Aesthetic judgements are only interior mental acts; art objects, on the other hand, are produced and circulated in the external physical and social world. This production and circulation has to be sustained by certain social processes of an objective kind, which are connected to other social processes (exchange, politics, religion, kinship, etc.). Unless, for instance, there were secret societies such as Poro and Sande in West Africa, there would be no Poro and Sande masks. Poro and Sande masks can be regarded and evaluated aesthetically, by ourselves, or by the indigenous art public, only because of the presence of certain social institutions in that region. Even if one were to concede that something akin to 'aesthetics' exists as a feature of the ideational system of every culture, one would be far from possessing a theory which could account for the production and circulation of particular works of art in particular social milieux. In fact, as I have argued elsewhere (Gell 1995), I am far from convinced that every 'culture' has a component of its ideational system which is comparable to our own 'aesthetics'. I think that the desire to see the art of other cultures aesthetically tells us more about our own ideology and its quasi-religious veneration of art objects as aesthetic talismans, than it does about these other cultures. The project of 'indigenous aesthetics' is essentially geared to refining and expanding the aesthetic sensitivities of the Western art public by providing a cultural context within which non-Western art objects can be assimilated to the categories of Western aesthetic art-appreciation. This is not a bad thing in itself, but it still falls far short of being an anthropological theory of art production and circulation.

I say this for reasons that are unaffected by the correctness or otherwise of my views about the impossibility of using 'aesthetics' as a universal parameter of cultural description and comparison. Even if, as Price, Coote, Morphy, and others suppose, all cultures have an 'aesthetic', descriptive accounts of other cultures' aesthetics would not add up to an anthropological theory. Distinctively 'anthropological' theories have certain defining characteristics, which these accounts of evaluative schemes would lack. Evaluative schemes, of whatever kind, are only of anthropological interest in so far as they play a part within social processes of interaction, through which they are generated and sustained.

The anthropology of law, for instance, is not the study of legal–ethical principles —other peoples' ideas of right and wrong—but of disputes and their resolution, in the course of which disputants do often appeal to such principles. Similarly, the anthropology of art cannot be the study of the aesthetic principles of this or that culture, but of the mobilization of aesthetic principles (or something like them) in the course of social interaction. The aesthetic theory of art just does not resemble, in any salient respect, any existing anthropological theory about social processes. What it resembles is existing Western art theory—which of course it is, applied no longer to 'Western' art, but to exotic or popular art. To develop a distinctively anthropological theory of art it is insufficient to 'borrow' existing art theory and apply it to a new object; one must develop a new variant of *existing anthropological theory*, and apply it to art. It is not that I want to be more original than my colleagues who have applied the existing theory of art to exotic objects, I just want to be unoriginal in a new way. 'Existing anthropological theories' are not about art; they are about topics like kinship, subsistence economics, gender, religion, and the like. The objective, therefore, is to create a theory about art which is anthropological because it resembles these other theories that one can confidently describe as anthropological. Of course, this imitative strategy very much depends on what sort of a subject one considers anthropology to be; and how this subject differs from neighbouring ones.

What constitutes the defining characteristic of 'anthropological theories', as a class, and what grounds have I for asserting that codifying aesthetic-evaluative schemes would not fall under such a rubric? My view is that in so far as anthropology has a specific subject-matter at all, that subject-matter is 'social relationships'—relationships between participants in social systems of various kinds. I recognize that many anthropologists in the tradition of Boas and Kroeber, Price among them, consider that the subject-matter of anthropology is 'culture'. The problem with this formulation is that one only discovers what anybody's 'culture' consists of by observing and recording their cultural behaviour in some specific setting, that is, how they relate to specific 'others' in social interactions. Culture has no existence independently of its manifestations in social interactions; this is true even if one sits someone down and asks them to 'tell us about your culture'—in this case the interaction in question is the one between the inquiring anthropologist and the (probably rather bemused) informant.

The problem with the 'indigenous aesthetics' programme, in my view, is that it tends to reify the 'aesthetic response' independently of the social context of its manifestations (and that Boasian anthropology in general reifies culture). In so far as there can be an anthropological theory of 'aesthetics', such a theory would try to explain why social agents, in particular settings, produce the responses that they do to particular works of art. I think that this can be distinguished from the laudable, but essentially non-anthropological task of providing a 'context' for non-Western art such that this art can become accessible to a Western art-public. However, the responses of the indigenous art 'public' to indigenous art is hardly exhausted by the enumeration of those contexts in which something like an evaluative aesthetic scheme is deployed in 'appreciating' art. Such contexts may be rare or non-existent, yet 'what looks to us like art' is none the less produced and circulated.

A purely cultural, aesthetic, 'appreciative' approach to art objects is an anthropological dead end. Instead, the question which interests me is the possibility of formulating a 'theory of art' which fits naturally into the context of anthropology, given the premiss that anthropological theories are 'recognizable' initially, as theories about social relationships, and not anything else. The simplest way to imagine this is to suppose that there could be a species of anthropological theory in which *persons* or 'social agents' are, in certain contexts, substituted for by *art objects*.

1.2. *The Art Object*

This immediately raises the question of the definition of the 'art object', and indeed, of 'art' itself. Howard Morphy (1994: 648–85) in a recent discussion of the problem of the 'definition of art' in the anthropological context, considers, and rejects, the (Western) institutional definition of art, that 'art' is whatever is treated as art by members of the institutionally recognized art world (Danto 1964)—critics, dealers, collectors, theoreticians, etc. This is fair enough: there is no 'art world' to speak of in many of the societies which anthropologists concern themselves with, yet these societies produce works some of which are recognized as 'art' by our 'art world'. According to the 'institutional theory of art', most indigenous art is only 'art' (in the sense we mean by 'art') because we think it is, not because the people who make it think so. Accepting the art world's definition of art obliges the anthropologist to bring to bear on the art of other cultures a frame of reference of an overtly metropolitan character. To some extent this is inevitable (anthropology is a metropolitan activity, just like art criticism) but Morphy is understandably disinclined to accept the verdict of the (anthropologically uninformed) Western art world as to the definition of 'art' beyond the physical frontiers of the West. He proposes, instead, a dualistic definition; art objects are those 'having semantic and/or aesthetic properties that are used for presentational or representational purposes' (ibid. 655), that is, either art objects are sign-vehicles, conveying 'meaning', or they are objects made in order to provoke a culturally endorsed aesthetic response, or both of these simultaneously.

I find both of these conditions for art object status questionable. I have already expressed the opinion that 'aesthetic properties' cannot be abstracted, anthropologically, from the social processes surrounding the deployment of candidate 'art objects' in specific social settings. I doubt, for example, that a

warrior on a battlefield is 'aesthetically' interested in the design on an opposing
warrior's shield; yet it was so as to be seen by this warrior (and to frighten him)
that the design was placed there. The shield, if it resembles the one in the frontis-
piece (p. xxiv), is indisputably a work of art of the kind interesting to the
anthropologist, but its aesthetic properties (for us) are totally irrelevant to its
anthropological implications. Anthropologically, it is not a 'beautiful' shield,
but a fear-inducing shield. The innumerable shades of social/emotional responses
to artefacts (of terror, desire, awe, fascination, etc.) in the unfolding patterns
of social life cannot be encompassed or reduced to aesthetic feelings; not without making the aesthetic response so generalized as to be altogether meaningless. The effect of the 'aestheticization' of response-theory is simply to equate
the reactions of the ethnographic Other, as far as possible, to our own. In fact,
responses to artefacts are never such as to single out, among the spectrum of
available artefacts, those that are attended to 'aesthetically' and those that are
not.

Nor am I happy with the idea that the work of art is recognizable, generically, in that it participates in a 'visual' code for the communication of meaning.
I entirely reject the idea that anything, except language itself, has 'meaning' in
the intended sense. Language is a unique institution (with a biological basis).
Using language, we can talk about objects and attribute 'meanings' to them in
the sense of 'find something to say about them' but visual art objects are not
part of language for this reason, nor do they constitute an alternative language.
Visual art objects are objects about which we may, and commonly do, speak—
but they themselves either do not speak, or they utter natural language in
graphemic code. We talk about objects, using signs, but art objects are not,
except in special cases, signs themselves, with 'meanings'; and if they do have
meanings, then they are *part of language* (i.e. graphic signs), not a separate
'visual' language. I shall return to this subject at intervals, since my polemic
against the idea of a 'language of art' has many different aspects to it, which are
better dealt with separately. For the present, let me simply warn the reader that
I have avoided the use of the notion of 'symbolic meaning' throughout this
work. This refusal to discuss art in terms of symbols and meanings may occasion some surprise, since the domain of 'art' and the symbolic are held by many
to be more or less coextensive. In place of symbolic communication, I place all
the emphasis on *agency, intention, causation, result*, and *transformation*. I view
art as a system of action, intended to change the world rather than encode symbolic propositions about it. The 'action'-centred approach to art is inherently
more anthropological than the alternative semiotic approach because it is preoccupied with the practical mediatory role of art objects in the social process,
rather than with the interpretation of objects 'as if' they were texts.

Having rejected Morphy's two criteria for discriminating the class of 'art
objects' for the purposes of the anthropology of art, I am, of course, still left
with the unsolved problem of proposing a criterion for art object status.

Fortunately, however, the anthropological theory of art does not need to provide a criterion for art object status which is independent of the theory itself. The anthropologist is not obliged to define the art object, in advance, in a way satisfactory to aestheticians, or philosophers, or art historians, or anybody else. The definition of the art object I make use of is not institutional, nor is it aesthetic or semiotic; the definition is *theoretical*. The art object is whatever is inserted into the 'slot' provided for art objects in the system of terms and relations envisaged in the theory (to be outlined later). Nothing is decidable in advance about the nature of this object, because the theory is premised on the idea that the nature of the art object is a function of the social–relational matrix in which it is embedded. It has no 'intrinsic' nature, independent of the relational context. Most of the art objects I shall actually discuss are well-known ones that we have no difficulty in identifying as 'art'; for instance, the Mona Lisa. Inasmuch as we recognize a pre-theoretical category of art objects—split into the two major subcategories of 'Western' art objects and 'Indigenous' or 'Ethnographic' art objects—I conduct the discussion in terms of 'prototypical' members of these categories, for convenience's sake. But in fact anything whatsoever could, conceivably, be an art object from the anthropological point of view, including living persons, because the anthropological theory of art (which we can roughly define as the 'social relations in the vicinity of objects mediating social agency') merges seamlessly with the social anthropology of persons and their bodies. Thus, from the point of view of the anthropology of art, an idol in a temple believed to be the body of the divinity, and a spirit-medium, who likewise provides the divinity with a temporary body, are treated as theoretically on a par, despite the fact that the former is an artefact and the latter is a human being.

1.3. *Art Sociology*

I have just provisionally defined the 'anthropology of art' as the theoretical study of 'social relations in the vicinity of objects mediating social agency' and I have suggested that in order for the anthropology of art to be specifically anthropological, it has to proceed on the basis that, in relevant theoretical respects, art objects are the equivalent of persons, or more precisely, social agents. Are there no alternatives to this seemingly radical proposition? Well, one might draw back from the abyss, and agree that even if the anthropological theory of art were not to be 'cross-cultural aesthetics' or a branch of semiotics, then it could still be a sociology of art 'institutions' which would not necessarily involve the radical affirmation of the personhood of art objects. There is, indeed, a flourishing 'sociology of art' which concerns itself precisely with the institutional parameters of art production, reception, and circulation. However, it is not coincidental that the 'sociology of art' (institutions) has been primarily concerned with Western art, or, failing that, the art of advanced states with bureaucracies, such as China, Japan, etc. There cannot be an 'institutional' sociology of art unless the relevant institutions are extant; that is, an art public, public or private patronage of artists, art critics, art museums, academies, art schools, and so on.

Writers who deal with the sociology of art, such as Berger (1972) and Bourdieu (1968, 1984), concern themselves with particular institutional characteristics of mass societies, rather than with the network of relationships surrounding particular artworks in specific interactive settings. This division of labour is characteristic; anthropology is more concerned with the immediate context of social interactions and their 'personal' dimensions, whereas sociology is more preoccupied with institutions. Of course, there is continuity between the sociological/institutional perspective and the anthropological/relational one. Anthropologists cannot ignore institutions; the anthropology of art has to consider the institutional framework of the production and circulation of artworks, in so far as such institutions exist. But it remains true to say that there are many societies in which the 'institutions' which provide the context for the production and circulation of art are not specialized 'art' institutions as such, but institutions of more general scope; for example, cults, exchange systems, etc. The anthropology of art would forever remain a very undeveloped field were it to restrict itself to institutionalized art production and circulation comparable to that which can readily be studied in the context of advanced bureaucratic/industrial states.

As it is, the 'sociology of art' is represented in the 'anthropology of art' primarily in the guise of studies of the *market* in 'ethnographic' art, such as the distinguished recent work by Steiner (1994). Morphy (1991), Price (1989), Thomas (1991), and others have written very illuminatingly about the reception of non-Western art by the Western art-public; but these studies concern themselves with the (institutionalized) art world of the West, and the responses by indigenous people to the reception of their artistic production by this alien art world. I think one can distinguish between these investigations of the reception and appropriation of non-Western art, and the scope of a genuinely anthropological theory of art, which is not to denigrate such studies in any way. One has to ask whether a given work of art was actually produced with this reception or appropriation in mind. In the contemporary world, much 'ethnographic' art is actually produced for the metropolitan market; in which case there is no possible way of dealing with it except in this specific framework. However, it also remains true that in the past, and still today, art was and is produced for much more limited circulation, independently of any reception which may be accorded to this art across cultural and institutional boundaries. These local contexts, in which art is produced not as a function of the existence of specific 'art' institutions, but as a by-product of the mediation of social life and the existence of institutions of a more general-purpose kind, justify the assertion of at least relative autonomy for an anthropology of art not circumscribed by the presence of institutions of any specific, art-related, kind.

It seems, then, that the anthropology of art can be at least provisionally separated from the study of art institutions or the 'art world'. Which implies the need to return to, and reconsider, the proposition advanced above. To suggest that art objects, to figure in an 'anthropological' theory of art, have to be considered as 'persons', seems a bizarre notion. But only if one fails to bear in mind that the entire historical tendency of anthropology has been towards a radical defamiliarization and relativization of the notion of 'persons'. Since the outset of the discipline, anthropology has been signally preoccupied with a series of problems to do with ostensibly peculiar relations between persons and 'things' which somehow 'appear as', or do duty as, persons. This basic theme was initially announced by Tylor in *Primitive Culture* (1875), where, it will be recalled, he discusses 'animism' (i.e. the attribution of life and sensibility to inanimate things, plants, animals, etc.) as the defining attribute of 'primitive' culture, if not culture in general. Frazer returns to precisely the same theme in his voluminous studies of sympathetic and contagious magic. Identical preoccupations surface, in a different way, in the work of Malinowski and Mauss, this time in relation to 'exchange' as well as the classical anthropological theme of magic, about which each also wrote extensively.

The proposition just advanced, that the anthropological theory of art is the theory of art which 'considers art objects as persons' is, I hope, immediately and legibly Maussian. Given that prestations or 'gifts' are treated in Maussian exchange theory as (extensions of) persons, then there is obviously scope for seeing art objects as 'persons' in the same way. In fact, it might not be going too far to suggest that in so far as Mauss's theory of exchange is the exemplary, prototypical, 'anthropological theory' then the way to produce an 'anthropological theory of art' would be to construct a theory which resembles Mauss's, but which was about art objects rather than prestations. Lévi-Strauss's kinship theory is Mauss with 'prestations' replaced by 'women'; the proposed 'anthropological theory of art' would be Mauss with 'prestations' replaced by 'art objects'. Actually, this would be a travesty of the theory I am about to produce, but I make the analogy in order to guide the reader as to my basic intentions. The point I am making is that an anthropological theory of any given topic is only 'anthropological' to the extent that it resembles, in key respects, *other* anthropological theories, otherwise the designation 'anthropological' has no meaning. My aim is to produce an anthropological theory of art which has affinities towards other anthropological theories, not just Mauss's of course, but various others as well. One of my basic objections to the 'cross-cultural aesthetics' and 'semiotics' theories of ethnographic art is that the theoretical affinities of these approaches lie in (Western) aesthetics and art-theory, not autonomously within anthropology itself. It may be that there is no useful theory of art that can be founded on or derived from existing anthropological theory, but until one has made the experiment to construct a genuinely anthropological theory of art, this question cannot be decided.

1.4. *The Silhouette of an Anthropological Theory*

The position I have reached is that an anthropological theory of art is one which 'looks like' an anthropological theory, in which certain of the *relata*, whose relations are described in the theory, are works of art. But what do 'anthropological' theories look like? Can one really give an identificatory silhouette of an anthropological theory as opposed to any other kind of theory? Well, possibly not, in that anthropology is a broad church and is only very ambiguously distinct from other disciplines, such as sociology, history, social geography, social and cognitive psychology, and so on. This much I readily concede. On the other hand, let us consider what anthropologists do best from the viewpoint of neighbouring disciplines. Anthropology is, to put it bluntly, considered good at providing close-grained analyses of *apparently irrational* behaviour, performances, utterances, etc. (The 'my brother is a green parrot' problem: Sperber 1985; Hollis 1970.) Since almost all behaviour is, from somebody's point of view, 'apparently irrational' anthropology has, possibly, a secure future. How do anthropologists solve problems about the apparent irrationality of human behaviour? They do so by locating, or contextualizing behaviour not so much in 'culture' (which is an abstraction) as in the dynamics of social interaction, which may indeed be conditioned by 'culture' but which is better seen as a real process, or dialectic, unfolding in time. The anthropological interpretative perspective on social behaviour is shared, needless to say, with sociology and social psychology, not to mention other disciplines. Anthropology differs from these in providing a particular *depth of focus*, which perhaps one could best describe as 'biographical', that is, the view taken by anthropology of social agents attempts to replicate the time perspective of these agents on themselves, whereas (historical) sociology is often, so to speak, supra-biographical and social or cognitive psychology are infra-biographical. Anthropology therefore tends to focus on the 'act' in the context of the 'life'— or more precisely, the 'stage of life'—of the agent. The fundamental periodicity of anthropology is the life cycle. This time perspective (fidelity to the biographical) dictates just how close to and how far away from the subject the anthropologist stands; if the anthropologist studies (say) cognition at the micro-scale typical of much laboratory cognitive psychology, the biographical perspective is lost and the anthropologist, in effect, is just doing cognitive psychology; conversely, if the anthropologist's perspective expands to the degree that the biographical 'life cycle' rhythm no longer delimits the scope of the discourse, he or she is doing history or sociology.

Perhaps this definition of anthropology will not be to the liking of all, but I would argue that it does in fact encompass most of the work which is regarded as typically 'anthropological'. This specifically biographical depth of focus has of course also a spatial correlate; the spaces of anthropology are those which are traversed by agents in the course of their biographies, be they narrow, or, as is becoming increasingly the case, wide or even world-wide. Moreover, it dictates a certain view of social relations. Anthropologists typically view relationships in a 'biographical' context, by which I mean that relationships are seen as part of a biographical series entered into at different phases of the life cycle. 'Sociological' relations, are, so to speak, perennial, or supra-biographical, like the relation between the classes in capitalism, or the relationship between status-groups (castes) in hierarchical societies. 'Psychological' relations, on the other hand, are infra-biographical, often no more than momentary 'encounters', as, for instance, in experimental settings in which subjects are required to interact with one another, and with the experimenter, in ways which have no biographical precedents or consequences. Anthropological relationships are real and biographically consequential ones, which articulate to the agent's biographical 'life project'.

If these stipulations are correct, then the characteristic silhouette of an 'anthropological theory' is beginning to emerge. Anthropological theories are distinctive in that they are typically about social relationships; these, in turn, occupy a certain biographical space, over which culture is picked up, transformed, and passed on, through a series of life-stages. The study of relationships over the life course (the relationships through which culture is acquired and reproduced) and the life-projects which agents seek to realize through their relations with others, allows anthropologists to perform their allotted intellectual task, which is to explain why people behave as they do, even if this behaviour seems irrational, or cruel, or amazingly saintly and disinterested, as may be. The aim of anthropological theory is to make sense of behaviour in the context of social relations. Correspondingly, the objective of the anthropological theory of art is to account for the production and circulation of art objects as a function of this relational context.

2

The Theory of the Art Nexus

2.1. *Constructing a Theory: Terms and Relations*

To construct such a theory it is first of all necessary to define certain theoretical entities (terms) and relations. Just now, I suggested that such a theory would 'look like' familiar anthropological theories, such as the theory of exchange, or the theory of kinship, but that it would replace some of the terms of such theories with 'art objects'.

However, this raises immediate difficulties, in that 'art objects', 'works of art', or 'artworks' may form a readily identifiable class of objects in some art systems, but this is hardly true of all of them, especially not in anthropological contexts. In effect, if we make 'the work of art' the corner-stone of the anthropological theory of art, the theory itself becomes instantly otiose, for reasons which have already been alluded to. To discuss 'works of art' is to discuss entities which have been given a prior *institutional* definition as such. The institutional recognition (or 'enfranchisement') of art objects is the subject-matter of the sociology of art, which deals with issues which are complementary to the anthropology of art, but do not coincide with it. Of course, some (in fact, many, or even all) of the objects which fall within the scope of the sociology of art may also be considered 'anthropologically' as entities in whose neighbourhoods social relationships are formed; but 'work of art' status is irrelevant to this. The anthropology of art, if it is to be distinguished from the sociology of art, cannot restrict its scope to 'official' art institutions and recognized works of art. It cannot, in fact, talk about 'works of art' at all, not only because of the institutional implications of 'work of art' status, but because this term has undesirably exclusive connotations. An object which has been 'enfranchised' as an art object, becomes an art object *exclusively*, from the standpoint of theory, and can only be discussed in terms of the parameters of art-theory, which is what being 'enfranchised' in this way is all about. The anthropological theory of art cannot afford to have as its primary theoretical term a category or taxon of objects which are 'exclusively' art objects because the whole tendency of this theory, as I have been suggesting, is to explore a domain in which 'objects' merge with 'people' by virtue of the existence of social relations between persons and things, and persons and persons *via* things.

I do not promise never to mention art objects again; in fact, I shall do so repeatedly, since excessive terminological consistency is the enemy of intelligibility, my primary objective here. But I do not intend to use 'art object' or 'work of art' or 'artwork' as technical terms, nor to discuss when an object is an 'art object' and when it is something else. The technical term I am going to employ is 'index'. This requires explanation.

2.2. *The Index*

The anthropology of art would not be the anthropology of *art*, unless it were confined to the subset of social relations in which some 'object' were related to a social agent in a distinctive, 'art-like' way. We have dismissed the idea that objects are related to social agents 'in an art-like way' if (and only if) social agents regard these objects 'aesthetically'. But in this case, what alternative means can be proposed to distinguish art-like relations between persons and things from relations which are not art-like? To simplify the problem, I shall henceforth confine the discussion to the instance of visual art, or at least, 'visible' art, excluding verbal and musical art, though I recognize that in practice these are usually inseparable. So the 'things' of which I speak may be understood to be real, physical things, unique and identifiable, not performances, readings, reproductions, etc. These stipulations would be out of place in most discussions of art, but they are necessary here if only because difficulties can best be surmounted one at a time. And it certainly is very difficult to propose a criterion which would distinguish the types of social relations falling under the scope of the 'anthropology of art' from any other social relations.

I propose that 'art-like situations' can be discriminated as those in which the material 'index' (the visible, physical, 'thing') permits a particular cognitive operation which I identify as *the abduction of agency*. An 'index' in Piercean semiotics is a 'natural sign', that is, an entity from which the observer can make a *causal inference* of some kind, or an inference about the intentions or capabilities of another person. The usual example of an 'index' is visible smoke, betokening 'fire'. Fire causes smoke, hence smoke is an 'index' of fire. Another very common example of an index is the human smile, indexing a friendly attitude. However, as we all know, smoke can arise in the absence of fire, and smiles may deceive. The cognitive operation through which we infer the presence of fire (given smoke) or friendliness (given the smile) is not like the cognitive operation by means of which we 'know' that $2 + 2 = 4$, or that if somebody utters the word 'dog' he means 'canine' and not 'railway train' or 'butterfly'. Indexes are not part of a calculus (a set of tautologies, like mathematics) nor are they components of a natural or artificial language in which terms have meanings established by convention. Nor are inferences from indexes arrived at by induction or deduction. We have not made a test, and established that by a law of nature, smoke means fire. In fact, we know that smoke may not mean fire, since we know of fire-less ways of producing smoke, or the appearance of smoke. Since smoke as an index of fire does not follow from any known law of nature, deductively or inductively arrived at, and is neither a tautology nor a convention of language, we need another technical term to designate the mode of inference (or cognitive operation) we bring to bear on indexes.

2.3. *Abduction*

The term employed in logic and semiotics for such inferences is 'abduction'. Abduction is a case of synthetic inference 'where we find some very curious circumstances, which would be explained by the supposition that it was a case of some general rule, and thereupon adopt that supposition' (Eco 1976: 131, citing Pierce ii. 624). Elsewhere, Eco writes 'Abduction . . . is a tentative and hazardous tracing of a system of signification rules which allow the sign to acquire its meaning. . . . [it] occurs with those natural signs which the Stoics called indicative and which are thought to be signs, yet without knowing what they signify' (Eco 1984: 40). Abduction covers the grey area where semiotic inference (of meanings from signs) merges with *hypothetical inferences* of a non-semiotic (or not conventionally semiotic) kind, such as Kepler's inference from the apparent motion of Mars in the night sky, that the planet travelled in an elliptical path:

Abduction is 'induction in the service of explanation, in which a new empirical rule is created to render predictable what would otherwise be mysterious' . . . Abduction is a variety of nondemonstrative inference, based on the logical fallacy of affirming the antecedent from the consequent ('if p then q; but q; therefore p'). Given true premises, it yields conclusions that are not necessarily true. Nevertheless, abduction is an indispensable inference principle, because it is the basic mechanism that makes it possible to constrain the indefinitely large number of explanations compatible with any event. (Boyer 1994: 147, citing J. Holland *et al.* 1986: 89)

I have a particular reason for using the terminology of 'indexical signs' and 'abductions' therefrom in the present connection. No reasonable person could suppose that art-like relations between people and things do not involve at least some form of semiosis; howsoever one approaches the subject there seems something irreducibly semiotic about art. On the other hand, I am particularly anxious to avoid the slightest imputation that (visual) art is 'like language' and that the relevant forms of semiosis are language-like. Discovering the orbits of the planets is not in the least analogous to interpreting a sentence in any natural language. Kepler did not discover the 'grammar' of planetary motions, for there is no equivalent to grammar in nature. On the other hand, scientists often speak (metaphorically) of their data as 'meaning' this or that, in other words permitting certain inferences which, if they do not appeal to established physical laws, are abductions. The usefulness of the concept of abduction is that it designates a class of semiotic inferences which are, by definition, wholly distinct from the semiotic inferences we bring to bear on the understanding of language, whose 'literal' understanding is a matter of observing semiotic conventions, not entertaining hypotheses derived *ad hoc* from the 'case' under consideration (Eco 1984: 40). Abduction, though a semiotic concept (actually, it belongs to logic rather than semiotics) is useful in that it functions to set bounds to linguistic semiosis proper, so that we cease to be tempted to apply linguistic models where they do not apply, while remaining free to posit inferences of a non-linguistic kind.

For our purposes, a more perspicuous example of abductive inference from an index is the instance of smiling 'meaning' friendliness. Very much part of the theory I am proposing is the idea that we approach art objects (and members of a larger class of indexes of agency) as if they had 'physiognomies' like people. When we see a picture of a smiling person, we attribute an attitude of friendliness to 'the person in the picture' and (if there is one) the sitter or 'subject' of the picture. We respond to the picture in this way because the appearance of smiling triggers a (hedged) inference that (unless they are pretending) this person is friendly, just as a real person's smile would trigger the same inference. We have, in short, access to 'another mind' in this way, a real mind or a depicted mind, but in either case the mind of a well-disposed person. Without pausing to unravel the very difficult question as to the nature of the relationship between real and depicted persons, the point I want to emphasize here is that the means we generally have to form a notion of the disposition and intentions of 'social others' is via a large number of abductions from indexes which are neither 'semiotic conventions' or 'laws of nature' but something in between. Furthermore, the inferential schemes (abductions) we bring to 'indexical signs' are frequently very like, if not actually identical to, the ones we bring to bear on social others. These may seem very elementary points, but they are essential to the anthropology of art.

The minimal definition of the (visual) 'art' situation therefore involves the presence of some index from which abductions (belonging to many different species) may be made. This, by itself is insufficiently restrictive, since it will be apparent that, formal reasoning and linguistic semiosis apart, the greater part of 'thinking' consists of abductions of one kind or another. To restrict the scope of the discussion, I propose that the category of indexes relevant to our theory are those which permit the abduction of 'agency' and specifically 'social agency'. This excludes instances such as scientific inferences about the orbits of planets (unless one imagines that the planets are social agents, which of course many people do). However, the restriction is narrower than this, and excludes much else besides scientific hypothesis-formation. The stipulation I make is that the *index is itself seen as the outcome, and/or the instrument of, social agency*. A 'natural sign' like 'smoke' is not seen as the outcome of any social agency, but as the outcome of a natural causal process, combustion, so, as an index of its non-social cause, it is of no interest to us. On the other hand, if smoke is seen as the index of fire-setting by human agents (burning swiddens, say) then the abduction of agency occurs and smoke becomes an artefactual index, as well as a 'natural sign'. To give another example, let us suppose that, strolling along the beach, we encounter a stone which is chipped in a rather suggestive way. Is it perhaps a prehistoric handaxe? It has become an 'artefact' and hence qualifies for consideration. It is a tool, hence an index of agency; both the agency of its maker and of the man who used it. It may not be very 'interesting' as a candidate object for theoretical consideration in the 'anthropology of art' context, but it certainly may be said to possess the minimum qualifications, since we have no a priori means of distinguishing 'artefacts' from 'works of art' (Gell 1996). This would be true even if I concluded that the chipped stone was not actually made by a prehistoric artisan, but, having taken it home anyway, I decide to use it as an ornament for my mantelpiece. Then it has become an index of my agency, and qualifies yet again (besides which it is now obviously a 'work of art' i.e. a 'found object').

2.4. *The Social Agent*

However, as is generally the case with definitions, the stipulation that the index must be 'seen as the outcome, and/or the instrument of, social agency' is itself dependent on a still undefined concept, that of 'social agent'—the one who exercises social agency. Of course it is not difficult to give examples of social agents and social agency. Any person must be considered a social agent, at least potentially.

Agency is attributable to those persons (and things, see below) who/which are seen as initiating causal sequences of a particular type, that is, events caused by acts of mind or will or intention, rather than the mere concatenation of physical events. An agent is one who 'causes events to happen' in their vicinity. As a result of this exercise of agency, certain events transpire (not necessarily the specific events which were 'intended' by the agent). Whereas chains of physical/material cause-and-effect consist of 'happenings' which can be explained by physical laws which ultimately govern the universe as a whole, agents initiate 'actions' which are 'caused' by themselves, by their intentions, not by the physical laws of the cosmos. An agent is the source, the origin, of causal events, independently of the state of the physical universe.

Actually, the nature of the relations between the agent's beliefs, intentions, etc. and the external events he/she causes to happen by 'acting' are philosophically very debatable. Philosophers are far from agreed as to the nature of 'minds' harbouring 'intentions' and the relation between inner intentions and real-world events. Sociologists, also, have every reason to be aware that agents' actions very often have 'unintended consequences' so that it cannot be said that real-world (social) events are just transcriptions of what agents intended to happen. Fortunately, in order to carry on this particular discussion, I do not have to solve problems which have preoccupied philosophers for centuries. For the anthropologist, the problem of 'agency' is not a matter of prescribing the most rational or defensible notion of agency, in that the anthropologist's task is to describe forms of thought which could not stand up to much philosophical scrutiny but which are none the less, socially and cognitively practicable.

For the anthropologist 'folk' notions of agency, extracted from everyday practices and discursive forms, are of concern, not 'philosophically defensible' notions of agency. Some philosophers believe that 'folk' notions about agency, intention, mind, etc. constitute a set of philosophically defensible beliefs, but this is of no particular concern to us. I am going to take seriously notions about agency which even these philosophers would probably not want to defend, for example that agency can inhere in graven images, not to mention motor cars (see below). I do so because, in practice, people do attribute intentions and awareness to objects like cars and images of the gods. The idea of agency is a culturally prescribed framework for thinking about causation, when what happens is (in some vague sense) supposed to be intended in advance by some person-agent or thing-agent. Whenever an event is believed to happen because of an 'intention' lodged in the person or thing which initiates the causal sequence, that is an instance of 'agency'.

Putting the word 'social' in front of the word 'agent' is in a sense redundant, in so far as the word 'agency' primarily serves to discriminate between 'happenings' (caused by physical laws) and 'actions' (caused by prior intentions). 'Prior intentions' implies the attribution to the agent of a mind akin to a human one, if not identical. Animals and material objects can have minds and intentions attributed to them, but these are always, in some residual sense, human minds, because we have access 'from the inside' only to human minds, indeed to only one of these, our own. Human minds are inevitably 'social' minds, to the extent that we only know our own minds in a social context of some kind. 'Action' cannot really be conceptualized in other than social terms. Moreover, the kinds of agency which are attributed to art objects (or indexes of agency) are inherently and irreducibly social in that art objects never (in any relevant way) emerge as agents except in very specific social contexts. Art objects are not 'self-sufficient' agents, but only 'secondary' agents in conjunction with certain specific (human) associates, whose identities I discuss below. The philosophical theory of 'agents' presupposes the autonomy and self-sufficiency of the human agent; but I am more concerned with the kind of second-class agency which artefacts acquire once they become enmeshed in a texture of social relationships. However, within this relational texture, artefacts can quite well be treated as agents in a variety of ways.

2.5. *'Things' as Social Agents*

The immediate 'other' in a social relationship does not have to be another 'human being'. My whole argument depends on this not being the case. Social agency can be exercised relative to 'things' and social agency can be exercised

by 'things' (and also animals). The concept of social agency has to be formulated in this very permissive manner for empirical as well as theoretical reasons.
It just happens to be patently the case that persons form what are evidently
social relations with 'things'. Consider a little girl with her doll. She loves her
doll. Her doll is her best friend (she says). Would she toss her doll overboard
from a lifeboat in order to save her bossy elder brother from drowning? No
way. This may seem a trivial example, and the kinds of relations small girls
form with their dolls are far from being 'typical' of human social behaviour.
But it is not a trivial example at all; in fact it is an archetypal instance of the
subject-matter of the anthropology of art. We only think it is not because it is
an affront to our dignity to make comparisons between small girls showering
affection on their dolls and us, mature souls, admiring Michelangelo's *David*.
But what is *David* if it is not a big doll for grown-ups? This is not really a matter of devaluing *David* so much as revaluing little girls' dolls, which are truly
remarkable objects, all things considered. They are certainly social beings—
'members of the family', for a time at any rate.

From dolls to idols is but a short step, and from idols to sculptures by
Michelangelo another, hardly longer. But I do not wish to confine the notion
of 'social relations between persons and things' to instances of this order, in
which the 'thing' is a representation of a human being, as a doll is. The concept required here is much broader. The ways in which social agency can be
invested in things, or can emanate from things, are exceedingly diverse (see
Miller 1987 for a theoretical analysis of 'objectification').

Take, for instance, the relationship between human beings and cars. A car,
just as a possession and a means of transport is not intrinsically a locus of
agency, either the owner's agency or its own. But it is in fact very difficult for
a car owner not to regard a car as a body-part, a prosthesis, something invested
with his (or her) own social agency *vis-à-vis* other social agents. Just as a sales-
man confronts a potential client with his body (his good teeth and well-brushed
hair, bodily indexes of business competence) so he confronts the buyer with his
car (a Mondeo, late registration, black) another, detachable, part of his body
available for inspection and approval. Conversely, an injury suffered by the car
is a personal blow, an outrage, even though the damage can be made good and
the insurance company will pay. Not only is the car a locus of the owner's
agency, and a conduit through which the agency of others (bad drivers, vandals)
may affect him—it is also the locus of an 'autonomous' agency of its own.

The car does not just reflect the owner's personhood, it has personhood as a
car. For example, I possess a Toyota which I esteem rather than abjectly love,
but since Toyotas are 'sensible' and rather dispassionate cars, my Toyota does
not mind (it is, after all, Japanese—cars have distinct ethnicities). In my family, this Toyota has a personal name, Toyolly, or 'Olly' for short. My Toyota
is reliable and considerate; it only breaks down in relatively minor ways at
times when it 'knows' that no great inconvenience will result. If, God forbid,

my Toyota were to break down in the middle of the night, far from home, I should consider this an act of gross treachery for which I would hold the car personally and morally culpable, not myself or the garage mechanics who service it. Rationally, I know that such sentiments are somewhat bizarre, but I also know that 99 per cent of car owners attribute personality to their cars in much the same way that I do, and that such imaginings contribute to a satisfactory *modus vivendi* in a world of mechanical devices. In effect, this is a form of 'religious belief' (vehicular animism) which I accept because it is part of 'car culture'—an important element in the *de facto* culture of twentieth-century Britain. Because this is a form of 'animism' which I actually and habitually practise, there is every reason to make mention of it as a template for imagining forms of animism that I do not happen to share, such as the worship of idols (see Chapter 7 below, and particularly Sections 7.8–9, where the discussion of the 'agency' of images is taken up in greater detail).

So, 'things' such as dolls and cars can appear as 'agents' in particular social situations; and so—we may argue—can 'works of art'. While some form of hedged agreement to these propositions would, perhaps, be widely conceded in the current climate of conceptual relativism and pragmatism, it would be facile in the extreme not to observe that unwelcome contradictions arrive in their wake.

2.5.1. Paradox Elimination

An agent is defined as one who has the capacity to initiate causal events in his/her vicinity, which cannot be ascribed to the current state of the physical cosmos, but only to a special category of mental states; that is, intentions. It is contradictory to assert that 'things' such as dolls and cars can behave as 'agents' in contexts of human social interactions, since 'things' cannot, by definition have intentions, and moreover, such causal events as occur in their vicinity are 'happenings' (produced by physical causes) not 'actions' referable to the agency exercised by the thing. The little girl may, possibly, imagine that her doll is another agent, but we are obliged to regard this as an erroneous idea. We can preoccupy ourselves with detecting the cognitive and emotional factors which engender such erroneous ideas—but this is very different from proposing a theory, as I seem to be bent on doing, which accepts such palpable errors in agency-attribution as basic postulates. This appears a dangerous course indeed. A 'sociology of action' premised on the intentional nature of agency, undermines itself fatally by introducing the possibility that 'things' could be agents, because the whole interpretative enterprise is founded on the strict separation between 'agency'—exercised by sentient, encultured, human beings—and the kind of physical causation which explains the behaviour of mere things. However, this paradox can be mitigated, initially, in the light of the following considerations.

Whatever happens, human agency is exercised within the material world. Were the kinds of material cause and effect with which we are familiar not in place, intentional action, action initiated in a social context and with social objectives in view, would be impossible. We can accept that the causal chains which are initiated by intentional agents come into being as states of mind, and that they are orientated towards the states of mind of social 'others' (i.e. 'patients': see below)—but unless there is some kind of physical mediation, which always does exploit the manifold causal properties of the ambient physical world (the environment, the human body, etc.), agent and patient will not interact. Therefore, 'things' with their thing-ly causal properties are as essential to the exercise of agency as states of mind. In fact, it is only because the *causal milieu* in the vicinity of an agent assumes a certain configuration, from which an intention may be abducted, that we recognize the presence of another agent. We recognize agency, *ex post facto*, in the anomalous configuration of the causal milieu—but we cannot detect it in advance, that is, we cannot tell that someone is an agent before they *act as an agent*, before they disturb the causal milieu in such a way as can only be attributed to their agency. Because the attribution of agency rests on the detection of the effects of agency in the causal milieu, rather than an unmediated intuition, it is not paradoxical to understand agency as a factor of the ambience as a whole, a global characteristic of the world of people and things in which we live, rather than as an attribute of the human psyche, exclusively. The little girl's doll is not a self-sufficient agent like an (idealized) human being, even the girl herself does not think so. But the doll is an emanation or manifestation of agency (actually, primarily the child's own), a mirror, vehicle, or channel of agency, and hence a source of such potent experiences of the 'co-presence' of an agent as to make no difference.

I am prepared to make a distinction between 'primary' agents, that is, intentional beings who are categorically distinguished from 'mere' things or artefacts, and 'secondary' agents, which are artefacts, dolls, cars, works of art, etc. through which primary agents distribute their agency in the causal milieu, and thus render their agency effective. But to call artefactual agents 'secondary' is not to concede that they are not agents at all, or agents only 'in a manner of speaking'. Take, for instance, the anti-personnel mines which have caused so many deaths and mutilations in Cambodia in recent years. Pol Pot's soldiers, who laid these mines, were, clearly, the agents responsible for these crimes against innocent people. The mines themselves were just 'instruments' or 'tools' of destruction, not 'agents of destruction' in the sense we mean when pinning moral responsibility on Pol Pot's men, who could have acted differently, while the mines *could not help* exploding once trodden on. It seems senseless to attribute 'agency' to a mere lethal mechanical device, rather than its culpable user.

But not so fast. A soldier is not just a man, but a man with a gun, or in this case with a box of mines to sow. The soldier's weapons are *parts* of him which make him what he is. We cannot speak of Pol Pot's soldiers without referring, in the same breath, to their weaponry, and the social context and military tactics which the possession of such weaponry implies. Pol Pot's men were capable of being the kind of (very malign) agents that they were only because of the artefacts they had at their disposal, which, so to speak, turned them from mere men into devils with extraordinary powers. Their kind of agency would be unthinkable except in conjunction with the spatio-temporally expanded capacity for violence which the possession of mines makes possible. Pol Pot's soldiers possessed (like all of us) what I shall later discuss as 'distributed personhood'. As agents, they were not just where their bodies were, but in many different places (and times) simultaneously. Those mines were components of their identities as human persons, just as much as their fingerprints or the litanies of hate and fear which inspired their actions.

If we think of an anti-personnel mine, not as a 'tool' made use of by a (conceptually independent) 'user', but, more realistically, as a component of a particular type of social identity and agency, then we can more readily see why a mine can be seen as an 'agent'—that is, but for this artefact, this agent (the soldier + mine) could not exist. In speaking of artefacts as 'secondary agents' I am referring to the fact that the origination and manifestation of agency takes place in a milieu which consists (in large part) of artefacts, and that agents, thus, 'are' and do not merely 'use' the artefacts which connect them to social others. Anti-personnel mines are not (primary) agents who initiate happenings through acts of will for which they are morally responsible, granted, but they are objective embodiments of the *power or capacity to will their use*, and hence moral entities in themselves. I describe artefacts as 'social agents' not because I wish to promulgate a form of material-culture mysticism, but only in view of the fact that objectification in artefact-form is how social agency manifests and realizes itself, via the proliferation of fragments of 'primary' intentional agents in their 'secondary' artefactual forms.

2.5.2. Agents and Patients

Many more examples of social agency being attributed to 'things' will be provided as the discussion proceeds, but there is another issue which needs to be dealt with in this connection. There is a special feature of the concept of agency that I am advancing to which I must draw particular attention. 'Agency' is usually discussed in relation to the permanent dispositional characteristics of particular entities: 'here is X, is it an agent or not?' And the answer is—'that depends on whether X has intentions, a mind, awareness, consciousness, etc.' The issue of 'agency' is thus raised in a classificatory context, classifying all the entities in the world into those that 'count' as agents, and those that do not. Most philosophers believe that only human beings are *pukka* agents, while a few more would add some of the mammals, such as chimpanzees, and some would also include computers with appropriately 'intelligent' software. It is important to emphasize that I am not raising the question of 'agency' in anything like this 'classificatory' sense. The concept of agency I employ is relational and context-dependent, not classificatory and context free. Thus, to revert to the 'car' example; though I would spontaneously attribute 'agency' to my car if it broke down in the middle of the night, far from home, with me in it, I do not think that my car has goals and intentions, as a vehicular agent, that are independent of the use that I and my family make of my car, with which it can co-operate or not. My car is a (potential) agent with respect to me as a 'patient', not in respect to itself, as a car. It is an agent only in so far as I am a patient, and it is a 'patient' (the counterpart of an agent) only is so far as I am an agent with respect to it.

The concept of agency I employ here is exclusively relational: for any agent, there is a patient, and conversely, for any patient, there is an agent. This considerably reduces the ontological havoc apparently caused by attributing agency freely to non-living things, such as cars. Cars are not human beings, but they act as agents, and suffer as patients 'in the (causal) vicinity' of human beings, such as their owners, vandals, and so on. Thus I am not really indulging in paradox or mysticism in describing, as I shall, a picture painted by an artist as a 'patient' with respect to his agency as an artist, or the victim of a cruel caricature as a 'patient' with respect to the image (agent) which traduces him. Philosophers may rest content with the notion that, in such locutions, the only *pukka* agents are the human ones, and that cars and caricatures (secondary agents) could never be *pukka* agents. I, on the other hand, am concerned not with the philosophical definition of agency *sub specie aeternitatis*. I am concerned with agent/patient relationships in the fleeting contexts and predicaments of social life, during which we certainly do, transactionally speaking, attribute agency to cars, images, buildings, and many other non-living, non-human, things.

In what follows, we will be concerned with 'social agents' who may be persons, things, animals, divinities, in fact, anything at all. All that is stipulated is that with respect to *any given transaction* between 'agents' one agent is exercising 'agency' while the other is (momentarily) a 'patient'. This follows from the essentially relational, transitive, and causal implications of our notion of 'agency'. To be an 'agent' one must act with respect to the 'patient'; the patient is the object which is causally affected by the agent's action. For the purposes of the theory being developed here, it will be assumed that in any given transaction in which agency is manifested, there is a 'patient' who or which is *another 'potential' agent*, capable of acting as an agent or being a locus of agency. This 'agent' is momentarily in the 'patient' position. Thus, in the 'car' example just considered, if my car breaks down in the middle of the night, I am in the 'patient' position and the car is the 'agent'. If I should respond to this emergency by shouting at, or maybe even punching or kicking my unfortunate vehicle, then I am the agent and the car is the patient, and so on. The various possibilities and combinations of agency/patiency will be described in detail later on.

It is important to understand, though, that 'patients' in agent/patient interactions are not entirely passive; they may resist. The concept of agency implies the overcoming of resistance, difficulty, inertia, etc. Art objects are characteristically 'difficult'. They are difficult to make, difficult to 'think', difficult to transact. They fascinate, compel, and entrap as well as delight the spectator. Their peculiarity, intransigence, and oddness is a key factor in their efficacy as social instruments. Moreover, in the vicinity of art objects, struggles for control are played out in which 'patients' intervene in the enchainment of intention, instrument, and result, as 'passive agents', that is, intermediaries between ultimate agents and ultimate patients. Agent/patient relations form nested hierarchies whose characteristics will be described in due course. The concept of the 'patient' is not, therefore a simple one, in that being a 'patient' may be a form of (derivative) agency.

2.6. *The Artist*

However, we still have not specified the situation sufficiently to circumscribe the scope of an 'anthropological theory of art'. Agency can be ascribed to 'things' without this giving rise to anything particularly recalling the production and circulation of 'art'. For this to be the case it seems necessary to specify the identity of the participants in social relations in the vicinity of the 'index' rather more precisely.

The kinds of 'index' with which the anthropological theory of art has to deal are usually (but not always) artefacts. These artefacts have the capacity to index their 'origins' in an act of *manufacture*. Any artefact, by virtue of being a manufactured thing, motivates an abduction which specifies the identity of the agent who made or originated it. Manufactured objects are 'caused' by their makers, just as smoke is caused by fire; hence manufactured objects are indexes of their makers. The index, as manufactured object, is in the 'patient' position in a social relationship with its maker, who is an agent, and without whose agency it would not exist. Since art-making is the kind of making with which we are primarily concerned, it might be most convenient to call the one to whom the authorship of the index (as a physical thing) is attributed, 'the artist'. Wherever it is appropriate, I shall do so, but it is important to note that the anthropology of art cannot be exclusively concerned with objects whose existence is attributed to the agency of 'artists', especially 'human' artists. Many objects which are in fact art objects manufactured by (human) artists, are not believed to have originated in that way; they are thought to be of divine origin or to have mysteriously made themselves. The origins of art objects can be forgotten or concealed, blocking off the abduction leading from the existence of the material index to the agency of an artist.

2.7. *The Recipient*

Art objects lead very transactional lives; being 'made by an artist' is only the first of these. Often an art object indexes, primarily, not the moment and agent of its manufacture, but some subsequent, purely transactional, 'origin'. This applies, for instance, to ceremonial valuables in Melanesia (such as Kula shells) whose actual makers (who are not in the Kula system) are forgotten—Kula shells 'originate' with whoever possessed them as a *kitoum*, that is, as unencumbered ceremonial property (Leach and Leach 1983).

Similarly, in the Victoria and Albert Museum, one may see the beautiful carved onyx cup of the Mogul emperor, Shah Jehan. This cup is Shah Jehan's *kitoum* for all that it is now British government property. But there is a difference, in that in Shah Jehan's cup, we see, first and foremost, the power of the Mogul emperor to command the services of craftsmen possessing more skill and inventiveness than any to be found nowadays. Shah Jehan's agency is not as a maker, but as a 'patron' of art, and his cup indexes his glory in this respect, which contemporary potentates can only emulate in feeble, vulgar, ways.

Thus a second abduction of agency which an index in the form of an artefact normally motivates is the abduction of its 'destination', its intended reception. Artists do not (usually) make art objects for no reason, they make them in order that they should be seen by a public, and/or acquired by a patron. Just as any art object indexes its origins in the activity of an artist, it also indexes its reception by a public, the public it was primarily made 'for'. A Ferrari sports car, parked in the street, indexes the class-fraction of 'millionaire playboys' for whom such cars are made. It also indexes the general public who can only admire such vehicles and envy their owners. A work of contemporary art indexes the contemporary art public, who constitute the intended recipients of such work. If the work is to be seen in the Saachi gallery, it indexes this famous collector and his patronage of contemporary art. And so on. In the course of their careers, art objects can have many receptions. While I am able to feel that I belong (as a gallery-goer and occasional reader of *Art Now* and similar periodicals) to the 'intended' public for contemporary art, I know perfectly well that the Egyptian art in the British Museum was never intended for my eyes. This art permits the vicarious abduction of its original, or intended reception, as a component of its current, non-intended reception.

The public, or 'recipients' of a work of art (index) are, according to the anthropological theory of art, in a social relationship with the index, either as 'patients' (in that the index causally affects them in some way) or as 'agents' in that, but for them, this index would not have come into existence (they have caused it). The relation between the index and its reception will be analysed in greater detail in due course. For the present it is sufficient to stipulate that an index has always to be seen in relation to some specific reception and that this reception may be active or passive, and is likely to be diverse.

2.8. *The Prototype*

To complete the specification of the network of social relationships in the vicinity of art objects, we need only one more concept, one which need not always apply, but which very commonly does. Most of the literature about 'art' is actually about representation. That representation is the most complicated philosophical and conceptual problem stemming from the production and circulation of works of art there is no doubt. Of course, by no means all 'art' actually is representational, even in the barest sense, and often it is the case that the 'representational content' of art is trivial, even if the art is representational (e.g. the bottles and guitars in Cubist still lifes, or the botanically arbitrary flowers and leaves in textile patterns). I do not propose to discuss the problem of representation as a philosophical problem in any detail. I should, however, state that I espouse the anti-Goodmanian view which has been gaining ground recently (Schier 1986). I do not believe that iconic representation is based on symbolic 'convention' (comparable to the 'conventions' which dictate that 'dog' means 'canine animal' in English). Goodman, in a well-known philosophical treatise (1976), asserts that any given icon, given the appropriate conventions for reception, could function as a 'representation' of any arbitrarily selected depicted object or 'referent'. The analogy between this proposition and Saussure's well-known postulate of the 'arbitrary nature of the sign' does not need to be underlined. I reject this implausible claim as an overgeneralization of linguistic semiotics. On the contrary, and in accordance with the traditional view, I believe that iconic representation is based on the actual resemblance in form between depictions and the entities they depict or are believed to depict. A picture of an existing thing resembles that thing in enough respects to be recognized as a depiction or model of it. A depiction of an imaginary thing (a god, for instance) resembles the picture that believers in that god have in their minds as to the god's appearance, which they have derived from other images of the same god, which this image resembles. The fact that 'the picture that people have in their minds' of the god's appearance is actually derived from their memories of images which purport to represent this appearance does not matter. What matters to me is only that people believe that the causal arrow is orientated in the other way; they believe that the god, as agent, 'caused' the image (index), as patient, to assume a particular appearance.

It is true that some 'representations' are very schematic, but only very few visual features of the entity being depicted need to be present in order to motivate abductions from the index as to the appearance (in a much more completely specified form) of the entity depicted. 'Recognition' on the basis of very under-specified cues is a well-explored part of the process of visual perception. Under-specified is not the same as 'not specified at all', or 'purely conventional'.

One can only speak of representation in visual art where there is resemblance, triggering recognition. One may need to be told that a given index is an iconic representation of a particular pictorial subject. 'Recognition' may not occur spontaneously, but once the necessary information has been supplied, the visual recognition cues must be present, or recognition will still not occur.

Meanwhile, there are indexes which refer to other entities (such as gods, again) which (*a*) are visible, but which (*b*) do not permit abductions as to the visual appearance of the entity (god) because they lack any visual recognition cues. Sometimes gods are 'represented' by stones, but the god does not 'look like' a stone in anybody's estimation, believer or non-believer alike. The anthropology of art has to consider such instances of 'aniconic' representation, as well as the ones involving more or less overt visual cues as to the appearance of the entity being represented. There are many forms of 'representation' in other words, only one of which is the representation of *visual form*. Approximately, the aniconic image of the god in the form of a stone is an index of the god's spatio-temporal presence, but not his appearance. But in this case, the spatial location of the stone is not 'arbitrarily' or 'conventionally' associated with the spatial location of the god; the stone functions as a 'natural sign' of the god's location just as smoke is a natural sign of the spatial location of fire.

In what follows I shall use the term 'the prototype' (of an index) to identify the entity which the index represents visually (as an icon, depiction, etc.) or non-visually, as in the example just considered. Not all indexes have prototypes or 'represent' anything distinct from themselves. Abstract geometric patterns have no discernible or relevant prototype, but such abstract decorative forms are of great importance theoretically, as I shall describe later. As with the artist (the originator of an index) and the recipient of an index, I hold that there are various types of social agency/patiency relationships linking indexes and their prototypes, where they exist. That is to say, there is a species of agency which is abducted from the index, such that the prototype is taken to be an 'agent' in relation to the index (causing it, for instance, to have the appearance that it actually has). Conversely, the prototype may be made into a social 'patient' via the index (as in 'volt sorcery', to be described later).

2.9. *Summary*

Let me briefly recapitulate the argument so far. The 'anthropological theory of art' is a theory of the social relations that obtain in the neighbourhood of works of art, or indexes. These social relationships form part of the relational texture of social life within the biographical (anthropological) frame of reference. Social relations only exist in so far as they are made manifest in actions. Performers of social actions are 'agents' and they act on 'patients' (who are social agents in the 'patient' position *vis-à-vis* an agent-in-action). Relations between social agents and patients, for the purposes of the anthropological theory of art, obtain between four 'terms' (entities which can be in relation). These are:

1. Indexes: material entities which motivate abductive inferences, cognitive interpretations, etc.;
2. Artists (or other 'originators'): to whom are ascribed, by abduction, causal responsibility for the existence and characteristics of the index;
3. Recipients: those in relation to whom, by abduction, indexes are considered to exert agency, or who exert agency via the index;
4. Prototypes: entities held, by abduction, to be represented in the index, often by virtue of visual resemblance, but not necessarily.

3

The Art Nexus and the Index

3.1. *The Table of Agent/Patient Relations between Four Basic Terms*

Where the four terms—Index, Artist, Recipient, and Prototype—coexist we have, so to speak, the 'canonical' nexus of relations in the neighbourhood of art objects, which the anthropology of art must describe and elucidate. But, as we will see, many instances can be cited in which 'artists' or 'recipients' or 'prototypes' may be lacking or only ambiguously present.

A theory of the kind being developed here consists primarily of a device for ordering and classifying the empirical material with which it deals, rather than offering law-like generalizations or predictions therefrom. The situations in which indexes of an art-like kind can form part of a nexus of social relations between agents are very diverse indeed, and it is necessary to classify them, before offering commentaries which will, in the nature of things, only apply to certain of the situations under consideration, and not to others. One convenient approach to the problem of classification is the construction of a table of combinations, such as the one I will introduce at this point. This table is based on the premiss that all four of the 'terms' so far distinguished can be considered as social agents of different kinds, and as such, are capable of being in the 'agent' or 'patient' position *vis-à-vis* one another (and in relation to themselves). Table 1 therefore opposes indexes, artists, prototypes, and recipients as, respectively, 'agents' (horizontally, reading downwards) and as 'patients' (vertically, reading across).

Turning to Table 1, I shall now embark on an account of agent/patient relations between opposed terms, using the suffixes -A and -P to indicate agent and patient status respectively. I consider first the index, in the 'agent' position.

3.2. *Index-A ⟶ Artist-P*

The index is the material thing which motivates abductions of an art-related kind. What we have to consider under this rubric are instances in which the material index dictates to the artist, who responds as 'patient' to its inherent agency. This, of course is the precise inversion of the relationship which we normally think of as obtaining between artists and indexes, which is Artist-A ⟶ Index-P. However, it is possible, if not very easy, to find examples. Thus, Father Roman Pane, who wrote an account of the religion of the inhabitants of the Antilles, at the behest of Christopher Columbus, reported that: 'Certain

Table 1. *The Art Nexus*

AGENT

		Artist	Index	Prototype	Recipient
P A T I E N T	Artist	Artist as source of creative act / Artist as witness to act of creation	Material inherently dictates to artist the form it assumes	Prototype controls artist's action, appearance of prototype imitated by artist. Realistic art.	Recipient cause of artist's action (as patron)
	Index	Material stuff shaped by artist's agency and intention	Index as cause of itself: 'self-made' / Index as a 'made thing'	Prototype dictates the form taken by index	Recipient the cause of the origination and form taken by the index
	Prototype	Appearance of prototype dictated by artist. Imaginative art	Image or actions of prototype controlled by means of index, a locus of power over prototype	Prototype as cause of index / Prototype affected by index	Recipient has power over the prototype. Volt sorcery.
	Recipient	Recipient's response dictated by artist's skill, wit, magical powers, etc. Recipient captivated.	Index source of power over recipient. Recipient as 'spectator' submits to index.	Prototype has power over the recipient. Image of prototype used to control actions of recipient. Idolatry.	Recipient as patron / Recipient as spectator

trees were believed to send for sorcerers, to whom they gave orders how to shape their trunks into idols, and these "cemu" being then installed into temple-huts, received their prayers and inspired their priests and oracles' (Tylor 1875: 216). Even this terse statement is enough to establish the possibility that, in certain instances, it is an agency in the material of the index, which is held to control the artist, who is a patient with respect to this transaction.

The more common case is for the material index to dictate its form simply on the basis of traditional knowledge, rather than by occult instruction. Turner, in his account of Ndembu 'rituals of affliction' (1968: 72–5), describes the carving of figurines from the wood of the sacred Mukula tree. This tree secretes blood-resembling gum; in the ritual context it is identified as 'the shade' who is causing menstrual and reproductive problems to female patients. After being worshipped, the tree is ritually cut down, and its wood is carved into figurines resembling babies (*ankishi*). These figurines assist the afflicted women in regaining their fertility, via further ritual procedures. In the context of the ritual, it is clear that the tree which is worshipped in its living form and the carved 'babies' that are subsequently made of its wood, are both alternative forms of the fertile/destructive Mukula tree. It is the identity of the index in its living form which imposes form on the index in its subsequent, carved, state, the actual carving being the mere extraction of this inherent form. Perhaps analogous instances are not so hard to discover in the Western art doctrine of 'truth to materials', the idea that it behoves the artist (or craftsman, architect, etc.) to make from his materials what 'they' want, rather than what he wants. The act of carving, famously in the instance of Michelangelo's 'slaves', is often seen as a matter of 'liberating' forms which inhere in the uncut stone or wood.

In this connection, one may also note the more common instances in which the artist does not so much make, as 'recognize' the index. The idea of the 'found object' or the 'ready made' place the artist in the patient position with respect to the index, in that it is the index which inherently possesses the characteristics which motivate its selection by the artist as an art object, to which, none the less his name is attached as originator. Oriental art, especially Japanese, is particularly rich in the use of found objects for artistic purposes, for instance, the natural boulders which are deployed in Japanese gardens. These uncarved stones are, by common consent, among the most entrancing objects to be seen anywhere, and the Buddhist garden-designers who made use of them are far more revered than any stone-carvers from Japan. The West has an activist notion of artistic creativity, whereas the oriental art public esteems far more those 'quietist' modes of creativity in which success attends those who open themselves most to the inherent physiognomic appeal of natural objects. The same tradition exists in Indian tantric art, which involves the cult of natural, or slightly modified, river boulders, nuts of the coco-de-mer, and so on, as *lingam* and *yoni*, though in these instances no artist's name is attached to the object, as it is in Japan. The Indian examples really come under the heading of 'self-made' indexes, which will be discussed later under the heading of Index-A ⟶ Index-P.

Modern Western artists using found objects, most notably Duchamp, are ostensibly less passive. Duchamp claimed that his ready-mades, such as the snow-shovel, the bottle-rack, etc., possessed 'the beauty of indifference', that is, they were selected on the grounds that nobody could possibly imagine that Duchamp had any particular reason to select them, rather than something else (which was, in fact, far from being the case). Their selection was presented as a pure act of will on his part, an *acte gratuite* in the manner of Gide's amoralist hero, Lafcadio Wluiki. However, having 'no reason' to select something as an object of ready-made art, is of course, a reason, since it is motivated by the need to avoid selecting anything for whose selection some reason might be proposed. This was Duchamp's conceit. Consequently, even the purportedly 'arbitrary' ready-mades of Duchamp, forced themselves on the artist (as patient) who responded to the appeal of their arbitrariness and anonymity, just as the Buddhist landscape artists responded to their mutely speaking boulders.

3.3. *Index-A ⟶ Recipient-P*

This is the elementary formula for 'passive spectatorship', which is of course not at all difficult to conceptualize or exemplify. Whoever allows his or her attention to be attracted to an index, and submits to its power, appeal, or fascination, is a patient, responding to the agency inherent in the index. This agency may be physical, spiritual, political, etc. as well as 'aesthetic'. The warrior's shield (Fig. 1.2/1) is an index which, in context, possesses agency, having the power to demoralize the enemy warrior (the recipient/patient). It would be unwise to impose any theoretical restriction as to the type of agency which the index can mediate, since, as we will see, these may be exceedingly diverse. None the less, one may, under the rubric Index-A ⟶ Recipient-P, offer certain general points about the effect of the index on the recipient.

Reconsider, for a moment the Asmat shield which terrifies the opposing warrior. It is surely noteworthy that these designs produce terror by making terror manifest—these designs seem to have been *composed* in a mood of terror, and we are terrified by them (or can easily imagine being terrified by them) because, submitting to their fascination, we are obliged to share in the emotion which they objectify. The tiger which is about to pounce and devour its victim looks, above all, *terrified*—of itself, as it were—and the same is true of warriors bearing down with grimaces of fear and rage. The Asmat shield is a *false mirror*, which seems to show the victim his own terror, when in fact, it is another's—and in this way persuades him that he is terrified. Like the famous *trompe-l'œil* image (by Parmigianino) of the Medusa's head in the mirror of Perseus (in the Uffizi gallery) the shield terrifies by persuading us that *we are what it shows*.

The same 'false mirror' effect is observable in myriad other contexts, and may, according to Benjamin (see Taussig 1993; Benjamin 1933), constitute the very secret of mimesis; that is, to perceive (to internalize) is to imitate, and thus we become (and produce) what we perceive (see below, Sect. 7.2). At any rate, the spectacle of a painted saint at prayer is conducive to piety, of an amorous couple, to lustfulness, and so on, as has been endlessly commented on since ancient times. Without dilating any further on this venerable theme, we may suggest that the primary means through which the index affects the recipient is by subverting the recipient's *sense of self-possession* in some way. It may be that there is, as in the Asmat-shield case, a spontaneous convergence between the index and recipient such that the recipient takes on the nature of the index; but usually the mediation is much more roundabout, as will be described in due course. Indexes can work by alienating the spectator as well as by producing identification (e.g. Hyacinthe Rigaud's picture of Louis XIV, discussed below, which certainly is *not* intended to make the spectator feel 'regal' or to identify with the monarch, but to have exactly the reverse effect).

Nor can the formula Index-A ⟶ Recipient-P be restricted to those contexts in which the recipient is confined to *seeing* the index, as opposed to interacting with the index in some other way. For instance, kissing a holy icon will, some believers hope, elicit the agency of the image in relieving illness or poverty. Not all images with the same ostensible 'reference' are equally efficacious in this regard; only some images, for example, of the Virgin, have this quality. Worshipping the others may assist in one's salvation, but will not cure one's rheumatism. So it is the inherent agency of the material index, rather than the Virgin, which is at issue (whatever the priest says). Wherever images have to be *touched*, rather than merely looked at, there is an imputation that there is inherent agency in the material index, which is not to say that the agency of the prototype is excluded in these instances.

And here we encounter a difficulty in presentation. The formula for passive spectatorship, Index-A ⟶ Recipient-P is so fundamental and general that it is difficult to cite a 'pure' case. The 'holy icon of the Virgin which cures rheumatism' is probably more accurately represented as [[Prototype-A] → Index-A] ⟶ Recipient-P, than by the simple formula (the Prototype being the Virgin Mary). I intend to deal with three-place and four-place expressions later, however, where I will explain the significance of the brackets and provide a more perspicuous graphic representation. For the present, it will be sufficient to stipulate that where the index is not seen primarily as the outcome of an external artist's agency, and where it also has no prototype, its agency with respect to the recipient will be a pure case of Index-A ⟶ Recipient-P.

3.4. *Index-A ⟶ Prototype-P*

Here the index behaves as an agent with respect to its prototype. A familiar example of this is provided by Wilde's short story *The Portrait of Dorian Grey*, in which the ageing undergone by the picture in the attic causes the prototype to retain his youthful good looks indefinitely. The fact that this is a fictional example need not deter one from citing it, since anthropology has to deal with fictions as much as with real situations, the two often being hard to tell apart, anyway. Another type of instance of Index-A ⟶ Prototype-P is in sorcery, where the injury done to a representation of the victim causes injury to the victim; this very common type of image-sorcery ('volt sorcery') will play an important part in the argument later on. However, as with Index-A ⟶ Recipient-P, Index-A ⟶ Prototype-P is more commonly encountered with recipients or artists or sorcerers in the 'agent' position as well, in a three- or four-place expression.

Next, I consider the 'Index' in the 'Patient' position.

3.5. *Artist-A* ⟶ *Index-P*

This is the elementary formula for artistic agency. The index usually motivates the abduction of the agency of the person who made it. The index is, in these instances, a congealed 'trace' of the artist's creative performance. Much post-Renaissance Western art projects the artist's agency in a very salient manner. The brushwork in works by Van Gogh emanates an almost palpable sense of the artist's presence, smearing and dabbing the still viscous oil paint. Jackson Pollock's 'drip' paintings provide even more striking examples. They have no subject at all except the agency of Jackson Pollock himself; they are (non-representational) self-portraits of a man in frenzied ballistic activity.[1] Among the very earliest examples of art of any kind are the famous hand-prints which occur beside the cave paintings of Lascaux, Altamira, etc. These are particularly 'pure' cases of Artist-A ⟶ Index-P.

3.6. *Recipient-A* ⟶ *Index-P*

This is the elementary formula for 'patronage' and/or 'the spectator as agent'. In so far as a recipient can abduct his/her own agency from an index, this formula is satisfied. One does not have to lift a finger in order to feel that one has 'made' something. One may readily conceive that a great king (such as Louis XIV strolling in the grounds of Versailles) surveying the works he has commissioned and financed, regards himself as the author of the scene before his eyes, for all that these works have been created, in the material sense, by hosts of architects, artists, craftsmen, masons, gardeners, and other labourers. The patron as provider of the commission is an efficient cause of the index; his glorification is its final cause. The patron is the conduit of the social causation of such works of art; his agency is therefore readily abducted from it.

But it is not just great patrons such as Louis XIV who have to be considered in this connection. There is a more general sense, which has been given particular prominence in contemporary aesthetic theory, in which recipiency as spectatorship conceals a form of agency. 'Seeing' is a form of agency in psychological theories of perception which emphasize the way in which perception 'goes beyond the information given'. According to such theories, the mind of the perceiver actively 'constructs' the perceptual image of the thing perceived. Semiotic/interpretative theories of art give prominence to the fact that what a person sees in a picture, or, even more, gleans from an utterance or a text, is a function of their previous experience, their mind-set, their culture, etc. Readers, according to some critical theorists, have been promoted to a status hardly distinguishable from that once occupied by writers; and I think that gallery-goers

---

[1] On 'ballistic' activity, see below on Artist-A ⟶ Artist-P.

have shared, though to a lesser degree, in the transfer of agency from the originators of works of art to the recipients of works of art. I do not wish to discuss literary theory, since I am only interested in visual art. But one can hardly fail to take note of the fact that many members of the contemporary art public have actually internalized the view critics take of their agency as recipients of art, that is, they attribute creativity to themselves as spectators, who can 'make something' out of the raw material presented to them in the art gallery, in effect Recipient-A $\longrightarrow$ Index-P. Artists collude in this, disclaiming their own undivided agency and transferring partial responsibility for their art to its public.

The ideological congruence between the 'spectator as agent' theory and other aspects of Western individualism is too obvious to need underlining. Gallery-goers, who are mostly middle class and educated, are involved in life-projects which are predicated on individual freedom, autonomy, personal responsibility, and so on. They are hardly likely to abandon these existential attitudes on entering a gallery. They do not feel passive; after all, entering a gallery is something they do voluntarily, out of motives which can certainly be attributed to their own social agency.[2] In ages past, the art public more resembled, in its own estimation, the religious devotees who humbly submit to the power of the icon and who find causes for personal satisfaction in their very passivity before it (Index-A $\longrightarrow$ Recipient-P). But it is certainly true, now, that spectatorship is seen as a form of agency, even though the spectator role simultaneously involves the passive registering of a 'given' art object.

Such considerations aside, there is almost always a sense in which the recipients of a work of art can see their own agency in the index. Even if one is not 'the patron' who caused the work of art to be made, any spectator may infer that, in a more general sense, the work of art was made for him or her. A religious congregation, for instance, is entitled to think that their piety and devotion were contributory to the causation of the cathedral in which they worship, even though this cathedral was constructed centuries earlier, because they (not unreasonably) believe that the cathedral was erected *with them in mind*, the future generations of worshippers therein. They are, in other words, the teleological cause of the cathedral. Alternatively, in that gallery art is a commodity, gallery-goers as consumers can infer that their 'demand' for art is the factor ultimately responsible for its existence, just as the existence of any commodity on the market is an index of consumer demand for it.

---

[2] On the other hand, exactly the same degree of agency could be attributed to the thousands of pilgrims flocking to Mecca, to circumambulate and kiss the Kaaba, who are also voluntary pilgrims seeking salvation through their own efforts, not religious automata. The extent to which the culturally inculcated belief in agency of spectatorship is a screen, concealing from modern souls the extent to which their actions are driven by social imperatives, cannot be determined here. For our purposes what is important are the beliefs that people hold, not whether these beliefs are justified.

3.7. *Prototype-A ⟶ Index-P*

The agency of the prototype can frequently be abducted from the index. There are obvious ways in which 'prototypes' can have agency attributed to them. In our own art system this kind of agency is everywhere manifest, since it is essential to the notion of 'realistic representation'. Let me give an example. Who is responsible for the appearance of the Duke of Wellington in Goya's well-known portrait? We might be tempted to invoke Goya's name here, because we are so inclined to impute primary agency to artists with respect to works of art, but this is not so self-evident as it appears. Goya's task was to make a representation of the Duke of Wellington, the prototype of the index he produced. He could not produce a picture of a little girl with golden curls and tell the world that this represented the Duke; he would have been regarded as insane and the Duke would have been understandably displeased. In the circumstances, he had to produce a portrait depicting the features actually possessed by the Duke and regarded as characteristic of his persona, his Roman nose, serious demeanour, military attire, etc. It is reasonable to attribute agency to the Duke of Wellington with respect to his portrait by Goya, not because he wielded Goya's brushes, but because, in the social nexus which existed between Goya, his painting, and the Duke, he dictated the strokes Goya *had to make* with his brush, merely by possessing certain features which it was Goya's task to represent. The Duke, in other words, played a causal role with respect to the appearance of his portrait. However, this is not a 'pure case' of Prototype-A ⟶ Index-P in that Goya's mediation, as artist, is an essential feature of the situation: [[Duke/Prototype-A] → Goya/Artist-A] ⟶ Index-P would be a more accurate formula.

Actually, in this instance, the Duke of Wellington (as the possessor of a given physiognomy) is best considered a 'secondary agent', part of the causal milieu surrounding and permitting the manifestation of the 'primary' agency of the artist, Goya.

Photography was, once upon a time, considered to be an 'artist-less' mode of image-production, and is still so seen by some. The image which forms itself out of light emanating from the prototype provides a model for the 'pure' case.

3.8. *The Centrality of the Index*

These are all the abductions which can be drawn from the index as agent and as patient. Turning to Table 1, we see that there are quite a number of other agent–patient relationships to be considered. Thus we have Artist-A ⟶ Recipient-P, Artist-A ⟶ Prototype-P, Recipient-A ⟶ Prototype-P and so on. The relevant cells in Table 1 provide indications of the relationships involved. However, there is a theoretical problem associated with discussing them separately, one by one. A basic constraint on the theory being developed here is that unless there is an *index*, there can be no abductions of agency, and since the topic of this theoretical enterprise is precisely the abduction of agency from indexes, the index has to be present for analysis to proceed. One can construct formulae which lack the artist, or the recipient, or the prototype, but not ones which lack the index. It follows that a formula such as Artist-A $\longrightarrow$ Recipient-P is always implicitly [[Artist-A] $\rightarrow$ Index-A] $\longrightarrow$ Recipient-P, or some variant thereof, including the index. So cells in Table 1 which show binary relations between terms neither of which is an index are not theoretically 'well-formed' expressions.

However, for purposes of general guidance, I will later give a brief account of these illegitimately formed expressions, since there is no point in being pedantic. Then I will proceed to discuss the 'self-reciprocal' relations, Index-A $\longrightarrow$ Index-P, Artist-A $\longrightarrow$ Artist-P, Recipient-A $\longrightarrow$ Recipient-P, Prototype-A $\longrightarrow$ Prototype-P, of which the last three are not 'well formed' either. I particularly need to do so because the reader may be at a loss to imagine what may be intended by self-reciprocal relations, for example, an artist being an agent with respect to himself.

3.8.1. The Logic of 'Primary' and 'Secondary' Agents and Patients

Before turning to the 'illegitimate' expressions, I can specify the 'logic' of well-formed expressions rather more precisely; the centrality of the 'index' is not all there is to it. Let me return to the distinction, sketched in earlier, between 'primary' agents (entities endowed with the capacity to initiate actions/events through will or intention) and 'secondary' agents, entities not endowed with will or intention by themselves but essential to the formation, appearance, or manifestation of intentional actions. It will be apparent that 'indexes' are, normally, 'secondary' agents in this scene; they borrow their agency from some external source, which they mediate and transfer to the patient. It will be equally apparent that 'artists' are normally 'primary' agents. They initiate actions on their own behalf. This is true even if, as is often the case, they act under the direction of patrons. The artist may be a socially subordinate agent, a hired hand, but unless the artist wills it, the index he has been hired to make will never come into existence. In other words, 'subordinate' (but still 'primary') agency of this kind, is logically quite distinct from 'secondary' agency, as I have just defined it.

Approximately, then, artists are primary agents and indexes are secondary agents. What of recipients and prototypes? Recipients are just like artists; they are primary agents and/or primary patients, the sources, prime movers, or intended (social) targets of art-mediated agency. Unless recipients were primary agents, the art nexus would not be (as it is) a series of social transactions between persons, but a recondite type of causal interaction between things.

Prototypes are more ambiguously situated. In general, the prototype of an index is not an intentional or 'primary' agent; an apple (say) does not 'intend' to appear to us (or to a painter) as round, red and green, of certain dimensions, etc. Nor does it intend to be represented at all. It just has these visual characteristics, and these are part of the 'causal milieu' which the artist exploits, and contends with, in producing (as a primary agent) an index which will trigger 'recognition' as a representation of an apple. The apple is a 'secondary' agent though, in that it is only by 'submitting' to the apple, by allowing the apple to impress itself on him, that the artist can attain his goal (as an agent) of 'representing an apple'. Anyone who has tried and failed to draw a 'difficult' object, such as the human hand, will know what it is to be an artist in the 'patient' position, confronted by the prototype-as-agent.

However, prototypes are not always just 'secondary' agents, part of the causal milieu of art-making and circulation. Some entities, unlike apples, 'will' their appearance as intentional beings, and hence also will their appearance as subjects for portrayal. Anyone can see that the Louis XIV of Hyacinthe Rigaud's well-known portrait is looking as he wishes to look—he has devoted his whole career, it seems, to perfecting his expression of *hauteur*, and his very features have been moulded into a mask of power, as if they were of latex rather than living flesh. His pose and magnificent dress are equally manifestations of his royal power of command over appearances, especially his own. In an instance such as this, the distinction between patron (recipient) and prototype threatens to dissolve. Rigaud's agency, though still indisputably present and 'primary' is utterly subordinated to Louis XIV's as patron of the art-making process and also as the one who has the power to appear precisely as he wishes to appear (like a god). Here artist and patron/prototype jointly exercise 'primary' agency, whereas in the 'apple' case, the artist's agency is primary and the prototype's is secondary. In short, where the prototype is an object not normally thought capable of exercising primary agency 'in the world', then as the subject of representation, it will convey only secondary agency; but where the prototype of an index is an entity (such as a king, magician, divine being, etc.) endowed with the ability to intend its own appearance, then the prototype may be partly or wholly a primary agent as well as a secondary agent.

Now a word about the general logical format of the expressions I shall be developing in later sections. The pivot of the art nexus is always the index. The index, however, is never, or at least rarely, a 'primary' agent (or patient). The index is just the 'disturbance' in the causal milieu which reveals, and potentiates, agency exercised and patient-hood suffered on either side of it—by the primary agents, by recipients (patrons and spectators), by artists, and to a lesser extent, prototypes. The index is articulated in the causal milieu, whereas intentional agency and patient-hood somehow lie just outside it. The index is at once a prosthesis, an extra limb, of the patron and/or artist, while it is also the handle, attached to the patient-recipient, which is grasped and manipulated by external agents like these.

I provide a general depiction of the situation in Fig. 3.8.1/1, which shows the index as the region in the causal milieu in which the 'sphere of action' of the

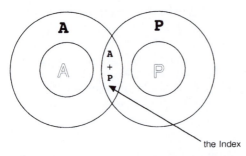

the Index

$\mathbb{A}$ = the primary agent, the artist, as an intentional being

A = the causal milieu over which the artist may exercise agency, the sphere of causal control and influence

$\mathbb{P}$ = the primary patient/recipient (spectator) as an intentional being

P = the causal milieu of the patient, the sphere within which the patient is vulnerable to control and influence via outside agents

A + **P** = the region where the sphere of agency of $\mathbb{A}$ overlaps the sphere of patiency (vulnerability) of $\mathbb{P}$. The Index is located in this region.

FIG. 3.8.1/1. The index as the pivot of the art nexus

primary agent and the 'sphere of vulnerability' of the primary patient meet and overlap.

There is thus a general pattern which underlies all the examples I will be discussing in the ensuing sections; all of which are really no more than variations on the pattern shown in Fig. 3.8.1/1. That is to say, we are concerned with relations between 'primary' agents and patients (artists, recipients) who figure, so to speak, at the points of origin and termination of art-mediated chains of transactions. These transactions manifest themselves in the causal milieu which they both share, in the form of 'secondary' or derivative agents and patients which are indexes, objectifications of agency distributed in the causal milieu:

> Primary agent ⟶ (secondary patient → secondary agent) ⟶ primary patient.

However, the interest of all this does not lie simply, I hope, in the elaboration of abstract models such as these. Let us return to a more informal exploration of the cells shown in Table 1, making use of relevant examples.

3.9. *The 'Illegitimate' Expressions*

1. Artist-A ⟶ Prototype-P. This is the general formula for 'imaginary' images made by artists. From our point of view, an index is an instance of 'imaginary' image-making, when its appearance is held to have been dictated

by the artist and to be an index of his agency as an imaginer of the appearances of things. William Blake's well-known pencil-sketch of *The Ghost of a Flea* is a pure case of imaginary art, and a pure case of artistic agency dictating the appearance of a (fictional) entity. Any picture of a unicorn is also 'imaginary' in that, as unicorns are as fictional as the ghosts of fleas, no artist has patiently attempted to delineate their forms 'from life'. On the other hand, the unicorn is a 'received image' which was not invented by the agency of any known artist who has represented a unicorn. An artist who depicts a unicorn is not dictating the form of the prototype, even though the prototype is fictional, so this is not Artist-A ⟶ Prototype-P, in the 'pure' sense. Meanwhile, each artist may invent various details of the unicorn he represents, so, in those particular respects, the formula would be satisfied. The inverse of Artist-A ⟶ Prototype-P is:

2. Prototype-A ⟶ Artist-P, which is the formula for 'realist' image-making. Here, the appearance of the prototype dictates what the artist does. I introduced this concept of 'realistic depiction' earlier under the heading of 'Prototype-A (Duke of Wellington) ⟶ Index-P (his portrait by Goya). The prototype, as social agent, in this case, impresses his/her/its appearance on the index, via the mediating agency of the artist, who is a 'patient' with respect to the prototype while remaining an 'agent' with respect to the index. In sum, the pair of expressions Artist-A ⟶ Prototype-P versus Prototype-A ⟶ Artist-P encodes the basic contrast between artistic activity as the origination of appearances versus artistic activity as the 'realistic' depiction or imitation of 'given' appearances. In practice, any given index may motivate the abduction of both of these formulae; that is, in certain respects, the index shows the artist's imagination at work, causing the prototype to have a particular appearance, while in other respects, the index shows the prototype causing the artist to reproduce, passively, its 'given' appearance.

3. Artist-A ⟶ Recipient-P. This formula expresses the power of the artist as a social agent over the recipient as a social patient. Many works of art inspire wonder, awe, fear, and other powerful emotions in the spectator. Artists, whose technical prowess enables them to produce these powerful effects on recipients, are (sometimes) heroes, magicians, persons of power and consequence (see e.g. Kris and Kurtz 1929; Forge 1966; Morphy 1991). The particular nature of the awe aroused by artistic activity is taken up below in a separate Section (5.2, below), besides which I have already written at some length on this topic elsewhere (Gell 1992*b*, 1993). The reciprocal of the artist-as-hero (Artist-A ⟶ Recipient-P) is:

4. Recipient-A ⟶ Artist-P, the formula for the 'artist as artisan', that is, a hired hand who does the recipient's bidding. Here the recipient figures as the 'patron' (see above, 3.6) rather than as the passive spectator. The pair of formulae Artist-A ⟶ Recipient-P/Recipient-A ⟶ Artist-P, as with the pair Artist-A ⟶ Prototype-P/Prototype-A ⟶ Artist-P may both be abducted from the same index simultaneously. That is to say, from one point of view,

the index may manifest the independent agency of the artist and his pre-eminence over the spectator, while the same index, from another point of view manifests the subordination of the artist and the pre-eminence of the patron.

5. Prototype-A $\longrightarrow$ Recipient-P. One might call this the 'idol' formula. Here the agency abducted from the index, by the patient-recipient, is that of the prototype, who, besides causing the index to assume a certain appearance, exercises social agency *vis-à-vis* the recipient. A typical instance of this is the practice of dictators, such as Mao and Stalin, in having enormous images of themselves posted on walls, keeping the population under continuous surveillance and control via their images. Later on in this book, I shall discuss the worship of images in considerable detail, so there is no need to adduce detailed examples at this stage. However, it is important to note that this formula is also 'reversible' in the same way as the ones I dealt with a moment ago. The inverse of Prototype-A $\longrightarrow$ Recipient-P is:

6. Recipient-A $\longrightarrow$ Prototype-P. This is the 'volt sorcery' formula. Volt sorcery is the practice of inflicting harm on the prototype of an index by inflicting harm on the index; for example, sticking pins into a wax image of the prototype. Volt sorcery will play a large part in the argument later, as well, so I shall not give any more details at this stage. In general Recipient-A $\longrightarrow$ Prototype-P refers to situations in which the prototype can be 'got at' in some way via his or her image. This may be as a result of malign artistic agency (a case of Artist-A $\longrightarrow$ Recipient-P) or the agency may stem not from the artist's activity in making the image, but the recipient's activity in defacing it. Painting a moustache on a picture of Mrs Thatcher is not necessarily 'artistic agency' so much as a (hostile) mode of reception, through which the recipients of Mrs Thatcher's image can obtain redress against the woman (prototype) they hate and despise. This reception-tactic is not necessarily mystical, that is, based on the supposition of 'sympathetic magic' in the manner of volt sorcery. A poster-defacer might quite rationally suppose that Mrs Thatcher herself, or at least some of her supporters, might see the defaced poster and feel bad as a result of being made aware of the extent of anti-Thatcher feeling.

It will be apparent that Prototype-A $\longrightarrow$ Recipient-P/Recipient-A $\longrightarrow$ Prototype-P form a couple; a single image can be an index of both of these relations simultaneously. Thus an idol is simultaneously an index through which the god mediates his agency over his devotees, who submit to him in the form of his image; but at the same time, the devotees actually have power over the god via his image, because it is they who have made, installed, and consecrated the idol, it is they who offer sacrifices and prayers etc., without which the god would hardly be so consequential. In fact, there is a great deal more in common between volt sorcery and idol-worship than initially meets the eye (see below, Ch. 7).

This completes our survey of the cells in Table 1 with the exception of the cells showing 'self-reciprocal' agency. To these I shall now turn.

3.10. *Index-A* ⟶ *Index-P*

An index can be seen as the 'cause' of itself. To convey an idea of this, imagine being a spectator at a performance of the Chinese State Circus's acrobatics team. At a certain point all the acrobats start clambering over one another and lo!—as if by magic they have turned themselves into a majestic human pyramid. But who or what has made this pyramid? Clearly, the acrobatics team. And of what does this pyramid consist?—the acrobatics team. The human pyramid as an index (and a kind of work of art) is a 'patient' in the sense that it is something that is made by someone (a collective someone, in this instance) but it is also an 'agent' in that the act of 'making' is one that it performs on itself; it is self-made. There are many works of art (indexes) which have characteristics similar to a human pyramid created by acrobats. For instance, long yams are displayed at annual festivals by the Abelam of the Sepik district, New Guinea, as cult objects. They are in fact decorated (painted and provided with masks) but the object on display is the yam itself, rather than the mask. Yams grow themselves. It is true that yam-growers can assist yams to grow, technically, by hollowing out the earth around the growing tuber, and socially, by refraining from sexual intercourse, which is deleterious (or more precisely, offensive) to yams. The yam must be magically protected, but the magic of yam-growing does not cause tuberous growth. The powers of growth inherent in yams is precisely why they are cultivated ceremonially and exhibited; they are objects of wonderment, attaining, sometimes, lengths of over ten feet. Yams of these dimensions are utterly inedible, their only destiny is to be looked at and to be a source of planting material (yams are, of course, alive and social agents, just like people). The ethnographer (Forge 1966) is quite explicit in stating that yams are 'art objects' categorically assimilated to the sculptures and painting which the Abelam also make and display.

Abelam yams provide a suitable example of indexes which exert agency with respect to themselves. This is the abductive inference drawn by the Abelam, but it is not in the least obscure; all living things are agents with respect to themselves in that their growth and form may be attributed to their own agency. What is counter-intuitive, from our point of view is that 'yams' should be considered person-like agents and 'works of art'. But of course horticulturalists frequently do personify their plants and the blooming back-gardens of England abound with unacknowledged animists. The behaviour of attenders at garden shows is exactly comparable to the behaviour of spectators at art shows except that it is generally less self-conscious and solemn. Highly nuanced aesthetic judgements are freely voiced on the subject of roses and cauliflowers by no-nonsense matrons who would hardly care to utter any opinions at all on 'works of art' explicitly identified as such. Such is the nature of our art world, which is no more rational than the one operated by the Abelam, but which is predicated on a different set of social relationships—social class relationships in

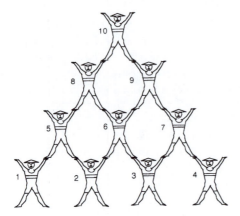

FIG. 3.10/1. The self-made index

particular (Bourdieu 1984). We find it hard to see things which 'grow by them-selves' as works of art because, for us, the activities of an 'artist' are intrinsic to the concept of art itself. But from the standpoint of the anthropology of art this is merely a relative matter, an axis of comparison between different art systems.

However, we do not have to consider only indexes which actually 'make themselves' under this heading. Agency is not just 'making' but any modality through which something affects something else. Indexes do commonly—indeed universally perhaps—exert agency over themselves in the sense that they consist of visual parts, and these parts are seen as affecting one another internally to the index.

To revert to the human pyramid formed by the acrobatics team; when we see this form we recognize that it is in stable equilibrium. Each acrobat is exert-ing the necessary force to maintain this equilibrium, but if one should make an unexpected movement, then we should fear to see the whole pyramid collapse. The forces in the structure, the agency exercised by one part (one acrobat) with respect to the others, are visually embodied in the structure as a whole (Fig. 3.10/1). What we see is a complex network of agent/patient relationships between individual acrobats, pairs and triads of acrobats, etc. *within* the index. Thus acrobat 6 can be seen as the agent who holds up 8 and 9, and the patient whom 2 and 3 hold up. Together with 5 and 7, he is part of a three-man team, jointly holding up 8, 9, and 10, and jointly sustained by 1, 2, 3, and 4, and so on. Innumerable relations of this kind can be extracted.

The important point is that it is not just in connection with works of art whose 'parts' consist of human acrobats that such part-to-part and part-to-whole agent/patient relations can be extracted (or abducted). The same is equally true of artefactual indexes of all kinds. Indeed, the kind of part-to-part and part-to-whole agent/patient (cause and effect) relationships within indexes

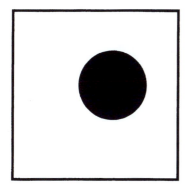

FIG. 3.10/2. The black disc looks as if it 'wanted' to return to the centre of the square. *Source*: Arnheim 1974

is the subject-matter of the most developed branch of the cognitive psychology of art, the part developed from Gestalt psychology by Rudolf Arnheim in his classic treatise on art and visual perception (1974). Fig. 3.10/2 comes from the opening pages of Arnheim's work, and it demonstrates a fundamental visual-cognitive phenomenon. Whereas if the black disc were positioned in the centre of the white square it would appear to be at rest, as it is in the figure the disc seems to be drawn towards the right against some kind of resistance or tension (ibid. 12–13). Parts of indexes (such as the disc, though of course, Arnheim does not use this language) are shown to be at the conductors of pictorial 'forces' affecting the appearance of balance, energy, growth, dynamics, etc. (*passim*). I have no intention of summarizing Arnheim's authoritative presentation of visual psychology at this stage; the important point to note is that the idea of agency internal to the (pictorial or sculptural) index is an exceedingly familiar one.

Abstract art exploits our perception of internal agency (or to be more precise, cause and effect) within the index to a great degree and in fairly obvious ways. Patches of colour seem to whirl around, hover, clash, and fragment as if they had internal sources of energy and were engaged in complex causal interactions. With representational art the situation is different, in that we have to distinguish between the 'internal' causal domain of the picture surface or sculptural form, and the external causal processes in the world to which the index relates. One of the most striking examples of 'apparent causality' in Western art are the perfectly modelled depressions in the soft flesh of Persephone's thigh, produced by the fingers of Pluto grasping her in Bernini's masterpiece of illusionistic sculpture (see Fig. 3.10/3). These marble depressions are 'representations' of the causal nexus between gripping fingers and yielding flesh; but I do not think we see them as such. Instead—so compelling is the illusion—we see these depressions as instances, rather than representations, of causality. This kind of *trompe l'œil* pseudo-causality (agent/patient

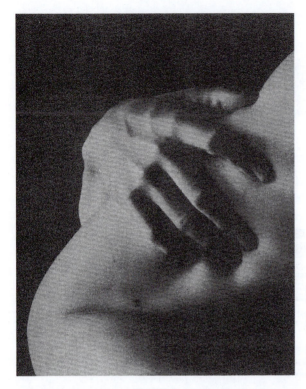

FIG. 3.10/3. Causality made visible: detail from *Pluto and Persephone* by Bernini. *Source*: H. Hibbard (1976), *Bernini* (2nd edn.; Harmondsworth: Penguin), plate 16

interaction) within the index is not necessarily confined to illusionistic Western art. Any representational index, which depicts causal interactions in the proto-type, can also be considered as a separate domain of causality unto itself, in which parts of the index causally interact with other parts of the index.

However, in the light of our previous discussion of primary and secondary agency, it is necessary to qualify the above in certain respects. Abstract patterns appear to show 'cause and effect' relations between motifs rather than 'agent/patient' relations between motifs, in that nothing makes us think that the motifs in patterns are sentient in themselves, that they have intentions or desires etc. Whereas the part-to-whole relations within the human pyramid testify to 'primary' intentionality on the part of acrobats whom we instantly recognize as intentional agents, the same is not true of the relations between the individual flower motifs on our floral drapes, be they ever so bustling. These motifs only have 'secondary' agency, they manifest the effect of agency/intentionality without possessing it intrinsically. These motifs only interact causally with one another, not intentionally. However, even in this case, we do see 'intentional activity' here, but it is displaced onto the imaginary creator of the pattern, rather than onto the physical constituents of the pattern. Complex causal relations, whether they are only 'suggested'—as in patterns and abstract art—or whether they are depicted directly, as in Bernini's *Pluto and Persephone*, testify to complex intentional agency not in the index itself, but 'off-stage', in the cunning mind of the artist.

3.11. *Artist-A* ⟶ *Artist-P*

Having explicated the sense in which an index, or candidate work of art, can exercise agency with respect to itself, let me turn to the kind of self-reciprocal agency which can be exercised by artists. Every artist is a patient with respect to the agency s/he exercises, indeed, artistic agency cannot proceed otherwise. Consider the act of drawing something that one has not attempted to draw before (a Chippendale chair, say). One desires to make an index which will refer to this chair. The act of drawing is preceded (whether the object to be drawn is present or not) by an act of visualization of the drawing to be made. One internally rehearses the line(s) which must be produced, and then draws them (a drawing is always really a drawing of a drawing, the drawing in one's head). Because one's hand is not actually directly controlled by the visualized or anticipated line that one wants to draw, but by some mysterious muscular alchemy which is utterly opaque to introspection, the line which appears on the paper is always something of a surprise. At this point one is a spectator of one's own efforts at drawing; that is, one has become a patient. Subliminally, one asks, 'would I recognize this (index) as the chair I wanted to draw?' just as if it had been drawn by somebody else.

Drawing, and most other artistic skills (carving, etc.) are what are known as 'ballistic' activities, muscular performances which take place at a rate such that cognitive processing of the 'outcome' of action only takes place after the act is complete, not while it is in progress. (The archetypal 'ballistic' behaviour is throwing.) Most often, if one is not very good at drawing, the result of one's ballistic chair-drawing gestures are frustrating: 'this chair is not the one I wished to draw—the legs are too long and it is all lop-sided'. The patient position of the would-be artist who cannot draw objects 'as intended' is a familiar predicament. Occasionally though, by a happy muscular fluke, the line drawn is actually superior to the one visualized beforehand.

This is the 'generate and test' sequence which is a fundamental feature of all complex cognitive performances. Dennett quotes Valéry as saying 'It takes two to invent anything. The one makes up the combinations; the other chooses, recognises what he wishes and what is important to him in the mass of things which the former has imparted to him. What we call genius is much less the work of the first one than the readiness of the second one to grasp the value of what has been laid before him and to choose it' (Dennett 1979: 71). Dennett devotes a chapter to vindicating Valéry's argument, though he disagrees that 'choosers' are necessarily more important than 'generators'. Valéry is obviously talking about Artist-A ⟶ Artist-P in precisely our sense. Of course, he is speaking of poetry, an art form which permits indefinitely many cycles of self-correction. This is not always possible in graphic/plastic art, where erasure by the 'chooser' may be difficult or impossible, and the whole enterprise may have to be restarted if the results of any given 'test' cycle are deemed unsatisfactory. However, one does see copious evidence of 'generate and test' in artists' preparatory drawings, especially those by such Renaissance masters of the art of drawing as Raphael and Michelangelo, many of whose exquisitely drawn forms emerge out of clouds of provisional strokes known as *abbozzi*.

Moreover, it is often the case, especially with more complicated drawings, paintings, or carvings that the final product comes as a surprise to the artist simply because it never was the 'final product' which was visualized beforehand, but only the successive generate-and-test cycles along the road to its completion. D'Azevedo cites the testimony of an African carver, who says:

I see the thing I have made [a *Sande* mask] coming out of the women's bush. It is now a proud man *jIna* [spirit] with plenty of women running after him. It is not possible to see anything more wonderful in this world. His face is shining, he looks this way and that, and all the people wonder about this beautiful and terrible thing. To me, it is like what I see when I am dreaming. I say to myself, this is what my *neme* [familiar spirit] has brought into my mind. I say, I have made this. How can a man make such a thing? It is a fearful thing that I can do. No other man can do it unless he has the right knowledge. No woman can do it. I feel that I have borne children.   (d'Azevedo in Forge 1973: 148)

The artist vacillates between the 'patient' response, the astonishment and awe that the Sande mask produces in him—'How can a man make such a thing?'—and self-approbation stemming from the fact that, after all, his was the agency which produced it—'It is a fearful thing I can do.' It would be impossible to find a more explicit instance of self-reciprocal artistic agency than this. The carver's statement that in carving the mask, he thinks he has 'borne children' and his evidently total commitment to the notion that the mask is a living, perceiving, being 'looking this way and that' is also very helpful testimony bolstering our general hypothesis that, anthropologically speaking, works of art are best considered as types of agents. The makers of our idols are no less enthusiastic idolaters than the rest of us, because, in some sense, they always remain passive spectators at the birth of their very own creations. Correctly expressed, this is really [[Artist-A] → Index-A] ⟶ Artist-P.

Finally, on this subject, I should signal a theme which will not fully surface for a long while yet. Artists do not just produce singular 'works', they have careers and produce an *œuvre* (I will reserve the French word for 'work' to mean 'lifetime work' or 'all the work to date' of an artist). Artists are not just patients with respect to the 'work' they are producing right now. They may also be in the patient position *vis-à-vis* all the work they have ever produced.

Some artists, for instance, seem unwilling to repeat themselves, or work for patrons who demand that they should not do so. For instance, it seems to me that Poussin, for whatever reason, rarely if ever repeated a composition at all closely. If Poussin, as I hazard, observed a principle which discouraged him from repeating his own work, then his every work, individually, was negatively determined by all the others, so as not to resemble them in composition (though of course his personal style remained relatively consistent). Renoir, on the other hand (as one may verify by visiting the Barnes collection, in Philadelphia), painted a large number of 'bathers' which resemble one another very closely indeed; and he did so, presumably, because he had (in Mr Barnes) a patron who was happiest if the next painting he purchased from Renoir resembled all the ones he had purchased from the same artist on previous occasions. In either case, the artist was in the 'patient' position with respect to his total *œuvre* at any given time, to the extent that his current work had to be related, in a specific way, to his previous works.

3.12. *Recipient-A ⟶ Recipient-P*

The category of 'recipients' splits into agents and patients in a very salient fashion, so much so that one might be tempted to deny that it was really a single category at all. The differentiation that I have in mind is that between 'passive spectators' (the general art public) and 'patrons'—those who actually commission artists to produce works of art, and whose agency, as patrons, is consequently indexed in the works of art they have caused to come into existence. Patronage is a very significant form of agency from the point of view of the anthropology of art. It seems very different from mere spectatorship, which involves being in the patient position *vis-à-vis* a work of art and being 'caused' to respond by it (being impressed, fascinated, etc.). On the other hand, art patrons are profoundly impressed, or can be, by the works of art that they have caused to come into existence by commissioning them. The Sande adepts (important, senior, women) who commissioned the carver whose words are cited above, are the same women whom he describes as 'running after' it, subject to its spiritual and masculine allure. Here, for comparison, is a quotation from a fourteenth-century observer, describing the public homage paid to Duccio's *Majesty of Christ* altarpiece for Siena cathedral by the patrons of the work:

And on the day that it [the new painting] was carried to the Duomo the shops were shut, and the Bishop conducted a great and devout company of priests and friars in solemn procession, accompanied by the nine signiors, and all the officers of the commune, and all the people, and one after another the worthiest with lighted candles in their hands took places near the picture, and behind came the women and children with great devotion. And they accompanied the said picture up to the Duomo, making the procession around the Campo, as is the custom, all the bells ringing joyously, out of reverence for so noble a picture as is this. (MS of *c.*1311, cited in Holt vol. i 1957: 135)

The bishop and lay authorities (the 'nine signiors') who commissioned the work, glorified themselves by conspicuously showing reverence, in public, towards the product of their own agency (mediated by Duccio). They were, of course, also revering Christ, the Virgin, and the Saints, but it was really the picture itself which was the object towards which reverence was being shown, because, at that time, such holy icons were believed to protect the specific interests of the commune which harboured them. Duccio's picture was to replace an older icon, the *Madonna of the Large Eyes* (removed to the church of St Bonifacio), to which was attributed the victory of the Sienese forces over the Florentines at the recent battle of Monte Aperto. So it was most important that the new picture should 'realize' that the whole town was depending on it to 'keep us from the hands of traitors and enemies of Siena' (ibid.).

In other words, the very essence of successful performance of the 'patron' role, necessitates a show of reverence towards the products of patronage. The patron is *primus inter pares* among the general art public. Unless the patron is visibly and/or privately impressed by the index of which s/he is patron, the very act of patronage is a failure, and the resources which have been invested in the commission have been wasted. It follows that patronage has, intrinsically, a phase in which the patron/agent [Recipient-A] is a patient [Recipient-P].

3.13. *Prototype-A* $\longrightarrow$ *Prototype-P*

The prototype of an index can be a patient with respect to the index which, by representing him or her, incorporates his or her agency. Consider the case of Councillor (later Mayor) H, hailing from an old-established industrial town. Councillor H's party is more or less permanently in power in the town, and H, who is an intelligent and efficient businessman, rises gradually through membership and chairmanship of committees to the position of leader of the Council, which he occupies successfully for a number of years. The town flourishes; at the appropriate time, he relinquishes the leadership to a younger colleague, and accepts the mayoralty. He presides with dignity over public functions, and, behind the scenes, helps to secure no end of lucrative grants and contracts for his community. He is universally popular, even winning the respect of his sometime political opponents. To commemorate his term as mayor, the Council unanimously propose that he should sit for his portrait, which will hang in the council chamber, in an honoured place. He agrees, partly because he knows how pleased his wife will be, and partly because he obtains an assurance that he will not have to endure long sittings in the artist's studio, which, as a still very busy man, he has no time for. And so it proves; the artist only needs an hour to dash off a number of quick sketches, and take a large number of photographs from various angles and distances.

The appointed day arrives; the Council is assembled, and, seated on the mayoral throne, H watches as the curtain is drawn apart and his image is revealed. As the inevitable, and prolonged, speeches proceed, H has a good opportunity to scrutinize his portrait. As he does so, he is assailed by panic and despair. For the portrait appears to him not to be a representation of a man, but of some vegetable, a turnip in fact, with a revolting purplish sheen to it, disfigured by nameless appendages. He is not a vain man; in fact it is years since he looked at himself for more than a moment at a time, for he is even accustomed to shave in the back of his limousine on the way to work, rather than waste precious moments before the bathroom mirror. But it is a terrible shock to him to discover how ugly he really is, and the effect is made worse by the contrast between his impossible turnip-head and the splendour of the mayoral costume he wears. He cannot blame the portraitist for his discomfiture, because he is intelligent enough to appreciate that the portrait is faithful to his actual appearance; the artist did not wield either his camera, or his brushes, inexpertly. Would that he had!—but H, who began life as an apprentice and imbibed the Protestant ethic, knows honest workmanship when he sees it. 'Is this how I am going to be remembered forever,' he wonders, 'as a turnip? What does my appearance matter anyway? Why does my *face*, of all the things to do with me, have to be remembered?' He wishes he could have been memorialized aniconically, by something in the nature of an inscribed plaque—but you have to be dead for that. In the end, there is nobody he can blame for what has happened but himself, his own ugly mug. If he were better-looking, his portrait would not have been such a horrid thing. As it is, H is his own victim, the victim of the direct causal influence his actual appearance [Prototype-A] has of the actual appearance of his portrait, which is so damaging to him [Prototype-P].

This, I admit, is an invented example. But there are numerous real instances of sitters for portraits feeling victimized. I might cite the well-documented antipathy felt by Winston Churchill towards the portrait made of him by Graham Sutherland (whose public circulation he prevented). This portrait is widely regarded by critics as a penetrating study of the great leader, very 'true to life'. Churchill himself infinitely preferred the heroic photographic portrait by Karsh, as well he might have, in defiance of contemporary opinion which detects much less authenticity in Karsh's photograph than in Sutherland's painting. Churchill was vain enough to blame Sutherland, in public, for the ugliness of his image, rather than himself, unlike our honest H, who knows where agency really lies in the coming-into-being of ugly portraits. But I think he must have had private doubts—otherwise his reaction would not have been so violent.

This type of self-reciprocal agency/patiency exercised by the prototype of an index with regard to itself is actually very familiar to us. If we look into the mirror, and dislike what we see, or indeed approve of what we see, we are responding, as patients, to an index (the mirror image) of which we are the agents. Portraiture is only a special instance of this, mediated by the activities of an artist, or a photographer. Wherever there is really or supposedly a causal relationship such that the prototype is the cause of the index, it must be that the index is at least potentially able to cause effects (dismay, etc.) in the prototype. A very pure 'artist-less' case of Prototype-A $\longrightarrow$ Prototype-P is provided by the myth of Narcissus, whose beguilement by his own reflection (index) in a pool caused him to fall in, and drown. However, mostly the effects of the index on the prototype are not primarily caused by the index, but simply mediated by the index, and agency lies with the artist or the recipient. In the Churchill/ Sutherland case, Churchill considered himself the victim of the agency of the artist, rather than his own agency as an ugly person.

4

The Involution of the Index in the Art Nexus

4.1. *Hierarchical Embedding of Agent/Patient Relations*

This completes our survey of binary relations. As the reader will have noticed, in the discussion of these relations, it has often been necessary to refer to more complicated relations, involving more than two terms. An example of such an expression, would be:

$$[\,[\,[\text{Prototype-A}] \rightarrow \text{Artist-A}] \rightarrow \text{Index-A}] \longrightarrow \text{Recipient-P}.$$

This expression refers to a nexus of agent/patient relationships such that the recipient is the 'patient' and the agent acting on him is the index. This is the relationship between a (secondary) agent (the index) and a 'primary' patient, in this instance, the recipient. I adopt the graphic convention of always indicating the relationship between the index-agent and the 'primary' patient in a relation by the use of a long arrow '$\longrightarrow$' as opposed to the short arrow '$\rightarrow$' indicating subordinate agent/patient relations. Because of the centrality of the index (see above, 3.8) it is always immediately to the left (or occasionally to the right) of the long arrow. Agents are always placed to the left of patients; the terminations '-A' and '-P' are really redundant because any term to the left of another is always interpreted as an 'agent' with respect to it; however, I retain the '-A' and '-P' suffixes because they make the resulting formulae more readily intelligible, or at least, I hope they do.

The index in the above formula is not acting on the recipient autonomously. It may be the focal carrier of agency, but it is serving to mediate other types of agency affecting the patient/recipient. The recipient's response to the index incorporates the abduction that the index is a 'made thing', the outcome of the agency of an artist. That is to say, the index is an agent with respect to the recipient by virtue of the fact that the recipient abducts the agency of the artist from it. The index is an agent (with respect to the recipient) but it is simultaneously a patient, with respect to the agency of the artist, which it mediates. This 'indirect' relationship between the recipient as patient and the artist as agent is expressed in our formula via the brackets. The term 'index' *includes within itself* another term, 'artist'; thus, '[Index]' expands to become '[[Artist] Index]'. Adding '-A' and '-P' suffixes, and the agency arrow indicating that the artist is an agent with respect to the index, this becomes: [[Artist-A] $\rightarrow$ Index-A] $\longrightarrow$ Recipient-P.

Finally, in the above formula, the prototype also makes an appearance as an agent with respect to the artist, the index, and the recipient. This can only occur when the abduction is made that the activities of the artist are subordinated to the prototype, for example, to the appearance of the prototype, as in realistic forms of art, such as portraiture. From a certain point of view, a portrait is an index of the appearance of the sitter, mediated by the artist's performance in creating an index, which mediates the prototype's appearance to the recipient. The sitter's appearance caused the index to appear as it does. This is expressed by enclosing the prototype in the 'artist' brackets, '[[Artist] Index]' becomes '[[[Prototype] Artist] Index]', which finally with the addition of the '-A' and '-P' suffixes, and the agency arrows, becomes [[[Prototype-A] → Artist-A] → Index-A] ⟶ Recipient-P, our starting-point.

4.2. *The Effect of Substitutions*

What purpose does such a formula serve? I am only too well aware that many people find formalization objectionable, especially the kind of people who interest themselves in artistic matters, many of whom (like me, in fact) suffered exceedingly during maths lessons at school. I dare say all these symbols, even though I have kept them to the minimum and made them as perspicuous as possible, seem to have little to do with 'art'. None the less, there is some point in formalization if it genuinely assists one in thinking clearly. The formula under discussion, I claim, encapsulates in the most economical way, *just one* of the myriad possibilities which exist for art objects to mediate social relations. In more impressionistic language,

$$[[[\text{Prototype-A}] \rightarrow \text{Artist-A}] \rightarrow \text{Index-A}] \longrightarrow \text{Recipient-P}$$

picks out the situation in which a 'passive' spectator is causally affected by the appearance (or other attributes) of a prototype of an artwork (the index), when this attribute is seen as itself causal of the spectator's response. This is a very common situation. A good example of this would be our response to Reynolds's portrait of Dr Johnson (Fig. 4.2/1). This portrait, excellent example though it is of Reynolds's art, is none the less seen primarily as an icon of Dr Johnson, a culture hero of the English. Reynolds, in painting his portrait, is understood by us to be as much in awe of the lexicographer as we are ourselves, and this has affected the way in which the sitter is portrayed. The situation is quite otherwise in the case of a portrait, or ostensible portrait, such as the *Mona Lisa*, by Leonardo da Vinci. The priorities are reversed in this instance; the features, or some semblance of the features, once possessed by the woman referred to in Leonardo's picture, are significant only in so far as they mediate our awareness Leonardo's art as a painter:

$$[[[\text{Artist-A}] \rightarrow \text{Prototype-A}] \rightarrow \text{Index-A}] \longrightarrow \text{Recipient-P};$$

FIG. 4.2/1. The prototype as agent: *Samuel Johnson* by Reynolds. *Source*: Tate Gallery, London

that is, Leonardo is seen as responsible for the Mona Lisa's appearance, or at least, what is fascinating and compelling about her appearance from the patient/ recipient's point of view; whereas Reynolds is *not* seen as responsible for the compelling aspects of Dr Johnson's appearance.

By making substitutions within the formula—in this case, by switching the relative positions of the artist and the prototype in an otherwise identical formula—we can express the basic difference between representations in which the ultimate source of agency over the index is attributed to the artist (as in the Mona Lisa case), and those representations in which ultimate agency seems to rest with the prototype (as in the case of Dr Johnson). Our formulae are designed therefore to provide models which can be manipulated and transformed at will, so as to discriminate between *all possible combinations* of agent/ patient relations between terms.

4.3. *Tree-Structures*

Underlying our formulae are tree-structures as represented in Fig. 4.3/1. This graphic convention is less economical, but more perspicuous than the formulae using brackets. In particular, it brings out the crucial idea that the 'index

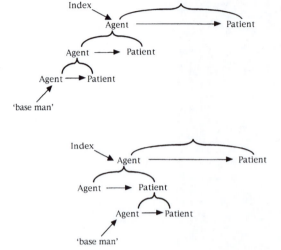

FIG. 4.3/1. The multiple levels
of agency within the index

as agent' encompasses, within itself, hierarchically subordinate 'patient' relationships, and conversely, the index as patient contains subordinated agency relations. The index, in other words, has an involute hierarchical structure, permitting abductions of agency at multiple levels simultaneously.

The tree-structure shown in Fig. 4.3/1 is not the only possible one. For formulae with four terms, such as the one we have been considering, there are also four more possibilities (Fig. 4.3/2).

An example of the second type of 'tree'—the kind in which both agents and patients are to be found on either side of the 'primary' agent/patient relations would be:

$$[\,[\text{Recipient-A}] \to \text{Index-A}] \longrightarrow [\text{Artist-P} \to [\text{Prototype-P}]\,].$$

This corresponds to a situation in which the artist is a 'patient' with respect to the index, which mediates the 'patient' relationship he has with the recipient; with respect to the reference of the image, however, he is the agent. 'Recipient-A' in a formula like this, means generally the recipient as patron or prime mover. 'Artist-P' implies that the artist's passive acceptance of the patron's demands on him are what we abduct from the index; on the other hand, the prototype of the index (in this formula) is contributed by the agency of the artist. What kind of real-life index might motivate the abduction of agency 'distributed' in this way? Well, consider a school situation as follows; the teacher (recipient/patron) enters, and says: 'today, class, I want you all to paint something from your own imaginations, so get busy! . . .'. The young artists accordingly set to and produce their indexes—under orders. The resulting works of art index the agency of the teacher; but for the teacher giving the class its instructions, none of these exercises in imaginative art would exist. School

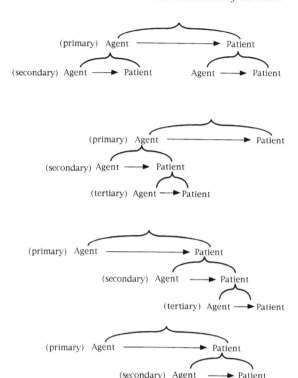

FIG. 4.3/2. The hierarchical embeddedness of agent–patient relations

art is, or at least was, indicative of the lives children lead as 'patients'. School art is produced at the behest of adults, so as to please them, or at least not offend them. Anthropologically speaking, the important feature of school art is what it tells us about the social relations between adults in authority and the children in their charge. On the other hand, the teacher has not, on this occasion, told the children in the class what to represent, so although each child attempts to paint something which will be acceptable to the teacher (no 'rude' people, no bleeding corpses, plenty of views of mountains and botanically questionable flower-pieces), each is obliged to exercise agency within the 'patient' role. Hence the requirements of the formula given above would be met.

Finally, let us take another instance, this time of Artist-A $\longrightarrow$ [Index-P $\rightarrow$ [Prototype-P $\rightarrow$ [Recipient-P]]]. This formula shows the artist as sole agent, exercising agency over the index, which mediates his agency over the prototype, which in turn mediates his agency over the recipient. This, so to speak, is the 'artistic genius' formula. A suitable example might be provided by the work of Salvador Dalí, a painter who played the 'genius' role to the hilt, before an adoring public. Any painting by Dalí (e.g. *The Persistence of Memory* a.k.a. *The Soft*

Watch) can be seen, and frequently is seen, primarily as an index of his agency
as a painter. Dalí's painterly agency is emphasized by the brilliant technical
finish of his work. Moreover, the prototype of a Dalí (the representational content) is supposedly Dalí's private dream-world, rather than anything in the real,
external, world, which he was striving to represent. Hence the prototype is in
the 'patient' position, relative to Dalí's agency as the producer of the index. *The
Persistence of Memory* is a Surrealist 'self-portrait' of Dalí. Finally, the recipient
is not a patron, but a passive spectator, whom Dalí regarded with a fine show
of aristocratic contempt. The aim of Dalí's art was to dominate the spectator
by subverting and deranging his or her petit bourgeois sensibilities. Sadistic,
domineering artists like Dalí do not target their art at a public of fellow-sadists,
but at a masochistic public which revels in being outraged and loves the
oppressor. Hence it is appropriate to indicate the recipient as a 'patient' here.

There are, according to my laborious calculations, thirty-six formulae which
can be derived by combining index, artist, recipient, and prototype in agent/
patient relations corresponding to the tree-structures shown in Figs. 4.3/1–2,
and keeping to the stipulation that the 'index' has to figure either as the primary agent or as the primary patient. However, the reader will be relieved to be
told that I do not intend to provide instances of every single one of them,
though perhaps examples might be found. There would be little point in doing
so though; these formulae just provide a means of distinguishing between different distributions of agent/patient relations in the vicinity of works of art;
they do not predict them or explain them. And, as we will see, in order to provide appropriate models for very common modes of artistic agency, we need to
add some further refinements. There is, in particular, no empirical reason why
any of our four basic 'terms' should appear only once in a given formula. We
already know this, because in the instances of self-reciprocal agency discussed
earlier, the same term necessarily occurs twice, as an agent or a patient. But
before I conclude the discussion of four-term formulae and their associated
tree-structures, there are some further points which require discussion.

The first of these is methodological; it concerns the degree to which each
formula is to be understood as a schematic description of an 'objectively' different situation, as opposed to a different 'perspective' on a situation which
remains the same. We can conveniently discuss this problem with reference
to two examples that have already been introduced; Dalí's *Soft Watch* and the
Mona Lisa, by Leonardo, for which I gave the formula:

(Leonardo) [[[Artist-A] → Prototype-A] → Index-A] ⟶ Recipient-P

while for the Dalí I gave the formula:

(Dalí) Artist-A ⟶ [Index-P → [Prototype-P → [Recipient-P]]].

The difference between these two formulae is produced by a shift of the 'index'
term from the left of the focal agency arrow (⟶) in the *Mona Lisa* formula,
to the right, in the *Soft Watch* formula. It is far from being my contention that

this shift results from any objective feature present in either of these paintings. The shift is a shift in 'perspective' on the nexus of relationships around these paintings. The 'Dalí' formula puts the spotlight on the artist; his person and activity are out in the open and thematic from the observer's point of view. All other factors in the situation are seen as subordinated to him; the canvases on show are, above all, 'Dalís'—passive impressions of his dominant personality, mediating his agency over his public. The cult of personality is, anthropologically speaking, the salient social transaction from this perspective. We could, however, refuse to take this point of view; focusing instead on Dalí's painting as the overt agent, rather than on Dalí the painter as the focus of our attention. Then our perspective would correspond to the *Mona Lisa* formula. *The Persistence of Memory* is a distinguished painting, deserving of serious art-historical consideration independently of the cult of personality surrounding Dalí. Conversely, there is reason to suspect that Leonardo exercised agency not only over his painted canvases, but also in initiating a cult of personality of his own, which is part of his historical legacy, just as in the Dalí case. From the point of view of the da Vinci cultists, the *Mona Lisa* is thematically perceived, not as an image, but as a sacred relic of Leonardo, the semi-divine creative hero. So we may be at liberty to redescribe the nexus of relations surrounding the *Mona Lisa* from this alternative perspective, in terms of the formula we previously used for Dalí.

What changes, and what remains the same, if we make these substitutions or redescriptions? In a sense, the difference between placing the index in the agent or patient position is rhetorical; akin, in fact, to the rhetorical difference between (i) 'Leonardo da Vinci painted the *Mona Lisa*' and the equivalent 'passive' construction (ii) 'The *Mona Lisa* was painted by Leonardo da Vinci'. Although responsibility for the *Mona Lisa* is in both cases attributed to Leonardo, only in (i) is Leonardo the subject or topic of the sentence, whereas in (ii) the *Mona Lisa* is. Sentence (i) corresponds to the formula in which the index comes to the right of the 'agency' arrow, whereas sentence (ii) corresponds to the case where agency can be attributed to the index, as in: 'The *Mona Lisa* (which was painted by Leonardo da Vinci), blew my mind away when I was a kid'. In fact, passive constructions largely exist for use in relative clauses like this. This sentence does not mean quite the same as one in which Leonardo da Vinci figures as main subject: 'Leonardo da Vinci (who painted the *Mona Lisa*) blew my mind away when I was a kid'. The same basic information is there, but a different syntactical pattern implies a distinctly different 'analysis' of the world. Which analysis is the appropriate one is a matter of social or psychological judgement. On this basis I would argue that although the decision to treat the index as primary agent or primary patient is a matter of choice not dictated by the 'basic facts' of a situation, the choice is not arbitrary, but is motivated by sociological or psychological considerations of appropriateness.

The next point is related to this. In the formulae I have presented, it has been stipulated that the index is always focal or central agent or patient.

'Central' means 'visible', 'overt', 'immediate'; it does not necessarily mean 'most important'. In particular, it does not mean, 'most endowed with original agency' when the index is the agent, or 'ultimate object of agency' when it is the patient. In a formula of the 'Leonardo' type:

$$[\,[\,[\text{Artist-A}] \rightarrow \text{Prototype-A}] \rightarrow \text{Index-A}] \longrightarrow \text{Recipient-P}$$

Leonardo, as artist, is well to the left of the arrow of primary agency, which, in this case, is the agency of the index over the spectator, whose mind is being affected, thereby causing him later to remark 'the *Mona Lisa*, which was painted by Leonardo da Vinci, blew my mind away when I was a kid'. Leonardo, via his origination of the appearance of the lady in his picture, and his representation of this appearance in the index, is the 'hidden agent' to whom access is gained at two removes, primarily via the index, and secondarily via the appearance of the lady represented in the index. Leonardo is like God, invisible himself, but visible via his works. Anthropologists will be very familiar with this kind of thing. As a Melanesianist, I find the Melanesian idiom of the 'base' or 'root' (of something) springing to mind here. This idiom is used by Melanesians to indicate the ultimate cause or origination of something. At a pig-festival, for instance, where hundreds of people congregate to conduct pig-exchanges with one another, each seemingly motivated by their own interests and exchange partnerships, one or two leading men (such as Onka, a famous 'big man' of the Mount Hagen tribes in A. Strathern 1971) will be singled out as the base-men or root-men of the occasion, those whose primary will and agency is manifested, not just in their own acts as pig-exchangers, but in the acts of will and agency manifested by everybody else present as well.

In the formula given above, Leonardo da Vinci is the base-man or root-man, since even if the primary agent is the index (from which his agency is abducted at two removes) he stands at the 'origin'. Schematically, therefore, in a bracketed expression such as:

$$[\,[\,[\text{A}] \rightarrow \text{B}] \rightarrow \text{C}]$$

'A' is in 'base' position, or, we might even say, 'bass' position, since like the bass line in music, the one in this position exercises mediated agency over all ascending levels. However, the analogy is perhaps inexact, in that the same type of tree-structure can be made to apply in the case of patients as well as agents. Thus in the Dalí formula, the recipients, Dalí's public, suffer his agency through a double mediation, consisting, first of all, of his dream-world imagery, which disrupts their normal sense of the real, and secondly of his technical mastery, which disrupts their preconceptions about (Dalí's) agency, since it seems supernaturally proficient (see Gell 1992*b*). This gives rise to the inverse structure:

$$[\text{D} \rightarrow [\text{E} \rightarrow [\text{F}]\,]\,]$$

where 'F' are the recipients in 'base' position as patients, and 'D' is the index as primary patient.

There is nothing to prevent multiple-nested expressions like these occurring on both sides of the 'central' agent/patient arrow, as in:

$$[[[A] \to B] \to C] \longrightarrow [D \to [E \to [F]]].$$

The only reason why we have not encountered any formulae of this type so far is that in the ones considered so far there have only been four terms, and each (the index, the artist, the recipient, and the prototype) has occurred only once. But this restriction is by no means stipulated. For instance, the recipient can easily appear twice, once as 'the patron' and again as 'the public'. For instance, let us suppose that the index is Michelangelo's *Moses*, which, everybody knows, was carved in order to memorialize Pope Julius II. This work indexes Michelangelo's agency, but he was not 'prime mover'; indeed, it is fair to say that this carving (and the 'slaves' which were to accompany it) expresses, in part, Michelangelo's experience as a patient, working for great patrons, who were more powerful and consequential than (even) he was. Moses (the prototype) is a metaphor for the Pope, and Moses, in our mythology, is archetypally a 'base-man'. A formula for this index must therefore include the recipient twice; once to represent the patron who acted as prime mover, eliciting Michelangelo's agency as a carver, and secondly to represent the public who are simply patients, awed and overwhelmed by Michelangelo's artistic agency, through which they become subject to the indirect (social/political) agency of Julius II. To express this, it is necessary to resort to superscript numberings to distinguish the two types of recipient:

$$[[[[\text{Recipient-A}^1] \to \text{Prototype-A}] \to \text{Artist-A}] \to \text{Index-A}] \longrightarrow \text{Recipient-P}^2$$

where Recipient-A^1 = Julius II, Prototype-A = Moses, Artist-A = Michelangelo, and Recipient-P^2 = the general public.

4.4. *Some more Complex Tree-Structures: The Nail Fetish*

In order to explore some of the complexities of tree-structures let us consider a type of image well known to visitors to ethnographic art museums; I refer to the 'nail fetishes' of the Congo region of West Africa (Fig. 4.4/1). These startling figures, anthropomorphic in form, are instantly identifiable because of the nails driven into their bodies, a violation of the notion of the (semi-sacred) artwork which greatly adds to the 'aesthetic' *frisson* they provoke in Western spectators, who perhaps wonder what Michelangelo's *David* would look like, given the same treatment. However, the apparent rhyme between these carvings and Western images of suffering and violation is fortuitous, and the actual network of agency-relations which surrounded them in their original setting

FIG. 4.4/1. Nail fetish figures from the Congo region of Africa. British Museum, London, MM023467. Musée de l'Homme, Paris. Kongo, Loango region

is much more interesting than the facile imagery of victimization which is all that uninstructed aesthetes can extract from them.

According to the missionary anthropologist Dennett, who worked in the Congo at a time when the colonial government was busily engaged in rooting out nail fetishes in the belief that they were fountainheads of native sedition, these images were essentially judicial in function; they belong to the same category as the 'judicial masks' which presided over legal proceedings in many parts of West Africa. The judicial mask punishes those who lie on oath; the nail fetish, in rather similar fashion, registers promises and oaths, and punishes

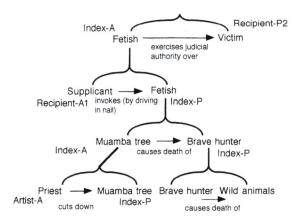

FIG. 4.4/2. The fetish as an index of cumulative agency and as the visible knot tying together an invisible skein of spatio-temporal relations

those who contravene them. According to Dennett, when such a judicial fetish was to be made:

A palaver [meeting] is held, and it is decided whose Kulu [soul] it is that is to enter into the Muamba tree and to preside over the fetish to be made. A boy of great spirit, or else, above all, a great and daring hunter, is chosen. Then they go into the bush and call his name. The Nganga [priest] cuts down the tree, and blood is said to gush forth. A fowl is killed and its blood mingled with the blood that they say comes from the tree. The named one then dies, certainly within ten days. His life has been sacrificed for what the Zinganga consider the welfare of the people. They say that the named one never fails to die . . . People pass before these fetishes (Zinkici Mbowu) calling on them to kill them if they do, or have done, such and such a thing. Others go to them and insist upon their killing so and so, who has done, or is about to do them some fearful injury. And as they swear and make their demand, a nail is driven into the fetish, and the palaver [business] is settled so far as they are concerned. The Kulu of the man whose life was sacrificed upon the cutting of the tree sees to the rest. (R. Dennett 1906: 93)

There are pronounced resonances between this ritual sequence and the making of the *ankishi* figurines from the blood-exuding Mukula tree among the Ndembu (see above, Sect. 3.2). Structurally, the situation is [[[[Artist-A] → Index¹-A] → Recipient¹-A] → Index²-A] ⟶ [Recipient²-P]. But this hardly does justice to the complexity of the situation, which is more perspicuously shown in a tree diagram, as in Fig. 4.4/2. This tree diagram contains features not encountered before. First, in the formation of the 'index' (the fetish) it is, by turns, passive (the tree which is cut down), then active (the tree which metonymically brings about the death of the hunter whose name it bears), then passive again (the fetish which has nails driven into it, 'attaching' the supplicant's requests to it), then, finally, active again (as it executes its judicial functions). The index is doubly active because, in the process of its formation it has been doubly passive; it has the capacity to act (as a fetish), *because it has been acted upon*, both as a tree, and, simultaneously, as a hunter who dies 'for the welfare of the people'. It demonstrates, in Bloch's terms, 'rebounding violence' (1991). Secondly, the tree diagram bifurcates at the base; the nail fetish has not one 'root-man' but two, the priest and the hunter, the former being responsible for the creation of the index as an artefact, the latter being responsible for its efficacy, which is underwritten by the hunter's efficacy in slaughtering game animals.

An instructed person, approaching such a fetish, does not see a mere thing, a form, to which he may or may not respond aesthetically. Instead, what is seen is the visible knot which ties together an invisible skein of relations, fanning out into social space and social time. These relations are not referred to symbolically, as if they could exist independently of their manifestation in this particular form; for these relations have produced this particular thing in its concrete, factual, presence; and it is because these relations exist(ed) that the fetish can exercise its judicial role. However, I shall defer further discussion of this theme until a later chapter, devoted to the whole subject of idolatry. The purpose of this discussion is only to show the 'involute' character of the index, which may objectify a whole series of relations in a single visible form.

Having disparaged the Western response which sees the nail fetish as an image of suffering, let me now turn to another example in which the sufferings of the index do genuinely connote the suffering of the prototype. However, the 'work of art' I have in mind, though belonging to the West, has so far not entered the canon of Western art. I refer to the *'Slashed' Rokeby Venus*, the work of a suffragette artist, Mary Richardson (and Velázquez). This work only existed for a few months, before it was superseded by the 'restored *Rokeby Venus*' which can be seen in the National Gallery today (by Velázquez and the Museum's picture-restoration staff). Fortunately, Mary Richardson's version of the picture was photographed, and this image is reproduced by Freedberg (1989: 411). See Fig. 4.4/3.

Freedberg devotes a whole chapter of his work to the attacks made on important works of art by so-called fanatics, such as Mary Richardson ('Slasher Mary') who attacked the *Rokeby Venus* with a kitchen knife in 1914. Freedberg makes the point that, though the Gallery officials always express incredulity and dismay after such attacks, ascribing them to insane malice, there always does prove to be a strong religious or political motive present in the mind of the attacker. For instance, it was not by chance that the latest picture to be attacked in the National Gallery (in 1978) was Poussin's *The Golden Calf* nor that the attacker's thrusts were aimed at the *Golden Calf* itself. Nothing was made of this at the time, but Freedberg argues, surely correctly, that this picture was chosen precisely because it depicts idolatry in progress. The attack was directed against idolatry, and with reason, because in the National Gallery, even if we do not commit full-blown idolatry, we do verge on it all the time.

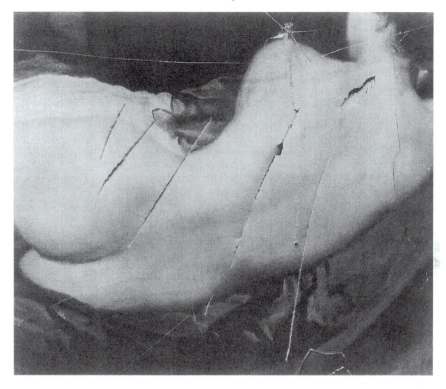

FIG. 4.4/3. *Mrs Pankhurst* by Mary Richardson: the *Rokeby Venus* by Velázquez slashed by Mary Richardson, 1914. *Source*: The National Gallery, London

This attack was consigned to the category of 'arbitrary' outrages committed by schizophrenics because to admit otherwise is to drop the defences we erect between ourselves and images which move us. Freedberg says that 'the iconoclastic act is so frightening' because:

It opens realms of power and fear that we may sense but cannot quite grasp. When the iconoclast reacts with violence to the image and vehemently and dramatically attempts to break its hold on him or her, then we begin to have some sense of its potential—if we do not perceive it in the flash of light that blinds us, finally, to its art. But these days we have become more sophisticated, and thereby more confused. We allow that art can be troubling too, and we come full circle. We have learned to turn the troubling image into something we can safely call art. (Freedberg 1989: 425)

Freedberg makes a pointed contrast between the ostensible violence of much contemporary Western art, which smooth-talking critics and collectors praise to the skies (because it is art) and the shock-horror reactions that actual violence against works of art provokes in the same quarters. But it is a moot point whether the outsiders who, due to mental instability or strong political motives, overcome the taboo against defacing masterpieces in museums, are not the more demonstrably in thrall to art. Such persons, as Freedberg puts it, are 'blinded', by art—blinded, that is, to the fact that art is not the real thing. Although, in the twentieth century, such attitudes can only really express themselves in acts of extreme deviance, they are natural and basic, rather than obscure and fantastic. Art-destruction is art-making in reverse; but it has the same basic conceptual structure. Iconoclasts exercise a type of 'artistic agency'.

Let us examine the case of 'Slasher Mary' and the *Rokeby Venus*, the most famous act of iconoclasm of the 'modern' period, and moreover, one not due to obvious insanity but to clear ideological motives. Mary Richardson gave this account of her action in 1914 'I have tried to destroy the picture of the most beautiful woman in mythological history as a protest against the government for destroying Mrs Pankhurst, the most beautiful character in modern history' (Freedberg 1989: 502). From this and from a later interview, it is quite clear that Richardson equated the woman in the picture (Venus) with Emmeline Pankhurst, and the 'sufferings' of the picture with Mrs Pankhurst's sufferings in prison. In other words, this is an instance of volt sorcery (see below) in reverse; the sufferings of the victim cause a change in the appearance of the representation. Examining the photograph of the *Rokeby Venus* after the attack, we note that the deepest slash is aimed at the heart; Venus has been stabbed in the back—a very political way to die. In effect, Mary Richardson was an artist who produced a 'new', modern, *Rokeby Venus*, now a representation of Emmeline Pankhurst (standing for modern womanhood as Venus stood for mythological womanhood). The *'Slashed' Rokeby Venus* by Richardson, is, without question, a more powerful image than the old one by Velázquez, though infinitely less aesthetic, because the image bears traces which testify directly to, rather than simply represent, the violence women endure, or believe they endure. The contrast between the supremely controlled and detached agency exercised by Velázquez in creating the painted image of Venus, and the frenzied gestures of Richardson defacing the image so that its 'death' corresponds to that of Pankhurst create the space in which the life of images and persons meet and merge together. Richardson endowed the *Rokeby Venus* with a life it never possessed before by 'killing' it and turning it into a beautiful corpse. The restoration of the picture to its original condition, though of course necessary and desirable, was also a means of re-erecting the barrier which prevents such images troubling us unduly, politically, sexually, or in any other way.

The structure of the agent/patient relations surrounding Richardson's *'Slashed' Rokeby Venus* are depicted in Fig. 4.4/4. Here we have a complete duplication of prototype, artist and index and recipient; the two prototypes are Venus and Mrs Pankhurst, the two artists are Velázquez and Mary Richardson, the two indexes are the *Rokeby Venus* in its intact and slashed

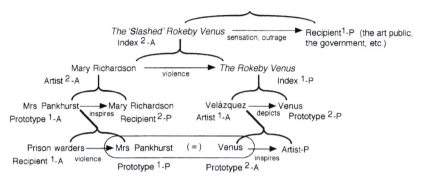

FIG. 4.4/4. The shared biographical spaces of persons and images

state, the two recipients are Mary Richardson and the outraged art public. The resulting tree diagram consequently bifurcates, though the two branches also implicitly join again at the base, as a result of the quasi-identity between the 'mythological' heroine, Venus, and her 'modern' counterpart, Mrs Pankhurst —note also the implicit identity between Recipient-A (the prison warders, agents of the repressive government) and Recipient-P (the outraged public).

5

The Origination of the Index

5.1. *Agency*

The fact that I have chosen to employ a single graphic symbol, an arrow, could be taken to imply that 'agency' has some quintessential, generic form, of which the various types of agency so far mentioned are species. This inference would be incorrect; the agency arrow implies no particular kind of agency, only the polarity of agent/patient relations. I set no limit whatsoever to the type of 'action' involved. Sometimes this action is psychological; for example, the 'action' of an index in impressing a spectator with its technical excellence, or arousing the spectator erotically; while at other times the action may be physical, as happens, for instance, if the index is a holy icon which cures the rheumatism of the one who kisses it, rather than merely looks at it. Conventional 'theories of art' are mostly predicated on one, or a limited selection, of 'kinds of agency'. Thus, aesthetic theories of art are predicated on the idea that artists are exclusively aesthetic agents, who produce works of art which manifest their aesthetic intentions, and that these intentions are communicated to the public which views their works in the light of approximately the same set of aesthetic intentions, vicariously entertained. In an ideal art world, such might indeed be the case, and nobody would have recourse to works of art with anything in mind except the garnering of aesthetic experiences, and certainly not in the hope of being cured of rheumatism. Semiologic or interpretative theories of art assume that works of art are vehicles of meaning (signs, symbols) which spectators have to decode on the basis of their familiarity with the semiological system used by the artist to encode the meanings they contain. I do not deny that works of art are sometimes intended and received as objects of aesthetic appreciation, and that it is sometimes the case that works of art function semiotically, but I specifically reject the notion that they always do.

The kind of agency exercised in the vicinity of works of art varies considerably, depending on a number of contextual factors. In gross terms, it may be supposed that whatever type of action a person may perform *vis-à-vis* another person, may be performed also by a work of art, in the realms of the imagination if not in reality—not that we are always in a position to decide what is 'real' and what is not. The anthropology of art, to reiterate, is just anthropology itself, except that it deals with those situations in which there is an 'index of agency' which is normally some kind of artefact.

There are instances in which the index may actually be a person. A case in point is possession by the deity. In Nepal (and elsewhere in the Hindu world) young girls are worshipped as the goddess Durga (Allen 1976). The *kumari* (living goddess) is an index of the deity, and it is impossible to distinguish between the cult of the living goddess during the festival, and the cult of idols (*murti*) of the same goddess at other times. The young maiden is also a *murti*— an image of the goddess—but a living one.[1] The living idol of the goddess finds a secular counterpart in Western contemporary performance art. The actress Tilda Swinton was recently exhibited in a gallery as a living (immobile, sleeping) work of art, and there are numerous similar examples.

Any dramatic performance involves one person (an actor) serving as the index of another; that is, the character being enacted. Acting is, in general, a form of representational art, and it can be expressed by an identical formula:

$$[\,[\,[\text{Artist-A}] \rightarrow \text{Prototype-A}] \rightarrow \text{Index-A}] \longrightarrow \text{Recipient-P}$$

where Artist = playwright, Prototype = character, Index = actor, and Recipient = audience. And of course, the dramaturgical situation may be modified at will, just as the situation *vis-à-vis* works of art in the form of artefacts may be. Thus, in ostensibly 'involuntary' dramatic roles (such as possession by the deity), the formula would involve the index in 'patient' position:

$$\text{Prototype-A} \longrightarrow [\text{Index-P} \rightarrow [\text{Recipient-P}]\,]$$

where the Prototype is the deity, the Index is the possessed shaman, and the Recipient is the congregation.

These remarks will be sufficient to indicate that there is seamless continuity between modes of artistic action which involve 'performance' and those which are mediated via artefacts. The distinction has no theoretical significance. Every artefact is a 'performance' in that it motivates the abduction of its coming-into-being in the world. Any object that one encounters in the world invites the question 'how did this thing get to be here?' Mostly, the answers to such questions are so taken for granted as not to play any part in one's conscious mental life (but somewhere or other in one's psyche, there must be a device which identifies the familiar *as* familiar). Only geologists, who are trained to do so, ask, when they see a mountain range, how that came into being. But with artefacts, which are the product of types of agency which we possess generically, the situation is often very different, and we do indeed consciously attend to their origins. This means playing out their origin-stories mentally, reconstructing their histories as a sequence of actions performed by another agent (the artist), or a multitude of agents, in the instance of collective works of art such as cathedrals. We cannot, in general, take up a point of view on the origination of an artefact which is the point of view of the artefact itself. Our natural point of vantage is that of the originating person, the artist,

---

[1] For more on the *kumari* cult of living goddesses see below, Sect. 7.12.

because we, also, are persons. We imagine the origination of a painting from
the vicariously entertained standpoint of the painter, not (as we might) from
the standpoint of the paint or canvas. Only when the artefact actually is a person (as in the case of possession by the divinity, just mentioned) might we adopt
the index's point of view, but this involves an implicit refusal of the scenario
of possession, in that the possessed person is temporarily in abeyance, having
become the vehicle of the personhood of the divinity. So as a general rule, it is
fair to say that indexes, from the spectators' point of view, only mediate personhood rather than possess it intrinsically. However, the personhood of the artist,
the prototype, or the recipient can fully invest the index in artefactual form, so
that to all intents and purposes it becomes a person, or at least a partial person.
It is a congealed residue of performance and agency in object-form, through
which access to other persons can be attained, and via which their agency can
be communicated.

5.2. *Captivation*

Theoretically, there is no limit to the kind of agency which can be mediated by
indexes, but it would be disingenuous on my part to suggest that I do not attach
more priority to certain types of agency than to others. Where indexes are very
recognizably works of art, made with technical expertise and imagination of a
high order, which exploit the intrinsic mechanisms of visual cognition with
subtle psychological insight, then we are dealing with a canonical form of artistic agency which deserves specific discussion. Many indexes are crude and
uninteresting artefacts, whose importance rests solely on their mediatory function in a particular social context—for instance, the figurines used in African
divination—and while these certainly fall within the scope of the anthropology of art they have no significance as 'works of art', because nobody attends
to their making as a particularly salient feature of their agency. It is otherwise with artefacts which announce themselves as miraculous creations. The
'coming into being' of these objects is explicitly attended to, because their
power partly rests on the fact that their origination is inexplicable except as a
magical, supernatural, occurrence.

   In cultures which produce art at all, most adults (of the right gender, where
art production is gendered) have, at some stage, attempted to originate works
of art, at least of a trivial or ephemeral nature. Specialized art production, as
social practice, implies that most adults are either failed, or relatively unsuc-
cessful artists; only a few talented individuals, and/or individuals who receive
institutional encouragement, specialize in the production of really fine work.
They are the artists. The biographical probability that passive recipients of
works of art have some background practical experience of the art-making
process—whether this is formal school instruction in 'art' in the West, or
just childhood experimentation with whittling sticks and tracing patterns in

the dust in non-Western cultures—ensures that the reception of a work of art occurs in the light of the *possibility* that the recipient could, technically, approach the same task of art-making, himself or herself.

Thus, part of my experience as a recipient of Vermeer's *Lacemaker* is the contemplation of the possibility that I, not Vermeer, could have produced this painting—not in this world, I hasten to add, but in some other 'possible world' in which I would be a much better painter than I actually am. At the same time, I am acutely aware of the counterfactuality of this apparently feasible world: even though I know (generically) how to mix paint, and I can draw after my fashion, I also know that I could not even produce a decent copy of *The Lacemaker*, let alone originate a comparable masterpiece (*The Seamstress* by Alfred Van Gell). Gazing at the picture, my jaw drops, in admiration— and defeat. This defeat is, however, profitable to me also, to the extent that in mentally retracing Vermeer's origination of his picture, the technical and imaginative performance which culminated in the finished work, I do manage, exercising such powers as I possess, to attain a certain point, before I break off in bewilderment and can follow Vermeer no longer through the maze of his artistic agency. Up to a point, I can be Vermeer, I can identify with his artistic procedure and see his picture, vicariously, as a product of my bodily engagement with the world and with the materials artists manipulate. But once the point of incommensurability is reached, the point at which it is no longer possible to identify Vermeer's agency with my own, then I am left suspended between two worlds; the world in which I ordinarily live, in which objects have rational explanations and knowable origins, and the world adumbrated in the picture, which defeats explanation. Between these two worlds, I am trapped in a logical bind; I must accept that Vermeer's painting is part of 'my' world—for here it is, physically before me—while at the same time it cannot belong to this world because I only know this world through my experience of being an agent within it, and I cannot achieve the necessary congruence between my experi- ence of agency and the agency (Vermeer's) which originated the painting.

This is captivation, the primordial kind of artistic agency. It is far from difficult to cite instances of the deployment of captivation in practical contexts other than the art gallery. In an earlier publication (Gell 1992*b*), I discussed the efficacy of Trobriand canoe prow-boards as psychological weapons in the context of overseas Kula exchanges (Fig. 5.2/1). These boards are richly carved and painted, and they are the first thing that the Trobrianders' over- seas exchange-partners get to see when the Trobriand flotilla arrives on their shores, before exchange operations get under way. The purpose of these beau- tiful carvings is to demoralize the opposition, so that they will lose the capacity to drive hard bargains or resist the Trobrianders' blandishments and plausible falsehoods. Neither the Trobrianders nor their exchange-partners operate a category of 'art' as such; from their point of view the efficacy of these boards stems from the powerful magical associations they have. A prow-board is an

FIG. 5.2/1. Trobriand canoe prow-board. *Source*: Shirley Campbell

index of superior artistic agency, and it demoralizes the opposition because they cannot mentally encompass the process of its origination, just as I cannot mentally encompass the origination of a Vermeer.

But the paradox of the incommensurability of creative powers is understood in different terms; the artistic agency on display is magical, the result of the artist's ingestion of a magical tradition and substances which communicate carving skill. Magic, in the Trobriands or anywhere else, is not 'normal' even though magic may be in everyday use for a variety of purposes. The Trobrianders live in exactly the same world as we do and operate exactly the same conceptual categories so far as 'ordinary' cause and effect goes. With magic, it is different; magic produces extraordinary effects by means which do not articulate to the agent's 'normal' sense of self, embodiedness, agency, and being in the world. Thus, the fact that the boards are said by the Trobrianders to be 'magically' efficacious in demoralizing the opposition is just a transcription of the experience of captivation into the language of magical causation, which we are also tempted to use to describe the same type of 'uncanny' sensation which great works of Western art produce in Western spectators. Artistic agency, especially of the virtuoso character so obviously present in Trobriand carving, is socially efficacious because it establishes an inequality between the agency responsible for the production of the work of art, and the spectators; in the Trobriands this inequality is attributed to superior magic; in the West, to artistic inspiration or genius. Neither 'explanation' is really explanatory, each only serves to register the disparity of powers between artists and spectators. This fundamental inequality of powers is carried over into the wider social transactions within which the art object is embedded and mobilized; the kula exchange. The Trobrianders, if their artistic magic works as it should, are one-up before the exchanges even begin; having demonstrated the magical potency they possess in the artistic domain, the implication is that their exchange-facilitation magic is equally effective. They are irresistible, and their exchange-partners will find themselves, willy-nilly, disgorging their best valuables without demur.

I have no wish to recapitulate any more of the points I made on the basis of the Trobriand example in my previous paper (Gell 1992*b*). There are some additional comments though, which may serve to relate the notion of captivation as a form of artistic agency to the general argument being advanced here. Captivation or fascination—the demoralization produced by the spectacle of unimaginable virtuosity—ensues from the spectator becoming trapped within the index because the index embodies agency which is essentially indecipherable. Partly this comes from the spectator's inability mentally to rehearse the origination of the index from the point of view of the originator, the artist. The 'blockage' in cognition arises at the point when the spectator cannot follow the sequence of steps in the artist's 'performance' (the 'performance' which is objectively congealed in the finished work). The raw material of the work (wood) can be inferred from the finished product, and the basic technical steps—carving and painting; but not the critical path of specific technical processes along the way which actually effect the transformation from raw material to finished product. In other words, it is the complexity of the artistic decision-making process (generate and test) which defeats spectatorial recapitulation. This relates to the earlier discussion of artistic decision-making and proprioception under the heading Artist-A $\longrightarrow$ Artist-P (above, Sect. 3.11).

But captivation has other sources as well. The emphasis I have been placing on artistic agency has empirical support, in that we in the West do hero-worship artists, and the Trobrianders do place inordinate value on artistic prowess, though they associate this with possession of magical resources, rather than genius. But there are many types of abductions of agency from the index, and the abduction of origination in artistic agency is only one of them. Perhaps, though I do not think so, I place so much emphasis on captivation through artistic virtuosity as a mode of agency because I myself am a 'Sunday painter', and I consequently have a propensity to imagine, when I see a Vermeer, that I am Vermeer, painting thus and thus. The tragedy of amateur artists like me is that because they can partially recapitulate the performances of their artistic idols, they know much better than non-artists how abjectly they fail to achieve true virtuosity. Others, whose own practical acquaintance with wielding pencils and brushes is lost in the mists of childhood, or has been expunged with other degrading adolescent experiences, may never experience the impulse to measure themselves against the great artists. On the other hand, I have never even attempted to play the cello, yet I think I respond to Rostropovich recordings in terms of imaginary manipulations of an imaginary cello, with approximately the same results as my imaginary efforts to paint Vermeer's pictures; so I do not think immediate practical experience as a 'failed' virtuoso is necessary in order to become captivated by virtuosity.

Whatever the intersubjective validity of the analysis of captivation in terms of indecipherable agency may be, I would agree that captivation can occur in other ways. Much art criticism downplays virtuosity and indeed artistic agency altogether, and concentrates on the visual-aesthetic properties of art objects much as if they had come into being by themselves, quite without the physical intervention of any artist. The art object 'in itself' is the focus of attention, rather than the process of its origination through the bodily activities of an artist. Leaving artistic agency to one side therefore, I shall now turn the spotlight on the nature of the captivation exerted by the index in and of itself, rather than as the outcome of the prior agency of an artist.

6

The Critique of the Index

6.1. *On Decorative Art*

Since these reflections on art are directed in the main at the existing anthropology-of-art confraternity, I can make a start—and perhaps make amends—
by considering, first of all, a classical theme in the anthropology-of-art literature, namely, the significance of 'geometric' (i.e. non-representational, or
marginally representational) decorative designs. Most 'Western' art-theory is
about representational art, and so is most of the philosophy of art, in so far as
these two may be distinguished. But it is fair to say that most of the art in the
collections held in ethnological museums—if not on display there—is 'decorative' art, usually applied to artefacts such as pots, mats, and so forth. Many of
the more interesting studies which have been produced by anthropologists
concerned with art (e.g. Kaeppler 1978; Hanson 1983; Price and Price 1980)
have to do with this kind of art. Certainly the most massive compilation of data
for the study of non-Western art (Carpenter and Schuster 1986) deals primarily with ostensibly decorative art, though these authors' approach is predicated
on the idea that apparently decorative forms have universal symbolic meaning.

There is another reason for commencing the substantive discussion of 'the
anthropology of art' with a consideration of decorative art, and that is the elimination of a form of gender bias which is prevalent in much of the anthropology-
of-art literature (this work included), which pays most attention to contexts
of art production dominated by men, such as gender-exclusive male cult rituals.
It is in the context of male cults, or cult activities dominated by men, that
art production occurs in forms which bear the most immediate comparison
with Western 'fine' art; but this is no reason for always giving this type of art
production pride of place, analytically. The development of (Western) abstract
art during the twentieth century, and the simultaneous rise of 'design' to a status
rivalling, or even exceeding, the prestige of fine art, indicates a change in
attitude which may also be extended to the non-representational art and/or
'design' produced by non-Western artists. Many, even most, decorative artists
world-wide are women, because of the frequency with which the division of labour
in agrarian/subsistence societies assigns textile production, pottery, basketry, and
the like, to women. Which is not to say that there are not male decorative artists
as well. The advantage of beginning with decorative art, however, is that we
are, so to speak, in a neutral terrain, not one riven with violent ideological and
institutional tussles, as is the case with much high-status ritual art.

6.2. *Attachment*

Decorative patterns applied to artefacts attach people to things, and to the social projects those things entail. A child may more readily be induced to go to bed—which children are often disinclined to do—if the bed in question has sheets and a pillowcase richly embellished with spaceships, dinosaurs, or even polka dots, be they sufficiently jolly and attractive. The decoration of objects is a component of a social technology, which I have elsewhere called the technology of enchantment (Gell 1992*b*). This psychological technology encourages and sustains the motivations necessitated by social life. The world is filled with decorated objects because decoration is often essential to the psychological functionality of artefacts, which cannot be dissociated from the other types of functionality they possess, notably their practical, or social functionality. Undecorated children's bedsheets would be less functional in conferring protection and comfort during sleep than decorated ones because children would be less inclined to sleep in them. They would be less socially functional, because comfortable, protected, sleeping infants are a prime objective pursued by parents. In other words, the distinction we make between 'mere' decoration and function is unwarranted; decoration is intrinsically functional, or else its presence would be inexplicable.

Any bamboo tube, or container of suitable size and shape, could do duty as a lime-container, such as the ones I illustrate in Fig. 6.2/1 from the Iatmul (New Guinea). But a plain container would hardly be as functional, given that a man's lime-container, in the context of Iatmul social life, is a most important index of its owner's personhood. For instance, rattling the lime-stick in the lime-container is a means of communicating passionate emotion in oratorical performances (Bateson 1973; Forge 1973). The decoration, which is distinctive, binds the lime-container to its owner in a most intimate fashion; it is less a possession than a prosthesis, a bodily organ acquired via manufacture and exchange rather than by biological growth. The objectification of personhood in artefacts and exchange items is a familiar anthropological theme, on which it is unnecessary to dwell (e.g. Munn 1973, 1986; M. Strathern 1988). However, anthropology has yet to theorize the nature of the attachment between persons and things mediated by surface decoration, and that, rather than the provision of a more ethnographic context, is the task before us. Examining this gourd container, we are able to see that it is decorated with beautiful patterns, formed from motifs that do not obviously resemble real-world objects. The gourd's decoration is a free exercise in the deployment of curves, ovals, and spirals and circles, in symmetrical or repetitive arrangements. So far, I have not said anything about such ostensibly 'aesthetic' features of the index as symmetry, elegance, etc. and it might have been assumed that I never intended to, having ruled out the 'aesthetic' approach to the work of art in advance. This would be a mistake, however, since the 'technology of enchantment' approach which I

FIG. 6.2/1. Iatmul lime-containers. *Source*: The Museum of Archaeology and Anthropology, Cambridge 35–83, 35–91, 30–374, 35–82, 35–88

alluded to before (which is the psychological aspect of the anthropology of art) conjoins a theory of social efficacy with considerations which, if not aesthetic, are definitely cognitive in nature, because cognition and sociality are one.

How can such cognitive considerations be integrated into the theoretical framework advanced hitherto—the four basic terms, index, artist, prototype, recipient, agent/patient relationships, and so on? On the assumption that, where decorative patterns are concerned, there either is no prototype, or the prototype is not salient, the 'pattern' and the index are one and the same, which would imply that the whole discussion would have to be carried out in terms of artist, index, and recipient. This seems a rather limited set of concepts for handling complicated cognitive, even possible aesthetic, problems. How may this be accomplished?

6.3. *Decorative Pattern* = *Index-A* ⟶ *Index-P*

In Section 3.10 above, I established the idea that among the abductions of agency we derive from the index are agent/patient relationships between parts of the index *vis-à-vis* other parts of the index. Thus, in an abstract picture, one patch of colour seems to be 'pushing against' another patch of colour, even though there are no objects in the external world with which we can identify these patches of colour. The causal interaction we perceive is internal to the index itself. Part-to-part 'causal interaction' internal to the index is the basis of 'decorative' art, which is just another name for abstract art. Decorative art involving the use of 'patterns' exploits the particularly (visually) salient part-to-part relationships produced by the repetition and symmetrical arrangement of motifs.

The application of a decorative pattern to an artefact multiplies the number of its parts and the density of their internal relationships. The lime-containers in Fig. 6.2/1, were they lacking in decoration, would be simple tubular forms lacking in salient part-to-whole relationships. As it is, many separate parts may be distinguished, and relationships between these parts. Each of these parts may be considered a subordinate index within the index as a whole.

Parts of indexes convey agency just as indexes as wholes do. In the case of decorative art as opposed to representational art, it is not the diversity of the parts that communicates significant artistic agency, but their disposition with respect to one another. In other words, the parts of the index exert causal influence over one another and testify to the agency of the index as a whole, in that it is in the disposition of the parts of the index that the artist's agency is primarily made apparent. We are, indeed, accustomed to speak of decorated surfaces (as well as representational indexes with a lot of physical action in them) as 'animated'. This idiom reflects the fact that the motifs in decorative art often do seem to be engaged in a mazy dance in which our eyes become readily lost. We need a formula which captures the inherent agency in decorative forms, forms which do not simply refer to (represent) agency in the external world, but which produce agency in the physical body of the index itself, so that it becomes a 'living thing' without recourse to the imitation of any living thing. Decoration makes objects come alive in a non-representational way. Since this feat is accomplished via part-to-whole relationships internal to the index, the decorative index could be represented as in Fig. 6.3/1 or:

$$[\,[\,[\text{Index-A motif}^{\text{part}}] \rightarrow \text{Index-A}^{\text{part/whole}}] \rightarrow \text{Index-A whole}] \longrightarrow \text{Recipient-P.}$$

The root of a pattern is the motif, which enters into relationships with neighbouring motifs, relations which animate the index as a whole. However, we can describe the relevant part-to-part and part-to-whole relationships in patterns much more precisely. Patterns can be distinguished from all other

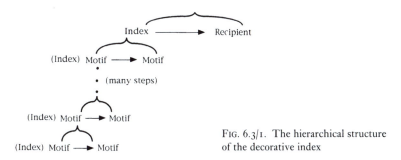

FIG. 6.3/1. The hierarchical structure of the decorative index

indexes by virtue of the fact that they have salient visual properties of repetit-iveness and symmetry.[1] It would be wrong to imagine that because symmetry and repetition are mathematical properties of forms, that it is not these prop-erties which most readily provoke the illusion—if it is only that—of immanent causality in the index. Nothing could be more animated than the tessellations (tiling patterns) devised by Islamic decorative artisans and book illuminators. The religiously imposed ban on the representation of living forms only served, it seems, to inspire ever more effective inducements to captivation by visual artifice, the non-mimetic appearance of animation.

6.4. *Symmetry and the Appearance of Animation*

How do mathematical relations induce animacy in this way? The actual math-ematical basis of patterned forms is not hard to grasp conceptually, though it is more difficult to apply. All patterns are variations on only four 'rigid motions in the plane', to which repeated motifs can be subjected. These are, (1) reflec-tion, (2) translation, (3) rotation, and (4) glide reflection. These four motions are shown and explained in Fig. 6.4/1. The simplest type of decorative pattern is the one-dimensional band pattern of the type shown in Fig. 6.4/2. This pat-tern (a Greek key) consists of the successive 'translations' of a single motif along a line. It seems to move, because we 'read' it as we would a line of text, by moving our attention from motif to motif, which we must do, in order to observe its symmetry, and hence its patterned-ness. The process of 'seeing' this pattern is a matter of registering the fact that motif A is identical to, and to the left of, B, and C and D, and so on.[2] Because the process of perceiving this pattern involves mentally translating the motif to the right, so as to lay the motif down on its neighbour and register the congruence between them,

---

[1] In psychology, the phrase 'pattern recognition' is used sometimes to refer to the perception of any form, e.g. recognizing the characteristic 'patterns' of the letters of the alphabet. This is a quite different use of the word 'pattern' to the one intended here. For our purposes pattern implies symmetry and repetition.

[2] I say, to the left of, because of my visual habituation to this procedure; I dare say that if I were only accustomed to reading Arabic or Japanese script, I should start at the right and read the pattern to the left.

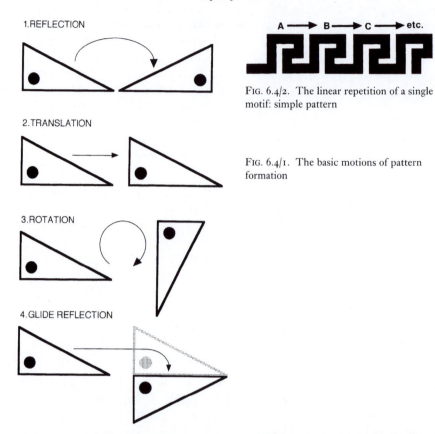

1.REFLECTION

2.TRANSLATION

3.ROTATION

4.GLIDE REFLECTION

A ⟶ B ⟶ C ⟶ etc.

Fig. 6.4/2. The linear repetition of a single motif: simple pattern

Fig. 6.4/1. The basic motions of pattern formation

agency and motion seems to inhere in the motifs themselves. The projection, or externalization, of the agency involved in perception (the perceptual act) into the thing perceived is, cognitively speaking, the source of its animation. It is unhelpful to describe the animation inherent in patterns as an illusion, as if it were some species of mistake. There is no mistake involved in describing the sun as 'moving' through the sky. Actually, it is the observer who is moving, not the sun, but the sun's movement is not a purely subjective phenomenon, like a dream. Similarly, we do not dream that the constituent motifs in patterns move, because these movements stem ultimately from the real movements of our bodies and perceptual organs, scanning the environment.

Psychological experiments on apparent motion and apparent causality (such as the famous experiments of Michotte) reveal how ready human subjects are to attribute motion and mutual causal interaction to the barest of stimuli. Nevertheless, even if one can provide a cognitive explanation for the animated appearance of patterned forms—as a phenomenon of apparent motion whereby the dynamic aspect of the act of perception is subjectively experienced as a dynamic property of the object being perceived—that still does not explain why patterned-ness is such a common property of artefacts, especially objects which are personal possessions and utensils, such as clothes, vessels, and so on. In order to understand this, one has to consider rather more complicated and realistic examples. Most significantly patterned objects and utensils are not decorated with 'simple' patterns, but with subtle and complicated ones, often comprising a great many motifs deployed in two dimensions simultaneously, and involving more recondite motions in the plane than simple translation. Sheer complexity, involution, and the simultaneous suggestion of a great many formal relationships between motifs is a characteristic of decorative art in general. One cannot understand decorative art by generalizing from simple, easily interpreted, examples, because the *telos* of decorative art lies in the opposite direction, towards the complex, the ambiguous, and the multitudinous.

Complicated patterns lie on the borderline between visual 'textures' and 'shapes'. Gibson, in his account of visual perception in naturalistic (or 'ecological' contexts), makes a sharp distinction between the perception of textures, which are structured surfaces (the sky, a green lawn, a brick wall) and the perception of shapes (a ball, a rod, a cup, etc.). Textures are perceived hierarchically constituted out of components (patches of white and blue, blades of grass, individual bricks, etc.) but these are not picked out individually; they are not attended to as objects but as components of a surface. We can respond to patterns as undifferentiated textures, and often do, but not when we attend to them *as* patterns. However, when we do this, we cannot entirely abstract them as 'shapes' either; they retain their essential 'texture' characteristic of internal hierarchy, division into motifs, blocs of motifs, and vague fringes.

6.5. *Complex Patterns*

Contrast, for instance, the Greek key (Fig. 6.4/2) with the design in Fig. 6.5/1, which is only a step up in complexity. It is quite hard, if one has not actually traced it out, to see how it is organized. We perceive it simultaneously as a texture and as an arrangement of shapes (but precisely what arrangement is harder to say). Still more beguiling are patterns which reverse figure and ground, as in Fig. 6.5/2. This is a 'change' (colour-reversal) pattern based on glide reflection along two parallel axes, along one of which the axe-like motif glides onto a same-colour motif (white on white) and along the other of which the motif glides onto an opposite colour motif of the same shape (white onto black). It is one thing to be informed that the pattern in Fig. 6.5/2 is based on this particular mathematical relationship, but it is very difficult to mentally follow through the two types of glide reflection, so that one can actually project the relationships onto the pattern.

In practice (and without the assistance of Washburn and Crowe), I think what happens is approximately as follows; what we do is single out, initially, a

FIG. 6.5/2. The pattern as mind trap: glide reflection and figure–ground reversal. *Source*: Washburn and Crowe 1992: fig. 5.5a

FIG. 6.5/1. The multidimensional orientation of a single motif: complex pattern

candidate motif, approximately, the axe-like shape (cf. Fig. 6.5/2) which we spontaneously see as being repeated (by translation) in rows and columns, and we may also be dimly aware that the 'ground' on which this shape is laid has the same shapes inscribed on it, but in reverse colour. What, however, is likely to defeat us is seeing the relation between the figure and the ground, and the relation of the leftwards-pointing and rightwards-pointing occurrences of our candidate 'basic' motif. So in fact we just mentally resign ourselves to just *not quite understanding* these complex relationships, we write them in as 'beyond our ken'. We experience this as a kind of pleasurable frustration; we are drawn into the pattern and held inside it, impaled, as it were, on its bristling hooks and spines. This pattern is a mind-trap (cf. Gell 1996), we are hooked, and this causes us to relate in a certain way to the artefact which the pattern embellishes.

6.6. *Complex Patterns as 'Unfinished Business'*

Patterns, by their multiplicity and the difficulty we have in grasping their mathematical or geometrical basis by mere visual inspection, generate relationships *over time* between persons and things, because what they present to the mind is, cognitively speaking, always 'unfinished business'. Who, possessed of an intricate oriental carpet, can say that they have entirely come to grips with its pattern; yet how often the eye rests on it and singles out now this relation, this symmetry, now that. The process can continue interminably; the pattern is inexhaustible, the relationship between carpet and owner, for life. Anthropologists have long recognized that social relationships, to endure over time, have to be founded on 'unfinished business'. The essence of exchange, as a binding social force, is the delay, or lag, between transactions which, if the exchange relation is to endure, should never result in perfect reciprocation, but always in some renewed, residual, imbalance. So it is with patterns; they slow perception down, or even halt it, so that the decorated object is never fully possessed at all, but is always in the process of becoming possessed. This, I argue, sets up a biographical relation—an unfinished exchange—between the decorated index and the recipient.

6.7. *Taste and Tackiness*

It could be objected that the argument of the preceding section is beside the point. Decorated objects please people because they confer aesthetic pleasure, and that is why they are desirable, not because they are cognitively resistant to analysis, as I have claimed. People just 'like' pretty patterns. To this objection I would answer that, first, not everybody does like pretty (complicated, animated, etc.) patterns, and secondly that mere aesthetic 'liking' cannot explain the types of social relationships which are mediated by patterned artefacts.

Aesthetic pleasure is consummatory, an end in itself, and there is nothing empirically to show that the decorated objects with which the world abounds are contemplated except in specific situational contexts in which their aesthetic properties are never the sole focus of interest. Melanesian big-men do not sit around aesthetically contemplating lime-containers; on the contrary, they treat them as mediating objects. Lime-containers are not self-sufficient sources of delight, but vehicles of personhood, to be owned, exchanged, and displayed. Aesthetic theories of art imply that any two recipients of an artwork, if they have the same aesthetic tastes (which would apply, *a fortiori,* to two Melanesian big-men) will have the same response to the aesthetic properties of any given object. But this is never the case in practice; so far as these big-men are concerned, the inherent quality present in an index (such as a lime-container) is modulated by the identity and status of the gourd's owner. The aesthetic properties of a lime-container are salient only to the extent that they mediate social agency back and forth within the social field.

Similarly, I would deny that the contemplation of an oriental carpet that one does not own is the same kind of experience as the contemplation of a carpet that is one's personal possession. The possessor of a carpet of complicated oriental design, as in the well-known Henry James story, sees in its coils an image of his own unfinished life. It is quite otherwise with somebody else's carpet, which is just a snare for unrealizable desire. Aestheticians will no doubt be horrified at the expression of such sentiments, but anthropologically, it is abundantly obvious that aesthetic responses are subordinate to responses stemming from the social identities and differences mediated by the index. Since the pure aesthetic response is a myth, it cannot be invoked to explain the very manifold types of attachment between persons and things. The aesthetic response always occurs within a social frame of some kind.

Secondly, when it comes to the specifically Western (or, indeed, Oriental) 'aesthetic attitude' it is objects devoid of precisely the kind of intricate surface decoration of the type I am interested in that have often excited the most extravagant admiration. Simple and undecorated forms are the most beautiful according to refined canons of taste, and equally, to those whose religious attitudes incline them towards asceticism and withdrawal. As E. Gombrich (1984) has shown, most committed aesthetes are far from keen on riotous decoration, which, however, survives and prospers, even in the face of aesthetic condemnation from on high, because it is socially efficacious. I, personally, in my incarnation as a person of refined tastes, admire even to excess ultra-plain Shaker furniture, but anthropologically, I know that this furniture came into existence in a community which specifically, on theological grounds, outlawed the kinds of mediation which decorated objects allow in less puritanical social milieux. Shaker chairs were made plain so that Shakers would not be attached to chairs, or other earthly things, but exclusively to Lord Jesus. Kantian high-bourgeois aesthetics cannot explain decoration because Kantian aesthetics is *against* decoration.

Most people are not like Shakers, they prefer to load surfaces with decoration in order to draw persons into worldly projects. An ornate Victorian chair is not half so beautiful as a Shaker one, but it communicates much more strongly, not just the idea of sitting comfortably, but also a host of other domestic and social implications of a this-worldly variety.

Gombrich (1984: 17–32) has traced the epidemiology of pro- and anti-decoration sentiment in the history of European taste. Puritan movements, such as the revolutionary modernism articulated by Adolf Loos, despise surface ornamentation, while romantic hedonists such as the 1960s hippies who customized their Volkswagens with flowers and stars, adore it. I am not going to recapitulate Gombrich's excellent history; instead I want to focus attention on what I have identified as the essential property of surface decoration, its cognitive resistance, the fact that once one submits to the allure of the pattern, one is liable to become hooked, or stuck, in it.

The fact that the word 'tacky' is the one selected (from a range of possibilities) by severe modernism to condemn the popular taste for riotous ornament and other lapses of taste is interesting in itself. Let me quote from Mary Douglas's summary of Sartre's account of 'viscosity' as an ignoble state of being (Douglas 1966: 38; Sartre 1943: 696 ff.):

The viscous is a state half-way between solid and liquid. It is like a cross-section in a process of change. It is unstable, but it does not flow. It is soft, yielding and compressible. There is no gliding on its surface. Its stickiness is a trap, it clings like a leech; it attacks the boundary between myself and it. Long columns falling off my fingers suggest my own substance flowing into a pool of stickiness . . . to touch stickiness is to risk diluting myself into viscosity . . .

Sartre is perturbed by the subversive effect of viscosity on the body/world boundary, but in the light of post-Maussian understandings of gifts as adhesive components of persons, strung between donors and recipients on loops of viscous (if imaginary) substance, we need not be so squeamish. Physical/tactile adhesiveness is perhaps genuinely disagreeable, but analogical, or cognitive, adhesiveness is not, otherwise we would not be so willing to have artefacts attached to us and so positively responsive to the adhesive qualities of surface decoration. Most non-modernist, non-puritan civilizations value decorativeness and allot it a specific role in the mediation of social life, the creation of attachment between persons and things.

6.8. *The Apotropaic Pattern*

The formula for the abstract pattern given previously:

$$[[[\text{Index-A motif}^{\text{part}}] \rightarrow \text{Index-A}^{\text{part/whole}}] \rightarrow \text{Index-A whole}] \longrightarrow \text{Recipient-P}.$$

refers to the essentially hierarchical nature of the index, the fact that it is composed of parts combined into a whole (this applies to all indexes, but is particularly salient in this context). My argument is that the deconstruction of this complex of hierarchical relationships endows the decorated object with a certain type of agency, which is the reciprocal of the agency exercised by the recipient in (attempting) to perceive it; his action is subjectively experienced as a passion, a pleasurable frustration. However, other types of agency may be present as well. In particular, the agency of the artist may be abducted from the pattern. Thus the formula can easily be expanded to:

$$[[[[\text{Artist-A}] \rightarrow \text{Index-A motif}^{\text{part}}] \rightarrow \text{Index-A}^{\text{part/whole}}] \rightarrow \text{Index-A whole}] \longrightarrow \text{Recipient-P}.$$

This agency can be agonistic or defensive as well as beneficial. I turn now to a series of examples in which the exercise of social agency turns on the employment of patterns as mediators of actively hostile, or defensive, intent. It might seem paradoxical that patterns, which bind persons to things, should be potential weapons in situations of conflict. A moment's reflection is sufficient to realize, first of all, that relations of conflict and struggle are just as 'social' as relations of solidarity, and secondly, that wherever one finds conflict there one finds abundant deployment of all kinds of decorative art. Much of this art is of the variety known as 'apotropaic'. Apotropaic art, which protects an agent (whom we will take to be the artist, for the present) against the recipient (usually the enemy in demonic rather than human form), is a prime instance of artistic agency, and hence a topic of central concern in the anthropology of art.

The apotropaic use of patterns is as protective devices, defensive screens or obstacles impeding passage. This 'apotropaic' use of patterns seems paradoxical

FIG. 6.8/1. Celtic knotwork: apotropaic pattern

in that the placing of patterns to keep demons at bay seems contrary to the use of patterns in other contexts as a means of bringing about attachment between people and artefacts. If patterns attract, wouldn't they also attract, rather than repel demons? But the paradox is apparent rather than real in that the apotropaic use of patterns depends on adhesiveness just as the use of patterns to attract people to things. Apotropaic patterns are demon-traps, in effect, demonic fly-paper, in which demons become hopelessly stuck, and are thus rendered harmless.

Take the Celtic knotwork pattern in Fig. 6.8/1. Knotwork like this was regarded as protective in that any evil spirit would be so fascinated by the entwined braids as to suffer from a paralysis of the will. Losing interest in whatever malevolent plan it had entertained previously, the demon would become stuck in the coils of the pattern and the object, person, or place protected by it would be saved. Not just intricate pattern, but sheer multiplicity can have this effect; I am told that even recently in Italy, peasants would hang a little bag of grain next to the bedstead, so that the Devil, approaching the sleeper in the bed, would be obliged to count the grains in the bag and would be thus diverted from inflicting harm. The interminableness of large numbers and complicated patterns work in the same way; but patterns are more interesting and certainly more artistic.

6.9. Kolam

A suitable example is provided by the kind of auspicious threshold designs known in Tamilnad (South India) as *kolam*, and by other names in other parts of southern and eastern India where similar threshold designs are also drawn (Fig. 6.9/1). In Tamilnad, *kolam* have two protective functions. First of all they are associated with the protective, fertile, and auspicious cobra deity (*naga*) and secondly they have an apotropaic function, repelling or ensnaring demons.

FIG. 6.9/1. *Kolam* threshold design: the pattern as topological snare

Kolam are made by women, who draw the design free-hand in lime, rice-powder, or some other white powder which they trickle through their fingers. The designs are made at dawn, especially during the time of year when there are many demons and spirits about, and are rubbed out by the passage of feet as the day wears on, to be renewed the next day (Layard 1937: 121, citing J. Dubois, and S. M. N. Sastri). Fig. 6.9/1 shows a typical *kolam* design. *Kolam* are sinuous, symmetrical figures which are usually very difficult to 'read' in the sense that it is difficult to see how the design has been constructed. They play topological games with the spectator and are thus akin to mazes. Let us take Fig. 6.9/1 apart and see what kind of cognitive teasing is going on here.

On first inspection, it seems to consist of a single line, pursuing a complex, sinuous path between the rows and columns of dots. However, this is an illusion in that this *kolam* is actually composed of four continuous loops of asymmetric configuration, superimposed on one another while being rotated in 90 degree steps. This *kolam* is, so to speak, the visual equivalent of a canon in four parts, in which each voice sings the same notes but not in phase; that is, after the lapse of one bar as in 'Frère Jacques'. The identical components (individual loops) of this are out of phase, not in time, but in space, being displaced by 90 degree rotations (Fig. 6.9/2).

What is most interesting about this *kolam* is that even if one 'knows' (intellectually) that this design is made up of four separate, but identical loops differently orientated, it is extremely frustrating to attempt to abstract individual loops from the overall design. And though I find I can, with some effort, do this for one loop at a time, I cannot do it for two loops simultaneously, still less three, or all four. Where simple geometric figures are concerned, 'seeing' (a triangle, say) is tantamount to mentally intending or projecting the construction of the figure, line by line. But this is impossible to do with complex figures like this *kolam*. Here seeing the figure is quite distinct from being able

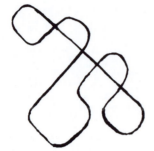

FIG. 6.9/2. The constitutive
element of the *kolam*

to mentally intend the process of its construction. Yet we 'write in' the fact that
it *is possible* to construct the figure, because here it is, it has been made by someone, and we might indeed have been lucky enough to have watched, entranced,
the deft movements of the woman who made it. So we end with a series of paradoxes. We want to see this figure as one continuous line, but we know it is four
separate loops, which, however, we cannot separately abstract from the overall
design. We know too that this design belongs to the real world, and was made,
apparently effortlessly, by this real woman; but we cannot retrace fully the process whereby the design came into the world, by the agency of this woman,
because we cannot reconstruct her skilled movements (and the intentions guiding them) from the design which has resulted from them.

   I attribute the cognitive stickiness of patterns to this blockage in the cognitive process of reconstructing the intentionality embodied in artefacts. Clearly,
no demon will readily cross a threshold set with sophisticated topological
snares such as this; the evil one will have to pause and ponder the problem, and
the impetus of its malevolence will be neutralized. Perhaps it is no coincidence
that Tamilnad, the state where women play these mathematical games, is also
the state from which most of India's world-renowned mathematicians and
computer wizards originate.

6.10. Kolam, *Tattoo, and the Cretan Maze*

In the earlier part of this century, designs frequently identical to *kolam* had an
alternative use as tattoo designs, defending not the threshold of the house, but
the skin, the threshold of the body. And this provides a link with the next stage
of my argument, which has to do with mazes. Fig. 6.10/1 taken from Layard
1937, shows a South Indian tattoo design published at the beginning of this
century, and for comparison, a 'map' of the labyrinth at Knossos (the one containing the Minotaur) as depicted on a Cretan coin of the seventh century BC.
Legendarily, this labyrinth was designed by the master-craftsman Daedalus,
and was modelled on another maze, the one which led to the Underworld. A
similar representation of the Cretan labyrinth is mentioned in book 6 of the

FIG. 6.10/1. Comparison of threshold, tattoo, and coin designs from Layard 1937: fig. 36: '(*a*) threshold design, *Kolam*, "the fort"; (*b*) tattoo pattern, "fort"; (*c*) conventionalized Cretan labyrinth design appearing on the coins of Knossos (for comparison)'

Aeneid, as being carved on the Cumaean gates, where it attracts the attention of Aeneas' men, prior to their leader's descent into the Underworld to consult the Cumaean Sibyl, who predicts that one day Rome will rule the world. Curiously, an exactly identical map of the labyrinth is to be found carved next to the entry into the great passage-grave at New Grange, in Ireland, which is indeed also a twisting tunnel leading, presumably, to the world of the dead. There are also representations of gods at the centre of labyrinths in the art of ancient Egypt.

Why do I mention these facts, which so excited the anthropologist Layard and the classical scholars of his period? Layard is now a forgotten figure in anthropology, and his interest in matters such as these ensured the demise of his reputation in an era dominated by the functionalism of Radcliffe-Brown and Malinowski. Layard was the last of the diffusionists of a psychological persuasion, who drew their theoretical framework from Rivers, and nowadays the only Layard works in print are those he wrote later on as a Jungian analyst, which are to be found, I am told, in 'Occult' bookstores. One can see why Layard abandoned academic anthropology and became a proponent of Jungian 'archetypes' in the light of the facts just mentioned. It is indeed astonishing that identical maze-patterns should be unearthed in South India, the ancient Mediterranean, Egypt, and the bogs of Ireland, especially so in that, as we will see, Layard found similar ideas linking 'maze' designs and entry into the land of the dead also in the New Hebrides (Vanuatu) in the midst of the Pacific ocean. I feel sympathy for Layard in that he was in a sense 'bounced' into pursuing a deeply untrendy diffusionist approach (for the time) by the sheer coherence of the data at his disposal, for which there does indeed appear no obvious explanation other than a Riversian or Jungian one.

I personally do not see why one should dismiss diffusionist explanations out of hand (cf. Lévi-Strauss 1963). But it is not the diffusionist hypothesis that I want to discuss here. Even if the 'Cretan maze' idea has spread across the globe from some specific place of origin, one would still have to explain the enhanced receptivity of very diverse civilizations to this idea, on a better basis than the preservation of ancient racial memories, as Jung proposes. One can afford to be agnostic about how exactly the labyrinth idea came to exist in so many different places with apparently the same associations, having to do with the passage between this world and the land of the dead. The problem I am concerned with is to understand the cognitive significance of this maze-pattern, which could equally well explain why it has travelled so far and wide and/or why it has been invented independently in so many mutually faraway places.

The Cretan labyrinth is not, technically, a 'maze' in that it has no branching passageways and so poses no navigational problems. Theseus would not really have needed Ariadne's thread to find his way into or out of the labyrinth if it were built as shown in Fig. 6.10/1. It is a 'meander' pattern, an exercise in finding the longest possible pathway between two spatially quite adjacent points. It evokes the idea of a navigational problem without actually offering one, rather, the problem is one of distance and the continuum. One could see the Cretan maze as a spatial version of Zeno's paradoxes of time and motion. Zeno argued, for instance, that an arrow in its flight must successively reach, and pass, an infinite number of points, that is, the half-way point, the three-quarters point, the 6/8 point, the 12/16 point, the 24/32 point, etc. etc. and that since this series of fractions is infinite, the arrow will never reach its destination. The Cretan maze is built up by connecting points serially (Fig. 6.10/2) so as to create a meander pattern which threatens to indefinitely extend the number of twistings and turnings in the path which must be traversed between the entry-door and the centre. In the Roman world, meander patterns (and genuine maze-patterns) were a popular device for mosaic floor-decoration in palaces, where their capacity to expand confined spaces indefinitely may indeed have been architectonically highly effective, as well as decorative (see Fig. 6.10/3, showing the great maze at Pula, in Croatia). Such mazes exemplify another way in which patterns can present cognitive obstacles. One knows there is a way through the maze; one may even know that the maze is created by the simple application of an iterative rule in connecting up lines and points, as is demonstrated in Fig. 6.10/2, but one cannot, all the same, see one's way through the maze except very laboriously by tracing out its winding course.

FIG. 6.10/2. The serial connection of points in the formation of the Cretan labyrinth design

FIG. 6.10/3. The Roman maze at Pula

This may help explain why mazes are associated with the passage between the worlds of the living and the dead. These worlds are close together (death is everywhere) yet far apart, separated by an impassable frontier. Aeneas' companions were prevented from entering the Cumaean gates by the fascination exerted over them by the maze design carved on the portal; in this respect they were akin to the demons waylaid by the *kolam* protecting the house, discussed earlier. But the connection between *kolam* and maze designs is closer than this, in that Indian (*kolam*-based) tattoo designs were specifically connected with entry into the world of the dead. Thus the tattoo design shown in Fig. 6.10/1, besides being formally identical to a *kolam*, is one of the class of Indian tattoo designs, occurring in many regions of the peninsular, which are identified as the 'fort' (i.e. City) of the land of the dead. Throughout India, especially among lower castes and tribes, it was considered a necessity for women, and sometimes men, to be tattooed, in order to avoid punishment in the land of the dead. The 'fort' design was considered to help the dead person (who retained her tattoos *post mortem*) to find their way to the land of the dead and be safely reunited with deceased kin. So the 'fort' is a map. At the same time, it is also a puzzle, in that these same people believe that Yama, the God of death, and his demons, will devour the untattooed, but will not harm the tattooed woman because they cannot solve the 'puzzle' that her tattoos present, that is to say, the tattoo is apotropaically protective of the body after death (Gell n.d. [1994]). So the *kolam* and the 'maze' tattoo both work in the same way—both stand for the idea of (demonic) attention being drawn into the pattern, being tantalized by it, while being thus rebuffed and rendered impotent.

6.11. *Sand-Drawings of Malakula and the Land of the Dead*

The idea of patterns as 'obstacles', that is to say, sticking-points, surfaces also in Malakula, the New Hebridean society investigated by Layard and his older contemporary Bernard Deacon, who died while he was in the field (both Deacon and Layard were pupils of Rivers). Malakula are perhaps unique in having contributed to the literature of anthropology not just as ethnographic subjects, but as originators of a method of diagrammatic representation in kinship theory. The diagram drawn by a Malakulan man for Deacon (using short and long sticks, and arcs traced on the sand) showing the operation of the Malakulan three- (or six-) class alliance system is plainly ancestral to subsequent anthropologists' efforts to create diagrams of the same kinds of institutions in Australia (Deacon 1934: Fig. 6.11/1; Lévi-Strauss 1969: Fig. 6.11/2). The reason why the Malakulans were so diagram-minded is that they practised pattern-construction as an art form and as part of the typical Vanuatan male competition to demonstrate knowledge and mastery. Deacon collected more than forty-five designs which were published after his death (Fig. 6.11/3). These designs were drawn on the beach by men, and would of course be washed away

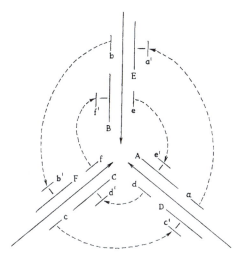

FIG. 6.11/1. Diagram traced by the Ambrym natives to explain their kinship system. (The long lines stand for men, and the short for women; the arrows separate the 'lines' within the same bilateral group.) Caption and diagram from Lévi-Strauss, *The Elementary Structures of Kinship. Source*: Lévi-Strauss 1969: fig. 5

FIG. 6.11/2. Lévi-Strauss's diagram to explain Aranda kinship in *The Savage Mind. Source*: Lévi-Strauss 1972

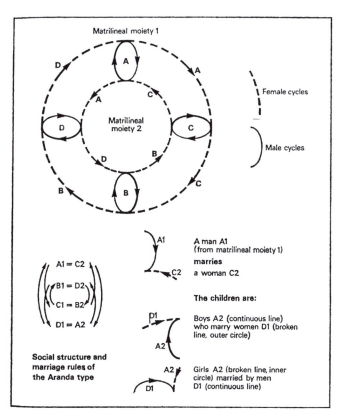

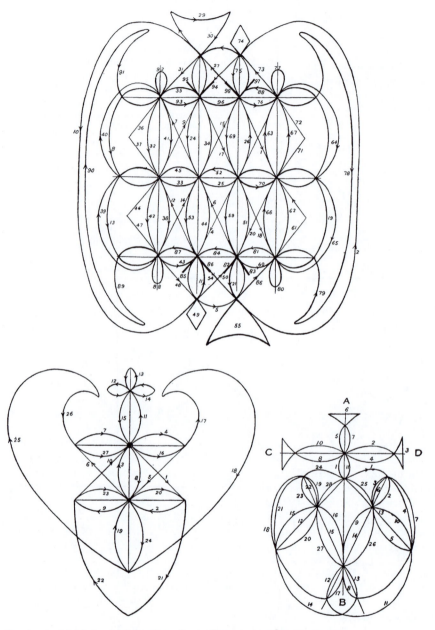

FIG. 6.11/3. Malakulan sand-drawings. *Source*: Deacon 1934: figs. 22, 23, 24

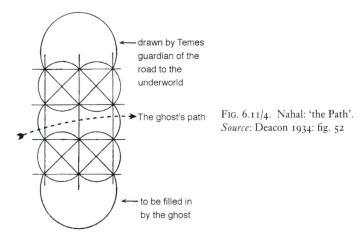

— drawn by Temes
guardian of the
road to the
underworld

— The ghost's path

Fig. 6.11/4. Nahal: 'the Path'.
Source: Deacon 1934: fig. 52

— to be filled in
by the ghost

by the incoming tide. As Deacon notes, what was important in Malakulan sand-drawing art, was not the artefact produced, but the 'performance' aspect of the procedure, the way in which an expert could delineate a complex figure, as in Fig. 6.11/3, without hesitation or deviation, in a single continuous movement from start to finish. Most of the designs are, in fact, continuous lines (drawn over a rectangular grid) though some involve superimposed figures, like the *kolam* considered earlier. However, let me now quote Deacon on the subject of the relationship between sand-drawing art and the 'obstacles' which have to be overcome on the way to the land of the dead.

Ghosts of the dead from Seniang district [*where Deacon worked*] pass along a 'road' to Wies, the land of the dead. At a certain point on their way they come to a rock called Lembwil Song [now] lying in the sea at the boundary between the Seniang and Mewun districts, but formerly it stood upright. The land of the dead is situated vaguely in the wooded open ground behind this rock and is surrounded by a high fence. Always sitting by the rock is a female ghost, Temes Savsap, and on the ground in front of her is drawn the completed geometrical figure known as *Nahal*, 'the Path' [Fig. 6.11/4]. The path which the ghost must traverse lies between the two halves of this figure.

As each ghost comes along the road the guardian ghost hurriedly rubs out one half of the figure. The ghost now comes up, but loses his track and cannot find it. He wanders about searching for a way to get past the Temes of the rock, but in vain. Only a knowledge of the completed geometrical figure can release him from this impasse. If he knows this figure, he at once completes the half which Temes Savsap rubbed out; and passes down the track through the middle of the figure. If, however, he does not know the figure, the Temes, seeing he will never find the road, eats him, and he never reaches the abode of the dead.   (Deacon 1934: 130)

Here 'pattern' is associated with the idea of a difficult journey, and obstacles which have to be overcome in order to proceed. 'Completing the pattern' (getting through the maze) is a task set this time, not for, but by, a demon, and the task is to outwit the demon by succeeding. We are a long way, here, from the idea that patterns appeal to the eyes or give aesthetic pleasure. I do not think that the Malakulans thought of these patterns as independent visual objects at all, but as performances, like dances, in which men could reveal their capability. Melanesian aesthetics is about efficacy, the capacity to accomplish tasks, not 'beauty'.

6.12. *Drawing and Dancing*

At this point one may draw attention to another source of insight in Layard's work, which was also utterly foreign to the mind-set of his anthropological contemporaries. Layard (1936) discusses the affinity between the choreography of Malakulan dance and the style of their graphic art. The ghost's task of completing the maze-like figure on the sand, is complemented by the performance of ceremonies connected with the induction of neophytes into the men's cult in the course of which a single dancer (called 'the hawk') has to thread his way through the ranks of the main body of dancers very much indeed as if he were negotiating a maze (Figs. 6.12/1, 6.12/2 from Layard 1936). Layard links this

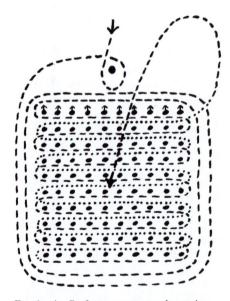 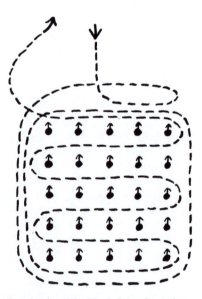

FIG. 6.12/1. Performance art complementing graphic art: the Malakulan dancer's path. 'The dots represent the main body of dancers, the arrows representing the direction in which they are facing. The broken lines represent the path traced by the Hawks. The dotted line represents the "Hawks' return track"' (Layard 1937: fig. 24)

FIG. 6.12/2. 'The Hawk flying from place to place' (Layard 1936: fig. 23) with the so-called 'Trojan Games' described in the *Iliad*, equestrian military exercises, witnessed by the Greeks, in which mounted youths executed a series of circuitous manœuvres supposedly tracing out the path of a labyrinth. But once again it is not the diffusionist thesis which concerns me, but the nature of the cognitive linkages being suggested here. It is surely useful to consider the act of drawing as akin to dancing, and the design as a kind of frozen residue left by this manual ballet. Indeed, just this analogy seems to have suggested itself to Merleau-Ponty, after witnessing a close-up, and slowed-down, cinematographic record of Matisse's hand and brush engaged in the act of painting.

This dancer-like nimbleness of the hand (and indeed the analogy with the hawk, the most precise of birds in its movements) emerges as a crucial element in the evaluation of plastic (sculptural) art in the Trobriands, for instance (cf. Gell 1992*b*). But, even more, it indicates the synergy between art forms and modalities of expression which conventional aesthetics tries to deal with separately, because they give pleasure to separate senses, the eye (visual art), the ear (music), or the kinetic sense (dance). If we can see visual patterns as frozen traces of dances, so we can also see dances as being half-way to becoming music, which indeed normally accompanies them. What unites drawing, music, and dancing is a certain cognitive indecipherability manifested in performance (see above, Sect. 5.2). Thus, to revert to the comparison made earlier between our *kolam* design and a four-part (musical) canon, we may observe that a four-part canon reveals its structure (because it is easy to hear the four successive entries of the theme) but also conceals it, in that it is near-impossible to hear all four parts simultaneously. So also the *kolam* reveals itself as constructed out of four superimposed figures, but just how, we cannot be certain. Drawing and music and dance tantalize our capacity to deal with wholes and parts, continuity and discontinuity, synchrony and succession. This analogy also reminds us of the fact that much art consists of virtuosic performances, and that although the performances involved in most visual art take place, so to speak, 'off-stage', none the less a painting by Rembrandt is a performance by Rembrandt, and is to be understood only as such, just as if it were a performance by one of today's dancers or musicians, alive and on-stage.

7

The Distributed Person

7.1. *Mimesis and Sorcery*

I now turn to the anthropological theory of representational art, that is to say, the production, circulation, and practical use of indexes that have relevant prototypes, something that geometric patterns lack. Most Western art is of this type, and most of art-theory is about representation, in one way or another. I shall try to avoid, as far as possible, discussing Western art, tempting though it is to do so. Instead, this part of the argument pivots around the classically 'anthropological' themes of sorcery and image-worship.

The basic thesis of this work, to recapitulate, is that works of art, images, icons, and the like have to be treated, in the context of an *anthropological* theory, as person-like; that is, sources of, and targets for, social agency. In this context, image-worship has a central place, since nowhere are images more obviously treated as human persons than in the context of worship and ceremonies. In this chapter, I present a general theory of idolatry, a practice I by no means regard as more misguided than any other religious observance; and I am, I hope, capable of sustaining a sympathetic attitude towards religion in general, despite not being a religious person myself. 'Idolatry' has had a bad press since the rise to world domination of Christianity and Islam, which have both inherited the anti-imagistic strain of biblical Judaism. Christianity, encumbered with its Graeco-Roman inheritance, has had to struggle more actively with recrudescences of *de facto* 'pagan' idolatry, and has experienced cataclysmic episodes of iconoclasm; Islam has more consistently resisted the lure of image-directed forms of worship. Protestantism, the most dynamic branch of Christianity in the past few centuries, has hardly been less puritanical about idolatry than Islam, and the consciences of the Catholics have been often pricked on this account as well, so that the net result is today that 'idolatry' is a pejorative word, which anthropologists, especially ones who claim to empathize with the religious sentiments of others, are not supposed to use. But rather than resort to some vague or misleading circumlocution I prefer to call the practice of worshipping images by its true name, deeming it better to explain idolatry, rather than rechristen it—by showing that it emanates, not from stupidity or superstition, but from the same fund of sympathy which allows us to understand the human, non-artefactual, 'other' as a copresent being, endowed with awareness, intentions, and passions akin to our own.

Granted that idolatry may be so called, I still have to explain why a book ostensibly about 'art' has to devote so many pages to a topic which appears to belong to the study of religion rather than aesthetics. Those who object to my anti-aesthetics stance will regard as irrelevant the 'religious function' of images they prefer to see in a totally non-religious frame of reference, from the standpoint of aesthetic contemplation. An image viewed as a source of religious power, salvation, exaltation, is not appreciated for its 'beauty', but for quite different reasons, the proponents of 'aesthetic experiences' would argue. I regard this as fallacious on two grounds. First of all, I cannot tell between religious and aesthetic exaltation; art-lovers, it seems to me, actually do worship images in most of the relevant senses, and explain away their *de facto* idolatry by rationalizing it as aesthetic awe. Thus, to write about art at all is, in fact, to write about either religion, or the substitute for religion which those who have abandoned the outward forms of received religions content themselves with. The Protestant-Puritan heritage combined with a special form of art-theoretical casuistry have established a special form of bad faith about the 'power of images' in the contemporary Western world, as Freedberg (1989) has persuasively argued (see below). We have neutralized our idols by reclassifying them as art; but we perform obeisances before them every bit as deep as those of the most committed idolater before his wooden god—I specifically include myself in this description. Secondly, from the anthropological point of view, we have to recognize that the 'aesthetic attitude' is a specific historical product of the religious crisis of the Enlightenment and the rise of Western science, and that it has no applicability to civilizations which have not internalized the Enlightenment as we have. In India (which figures largely in the ensuing discussion) idolatry flourishes as a form of religiosity, and nobody in their right minds would try to drive a wedge between the beautiful form and religious function of venerated idols. In India aesthetics, as in the ancient world, is subsumed under the philosophy of religion, that is, moral philosophy, as a matter of course. Consequently, it is only from a very parochial (blinkered) Western post-Enlightenment point of view that the separation between the beautiful and the holy, between religious experience and aesthetic experience, arises. Since this is so, the anthropologist writing about art inevitably contributes to the anthropology of religion, because the religious is—in some contexts, though not all—prior to the artistic.

Idols come in many varieties, but it is conventional to distinguish two polar types; (i) purely 'aniconic' idols, such as the *baitulia* (black meteoritic stones) worshipped in ancient Greece, versus (ii) 'iconic' idols, that is, indexes physically resembling a prototype, usually a human being, according to the formula $[[\text{Prototype-A} \rightarrow [\text{Artist-A}]] \longrightarrow \text{Index-P}$, where the prototype is the god, whose 'likeness' is mediated by the artist. However, before starting, it may be as well to clarify our reasons for not paying very much attention to this distinction. All idols, I think, are 'iconic'—including the so-called aniconic ones—whether

or not they look like some familiar object, such as a human body. An aniconic
idol is a 'realistic' representation of a god who either has no form (anywhere),
or has an 'arbitrary' form, in the particular 'body' he inhabits for the purposes
of being worshipped by his mortal devotees, here below. A meteoritic stone
is not a very, very, conventionalized or distorted 'portrait' of a god, who, elsewhere, looks like a human being. One need not imagine that worshippers of
stones would 'prefer' to worship more realistic portrayals of their gods, but
have to make do with unshaped stones for lack of any local stone-carvers of the
necessary ability. For such worshippers, the meteoritic stone is an index of the
god's spatio-temporal presence (and origins, in that the stone fell to earth from
heaven). The stone is a 'representative' of the god, like an ambassador, rather
than a visual icon. Just as an ambassador can represent his country in Moscow
one year, and the following year in Washington, the stone represents the god
at whatever spatial coordinates it happens to be; and it is movable. One such
'black stone' for instance, worshipped in Arabia as Cybele, was conveyed with
great ceremony to Rome, where it was installed into a cavity within the idol
of Magna Mater Idea, the goddess of members of the Imperial élite who favoured an 'internationalist' religious outlook (Dumézil 1980; on the significance
of such transactions, see below). The ideas of 'representing' (like a picture)
and 'representing' (like an ambassador) are distinct, but none the less linked.
An ambassador is a spatio-temporally detached fragment of his nation, who
travels abroad and with whom foreigners can speak, 'as if' they were speaking
to his national government. Although ambassadors are real persons, they are
also 'fictions', like pictures, and their embassies are fictional mini-states within
the state; just as pictures show us landscapes and personages who are 'not really
there'. Although the Chinese ambassador in London does not look like China,
or the Chinese government or people, he does *have to be visible*, and he does
visibly represent China on official occasions. He does not look like China, but
in London, China looks like him.

   One could not contrast a 'realistic' iconic ambassador to an 'unrealistic', aniconic ambassador, and no more, perhaps, should one contrast 'realistic' idols,
to unrealistic, aniconic idols. Whatever the idol looks like, that, in context, is
what the god looks like, so all idols are equally realistic, because the idol-form
is the visual form of the god made present in the idol. The contrast is not
between idols which resemble human beings to a greater or lesser degree, but
between gods who in idol-form (visually) resemble human beings to a greater
or lesser degree. Idols, in other words, are not depictions, not portraits, but
(artefactual) *bodies*. The formula cited above then $[[\text{Prototype-A} \rightarrow [\text{Artist-A}]]$
$\longrightarrow \text{Index-P}$ does not necessarily imply 'realistic' (i.e. anthropomorphic)
depiction of the prototype by the artist in the form of the image. When such
a formula is applied to portraiture, this implication exists, because there is
a living model for the portrait, and fidelity to this living model is the social
objective of portraiture. But in the context of idolatry, the agency involved is

religious. Where an idol is an artefact (rather than a natural object, such as a meteoritic stone), the nature of agency exerted by the prototype is to cause the artist to produce a *religiously stipulated* image according to the conventions for such images, which may be iconic/anthropomorphic or abstract and aniconic. In either case, the artist has to produce a 'faithful' rendition of the features of the accepted image of the body of the god, triggering 'recognition' of the god among his worshippers.

To assert that in the context of idolatry, the idol is not a 'depiction' of the god, but the body of the god in artefact-form is all very well, but I accept that any such assertion constitutes a paradox, and I must labour hard to dispel the puzzlement it must inevitably produce in the mind of any reasonable person. The mystery of the animation of idols, their genuine, if peculiar, personhood, has to be approached, like any difficult problem, via a series of incremental steps, not to mention detours through some unfamiliar territory. Rather than deal with idolatry in its most elaborated form, I shall introduce the subject by presenting an analysis of volt sorcery (*envoutement*)—the practice of inflicting harm on others via their images. This is a particularly pertinent case of agency mediated via representational indexes, and it has the advantage of removing the discussion, temporarily, from the sphere of 'religion proper', which involves the always problematic question of other-worldly entities such as gods. Volt sorcery takes place in this world and without the necessity for other-worldly divine or diabolic intervention, though it may be sought. As we will be able to observe, there is actually a smooth transition between this-worldly volt sorcery and religious image-worship orientated towards other-worldly beings. This will be explained in due course.

7.2. *The Mimetic Faculty*

Frazer, rather than Tylor, is the ancestral figure who presides over this discussion. Frazer, it will be recalled, distinguished two basic modes of 'magical' action; (i) contagious magic, the magic of contact, in which influence passes from one object to another, and (ii) sympathetic magic, which depends on shared properties, that is, if object A shares properties with object B, A has influence over B or vice versa. The Frazerian idea of 'imitative' sympathetic magic has had an enormous influence on aesthetics and the philosophy of art in the course of this century. Via Benjamin and Adorno, this influence seems set to continue; Taussig (1993) in a most exciting recent book, whose primary inspiration comes from Benjamin, has this to say about Frazer:

I am particularly taken by [Frazer's] proposition that the principle underlying the imitative component of sympathetic magic is that 'the magician infers that he can produce any effect he desires merely by imitating it'. (52) Leaving aside for the moment the thorny issue of how and with what success Frazer could put himself into the head of one of these magicians, and to what degree either the accuracy or usefulness of his

proposition depends on such a move, I want to dwell on *this notion of the copy, in magical practice, affecting the original to such a degree that the representation shares in or
acquires the properties of the represented.* To me this is a disturbing notion, foreign and
fascinating not because it so flagrantly contradicts the world about me but rather, that
once posited, I suspect if not its presence, then intimations thereof, in the strangely
familiar commonplace and unconscious habits of representation in the world about me.
(Taussig 1993: 47–8)

   Following Benjamin, Taussig bases his analysis of mimesis in the colonial
milieu (of the Cuna Indians) on a supposed 'mimetic faculty'. Benjamin thought
that the mimetic faculty, which in modern times has resulted in a world filled to
overflowing with images and simulacra, so that nothing seems real any more, had
its origin in a primitive compulsion to imitate, and thus gain access, to the world:

[Man's] gift of seeing resemblances is nothing other than a rudiment of the powerful
compulsion in former times to become and behave like something else. Perhaps there
is none of his higher functions in which his mimetic faculty does not play a decisive
role.   (1933; cited in Taussig 1993: 19)

Taussig's book bears witness to the productivity of Frazer's idea mediated
through Benjamin's surrealist imagination, but it is fair to say that the 'mimetic
faculty' is only rather vaguely delineated. The fact that so much human behaviour
is imitative does not necessarily imply the existence of a 'faculty' inherited from
the distant past. Almost all learned behaviour could be described as imitative, in
that it is based on the imitation of an internalized model. Mimesis, narrowly
defined, involves the actual production of images (indexes) whose salient property is prototype, via resemblance to the original, and within this category artefacts, having visual resemblance to the originals, can be accorded a separate status.
   What Frazer never explained is why the mutual resemblance of the image
and the original should be a conduit for mutual influence or agency. He attributed it to a mistaken hypothesis, akin to a scientific theory, but grounded in
error. The trouble is that if the practitioners of sympathetic magic could have
seen their practices as Frazer saw them, they would never have engaged in them
in the first place. By abstracting a generalizable 'principle' from the inchoate
world of practice, Frazer guaranteed his eventual misunderstanding of the data
he had at his disposal. Taussig, in his Benjaminesque reanalysis, argues that
the basis of sympathetic magic is not a tragic misunderstanding of the nature
of physical causality, but a consequence of epistemic awareness itself. To see
(or to know) is to be sensuously filled with that which is perceived, yielding
to it, mirroring it—and hence imitating it bodily (ibid. 45) (see above in
'Captivation', Sect. 5.2). But for the moment I will approach the sympathetic
magic problem from a different direction.
   Frazer's intellectualism treated magic as a form of mistaken causal thinking. Anti-Frazerians, ever since, have criticized Frazer for attributing 'causal'

intentions to behaviours which were symbolic or expressive (Beattie 1966). There is another approach, though, which can be adopted, which is not to condemn Frazer for having invoked causality at all (because magic is, after all, intended to cause things to happen) but to rethink the idea of 'cause'. Frazer's mistake was to impose a pseudo-scientific notion of physical cause and effect (encompassing the entire universe) on practices which depend on intentionality and purpose, which is precisely what is missing from scientific determinism. Magic is possible because *intentions cause events to happen in the vicinity of agents*, but this is a different species of causation from the kind of causation involved in the rising and setting of the sun, or the falling of Newton's apple etc. For instance: here before me is this boiled egg. What has caused this egg to be boiled? Clearly, there are two quite different answers to this—(i) because it was heated in a saucepan of water over a gas-flame, or (ii) because I, off my own bat, chose to bestir myself, take the egg from its box, fill the saucepan, light the gas, and boil the egg, because I wanted breakfast. From any practical point of view, type-(ii) 'causes' of eggs being boiled are infinitely more salient than type-(i) causes. If there were no breakfast-desiring agents like me about, there would be no hens' eggs (except in the South-East Asian jungle), no saucepans, no gas appliances, and the whole egg-boiling phenomenon would never transpire and never need to be physically explained. So, whatever the verdict of physics, the real *causal explanation* for why there are any boiled eggs is that I, and other breakfasters, *intend* that boiled eggs should exist.

There is nothing mystical involved in tracing the causation of events in one's vicinity to intentions or acts of willing or wishing performed by oneself or other agents in one's neighbourhood. That is how perfectly ordinary events do ordinarily happen—barring 'accidents', and who is ever to know that an accident has not been willed by somebody? Frazer's mistake was, so to speak, to imagine that magicians had some non-standard physical theory, whereas the truth is that 'magic' is what you have when you *do without* a physical theory on the grounds of its redundancy, relying on the idea, which is perfectly practicable, that the explanation of any given event (especially if socially salient) is that it is caused intentionally.

The causal arrow between desire and accomplishment reflects the practical fact that the more one desires something to happen, the more likely it is to happen (though it still may not). Magic registers and publicizes the strength of desire, increasing the (inductively supported) likelihood that the much-desired, emphatically expressed, outcome will transpire, as frequently happens with respect to those outcomes we loudly clamour for. 'All events happen because they are intended'—'I emphatically intend that X shall happen' *ergo* 'X shall come to pass'. This is not 'confused' physics, nor is it devoid of a basis in social experience, as Malinowski (1935) understood more clearly than any of his successors, with the possible exception of Tambiah (1985).

7.3. *Volt Sorcery*

The symbolic language developed in earlier sections of this essay can be applied to the kind of causality which is involved in Frazer's prime example of sympathetic (imitative) magic, which is also extensively discussed by Taussig, namely, that form of sorcery in which an image of the victim is made (often of wax or some vulnerable material), subjected to injury or destruction, with the result that the victim of the sorcery suffers the same injuries or is done away with entirely. This kind of sorcery is practised in innumerable forms, all over the world, as anyone who opens Frazer's book is able to discover.

This kind of sorcery can be practised in aniconic forms; the ancient Greeks, for instance, used to sorcerize one another by taking small pieces of lead, on which they would scratch the name of the victim, and the words 'I bind, I bind' before burying them in the ground. This would cause the victim to sicken and die. The comparison with volt sorcery, which uses the image of the victim in place of the inscribed lead is interesting, in that it suggests that 'visual representation' and 'binding' (and naming) are essentially akin to one another. 'Binding' is, indeed, a fundamental metaphor of magico-religious control which we will encounter below. The words 'I bind, I bind' provide a bridge between the linguistic side of magic (they are words) and the physical side of magic (they refer to a physical operation, carried out on the body of the victim). The action of making a representational image, of any kind, involves a kind of binding, in that the image of the prototype is bound to, or fixed and imprisoned within, the index.

Nervousness about being represented in an index (a photograph or portrait) is often discussed as if it were only a foible of innocent tribesmen, who believe that their souls are in danger of being stolen away therein. In fact, almost everyone has reasons for wishing to keep some degree of control over representations of themselves, rather than have them circulate freely. I might be resigned to having my face photographed and circulated, but I do not feel the same about my naked behind. There is no reason to invoke magical or animistic beliefs in order to substantiate the idea that persons are very vulnerable indeed to hostile representation via images, not just to cruel caricatures, but even via perfectly neutral portrayals, if these are treated with contumely or ridicule. It is not just that the person represented in an image is 'identified' with that image via a purely symbolic or conventional linkage; rather, it is because the agency of the person represented is actually impressed on the representation. I am the cause of the form that my representation takes, I am responsible for it. I cannot disown a photograph of my inelegant posterior, on the grounds that I did not press the shutter and cause this damaging image to come into existence. I can blame the photographer for taking the picture, but I cannot blame him for the way the picture came out.

The 'magical' aspect of volt sorcery is only an epiphenomenon of our failure to identify sufficiently with sorcerers and their victims, our estrangement from

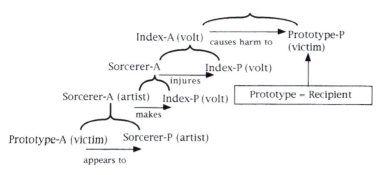

FIG. 7.3/1. Volt sorcery and the parodoxical agency of representation: the victim is both agent and patient

them, not the result of their enslavement by superstitious beliefs entirely different from our own. We suffer, as patients, from forms of agency mediated via images of ourselves, because, as social persons, we are present, not just in our singular bodies, but in everything in our surroundings which bears witness to our existence, our attributes, and our agency. Volt sorcery is not a more magical but just a more literal-minded exploitation of the predicament of representability in image form. It does not take leave of the everyday world, in appealing to some occult force, some magical principle of causation; on the contrary, it unites cause and effect all too closely, so that the causal nexus linking the image to the person represented is made reversible—the image can exercise a causal effect, in the opposite direction, over the person. The *modus operandi* of volt sorcery can readily be expressed using the diagrammatic conventions introduced earlier, as in Fig 7.3/1, or:

[[[Prototype-A] → Artist-A] → Index-A] ⟶ Prototype/Recipient-P.

The verisimilitude, so to speak, of volt sorcery resides in the fact that the victim appears twice; once as the prototype who causes the index to assume its particular form, and once as the recipient, whose injuries stem from the injuries that the index has received. The victim is ultimately the victim of his own agency, by a circuitous causal pathway. Vulnerability stems from the bare possibility of representation, which cannot be avoided. Sorcery beliefs endure, and are highly explanatory, because vulnerability to sorcery is the unintended consequence of the diffusion of the person into the milieu, via a thousand causal influences and pathways, not all of which can be monitored and controlled. Frazer himself noted that image-based sorcery is closely allied to the other kind of sorcery which depends on exuviae; hair, nail-clippings, food leftovers, excreta, and the like. Often, the volt is rendered more effective by the incorporation into it of the victim's exuviae, so that imitative magic, based on (visual) similarity, is allied with the other main kind of magic, based on contact. Once again, to describe this as 'magic' and to imagine that such sorcery is based on occult principles (or symbolic rituals) is quite misleading. There is nothing transcendental about the kind of causality involved in exuviae sorcery, though often sorcerers may enlist spiritual helpers in pursuing the objects of their hatred. Exuviae sorcery works (or seems likely to work) because of the intim- ate causal nexus between exuviae and the person responsible for them. These exuviae do not stand metonymically for the victim; they are physically detached fragments of the victim's 'distributed personhood'—that is, personhood dis- tributed in the milieu, beyond the body-boundary.

The interest of exuviae sorcery, from our point of view, is that it forges a direct link between the index as an image of the prototype, and the index as a (detached) *part* of the prototype. We are not accustomed to think of images (such as portraits, etc.) as parts of persons, limbs, as it were. In terms of the semiotic theory of representation, nothing would be more erroneous than to imagine that the substance of a sign (the visible or audible sign 'dog') were part of any dog, or dogs in general. But with indexes it is not the same as with proper signs. Abduction from an index does characteristically involve positing a substantive part–whole (or part–part) relation. Smoke is a kind of 'part' of fire, for instance. A person's smile (the cheshire cat excepted) is a part of the friendly person it betokens. From this point of view, it is not senseless to suppose that Constable's picture of Salisbury cathedral is a part of Salisbury cathedral. It is, what we would call, a 'spin-off' of Salisbury cathedral.

7.4. *The Epicurean Theory of 'Flying Simulacra' as Parts of the Body*

The convergence between images of things and parts of things can be approached from a philosophical angle. Yrjö Hirn (1900, cited by Frazer 1980 and discussed also by Taussig 1993: 51) made the suggestion that the magic of similarity and the magic of contact were really one and the same, because 'primitive' people anticipated, in their confusion, the philosophical doctrine of 'emanations'. Hirn writes:

For it is evident that a philosophical doctrine, if it fits in with the facts of primitive superstition, may be explanatory of those vague and latent notions which, without logical justification or systematical arrangement, lie in the mind of the magician and the idol- ater. Such a doctrine is presented to us in the familiar emanation-theories, according to which every image of a thing constitutes a concrete part of that thing itself. According to the clear and systematic statement of this doctrine given by the old Epicurean philosophers [*I will provide the relevant quotation from Lucretius below*] shadows, reflec- tions in a mirror, visions, and even mental representations of distant objects, are all caused by thin membranes, which continually detach themselves from the surfaces of all bodies and move onwards in all directions through space. If there are such things as necessary misconceptions, this is certainly one. Such general facts of sensuous experi- ence as reflection, shadow, and mirage will naturally appear as the result of a purely material decortication—as in a transfer picture. How near at hand this theory may lie even to the modern mind appears from the curious fact that such a man as Balzac fell back on it when attempting to explain the newly invented Daguerrotype, that most marvellous of image-phenomena. (Hirn 1900: 293–4; cf. on photographs as indexes of the real presence of persons, Barthes 1981 cited and discussed in Freedberg 1989: ch. 15)

The doctrine of emanations comes directly from Epicurus, but the most famous, and for my purposes the most interesting, statement of the doctrine is provided by Lucretius, who writes:

> I will attempt to lay before you a truth which most concerns . . . the existence of most things we call the idols [*simulacra*; in Greek, *eidola*] of things: these, like films peeled off from the surface of things, fly to and fro through the air . . . I say then that pictures of things and thin shapes are emitted from things off their surface, to which an image serves as a kind of film, or name it if you like a rind, because such image bears an appearance and form like to the thing whatever it is from whose body it is shed and wanders forth.This you may learn however dull of apprehension from what follows. [Many visible objects], . . . emit bodies some in a state of loose diffusion, like smoke which logs of oak, heat and fires emit; some of a closer and denser texture, like the gossamer coats which at times cicadas doff in summer, and the films which calves at their birth cast from the surface of their body, as well as the vesture which the slippery serpent puts off among the thorns; for often we see the brambles enriched with their flying spoils: since these cases occur, a thin image likewise must be emitted from things off their surface. (*De Rerum Natura* 4: 26 ff. trans. Munro, pp. 44–5)

Lucretius attributes the flying simulacra of things to a kind of internal jostling within objects, which causes the minute bodies 'in the front rank' to be discharged from the surface and to fly outwards. The simulacra are physical things though, and we see objects because simulacra enter our eyes and we can *feel* them 'since a particular figure felt by the hands in the dark is known to be the same which is seen by the bright light of day, touch and sight must be excited by quite similar causes'. Lucretius discusses a number of optical phenomena, notably images reflected by mirrors, but most interesting, perhaps, is the way in which he consistently draws analogies between vision by means of 'idols' and other physical forms of diffusion into the ambience, particularly smell and smoke, as well as the shedding of skins, rinds, and films from the surfaces of things. I shall have occasion, later, to return to the conceptual linkage between smoke, smell, skins, and visual appearances, which Küchler has identified as key elements in the ideology associated with a particularly well-known Melanesian art form, the Malangan carvings from northern New Britain (see below, Sect. 9.2). For the moment, though, I am interested in Hirn's point that if 'appearances' of things are material parts of things, then the kind of leverage which one obtains over a person or thing by having access to their image is comparable, or really identical, to the leverage which can be obtained by having access to some physical part of them; especially if we introduce the notion that persons may be 'distributed', i.e. all their 'parts' are not physically attached, but are distributed around the ambience, like the discarded 'gossamer coats of cicadas' in Lucretius' memorable instance, which are both images and parts of the living creature.

7.5. *From Sorcery to the Cult of Images*

I turn now to an ethnographic example which provides a bridge between volt sorcery, surely a discreditable practice, and the worship of images in the religious context. Volt sorcery provides a model for understanding the worship of images in general—indeed for 'objectification' in religious contexts generally. The material—and the idea—comes from Alain Babadzan's remarkable reanalysis of the religious practices of ancient Tahiti, and the deployment of images therein.

It may have been noticed that the victim of volt sorcery is involved in an involuntary process of *exchange*. This arises naturally from the fact that he appears twice in the formula, once as the contributor of something (his appearance) and once as the recipient of something (injuries matching those suffered by the volt, the index). He is an 'involuntary' agent; voluntary agency lies with the sorcerer—who may, of course, have been justifiably provoked.

The originality of Babadzan's account of Polynesian sorcery and idolatry arises from the subtle way in which he has observed both of these were variations on the well-known, but often tantalizing, explanation of the process of exchange provided by Ranapiri, the Maori intellectual, to Elsdon Best (cf. Mauss 1954; Sahlins 1974).

I will now speak of the *hau*, and the ceremony of *whangai hau*. That *hau* is not the *hau* (wind) that blows—not at all. I will carefully explain to you. Suppose that you possess a certain article, and that you give that article to me, without price. We make no bargain over it. Now, I give that article to a third person, who, after some time has elapsed, decides to make some return for it, and so he makes me a present of some article. Now, that article he gives me is the *hau* of the article I first received from you and then gave to him. The goods that I received for that item I must hand over to you. It would not be right for me to keep such goods for myself, whether they be desirable items or otherwise. I must hand them over to you, because they are a *hau* of the article you gave me . . .

I will explain something to you about the forest *hau*. The *mauri* was placed or implanted in the forest by the *tohunga*. It is the *mauri* that causes birds to be abundant in the forest, that they be slain and taken by man. These birds are the property of, belong to, the *mauri* . . . Hence it is said that offerings should be made to the *hau* of the forest. The *tohunga* (priests, adepts) eat the offering because the *mauri* is theirs: it was they who located it in the forest, who caused it to be. That is why some of the birds cooked at the sacred fire are set apart to be eaten by the priests only, in order that the *hau* of the forest-products, and the *mauri*, may return again to the forest—that is, to the *mauri*. (Best 1909: 439)

Babadzan explains that the exchange process described in Ranapiri's text involves three participants, the priests (*tohunga*), the '*hau* of the forest', and the hunters. The '*hau* of the forest' can be glossed as the 'principle of increase' in the forest; its fertility in other words. The priests make offerings of *mauri* to the *hau* of the forest. The *hau* of the forest responds by providing the hunters with birds to capture. A portion of these birds must be returned to the priests. The offering made by the priests and referred to as *mauri* are 'fertility stones'. The *mauri* forge the link between Ranapiri's famous text and our theme in this chapter, for *mauri* are *aniconic idols*. They are indexes, in other words: they are objectified repositories of the spirit (of increase) of the forest. They might just be special stones, but Best also tells us that sometimes they took the form of 'a hollow stone, in which hollow would be placed a lock of hair or some other item. These articles would be deposited at the base of a tree, or hidden in a hole, or by the side of a tree' (ibid. 438). Another form of *mauri* was created by immuring a (living) lizard within a hollow tree beside a bird-snaring site (ibid. 437). The significance of the *hollowness* of *mauri* idols will emerge in due course (below, Sect. 7.11).

Let us return to Babadzan's exposition of the ritual sequence, in which, in exchange for the birds they captured in the forest, Maori hunters were obliged to recompense the priests (*tohunga*) with a portion of the game they secured.

> The magic stones and the birds the hunters capture are thus, ritually, one and the same thing, one and the same *toanga* (gift) that the priests 'give' to the hunters, via the intermediary agency of the forest. (Babadzan 1993: 64, my trans.)

In other words, the forest is *obliged* to give birds to the hunters, because its life, its capacity to manifest productivity and fertility, is not its own; it has been placed there by the priests. 'The *hau* of the forest, which meanwhile is, in Maori theory, the very principle of the productivity of the forest, *is thus considered as the passive agent in a transmission of which the priests are the prime movers*' (ibid., italics in original, my translation). But there is a paradox here. How can a forest, or anything else for that matter, be a 'passive agent'—in a sense, this is a contradiction in terms, as passivity is defined as the absence of agency, and vice versa. What is meant is that the forest is passive in relation to the priests, the prime movers, but not that it has no intrinsic agency at all. There can only be a *mauri* of the forest, a physical objectification of the productivity of the forest, because the forest is (potentially) productive in itself; it is this 'agency' which has been co-opted by the agency of the priests.

The fundamental similarity between the situation just described and volt sorcery will perhaps be beginning to show itself: the *mauri* (objectified fertility) created by the priests and buried in the forest is both a representation of the productivity of the forest (*ex ante*) and a cause of the forest being fertile (*ex post*). Because *ex ante* fertility can be represented—i.e. objectified in an index—it comes under the control of those who control the index, the priests. The priests, in other words, make an index of the productivity of the forest and that makes the forest productive. They are rewarded by the hunters, who receive from the forest the fruit of its productivity, and who return it to the priests. The magic, so to speak, just *has* to work, because the index of productivity is caused by the productivity it causes; there is a perfect, but invisible, circularity. The objectification of the productivity of the forest differs from volt sorcery, of course, in one essential respect, namely, that the *mauri* represents the forest as prosperous and flourishing, whereas the volt represents the sorcery victim as injured, or even dead. But the mechanics are the same; the priests make the forest flourish by representing it as flourishing; on the other hand, the very same objectification could be used to injure and kill the forest, were it subjected to abuse. In fact, if enemies managed to find the *mauri* of the forest, they would destroy its effectiveness by reciting productivity-negating chants over it, bringing death to the owners, for now these same *mauri* would object-ify misery, and cause it. This is the equivalent of sticking pins into a volt to injure the victim represented as injured.

What is most interesting of all to note, though, in this connection (Babadzan 1993: 61) is that *hau* (fertility-principle) objectified in the *mauri*, is also the word used to refer to the exuviae used by a sorcerer to ensorcell his victim (citing Tregear 1891: 52). We now see why hollow *mauri* had 'locks of hair' placed inside them. Babadzan suggests a most satisfactory explanation of the synonymy between sorcery exuviae and the principle of fertility: both involve *growth*. Exuviae are parts of the body which have grown and become separate; this particularly applies to hair and nail-clippings; indeed, where adults are concerned, these are the most obvious manifestations of growth that the human body provides; and even if hair remains uncut, it still falls out and separates itself. Exuviae represent 'growth' because they are, so to speak, continually 'harvested' from the living body. Just as we harvest our *hau*, whenever we have a haircut, so when the hunters enter the forest to 'harvest' the birds there, they are harvesting the exuviae (*hau*) of the forest.

Exuviae sorcery is possible because of the fact that as the body grows, it sheds its parts, and these become distributed around the ambience. Here one may recall the remarkable resonance between Lucretius' instancing the skins shed by snakes and cicadas as prototypical simulacra or 'idols'; for these are, precisely, exuviae produced by growth and distributed around. In fact, the Epicurean theory saw the generation of simulacra as a 'growth' process—the 'shedding' of ephemeral skins from all things induced by a kind of 'pushing' from within.

The *mauri*, in its guise as a fertility stone rather than as an item of human exuviae, objectifies the growth of the forest because it is, conceptually, some-thing produced by that growth; it is the exuviae of the forest, which falls into the hands of the priests, who use it in the 'white' magic of prosperity-induction rather than the black magic of sorcery and dearth-induction.

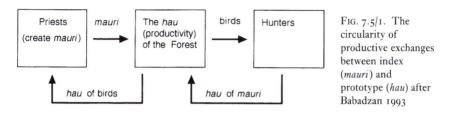

FIG. 7.5/1. The circularity of productive exchanges between index (*mauri*) and prototype (*hau*) after Babadzan 1993

Physically speaking, *mauri* fertility stones could take a variety of forms, as we have seen. Forest *mauri* were aniconic, but those used to promote the growth of sweet potatoes were carved as anthropormorphic images with open mouths, sometimes with their hands in a position suggesting the placing of food in the mouth. Ensuring that the poeple ate, they were shown eating—and they were of course fed themselves, with offerings of first-fruits and so on. Fig. 7.5/1 is a version of the figure Babadzan provides to summarize his general argument.

7.6. *Decortication and the Exchange of Indexes: Tahitian* To'o

The Tahitian equivalent of the Maori *mauri* stone took a variety of forms also. The productivity of fisheries was controlled by a type of *ti'i* (*tiki* = 'image') called *puna*. These 'fish' stones were elongated, like fish, and certain examples have fish-like gill slits on them. There are descriptions of the rituals associated with *puna* which make it clear that their use was entirely analogous to *mauri*. For agricultural purposes, Babadzan convincingly argues, a different type of stone was used, carved with anthropomorphic features, like the anthropomor-phic *mauri* buried in sweet-potato fields in New Zealand (ibid. 75–82). These growth stones were actually believed to grow, though only very slowly. Not much documentation that is relevant to agricultural rites in Tahiti has unfor-tunately survived, but it is safe to say that increase-rituals comparable to the much better documented Maori ones were practised there (ethnohistorically, Maori civilization and language have antecedents in the Society Islands, of which Tahiti is the most important). Perhaps the most important point to bear in mind is that the Tahitian word *tupu*, which basically means 'growth' also means, like *hau*, exuviae, usable for sorcery purposes. *Tupu* is the Tahitian equivalent of *hau*, in other words.

The interest of the Tahitian material discussed by Babadzan lies in a differ-ent direction than the mere replication of the Maori pattern of agricultural rites and the concepts of *hau*, *mauri*, etc. Maori society was effectively decentral-ized throughout, but in ancient Tahiti there was a proto-state with a centralized cult, the cult of Oro. Consequently, in relation to the Tahitian material, we are able, as it were, to pass from volt sorcery (a private affair) to public worship of the most majestic and awe-inspiring variety, involving the state god, the 'god of power', Oro.

FIG. 7.6/1. *Ti'i* in its benign form as a volcanic growth stone. *Source*: after Pierre volcanique 30 cm., Society Islands. Musée de l'Homme, Paris

Unlike *ti'i* images (see Fig. 7.6/1)—such as fish stones and anthropomorphic carvings, used in agriculture and sorcery—the objects at the centre of the Oro cult, and the cults of lesser gods, ancestors of important kin-groups, were not anthropomorphic, though they were (in a sense) representational, and they went by a different name, *to'o*. The word *to'o* means a 'prop' or staff or pillar. The *to'o* represent, mythologically, the pillar placed by the creator god to hold up the sky and preserve the *ao* (the world of light and of human life) from the encompassing powers of night, darkness, and divinity (the *po*). It is a moot point whether the *to'o* deserve to be considered representational (iconic) or non-representational (aniconic). As elongated billets of wood, slightly thicker at one end than at the other, they might be regarded as 'realistic representations' of pillars or props, which is what they are called. One could call them 'iconic' indexes of pillars, in that they refer to the mythological pillars which hold up the sky without actually being these pillars. On the other hand, they represent, aniconically, gods who have anthropomorphic attributes. Oro was not a pillar, as such. Rather, as the pillar which keeps heaven and earth apart— and thus connects them—the *to'o* is invested with the god's presence by virtue of contiguity rather than resemblance. Babadzan himself suggests that the *to'o* is formless because the god presides over the origination of everything that possesses form; as the giver of forms to all things, the god is himself formless. This deduction is well supported in the Tahitian creation chants (Henry 1928; cf. Gell 1993: 124 ff.). In this case, the *to'o* is again an iconic image, a formless image or formlessness, or all things *in statu nascendi*. Here, it seems to me that the supposed contrast between iconic and aniconic representation comprehensively breaks down. The *to'o* are wholly iconic and wholly aniconic at the same time. What is quite inarguable though is that they have a prototype, and that their prototype is the person of the god. They are also, like the humblest volt, open to manipulation by human beings. Through them, Oro himself, the mightiest being in the Tahitian universe, could be rendered a 'passive agent' via representation, just like the forest *hau* in the previous example, or the passive victim of volt sorcery.

Pursuing this theme, we are able to discover that the primary ritual procedure in which the *to'o* were involved, was a ritual of *decortication*, of the controlled production of divine exuviae. Following Babadzan's analysis of the existing sources, I will now describe this ritual sequence.

The primary *to'o* were embodiments of Oro. The Tahitian political system revolved around asserting control over the *marae* (temples) of Oro; whoever controlled the *to'o*, controlled the country, and rival chiefs fought bitterly over them. The important *to'o* stood at the pinnacle, so to speak, of a polity of images, and social rank among human beings was strictly and precisely correlated with the 'rank' of the *to'o* (and lower down the scale, *ti'i*, 'sorcery idols') in their charge. Social rank and political power were given regular and formal expression at a ritual called *pa'iatua*, which, translated, means the 'wrapping of the gods' (*pa'i* = wrap up, tie, bundle). (On wrapping in general see Gell 1993.)

Only during this ritual were *to'o* revealed to view, and even then, only to the most important and ritually protected priests and chiefs; the sight of a *to'o* would instantly result in the death of a lesser person, so filled were they with *mana* (a quality called *ra'a* in Tahitian). To protect them from view, *to'o* were at all other times tightly wrapped in bindings of sennit cordage and tapa bark-cloth, sometimes with roughly delineated facial features and limbs woven onto the outside (Fig. 7.6/2). The more important ones were kept in special containers for storage and transport. The ritual of *pa'iatua* consisted of the assembly of all the images in a district at the *marae*, for the purpose of the renewal of their outer wrappings, especially the outer wrapping of the primary *to'o* of Oro.

I need not describe the ceremony in any detail. Essentially, it consisted of a procession of the gods into the *marae*, led by the main god (completely hidden in its ark), with the lesser ones following in order of precedence, followed (and protected) by 'sorcerers' bearing not *to'o*, but *ti'i*, sorcery images (Fig. 7.6/3). Lesser gods and *ti'i* 'sorcery' images, Ellis tells us (and there is a sole surviving example in the British Museum to back this up) were not in the aniconic 'pillar' style, but were hollow anthropomorphic images, with an internal cavity for holding sacred feathers and/or sorcery exuviae (Ellis 1831: i. 339). All would assemble in and around the *marae*, according to their station. In a separate sanctuary, well away from public view, the *to'o* would be divested of their wrappings, oiled, and laid out in the sun. There then ensued an important exchange sequence.

The most symbolically significant 'currency' of political authority in Tahiti took the form of the feathers, the most important being red ones. Wearing red feathers was a sumptuary privilege of the highest chiefs, the *maro ura* (red feather girdle) was synonymous with occupancy of the paramount chiefship.

FIG. 7.6/2. *To'o* with Oro   FIG. 7.6/3. Sorcery *ti'i* with hollow back for feathers/exuviae.
the god hidden from view   *Source*: The British Museum, London, MM029679
and wrapped in bindings.
Source: Museum of
Archaeology and
Anthropology, Cambridge,
Z 6067

Feathers, needless to say, are the exuviae of birds, and birds have, everywhere in Polynesia (as so often elsewhere) heavenly associations. Red feathers are probably also associated with blood, another exuvial substance and index of life, growth, and reproductivity.[1] Oro was particularly associated with both feathers and redness. The primary act of homage to Oro was the presentation to him of red feathers, which would be woven into his sennit wrapping, attached to it by cords, or simply wrapped inside the covering.

[1] In Samoa the red feathers woven into the most prestigious fine mats forming chiefly dowries were associated with the hymeneal blood of the virgin *taupou*, the predestined reproducer of chiefly power.

When all were seated, the high priest opened the ark and took out the dreaded image, and as he uncovered it upon the mat, the others all uncovered theirs in unison . . . The minor gods then exposed, with their wrappers folded under them, remained in the hands of their owners, facing the *'ava'a* ready for presentation to the tutelar god [i.e. Oro] . . . When the image of the tutelar god was revealed from the profusion of red and yellow feathers lying upon its many coverings . . . Then followed the presentation of the minor gods by their owners in their proper turns, with offerings of new *ura* [red feather] amulets and loose feathers, which were given through the high priest to the tutelar god in exchange for some in his possession [i.e. which had just been unwrapped from the sennit wrapper of Oro]. This act was called *taritoara'a-atua* (the god's exchange) and was supposed to add new power from the greater god to the lesser ones. The fishermen's gods were presented last because they were from the sea. (Henry 1928: 166–7)

Babadzan provides the following schema of the feather exchange: new, non-sacred feathers passed from the lesser priests to the priests of the primary *to'o* (the 'main' Oro) and the feathers which had previously been in contact with the primary *to'o* were passed back to the inferior *to'o*. In this way a portion of the sanctity of the primary *to'o* was distributed to the assembly of lesser *to'o* in exchange for a tribute paid in the form of new feathers, a 'natural' product, as it were, potentially embodying power and fertility, but not yet able to generate it. Only feathers which, as Babadzan notes, had been intimately in contact with the primary image of Oro *for some time*, had this generative property (1993: 116). The feathers had to live and die with the god, quite literally, because it seems that to become divine exuviae, the primary god has to 'die' and scatter exuviae back into the world. This, Babadzan thinks, is the significance of the sequence as a whole, that is to say the unwrapping of the gods followed by wrapping them up again. Unwrapping brings the god into the world, wrapping him up again sends the god back to the nether world, the *po*. But because the god has died but left something behind (his feathers, his exuviae *tupu*) the power of the god is also left behind—in the hands of the chiefs and the priests of Oro. This inference is based on the fact that the Tahitian mortuary ritual for high chiefs involved the drying of the corpse in the sun, on a platform, followed by wrapping (binding) and decoration with red feathers. This was to keep the mighty dead under control, safely dead, and incapable, because of the massive bindings of bark-cloth enveloping them, from harming the living. Such treatment (wrapping and decoration with feathers) was reserved for corpses of powerful chiefs and for the *to'o*, so the implication is that the *to'o*, at the conclusion of the *pa'iatua* ceremony, is being treated as a 'powerful corpse'. The binding up of the *to'o* places Oro in the 'patient' position.[2]

---

[2] Related to this idea of 'binding' the god is the practice, which was common in antiquity, of restraining the images of the gods in temples with chains and manacles, to prevent them from escaping and transferring their protection to rival cities (cf. Freedberg 1989: 74–5).

The cult of the gods in the form of *to'o* and the accompanying feather exchanges can be seen as a kind of vastly magnified exercise in volt sorcery. Ostensibly, Oro rules the universe, but in practice his intervention in human affairs is controlled by the chiefs and priests, via indexes which are his parts, his exuviae, and the binding of the primary index of his person, the *to'o*. It will be recalled that the ancient Greek sorcerers wrote on the little lead plates representing their victims, the words 'I bind, I bind'. In the cult of the *to'o* we find this 'binding' of the god literally enacted, but the implications are the same. The prototype of an index is bound to the index by resemblance, and is thus subjected to control. The *to'o* were themselves tightly bound, and their power diffused into these bindings, especially the feathers, which then became the currency of political control.

This idea can perhaps be given a more general statement, so as to apply to all religious art. The great monuments that we have erected to God, the great basilicas and cathedrals, are indexes from which we abduct God's agency over the world, and over his mortal subjects, who have striven and laboured to please him, and have left these massive shells (or skins) in their wake, within which the faithful gather to worship the ultimate author of all this magnificence. Such, at any rate, is the orthodox view of religious magnificence, which represents basilicas and cathedrals as 'offerings' to God, who is all-powerful. However, it must also be recognized, first of all, that God is not really powerful at all unless his power is apparent in this-worldly indexes (behavioural ones, or, in the present case, material ones). The basic Miltonic paradox that God is at risk from his own creation, simply by having distributed himself in manifold forms (including Satan), applies to such material indexes of God's greatness in the following way. Humanity has a lien on God because his objectification is in their hands. Even if God is the ultimate author of his resemblance in the form of magnificent structures and works of art, it remains the case that, at a critical point in the sequence of causes, instruments, and results, human agency is essential. Since, in this world, God's presence is inherent in these works of human agency, he is bound to human purposes, the this-worldly prosperity and other-worldly salvation of his ostensible servants, rather than to purposes entirely his own. His agency is enmeshed in ours, by virtue of our capacity to make (and be) his simulacrum. With respect to our god, we are in just the same position as the Maori *tohunga* with respect to the *hau* of the forest.

Of course, the fact that we have trapped God inside his likenesses does not make all religious activity sorcery, as such. The homage paid to God in the basilica is not destructive or malignant, but it does make him the 'passive agent' of essentially human designs, just as the homage paid to the *to'o* made Oro the passive agent of the chiefs and high priests. I have no doubt that Christian theologians would have no difficulty in refuting such an imputation in a manner convincing, at least, to themselves, but the logic of the situation seems to me inescapable. The papal title 'Pontifex Maximus' (JVLIVS II PONTIFEX MAXIMVS blazoned over the apostle of St Peter's in Rome) attributes to the Pope the power to build bridges between earth and heaven. The analogy between the papal 'bridge' between earth and heaven, and the Tahitian *to'o*—the staff or prop which keeps heaven and earth apart (but also in communication)—seems too remarkable to pass without comment. And in St Peter's one can certainly detect the clear implication that God is the exchange-partner of his more important subjects such as Julius II if not the mass of his worshippers of low estate. St Peter's is the bridge; but the point is that the making of the bridge has been attributed unambiguously to the Pope, Julius II, his predecessors and successors. He, in exchange terms, is the primary donor, the holder of the *kitoum*, the 'unencumbered valuable' (Munn; see below, Sect. 9.3) which is sent out to find its match, the valuable which can be measured against it and returned for it. St Peter's, as a gift-object and an index of human agency, elicits a responsive counter-gift, which, paradoxically, is St Peter's itself, invested with divine power now available to mankind, like the feathers which, given to Oro, return from Oro as his embodiments.

However, let us not delay too long over such analogies, which may be regarded as unconvincing, or even offensive. I now want to turn to the worship of anthropomorphic images, among which neither the *to'o* nor St Peter's may be counted, at least, not at first glance.[3] The literature of idol-worship is, in the main, profoundly unsympathetic to this practice; it is almost as if learning to read and write disqualifies one from engaging in this practice with any enthusiasm. This rather supports the notion that there is a 'great divide' between the essentially non-sensuous mode of literate thinking and the sensuous, participatory mode of pre-literate thinking. However, there has been a reaction against the theory of the 'great divide' in recent years (Parry 1985) and there certainly exist numerous literate image-worshippers in the world today, and ancient, literate, civilizations whose religious practices centre on the paying of homage to images, such as Hinduism. The idea that only the uneducated or 'primitive' worship idols of stone, wood, and metal fashioned to resemble the human form, is a consequence of the convergence between anti-imagistic forms of religiosity (such as Judaism, Islam, and certain forms of Christian sectarianism and Protestantism) and the rise of a more generalized religious scepticism, which has ancient antecedents. Indeed, wherever religion exists, it is probable that scepticism also exists, whether or not this is expressed in public. Certainly, anthropologists have encountered innumerable examples of scepticism concerning the efficacy of rites among the illiterate and uneducated, so this cannot be attributed to literacy or the rise of 'science' alone.

---

[3] But cf. Wittkower on anthropomorphic elements in Renaissance theories of architectural proportion, Ackerman on Bernini's piazza, etc.

7.7. Darshan: *Witnessing as Agency*

Questions of the cultural foundations of belief and scepticism need not detain us, but it is still enormously difficult for Westerners and non-believers to empathize with idol-worshippers because of the bombardment with anti-idolatrous propaganda which we have experienced from the very moment we became conscious of such things. Perhaps the most insight-provoking accounts of image-worship belong to the literature of Hinduism, because followers of this religion are among the least self-conscious in showing devotion to images. A convenient introduction to the copious literature on image-worship in India has been provided by Diana Eck (1985). Worshipping images is obtaining *darshan* from the god, a particular type of blessing conveyed through the eyes. *Darshan* is something given by the god, a mode of the god's agency in the world, and the worshipper is a patient (the Recipient-P, in terms of our scheme). Living human beings can give *darshan*, as well as gods; a guru gives *darshan* when he or she makes an appearance before a gathering of disciples (see Babb 1987), and the same is true of an important politician appearing before an assembly of supporters, who have come to see, as much as to hear, their leader. *Darshan* is a gift or an offering, made by the superior to the inferior, and it consists of the 'gift of appearance' imagined as a material transfer of some blessing.

It seems to me that *darshan* is essentially similar to the other mode in which divine blessing/personhood is distributed in India: the distribution of sacred food, *prasad*, which is consumed by the god's devotees (of course, there are Christian parallels to this as well). *Prasad* is often conceptualized as the 'food leavings' (*jutha*) of the god, in a manner absolutely analogous to the exuviae used in sorcery. According to Eck, the conceptualization of *darshan* is closely allied to the role allotted in the Hindu tradition to the eye as an organ of inter-personal transactions.

Darshan, considered as a mode of divine agency is thus intimately connected to the concept of the evil eye. Divine idols, religious gurus, and politicians of renown transfer blessings via the steady and penetrating gaze with which they irradiate the assembly over which they preside. This is, so to speak, the positive 'white' aspect of evil-eye sorcery, which more imperfect beings transfer via their mean, envious, and ill-intentioned looks. To place oneself before the idol of the god, therefore, is to lay oneself open to the divine gaze and to internalize the divine image.

This is to examine the question from only one angle though; even in India, it takes an act of will on the part of the worshipper to worship the god, and the worshipper is also an agent with respect to the one being worshipped. The reception (as a patient) of *darshan* from the god is contingent on the transitive action of 'taking' (*darshan lena*) initiated by the recipient. Eck cites Stella Kramrisch's account of 'seeing' as transitive form of agency:

Seeing . . . is a going forth of the sight towards the object. Sight touches it and acquires its form. Touch is the ultimate connection by which the visible yields to being grasped. While the eye touches the object the vitality that pulsates in it is communicated . . . (Kramrisch 1976: 136)

These remarks of Kramrisch are informed by her knowledge of Sanskrit philosophical writings. Ancient Indian philosophers held views similar to those of the Platonists, that sight was an 'extromissive' sense, the eye sending out invisible beams or rays through the air, which touched the objects of sight at their surfaces. One philosopher, Caraka, argued that indeed we only have one sense, the sense of touch, of which sight, hearing, etc. are just more subtle forms (Sinha 1934). Other philosophers disagreed, but the consensus was none the less that seeing was, like touching, a form of contact. Epicurus' theory (see above), by contrast, is 'intromissive'; the *eidola* emanate from the object and enter the eye. But Lucretius shows that seeing was, even so, equated with touching by the Epicureans. The (gossamer, but physical) idols were touched at the surface of the eye, not at their own surfaces, via the eye-beams. I do not think that the Epicurean intromissive theory of vision by 'idols' had an Indian counterpart, so one could not attribute the prevalence of image-worship to its influence. But the alternative extromissive theory is, if anything, even more explanatory, because it forges a direct link between 'seeing' (*darshan*) and other types of physical interaction with the image, such as touching, anointing, and so on. These tactile forms of homage are very important elements in Hindu image-worship.

Certain Indian philosophers (Sinha 1934) made the analogy between seeing and the use of a stick by the blind, in order to ascertain the shape of external objects. This materialistic conception of seeing is reflected in Kramrisch's statement about *darshan*; seeing creates a physical bridge between one being and another. Hirn's basic insight that in relation to 'images' there really is no distinction between 'similarity' and 'contact' is fully brought into the open here, without the need to invoke the Epicurean parallel.

Darshan is thus very much of a two-way affair. The gaze directed by the god towards the worshipper confers his blessing; conversely, the worshipper reaches out and touches the god. The result is union with the god, a merging of consciousnesses according to the devotionalist interpretation. This brings back the issue of reciprocity and intersubjectivity in the relationship between the image (the index) and the recipient. It is clearly germane to the general thesis argued in these chapters that intersubjectivity between persons and indexes, particularly indexes which, like images of the gods, are human in form, should be possible. It cannot be denied that, from the point of view of the devotees worshipping the image of the god, the image of the god is a manifestation of a social Other, and that the god/devotee relationship is a social one, absolutely comparable to the relationship between the devotee and another human person. However, it is too easy just to accept this as an ethnographic, descriptive, fact, without a deeper questioning of the cognitive basis of this relationship. For all that the devotee asserts, and truly believes, that a union of minds is achieved between mortal devotee and immortal divinity, the devotee none the less also lives in a world of ordinary objects, mere things devoid of imputed subjectivity, in which the distinction between human beings—possessed of human-being-like consciousness and agency—and inert 'things' is readily drawn. The devotee does *know* that the image of the god is only an image, not made of flesh and blood; and if, perchance, the image moves, or speaks, or seems to drink milk, that is a miracle, a remarkable occurrence because so unexpected. Devotion is enhanced by such manifestations, but it is admitted that the gods only vouchsafe miracles when faith in them has reached a low ebb, and needs to be buttressed by extraordinary happenings. True devotion is attainable, ideally, without miracles of this or any other kind.

The animacy and imputed subjectivity of the idol is not attained except by surmounting the stark difference between an inert image and a living being. How does this happen?

So far as the Hindu material is concerned, the key to the process of animation seems, initially at least, to depend on the logic of looking and being seen. Imagistic devotion is a visual act (as opposed to prayer, etc.) and it is accomplished entirely by looking. Specifically, it is accomplished by looking into the eyes of the god; union comes from eye contact, not the study of all the other details the image may show, which indicate the identity and attributes of the god and which add to the general effect without being devotionally essential. The eyes of the god, which gaze at the devotee, mirror the action of the devotee, who gazes at the god. Sometimes (as in Jain temples) the eyes of images are set with little mirrors, so that the devotee can see himself or herself reflected in the image's eye in the act of looking. Even in the absence of actual mirrors, the image, so far as its ocular activity goes, reflects the action of the devotee (Fig. 7.7/1).

Animacy takes its origin from this ocular exchange, because, even if one does not take a mystical attitude towards images, one is none the less entitled to apply action verbs like 'look' (or 'smile', 'gesticulate', etc.) to them. A perfect sceptic can say, in fact is obliged to say, that an idol 'looks' in a particular direction; the remark would pass unnoticed because everybody accepts that the criterion for idols 'looking' is that their eyes should be open and pointed in a particular direction. The question is, what do idols see when they look? What the devotee sees is the idol looking at him or her, performing an act of looking, mirroring his or her own. It is not mysticism on the devotee's part which results in the practical inference that the image 'sees' the devotee, because we only ever know what other persons are seeing by knowing what they are looking at. The sceptic would say 'the idol is blind—it cannot see anything', but even so, to be blind is to be unable to see what one looks at, which hardly banishes the residual animacy of images, since a disability implies a potential

FIG. 7.7/1. Santoshi Ma. Colour lithograph, B. G. Sharma. *Source*: Sharma Picture Publications, Bombay, *c*.1960

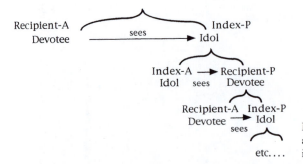

Fig. 7.7/2. Ocular exchange as the medium for intersubjectivities

ability. And the devotee need not draw this inference, in fact, cannot, because the situation is defined in terms of the devotee's own agency and result; the devotee looks and sees. The image-as-mirror is doing what the devotee is doing, therefore, the image also looks and sees. One does not even logically have to impute 'life' to an image to assert that an image can see; after all, people often speak of cameras as 'seeing' things, without implying that cameras have life.

But the inference that if idols can look, they can see, is not drawn explicitly; if it were, it might be open to sceptical objections. It is protected from judgement by a further consequence of the mirror-effect. This is the logical regression set up by seeing and being seen. Eye-contact, mutual looking, is a basic mechanism for intersubjectivity because to look into another's eyes is not just to see the other, but to see the other seeing you (I see you see me see you see me etc.). Eye-contact prompts self-awareness of how one appears to the other, at which point one sees oneself 'from the outside' as if one were, oneself, an object (or an idol). Eye-contact seems to give direct access to other minds because the subject sees herself as an object, from the point of view of the other as a subject. Eye-contact is the basic modality of 'second-order intentionality', awareness of the other (person) as an intentional subject. Thus, in image-worship, the devotee does not just see the idol, but sees herself (as an object) being seen by the idol (as a subject). The idol's 'seeing' is built into the devotee's own self-awareness at one remove as the object which is seen by the idol. She sees herself as the idol sees her, kneeling before it, gazing upwards. In that she can see herself seeing the idol, the idol must see her, because when she sees herself seeing the idol (from her point of view, a datum of immediate experience) the idol is seen by her as seeing her. The 'idol seeing her' is a *nested component* of 'her seeing herself seeing the idol'. The net result of the regression whereby devotee's and idol's perspectives become logically interdigitated with one another in this way is a kind of optical oscillation in which idol's and devotee's perspectives shift back and forth with such rapidity that interpersonal boundaries are effaced and 'union' is achieved. This mutual encompassment via eye-contact is represented diagrammatically in Fig. 7.7/2. I shall return to the significant role of the 'eyes' in idol-worship, below (Sect. 7.12) in connection with the consecration procedures for images.

7.8. *Animism and Anthropomorphism*

The worship of images, or aniconic indexes of divine presence, such as stones, springs, and trees, has preoccupied anthropologists from the beginning. Tylor, in the spirit of his times, sought an explanation in a purported difference of 'mentalities' between primitive and civilized people; primitive people were animists, whereas we are not. Tylor imagined that the belief in spirits, and 'the supernatural' generally, was implanted in the human mind through the experience of dreams, and arose from conceptual confusion, but this was merely a self-serving supposition on his part. In effect, the theory of animism is merely a classificatory device, which, like the concept of ritual, serves to separate behaviour that we think we can understand and sympathize with, from behaviour which seems to us superstitious and perverse.

However, the Tylorian concept of animism can be made into a more serviceable analytical tool if it is abstracted from the essentially pejorative context of Victorian positivistic thought. Guthrie, in a recent study of the foundations of religious belief, has argued that 'anthropomorphism'—the tendency to impute human attributes such as will, agency, and responsiveness to supposedly 'inanimate' entities—is an abiding feature of human cognition (Guthrie 1993). His cognitive argument is that, strategically, it is always safer to impute the highest degree of organization possible (such as animacy) to any given object of experience. It is better, he says, to presume that a boulder is a bear (and be wrong) than to presume that a bear is a boulder (and be wrong). His argument carries weight, and he certainly has no difficulty whatsoever in amassing copious examples of anthropomorphism, not just in religious contexts, but in everyday perception and cognition, in the arts, and even in the sciences. Quite rightly, Guthrie emphasizes that anthropomorphism is not a phenomenon restricted to children, so-called 'animists', or even to adult religious believers. As a non-religious adult, and a participant in an advanced technological civilization, I recognize that I consistently engage in anthropomorphic thinking, as my earlier remarks about cars will have made apparent. The trouble with Guthrie's argument is not that it lacks an empirical basis—far from it—but that to say that one attributes 'animacy' or 'anthropomorphism' to something does not explain what a thing must be or do to count as 'animate' or 'anthropomorphic'.

It is not animism, anthropomorphism, or anything like it, to attribute 'life' to a tree, which adults in our society agree is a living thing—though children under 5 or so may disagree (Carey 1985). On the other hand, it certainly is animism to attribute the capacity to 'hear' prayers to a stone idol, but that does not necessarily imply the belief that the stone or idol is 'alive' in a *biological* sense. This is abundantly evident from the furore which results when it is reported, as sometimes happens, that idols actually do 'come to life' in the sense of 'manifesting biological activity'. When particular statues bleed, or perspire, or move about, these are 'miracles'. But such happenings would not be miracles if the expectation was that all idols should behave in this way; in fact, they are generally expected not to. Idols may be animate without, in other words, being endowed with animal life or activity. In addition, there are automata, real or imaginary ones, which do really move, speak, and perform various human-like actions, but these are remarkable, not because they are alive, but because they are *not* alive, while maintaining the appearance of being so. It follows that 'ritual' animacy and the possession of 'life' in a biological sense are far from being the same thing.

Cognitive psychologists believe that the distinction between living things (biological organisms) and non-living things is one to which we are innately sensitive, and this is a finding which I do not need to contest. I have no doubt that worshippers, who address their prayers to stones, are perfectly capable of the category distinction between animals and plants (living things) and non-living things such as stones. The distinction between animacy and inanimacy that we require here cross-cuts the distinction between the living and non-living as 'natural kinds' (Boyer 1996: 86). The god who, at one moment, is manifested in a non-living thing, such as a stone or a statue, may be manifest in a living thing also, such as a possessed shaman, or a sacred goat or monkey. The worshippers, whose god appears in these contrasted forms, are perfectly cognizant of the difference between them. The imputation of 'animacy' to non-living things cannot, as Guthrie seems to suggest, rest on people making category mistakes about whether inanimate objects such as boulders are really biologically living things, such as bears.

7.8.1. Stocks and Stones

It seems that we must appeal to a different attribute from the possession of biological life to define 'animacy'. Should we say that the object is animate not because we attribute biological life to it, but subjectivity/intentionality, which is something quite different? As Boyer notes (1996: 92), 'the projection of human physical features [onto gods, spirits, etc.] in general results in a projection, tacit or otherwise, of intentional psychology, but a projection of intentional psychology does not generally entail a projection of any other human quality'. How can an entity possess 'intentional psychology', without being biologically alive? In this case, a worshipper who addresses prayers to a stone must believe, somehow, that the stone in question, though not a living thing, sees and hears as does the worshipper, thinks and reacts as he does, and moreover, has the power to plan and execute actions. It seems paradoxical to imagine that an admittedly non-living thing could possess these attributes. But not really, when one considers what heavy weather philosophers have made of accounting for 'intentionality' even among ordinary, living, breathing, human beings.

The question as to the manner in which representational indexes—idols—can be apprehended as social others, as repositories of agency and sensibility, seems to raise the question of 'apparently irrational' beliefs and practices. It is surely irrational, or at least strange, to speak to, offer food to, dress and bathe a mere piece of sculpture, rather than a living breathing human being. And so it is: those who do these things are just as aware of the 'strangeness' of their behaviour as we are, but they also hold, which we do not, that the cult of the idol is religiously efficacious, and will result in beneficial consequences for themselves and the masters they serve in their capacity as priests. It is not that the priests cannot distinguish between stocks and stones and persons, rather, they hold that in certain contexts stocks and stones possess unusual, occult, properties; of which the religiously uninstructed would remain ignorant, and the instructed but sceptical, wrong-headedly incredulous. According to Boyer (1996), religious ideas, such as the 'intentional psychology' of fetishes and idols, survive and prosper as components of cultural systems *just because* they are odd and counter-intuitive.

The question that we need to consider is the nature of the unusual occult capacities which idols possess, according to believers. What we need to know is how idol-worshippers square the circle between 'what they know'—and what we know they know—about stocks and stones, and what they know about persons and their capacities as intentional agents. They cannot confuse the two, but it remains possible that persons have attributes which can be also possessed by stocks and stones without prejudice to their *categorical* difference from persons. That is to say 'social agents' can be drawn from categories which are as different as chalk and cheese (in fact, rather more different) because 'social agency' is not defined in terms of 'basic' biological attributes (such as inanimate thing vs. incarnate person) but is relational—it does not matter, in ascribing 'social agent' status, what a thing (or a person) 'is' in itself; what matters is where it stands in a network of social relations. All that may be necessary for stocks and stones to become 'social agents' in the sense that we require, is that there should be actual human persons/agents 'in the neighbourhood' of these inert objects, not that they should be biologically human persons themselves.

This is not as bizarre a claim as it sounds. We certainly do not have to postulate a particular 'mentality' (primitive, uncritical, gullible, etc.) to account for idolatry; the worship of images is compatible with an extreme degree of philosophical and critical acumen, as the example of textual Hinduism amply demonstrates, besides numerous treatises on 'theurgy' (the creation of gods) from classical antiquity (e.g. Proclus). Rather than approach the problem from an initial assumption of the essential stupidity of idol-worshippers, we should remind ourselves of the difficulties which assail (very clever) philosophers, when they seek to account for the 'agency', not of stocks and stones, but of human beings themselves. If (Western) philosophers have a hard time pin-pointing exactly what makes the difference between human persons engaging in 'actions' and mere things obeying causal laws then we are in a better position to understand why some people appear to be (contextually) indifferent to this distinction.

The fact is that it remains a controversial philosophical problem to distinguish between 'actions' (stemming from agency) and 'happenings' resulting from material causation. What is the basis of the distinction we feel we must draw between a person performing the action of raising their arm (intentionally) and the same physical movement occurring involuntarily, say, as the result of some malfunctioning of the autonomous nervous system? In other words, there is a sense in which human beings are themselves 'stocks and stones'—only rather twitchy ones—and when human beings are asleep, insensible, or of course, dead, the resemblance becomes much closer. The 'philosophy of action' is devoted to devising and testing criteria for justifying the distinction that we intuitively make between our capacity to behave as person/agents and our simultaneous capacity to be, and behave as, things, or mere 'creatures' unendowed with full human agency.

I do not need to canvass, still less evaluate, all the theses which different philosophers have advanced in the search for a solution to this problem. My point is just that philosophers do detect a serious problem here; from which I think that we can reasonably infer that it is in fact awkward to differentiate between what people do 'as persons' and what people do 'as things'. And if philosophers (who know perfectly well that in the relevant senses persons and things are different) cannot always agree about 'just how' they differ, then the inverse proposition also holds; if pressed, we are not really very sure about 'just how' an idol is *not* a person—even though we are perfectly certain it isn't. We cannot rely on simple arguments like this: 'I am a person, I have a beating heart, a temperature of 98.4 degrees, etc. whereas this statue is stone-cold and has no heartbeat, *ergo*, it is not a person'. We could heat the statue to 98.4 degrees, give it a heart, etc. but it still would not qualify because it would only possess, after these modifications, attributes which human beings possess 'as things', not as persons/agents. Yet such are the arguments which are advanced against idolatry by sceptics:

Lala Lajpat Rai describes how the founder [of the Arya Samaj, a 'reformed' Hindu sect, opposed to the use of images] first got his insight into the wrongness of idolatry. He was set, as a lad of fourteen, to watch an image of the god Shiva, in a temple at night. He saw a mouse run over the god's body and the god remain motionless. The shock convinced him, Lajpat Rai wrote, that 'the image could not be Shiva himself, as was taught by the priesthood'.   (Bevan 1940: 34)

Such an argument could have been convincing only to one who had already (no doubt as a result of Christian-Protestant ascendancy in British India) decided that idol-worship was backward and futile. Shiva's indifference to the mouse could equally well have been interpreted as his superhuman asceticism manifesting itself—indeed comparable feats have been attempted by ascetics whose humanity is not in doubt. Some, for instance, are reputed to have induced birds to nest on their motionless bodies. Any such argument can cut both ways: if idols are not what they pretend to be, or are pretended to be, it is not because they are 'things'. Human beings are also 'things'. If an effigy possessed every single thing-attribute of a human being, it could still be 'just an effigy' and be unworthy of worship; conversely, an effigy could possess no identifiable thing-attribute of a human being and be worthy of devotion nevertheless.

Suppose we perform the thought experiment of gradually enriching an idol with more and more of the attributes of a 'genuine' living being. Temperature, heartbeat, mobility, the ability to utter words, to play tennis, to . . . well, you name it. Does the idol become more worship-able as a result? By no means: either, by this procedure, the idol becomes a common-or-garden human person, whom it would be senseless to worship, or the idol remains an idol but takes on the status of an automaton of extraordinary verisimilitude, worthy of exhibition and admiration in an establishment like Disneyland or Madame Tussaud's, but not of reverence or devotion. The criticism of idolatry on the grounds that idols are not 'alive' as human beings are (biologically) alive, or that idols are not realistic automata, but only statues, misses the point on both counts. The idol is worshipped because it is neither a person, nor a miraculous machine, but a god.

Whatever the attributes possessed by idols which render them religiously efficacious as a locus for person-to-person encounters with divinities, these attributes cannot be confirmed or disproved by physical tests such as the presence of a pulse, respiration, ingestion and elimination, the ability to move or speak, a natural distaste for mice, and so on. None of these attributes figures in philosophical attempts to distinguish between person/agents and mere things, machines, effigies, illusions, and so on. Currently, many philosophers agree that 'agency' implies the possession of a mind which 'intends' actions prior to performing them. 'Not moving' is an 'action' in this sense. 'Shiva (the god) did not move because he intended to stay still' is a perfectly reasonable interpretation for the scene witnessed by Dayananda, on the assumption that Shiva was, as the priests averred, present as a person/agent, in his image. He might have had various reasons for refraining from action; first (as just mentioned), because Shiva is the prototypical immobile ascetic, and secondly, because Shiva (who created the whole world) imbued stone, the material of his visible 'body' in this instance, with the property of absolute rigidity; Shiva was observing the 'rules' for stone objects, such as idols, which were of his own making, ultimately. Hindu theology, moreover, postulates that gods, such as Shiva, voluntarily 'sacrifice' their freedom of movement, imprisoning themselves in stone idols for the benefit of devotees.

This is the greatest grace of the Lord, that being free He becomes bound, being independent He becomes dependent for all His service on His devotee . . . In other forms
the man belonged to God but behold the supreme sacrifice of Isvara [Vishnu] here the
Almighty becomes the property of the devotee . . . He carries Him about, fans Him,
feeds Him, plays with Him—yea, the Infinite has become finite, that the child soul may
grasp, understand and love Him.   (Pillai Lokacarya, cited in Eck 1985: 46, diacritics
removed)

There are no a priori logico-philosophical grounds for rejecting the thesis
that Shiva 'intended to stand still, and thus stood still, when the mouse ran
over him' (and was an agent in so doing). Because there are no 'material tests'
for the possession, or non-possession, of agency, there is nothing to prevent
us from asserting, if we wish to, that the behaviour of a statue (standing
still) occurs because the statue has a mind, intends to stand still, and does as a
consequence of this prior intention stand still.

7.9. *External and Internal Conceptions of Agency*

How, in practice, do we attribute 'agency', 'intentional psychology'—the possession of a mind, consciousness, etc. to 'social others'? If we knew the answer
to this question we might be in a better position to define precisely what subset of human-like attributes idols as 'social others' are believed to possess, given
that they are probably not (on Boyer's argument) believed to possess all of
these attributes. I think it is fair to say that our attribution of 'intentional psychology' to anything (a person, an animal, a computer, a car, or a stone idol)
has two aspects to it, which at first glance seem to be rather distinct. The first
of these one could call the 'external aspect' or the 'practical' aspect of agency-
attribution. According to Wittgenstein, and a great many other subsequent
philosophers, the possession of a mind is something we attribute to others,
provisionally, on the basis of our intuition that their behaviour (e.g. their
linguistic behaviour) follows some 'rule' which, in principle, we may reconstruct (Winch 1958). If I can get along with the other in the give-and-take of
interaction, if our practical efforts to deal with one another work out, then the
other is a producer of intelligible (meaningful) behaviour, and hence has a
mind, intentions, volitions, etc. I cannot really tell, from the outside, whether
the 'other' is a zombie or an automaton, who/which mimics the behaviour of
an ordinary human being but does not have any of the 'inner experiences' we
habitually associate with this behaviour. But this does not matter because
the whole panoply of 'mind' is not a series of inner, private experiences at all,
but is out there, in the public domain, as language, practices, routines, rules
of the game, etc.; that is, 'forms of life'. Call this the 'externalist' theory of
agency-attribution.

However compelling in the hands of behaviouristically inclined philosophers, the 'externalist' theory of agency has a weakness, namely, that it does

not immediately square with psychological investigations of the way in which children and ordinary people (not philosophers) seem to approach the same problem. It seems that ordinary human beings are 'natural dualists', inclined, more or less from day one, to believe in some kind of 'ghost in the machine' and to attribute the behaviour of social others to the *mental representations these others have 'in their heads'*. Behaviour is caused by factors which well up from within the person, thoughts, wishes, intentions, etc. Minds are hidden away inside people, rather than being manifested in between them, in the public space in which interaction takes place, as the externalist theory seems to be saying. The 'internalist' theory of mind, according to the cognitive psychologists, is a 'module'—a kind of theory (or principle of interpretation) with which we are born, along with the principle that there is a basic distinction between living things and non-living things. When Boyer speaks of 'intentional psychology' he is referring to this (putatively innate) module.

Many philosophers believe that the notion that genuine 'persons' are beings whose behaviour is caused by the mental representations that they have 'in their heads' is not just a truth of common sense, but is perfectly defensible philosophically, if formulated with due care (e.g. Fodor 1994). However, we do not need to consider the arguments for and against the 'mentalist' (i.e. internalist) position in the philosophy of mind in any detail. All that we need to be aware of is that these two routes towards 'agency'-attributions exist. Let us consider further some of the differences between them. For a start, they each begin with a rather different problem-definition. The externalist theory is not really about the 'psyche' or 'consciousness'; it is an account of intersubjectivity rather than subjectivity, and it explains how it is that intersubjectivity is quite possible, even in the absence of some telepathic means of entering another person's skull and having his thoughts, feeling his pains, and so on. Because the externalist theory is about intersubjectivity, it is popular with sociologists, many of whom are much more behaviouristic in their thinking than they realize or acknowledge. To cite a case in point, the leading social theorist of today, Pierre Bourdieu, acknowledges a debt to both Wittgenstein and to the (subtle) behaviourist learning-theorist, Hull. Bourdieu's invaluable concept of the 'habitus'—the sedimented residue of past social interaction which structures ongoing interaction—is not a transcription of common-sense mentalism or 'folk psychology', but is precisely a notion of mind externalized in routine, practices, that is, the prevailing 'form of life'. Sociologists have to be 'externalists' because culture and social institutions are external, interactive, processual, historical realities, not states of mind. Sociologists cannot be 'pure' mentalists because, apart from anything else, they are concerned with actions in the light of their *consequences*, and we are all too well aware that our actions rarely if ever have precisely the consequences we hoped or expected them to have. So a theory which only relates actions to (inner, prior) intentions, even if adequate psychologically, is sociologically inadequate.

Since this is a treatise on the sociology of art, there are good reasons why I, in particular, should pay attention to the externalist theory of agency. The simplest solution to the problem of idolatry is an 'external' one on the following lines: idols are 'social others' to the extent that, and because, they obey the social rules laid down for idols as co-present others (gods) in idol-form. Thus, according to Eck (1985: 48), a Hindu deity in idol-form is essentially an honoured 'guest' to whom the devotee pays homage in the form of nurture (offering food, fanning the flies away, etc.). The appropriate behaviour for 'guests' of extremely high status, is, in fact, to do more or less exactly what idols do: accept what is offered with imperturbable dignity and impassivity. Idols 'produce intelligible behaviour' which conforms to certain expectations.

Of course, idols do not apparently 'do' anything; they generally just stand there, being immobile. This seems like an odd form of 'intelligible' behaviour, but it is not; the Life Guards outside Whitehall barracks produce exactly this type of 'intelligible' immobility and apparent insensibility as a behaviour, and they are quintessentially 'social others' while they do so. When evil-minded tourists poke umbrellas at their horses, they do not suddenly behave 'out of character' and curse their tormentors: they preserve their icy indifference. They are playing the game, and it is a game we can readily participate in. They are like the Sepik warriors whom Harrison describes as aspiring, in totemic ritual performances, to emulate the impervious spirituality of totemic *sacra*, the ceremonial effigies of spirits which line the interior of their long-house (Harrison 1983: 118).

This 'Dionysian' aggrandisement of the self, reserved for a select few, is viewed not as a celebration of subjectivity but as the reverse: the depersonalisation of the actors into human equivalents of ritual objects, like the masks, statuary and other sacra which figure in the men's cult as embodiments of ritual potency. Men contextually suspend their 'normal' social identities but gain power, in the form of the impact which highly-charged symbolic objects have on the subjectivities of others.

However, I agree that such an externalist interpretation of agency-attribution to idols seems too simple by half. Although the Life Guards may preserve their stony demeanours when their horses get poked, none the less, we know, and they know we know, that they are silently thinking 'bugger off' or words to that effect. And that is why their self-control is so remarkable and admirable. It is all very well to say that an idol which stands immobile is producing intelligible idol-behaviour according to the accepted social rules, but unless there is something going on inside the idol which corresponds to the 'inner life, unspoken thoughts, etc.' which we attribute to Life Guards, or Sepik warriors, then does this behaviour 'count'? There are two answers to this kind of objection. First of all, although idols may not produce much visible behaviour, they may none the less be very 'active' invisibly, that is, most of their actions take place 'off-stage' as it were. They can be making the crops grow, confounding traitors and plotters, or keeping the sun alight, or enjoying themselves in heaven, etc. And these actions (except perhaps the last) have visible consequences 'elsewhere', though not in any change in the bodily demeanour of the idol *per se*.

Secondly, an idol who does not respond actively (by moving or speaking) is none the less 'active' as a patient with respect to the agency of others. And this may be enough. Children's play with dolls can serve to illustrate this type of passive agency. Dolls, even those which open and close their eyes, emit cries, or even wet themselves, never produce any behaviour which is not directly under the control of the nurture-providing play-mother. The playing child knows this perfectly well, but that does not prevent them having the liveliest sensation that the doll is an alter ego and a significant social other. Doll play is so totally satisfying just because of this passivity; the doll does just whatever the child wants; submits to undressing and getting dressed again, sleeping, waking, and eating, and even, if necessary, being 'naughty' when the child is in the mood to inflict a smacking. The doll's 'thoughts' and inner life (which certainly are attributed to it while play is in progress) are a reflex of the child's own thoughts, which include the doll as a passive being whose thinking is done 'for it' just as dressing and undressing have to be done for it as well. The playing child thinks for her doll as well as doing everything else. We could interpret the thought-processes of idols along the same lines, that is, as something that devotees do for idols, which can none the less be attributed (in context) to them. Because idols (like dolls) are wholly 'passive' others, they exhibit 'passive agency', the kind of agency attributable to social others who or which, by definition, are only the *target* of agency, never the independent source. (The argument of this paragraph relates to the analysis of Hindu *darshan*, above, Sect. 7.7.)

However, I agree that neither of these responses quite measures up to the objection that idols, because of their behavioural ineffectuality, cannot be considered 'agents' in the full sense. There does seem to be a basic difference between the idol-like Life Guard whose mind seethes with unuttered curses, and the genuine idol whose dignified gaze betokens, for us, no such inner life. Whoever imagines that the idol is conscious, thinking, intentional, etc. is attributing 'mental states' to the idol which have implications, not just for the external relations between the idol and the devotee (and the form of life in which they co-participate), but for the 'inner structure' of the idol, that is, that it has something *inside* it 'which thinks' or 'with which it thinks'. The idol may not be biologically a 'living thing' but, if it has 'intentional psychology' attributed to it, then it has something like a spirit, a soul, an ego, lodged within it.

This is certainly true, ethnographically and psychologically, because of the innateness of the 'theory-of-mind module' which attributes intentionality to persons (and things as well, under certain circumstances) as a component of what Schutz calls 'the natural attitude'. The problems which assail spontaneous mentalism are not to do with demonstrating its existence, but with pursuing its implications. Let us say that 'intentional psychology' (that which is attributed to idols according to the 'internalist' approach to agency) consists of something like a 'conscious self' as experienced in the 'first person singular'. This is 'the Mind's "I"' (Hofstadter and Dennett 1982). The trouble with this mysterious 'I' is not that anybody truly disbelieves in it, but that nothing in the world, no physically identifiable thing, really seems to correspond to it. The externalist theory of mind does not seem to give one any real reason for believing in this entity in which we all do, none the less, believe: and on the basis of such a belief, interpret and predict the social behaviour of others. The philosophical problem of mentalism (of intentionalism generally) is succinctly summed up by Dennett in the following passage:

First, the only psychology that could possibly succeed in explaining the complexities of human activity must posit internal representations. This premise has been deemed obvious by just about everyone except the radical behaviorists . . . Descartes doubted almost everything *but* this. For the British Empiricists, the internal representations were called ideas, sensations, impressions; more recently psychologists have talked of hypotheses, maps, schemas, images, propositions, engrams, neural signals, even holograms and whole innate theories. So the first premise is quite invulnerable, or at any rate it has an impressive mandate . . . But, *second*, nothing is intrinsically a representation of anything; something is a representation only *for* or *to* someone; any representation or system of representations thus requires at least one *user* or *interpreter* of the representation who is external to it. Any such interpreter must have a variety of psychological or intentional traits . . . it must be capable of a variety of *comprehension*, and must have beliefs and goals (so it can *use* the representation to *inform* itself and thus assist it in reaching its goals). Such an interpreter is then a sort of homunculus.

Therefore, psychology *without* homunculi is impossible. But psychology *with* homunculi is doomed to circularity or infinite regress, so psychology is impossible. (Dennett 1979: 119–22)

Dennett argues that this problem is surmountable, not by getting rid of homunculi, but by having lots and lots of them; 'stupid' single-task homunculi doing low-level tasks and relaying the results to more intelligent homunculi doing higher-level processing tasks. There is not any one 'mind' but a pandemonium of homunculi generating representations and selecting among those that have been generated those which are of use in fulfilling the organism's needs. My purpose in citing Dennett on homunculi, however, is not to introduce his brilliant, artificial-intelligence-based theory of mind, which seeks to break the deadlock between the various compelling reasons to accept some modified form of behaviourism, and the need to explain consciousness as we actually experience it as psychological subjects. Dennettt, like all modern philosophers of mind, is writing about real human beings, not idols. The point that interests me is that Dennett is suggesting that in so far as we conceive of human beings as intentional agents because they generate and respond to mental representations, then we are obliged to 'split' them (internally) into two; the one who 'has' the representations (perceptions, ideas, etc.) and the one who interprets them (see Dennett, ibid., ch. 5). What I derive from this is the cognitive naturalness of the idea of the mind (or soul, spirit, etc.) as a homunculus; that is, like a person but *contained within* a person. That is to say, a predictable consequence of our (possibly innate) propensity to attribute 'intentional psychology' to humans, animals, etc. is attributing a *homunculus-like form* to this 'interpreter' lodged within the other, when the other is being attributed with an intentional psychology. That is to say, if we are to attempt to 'depict' the physical realization of the other's possession of an intentional psychology, the natural way to do this is to make a duplicate of the other in homuncular form (a representation of the inner person who interprets the other's representations) and lodge that homunculus inside the other's body.

Let us return to the idol. We have established, I hope, that the idol is acceptable as a social other on the basis of 'fitting in' to the role expectations for idols as a particular category of social agents, that is, primarily passive agents or agents whose agency is exercised 'off-stage'. Practically and physically, this is perfectly manageable; we just have to stipulate what the idol, to conform to its role expectations, shall look like, and manufacture an artefact which has the stipulated external characteristics. But what about making an idol which, on the basis of its actual physical characteristics, motivates the attribution to it of an intentional psychology? How might we do that?

Well, we might not want to: according to Boyer (1996) the attribution of intentional psychology (or other occult attributes) to non-living things is a potent religious idea precisely because it so markedly contradicts two basic assumptions about reality, (i) that living and non-living things are totally distinct, and that (ii) intentional psychology can only be attributed to living things. On this theory, there would be a strong (basically innate) cognitive preference for religious objects (attributed with intentional psychology) to be aniconic in form; the more blatantly the supposedly animate ritual object failed to measure up to the normal criteria for animacy, the more enthusiastically believers would worship it. However, this prediction is not borne out in practice; where the technical system of a particular religious community includes techniques for manufacturing iconic or anthropomorphic images, idols, etc., such idols are very often manufactured. Moreover, supposedly aniconic religious objects are often locally interpreted in 'iconic' ways. Goodman's well-known jibe against the notion of 'realism' in art (1976) certainly applies here, namely, that since everything 'resembles' everything else in at least *some* respects, everything can, under some interpretation, be regarded as 'depicting' anything you like. Consequently an uncarved stone can be an iconic representation of a god just as well as a minutely carved stone idol which looks much more 'realistic' to us.

However, I think that we can quite easily distinguish between idols in which iconism, the impulse to depict resemblance, is thematic, and those in which iconism is non-thematic, as in litholatry, pure and simple. So I rephrase the question; given that we are dealing with that class of idols in which iconic depiction of the object of veneration is thematic, how are we to indicate, by means of pictorial or sculptural 'mimesis', that the artefact is endowed with an intentional psychology? There is a simple answer to this: we cannot. There is nothing physical that we can imitate here, there is no mind in objective form that we can copy and insert into the appropriate place in the idol. No matter how realistically we imitate the outward appearance of the body, we fall short of depicting the soul which, however, we are determined to imitate in some fashion.

To say that there is no ideal solution is not to say that there are no half-measures. Even if we cannot depict the mind, we can at least depict the possibility that there is a mind we cannot depict. By way of a thought experiment, let us postulate an 'ideal aniconic idol'—a sphere of perfectly homogeneous material, actually black basalt. We may suppose that the spherical stone idol has a mind, intentions, sensibilities, etc. but there is nothing about the material characteristics of the sphere, as such, which articulates with these beliefs, which are entirely theological and abstract. But let us modify the spherical idol somewhat by drilling a hole in it, or maybe two holes, which would then probably be seen as 'eyes'. Once the sphere was equipped with 'orifices' of this kind it would be possible, not just to imagine, abstractly, that it had a mind, perceptions, intentions, etc. but to attach these imaginings to the formal contrast between the exterior of the sphere, into which the holes were drilled, and the interior, to which these holes give access. Adding features which apparently make the sphere more 'anthropomorphic' (by the addition of eyes, a mouth, etc.) do not just serve the purpose of making the sphere a more realistic 'depiction' of a human being, they render it more spiritual, more inward, by opening up *routes of access* to this inwardness. The 'internalist' theory of agency (in its informal guise as part of everyday thinking) motivates the development of 'representational', if not 'realistic' religious images, because the inner versus outer, mind versus body contrast prompts the development of images with 'marked' characteristics of inwardness versus outwardness. Paradoxically, the development of idols which depict the visible, superficial, features of the human body make possible the abduction of the 'invisible' mind, awareness, and will from the visible image. The more materially realistic the image, at least in certain key respects, the more spiritually it is seen.

It would be misleading to suppose, though, that the need to articulate visually the contrast between inner mind and outer body leads ineluctably towards representational art forms, though this happens. My argument is that the indexical form of the mind/body contrast, is primordially *spatial and concentric*; the mind is 'internal' enclosed, surrounded, by something (the body) that is non-mind. Now we begin to see why idols are so often hollow envelopes, with enclosures, like the hollow *mauri* stones, or the hollow sorcery-images we encountered in the preceding discussion of Polynesian idolatry (above, Sects. 7.5–6).

It is often the case that the human body (with an implied interior indicated by orifices) is used to index this primordial inside–outside relation. But there are other ways of achieving this as well. Suppose, instead of drilling 'eye' holes in the spherical idol, we leave it as it is, but place it in a box, an ark. At this moment it becomes possible to think of the spherical idol in a different way; we can easily suppose that the stone inside the box is the locus of agency, intention, etc. and the ark is the sacred 'vessel' which, body-like, contains and protects this locus of agency. Once the idol is in the ark we have, once more, the physical configuration necessary for thinking of the stone as 'opposed to' something else in the way that the mind (interior) is opposed to the body (exterior). The 'homunculus-effect', in other words, can be achieved without anthropomorphizing the index, so long as the crucial feature of concentricity and 'containment' is preserved.

7.10. *The Animation of Idols: The Externalist Strategy*

There are thus two basic strategies for converting (conceptually) stocks and stones into quasi-persons in artefact-form. The first of these strategies consists of animating the idol by simply stipulating for it a role as a social other. The second consists of providing it with a homunculus, or space for a homunculus, or turning it into a homunculus within some larger entity. I shall discuss the 'internal' animation of idols in the next section. Here is an example which gives us a good view of the externalist strategy in action. Contrary to what one might expect, the most important images of the gods of ancient Egypt were not the monumental carved figures that have survived to this day, but much smaller, conveniently heftable, idols, as the following description makes clear:

in the temple of Hathor at Denderah, there were, among others, the following sacred statues: Hathor, painted wood, copper, inlaid eyes, height 3 ells, 4 spans, and 2 fingers; Isis, painted acacia wood, eyes inlaid, height 1 ell; Horus, painted wood, inlaid eyes, height 1 ell and 1 finger. The largest, therefore, was scarcely of life size; the smallest only about 16 inches in height. The reason for this insignificance in size was that for certain acts of worship the images had to be easily portable.

The paltry size and material of these little wooden dolls were, however, atoned for by the splendour of their abode, and the reverence with which they were served. The shrine of the god was in the innermost chamber of the temple, which was in total darkness save on the entry of the officiating priest bearing artificial light. It consisted generally of a single block of stone, often, especially in the later periods, of enormous size, hewn into a house which surrounded with impenetrable walls the image of the god. The doorway in front was closed with bronze doors, or doors of wood overlaid with bronze or gold-silver alloy . . . after the daily ritual had been gone through, these doors were closed, fastened with a bolt, and then tied with a cord bearing a clay seal . . . Within the shrine, the image of the god reposed in a little ark, or portable inner shrine, which could be lifted out and placed upon the barque in which the deity made his journeys abroad on stated occasions.

The daily ritual of service to the image was in its main outlines the same in all the temples . . . the procedure was as follows. Early in the morning the priest of the day, after lustrations, entered the Holy of Holies, bearing incense in a censer, and stood before the shrine. He first loosened the door that closed the shrine, repeating as he did so a stereotyped phrase: 'The cord is broken, and the seal loosened,—I come, I bring thee the eye of Horus [i.e. light, the sun]' . . . As the doors of the shrine opened and the god was revealed, the priest prostrated himself and chanted 'The gates of heaven are opened, and the nine gods appear radiant, the god N is exalted upon his great throne . . . Thy beauty belongs to thee, O god N; thou naked one, clothe thyself.' Taking his vessels, the priest then began to perform the daily toilet of the god. He sprinkled water on the image twice from four jugs, clothed it with linen wrappings of white, green, red, and brown, and painted it with green and black paint. Finally, he fed the image, by laying before it bread, beef, geese, wine, and water, and decorated its table with flowers.   (Blaikie 1914: 132)

It is not hard to see the applicability of the externalist theory to the cult of the idols in the temples of ancient Egypt, cited above. The daily round to which the idols were subjected, being woken in the morning, washed, made up, served breakfast, and so on, imposed agency on them willy-nilly by making them patients in social exchanges which imply and confer agency necessarily. There is no 'as if' or make-believe about such performances; they would be pointless unless these life-endowing rituals were literal transpositions of the means in which we induce agency in social others in human form, such as children.

Indeed, it is very hard to read this description without being reminded of children's play with dolls. This is not altogether an appropriate comparison, except to the extent that children do not 'play' with dolls but actually make a cult of, or worship them. 'Play' behaviour is supposed to take place in conceptual brackets, which say 'this is play—so I am not doing what I appear to be doing' (Bateson 1936). Children, outside the temple, might play at being priests, and pretend to worship toy gods, but this type of make-believe is entirely distinct from the activities of the priests themselves. They were not at play, but at work. They were serious.

Nor is it quite right to say that their actions were 'symbolic'—though of course everything rather depends on how the word 'symbolic' is understood. Offering food to the image of the god is not a pantomime or dumb-show, as if there were some alternative way of feeding a god which was being alluded to, but not performed. Receiving food offerings is how the Egyptian gods ate their food. This is not to say that the act of feeding the god by placing an offering before it is not symbolic in the sense of 'meaningful', but the 'meaning' stemmed from the real (causal) outcome of this act of feeding; the god was no longer hungry. The essence of idolatry is that it permits *real physical interactions* to take place between persons and divinities. To treat such interactions as 'symbolic' is to miss the point. Images can be employed in worship in non-idolatrous ways, as aids to piety but not physical channels of access to the divinity—the Christian use of religious images is supposed to belong to this category, though in practice many Christians' use of images is *de facto* idolatrous, if not admitted to be so. We can only distinguish between idolatrous and non-idolatrous use of religious images because idolatry is in an important sense not 'symbolic' at all, whereas the use of images as aids to piety, rather than physical vehicles of divinity, is symbolic. The Egyptian ceremonies just adduced belong firmly in the category of idolatrous practices, and are thus real, practical, services performed for divine social others in image-form, not symbolic acts.

All the same, the way in which these idols were enmeshed in the structured routines of daily life can only provide a partial answer to the problem of idolatry. There are other features of the situation which seem to indicate the operation of different factors, which cannot be accounted for in terms of a purely 'externalist' notion of agency. For instance, as noted above, the purely externalist theory of agency makes no stipulations as to the physical or visual form of the object (index) which is treated as an agent. These Egyptian idols were, in fact, quite realistic representations of the outward appearance of human persons. The externalist theory of agency is not in a position to differentiate between 'iconic' idols, such as these, and 'aniconic' idols, such as stones, or the planks of wood, known as *baitulia*, which the Greeks worshipped (as Aphrodite, Zeus, etc.) before, and alongside, their subsequent cult of sculptural images of these gods. This indifference towards the iconic properties of idols is, in a sense, a point in favour of the 'externalist' theory; unless agency were a purely externally endowed property of idols, unconnected with their physical substance or form, then it is hard to see how the worship of aniconic idols such as stones or planks of wood would be possible. The externalist theory has got to be at least half-right, for this reason. Yet it cannot be wholly correct, or the impetus towards 'shaping' the idol—not just treating it as an agent, but making it look like or share physical attributes with a 'prototype'— would be inexplicable. Here one has to introduce the other theory of agency, the 'internalist' or homunculus theory. While it may be true that the agency of these idols derived in part from the way in which they were inserted into the relational texture of 'external' social praxis and language, this 'passive' agency is certainly not the whole story. These particular idols were in fact highly iconic, and moreover, the description given (by Blaikie, but deriving directly from Herodotus) emphasizes particularly their 'inlaid eyes'. In the next section I will describe in detail the consecration of contemporary idols, which crucially involves the animation of images by providing them with eyes. Eyes are, of all body orifices, those which signify 'interiority' (i.e. the possession of mind and intentionality) most immediately (see the previous discussion of *darshan*). The particular attention paid to the eyes of these idols arises, not from the need to represent the body realistically, but from the need to represent the body in such a way as to imply that the body is *only* a body, and that a much more important entity, the mind, is immured within it.

Thus, it is equally important to note that the animation of these idols was being achieved, simultaneously, in a quite different way. The description given above emphasizes, besides the realistic form of the idols, their extraordinary and impressive surroundings. They were kept, except when being served by the priests, in a box or ark, which, in turn, was kept in the darkest and most central sanctuary of a vast temple complex, consisting of innumerable lesser sanctuaries, shrines, courtyards, barracks and workshops, etc. If we situate ourselves, not inside the innermost sanctuary, but outside in the courtyard, with the ordinary worshippers (who rarely if ever saw the idols themselves) then we may readily imagine that the idols (immured in the temple complex, and animating it like a giant body) come to stand for 'mind' and interiority not just by physical resemblance to the human body, but by becoming the animating 'minds' of the huge, busy, and awe-inspiring temple complex. Just as the 'mind' is conceived of as an interior person, a homunculus, within the body, so the idols are homunculi within the 'body' of the temple. And it is true that idols, even very representational idols, are invariably presented in a setting, a temple, a shrine or an ark, a sacred space of some kind, which has the effect of emphasizing their interiority, their secludedness and (relative) inaccessibility, as well as their majesty. The seclusion of the idol has, automatically, the effect of motivating the abduction of agency, on the basis of the equation:

idol : temple :: mind : body.

These reflections lead towards a relativization of the contrast between the external and internal conceptions of agency, sentience, etc. with which I began this section. It is obvious that the homunculus, or 'inner person' conception of agency essentially reduplicates, within the human person, the relation which always exists between a human person and a texture of external relationships, but within the interior domain, within the body. This imagery leads to the 'homunculus within a homunculus' problem which besets this type of theory, according to its critics. But this 'problem' is also an advantage, in that it tends to blur the distinction between the 'induced' kind of animacy which is imposed externally on the idol by enmeshing it in praxis, language, social relations and routines, and the 'internal' agency which the idol is supposed to possess as a 'mind' encapsulated in a surrounding body. Just as the idol, externally, is at the centre of a concentric array of relations between persons, so the idol, internally, can be seen as a concentric array of relations between the 'inner' persons—

the pandemonium of homunculi—of which it is composed. Let us turn to an example which reveals this in a particularly graphic way.

7.11. *Concentric Idols and Fractal Personhood*

To exhibit the animation of the idol through the congruence between the external relational context within which the idol is set, and the internal nexus of relations between the mind and the body (as a relation between inner and outer 'persons') consider the Polynesian example in Fig. 7.11/1, a carving from Rurutu in the Austral Isles, which has been in London since 1822 and which can be seen at the Museum of Mankind. This carving, in Rurutu called A'a, but more commonly identified as Tangaroa, is arguably the finest extant piece of Polynesian sculpture. Almost every other Rurutan idol was consigned to the flames by the missionaries, but this one was preserved, initially to drum up subscriptions for the London Missionary Society so that they could afford to destroy other, no doubt equally fine, carvings elsewhere.

The most striking attribute of this carving is the way in which the features of the god are represented by little figures which repeat, in miniature, the overall form of the god as a whole. This god sprouts little gods all over its surface: mathematically, it is akin to the type of figure known as a 'fractal', a figure which demonstrates the property of *self-similiarity* at different scales of magnification/minification. Moreover, besides being a god made of many gods, the A'a is also a box or an ark. It is hollow inside, having a lid at the back, and it originally contained twenty-four or more additional, smaller images of Rurutan gods, which were removed and destroyed in 1822. For all we know, the gods inside the A'a were themselves hollow, though I think not. But whereas we think of boxes as less significant than their contents, the A'a, even though it is a box, is the primary image of Rurutan divinity, encompassing and subordinating all the subordinate gods who sprout from its surface and once resided in its interior. According to contemporary Rurutan traditions, the exterior gods encompassed by the A'a correspond to the kinship units (clans) comprising Rurutan society as a whole.[4] Many other important Polynesian

---

[4] Curiously though, contemporary Rurutans, according to the ethnographer Alain Babadzan have a quite different theory about the gods which, they know, were once inside the A'a. According to the Rurutan elders, there were three gods inside the A'a when it was made, by a Hero named Amaiterai. Amaiterai made the A'a after visiting a city none other than London, present resting-place of the A'a, which he reached in fulfilment of a species of knightly quest, imposed on him in order to win the hand of the adopted daughter of the King of Rurutu, who had been promised to his brother. In London Amaiterai encountered the God of Wisdom (who later was the God of the Christians, brought to Rurutu by the missionaries) whose image he replicated in the form of the famous A'a. The gods inside the A'a were three Polynesian gods originating in London: Room-etua-ore, alias Te Atua Metua, alias God the Father; Aura-roiteata, alias Te Atua tamaiti, alias God the Son; and Te atua aiteroa, alias Te Atua Varua Maita'i, alias God the Holy Spirit. In other words, the A'a is the Tabernacle in which the Trinity arrived on Rurutu, by the agency of a Rurutan hero, long before the missionaries themselves arrived. The A'a is in London, but it is present on Rurutu in the form of Christian belief.

FIG. 7.11/1. The fractal god: A'a from Ruruta. *Source*: The British Museum, MM 011977

FIG. 7.11/2. Genealogical personhood objectified: a staff god from the Cook Islands. *Source*: Museum of Archaeology and Anthropology, Cambridge, Z 6099

carvings represent personhood in the form of genealogy, as for instance the related carving, a 'staff god', from the Cook Islands shown in Fig. 7.11/2.

What is particularly remarkable about the A'a is the explicit way in which this image of a 'singular' divinity represents divinity as an assemblage of relations between (literally) homunculi. In so doing, the A'a obviates the contrast between one and many, and also between inner and outer. The surface of this image consists of amalgamated replications of itself, or alternatively, a succession of budding protuberances. Internally, the image consists of itself, replicated on a smaller scale, within its own interior cavity. As such, it images both the notion of personhood as the aggregate of external relations (the outcome of genealogy, fanning out in time and space) and at the same time the notion of personhood as the possession of an interior person, a homunculus, or, in this instance, an assemblage of homunculi. We cannot individuate the A'a in the way in which we normally individuate persons by identifying the boundaries of their person with the spatial boundaries of their bodies, for the A'a has no such boundaries; it is like a Russian doll, and in this respect, it irresistibly recalls the lines in *Peer Gynt* in which the hero compares the (moral, biographical) person to an onion, composed of a succession of concentric layers:

—Why, you're simply an onion—
and now, my good Peter, I'm going to peel you
and tears and entreaties won't help in the least.
[*Taking an onion, he strips it skin by skin*]
There goes the battered outer layer—
that's the shipwrecked man on the dinghy's keel.
This layer's the passenger—scrawny and thin,
But still with a bit of a taste of Peer Gynt.
Next underneath comes the gold-mining Self—
the juice, if it ever *had* any is gone.
This rough skin here, with the hardened patch
is the fur-trapping hunter from Hudson's Bay.
We'll throw that away without a word.
Next the archaeologist, short but vigorous;
and here's the prophet, juicy and fresh—
it stinks of lies, as the saying goes,
and would bring tears to an honest man's eyes.
This skin, curled and effeminate,
is the gentleman living his life of pleasure.
The next looks unhealthy and streaked with black—
black could mean either priests or niggers . . .
[*He peels off several layers at once.*]
What an incredible number of layers!
Don't we get to the heart of it soon?

[*He pulls the whole onion to pieces.*]
No, I'm damned if we do. Right down to the centre
there's nothing but layers—smaller and smaller . . .
Nature is witty!

(Ibsen 1966: 191)

Peer Gynt's onion is also a fractal, of the same essentially concentric form as
the A'a. Ibsen's idea, in utilizing this image is to show that there is no ultimate
basis to Peer Gynt's personhood; he is made of layers of biographical (relational) experience accreted together, for which none the less, he must take sole
responsibility. Perhaps it is not such a vast step to pass from Peer Gynt trapped
in the aporias of nineteenth-century materialism and individualism to the theological impulse which motivates the A'a, which depicts the divine creator, the
mind of which the world is the body, in the form of a body composed of other
bodies, *ad infinitum.*

   This idea is given contemporary expression in the work on personhood in
Melanesia, by writers such as Marilyn Strathern (1988; cf. Gell 1998) and Roy
Wagner (1991). Wagner, in particular, has developed the notion of 'Fractal
Personhood', which he mobilizes to overcome the typically 'Western' opposi-
tions between individual (ego) and society, parts and wholes, singular and plural.
The notion of genealogy, which is so signally expressed in our two Polynesian
examples (both idols, of course), is the key trope for making plurality singular
and singularity plural. Any individual person is 'multiple' in the sense of being
the precipitate of a multitude of genealogical relationships, each of which is
instantiated in his/her person; and conversely, an aggregate of persons, such as
a lineage or tribe, is 'one person' in consequence of being one genealogy: the
original ancestor is now instantiated, not as one body but as the many bodies
into which his one body has transformed itself. Wagner writes:

A fractal person is never a unit standing in relation to an aggregate, or an aggregate
standing in relation to a unit, but always an entity with relationship integrally implied.
Perhaps the most concrete illustration of integral relationship comes from the gener-
alised notion of reproduction and genealogy. People exist reproductively by being
'carried' as part of another, and 'carry' or engender others by making themselves
genealogical or reproductive 'factors' of these others. A genealogy is thus an enchainment of people, as indeed persons would be seen to 'bud' out of one another in a
speeded-up cinematic depiction of human life. Person as human being and person as
lineage or clan are equally arbitrary sectionings or identifications of this enchainment,
different projections of its fractality. But then enchainment through bodily reproduction is itself merely one of a number of instantiations of integral relationship, which is
also manifest, for instance, in the commonality of shared language.   (1991: 163)

   From the anthropological point of view, if not the philosophical one, the
solution to the conflict between the external notion of agency, deriving from
insertion in the social milieu, and the 'internalist' theory of agency, deriving

from an inner subjective self, is to be sought in this 'enchainment', the structural congruence between the inner self (which is relational) and the outer self (which is equally relational, but on an expanded scale). The 'genealogical theory of mind' which is explored, particularly, in Strathern's work (1988) seems perfectly expressed in the form of the A'a.

But this artwork, and its Polynesian cousins, is not unique. In fact, the possession of 'significant interiors' is a very common feature of sculptural works specifically intended for cult use, rather than as mere representations. Sculptural images which open up, like the A'a, to reveal other images, were manufactured in ancient Greece, and provided Alcibiades with a simile for his mentor, Socrates (as narrated by Plato in the *Symposium* 213–15):

I am here to speak in praise of Socrates, Gentlemen, and I will just do it by means of similes. Oh yes, he will perhaps think it is only for a bit of fun, but my simile will be for truth, not for fun. I say then, that he is exactly like a Silenos, the little figures that you see in statuaries' shops; the craftsmen make them, they hold panpipes or pipes, and they can be opened up down the middle or folded back, and then they show inside them, images of the gods. And I say further, that he is like Marsyas the Satyr [who was flayed by Apollo] . . .

Here the contrast is between the ugly exterior (body) and the divine interior (mind) of Socrates. The same kind of image was also developed in Christian cult art, though with a different theological implication. A class of holy statues called 'vierges ouvrantes' was made in the Middle Ages, though few have survived into the present, perhaps because these images were particularly conducive to idolatry, as the following passage from Camille's work of *The Gothic Idol* shows. 'Our Lady of Bolton' which used, before the Reformation, to stand in a chapel of Durham cathedral was:

a marveylous lyvely and bewtifull Image of the picture of our Ladie, so calld Lady of Boultone, which picture was made to open with gymmers [or two leaves] from her breasts downwards. And within this saide immage was wroughte and pictured the immage of our Saviour, merveylouse fynlie gilted holdynge uppe his hands, and holding betwixt his hands a fair large Crucifix of Christ, all of gold, the which Crucifix was to be taken fourthe every Good Fridaie, and every man did creepe unto it that was in that Church at that daye. And every principall daie the said image was opened, that every man might see pictured within her the Father, Son and the Holy Ghost, most curiouslye and fynely gilted. (Camille 1989: 230–1)

Camille illustrates a German example of such a 'vierge ouvrante' (Fig. 7.11/3). 'Our Lady of Bolton' was related to the more common type of Christian holy image in the form of a reliquary, in that she was, besides an image of the Virgin, a container for the golden crucifix which was paraded on Good Friday. (For an Indian parallel to a 'vierge ouvrante' cf. Fig. 7.11/4 showing Hanuman, the monkey god, opening his breast to reveal Rama and Sita.) Such images were controversial even when they were still in common use: Camille quotes

FIG. 7.11/3. 'Vierge
ouvrante'. *Source*: Camille
1989: pl. 124. Nuremberg
Germanisches National
Museum. Painted wood.
H. 126 cm

the theologian Gerson, in 1402, denouncing 'Carmelite' images which 'have
the Trinity in their abdomen as if the entire Trinity assumed flesh in the Virgin
Mary . . .' (1989: 232). These images were all too animate, they smacked of
necromancy rather than religion. Later on in the same book, Camille shows
how reliquary heads, containing the bones of saints, could become objects of
deep official suspicion, especially the silver and golden heads supposedly worshipped in pagan ceremonies by the Knights Templars, who were suppressed
in 1308 as a result (ibid. 271–7). The notorious 'talking head' reputedly devised
by Roger Bacon is another variation on the same theme (ibid. 246–7). But the
relation between religious art and sorcery runs very deep, we have already seen.

No such opprobrium attached to more ordinary reliquaries in human form, of
which there are many famous examples, such as those illustrated and discussed
by Freedberg (1989: 92–5, figs. 30–2). This author also remarks on the fact
that in the Middle Ages, churches could not be consecrated at all unless they
had holy relics installed in them. Just as relics animated the reliquary image,
rendering it a particularly holy object (an object with a mind, or perhaps more
precisely, a spirit, within it) so the church (fabric) as a whole became a 'body'
whose animation also required the insertion of a relic. The normal place for the

FIG. 7.11/4. An Indian parallel to 'vierge ouvrante': the monkey god Hanuman reveals Rama and Sita in his breast. *Source*: A. Mookerjee (1980), *Ritual Art of India* (London: Thames & Hudson), plate 80. Kalighat school, south Calcutta, *c*.1850. Gouache on paper

insertion of relics into the fabric of a church was inside the altarpiece, in the altar itself, or buried beneath it.

The insertion of animating relics into images raises a fresh question, however, that of consecration—the management of the transition between the religious image as a 'mere' manufactured thing and a vehicle of power, capable of acting intentionally and responding to the intentions of devotees. We shall consider this aspect of idolatry in the next section.

7.12. *The Rites of Consecration*

It is fair to say that the worship of images or idols is most extensively practised, nowadays, in south Asia, among Hindus and (in a rather more qualified way) among Buddhists. Here images are still being produced and installed in holy places in great numbers and here it is possible for anthropologists to observe the rites of consecration in detail. I shall therefore conduct the argument of this section with reference to three well-known south Asian examples, the consecration of the idol of Jagganath in Puri (Eschmann *et al.* 1978), the account given by Richard Gombrich (1966) of the installation of a statue of the Buddha in a Sinhalese monastery, and finally, the account given by Michael Allen (1976) of the consecration of the 'living image' of the goddess Taleju (Durga) in Kathmandu.

The images of Jagganath, his brothers, Balabadhra and Subadhra, and his wife Sudarsana in the temple of Puri (Orissa) are among the most revered idols in the whole of India, but, though anthropomorphic, these images are (visually speaking) quite obviously cylindrical sections of tree-trunk, dressed up and equipped with vestigial upper limbs and very, very, large eyes. The images are not old in physical terms, though their design is indeed ancient, since they have to be renewed every twelve, or at most every nineteen years, in the course of a ceremony called *navakalevara*. A detailed description of this ceremony (contributed by G. C. Tripathi) is provided in Eschmann's work on the history and affinities in 'tribal' religion of the Puri Jagganath cult. The tribal affinities of this important Hindu cult are not in doubt; I myself worked in the same region of India (Bastar district, which abuts onto the Orissa highlands to the west) among tribal Muria Gonds, whose images of divinities were aniconic wooden posts, without limbs or eyes, but otherwise highly resembling the Jagganath images, though on a reduced scale (A. Gell 1978; cf. S. Gell 1992).

Tripathi's account of *navakalevara* is a first-rate exercise in ethnographic description, which I cannot unfortunately summarize in any detail. The ceremony of renewal has five phases, as follows:

1. To find out the *daru* (sacred wood) with the prescribed characteristics and to bring it to the temple (involving a sacrifice to ward of evil spirits etc. and to sanctify the tree before felling it);
2. The carving of the wooden structure of the images;
3. The consecration of the images by the insertion of the 'life-substance' (*brahmapadartha*) into them;
4. The burial of the old figures, the funeral and purificatory rites of the Daitas (temple servitors, of low caste);
5. Giving the images their final form by means of several coverings of cloth etc. and by applying paint to them (Eschmann 1978: 230).

I omit the first two phases in this process, except to mention that the efficacy of the images depends, initially, on the auspicious location and form of the *daru* tree (it must grow by water, be surrounded by three mountains, have dark, 'red' bark, a straight trunk, with four branches, etc.). Numerous ceremonies accompany the felling, transport, and carpentering of the *daru* tree. The images are made by temple servitors of low caste but high ritual privilege, the Daitas, ex-tribals who alone know how to create this type of wooden image, according to precise rules, important aspects of their work being kept secret by them, even from the Brahmin priests. Among the most important of their secrets is the actual nature of the 'life-substance' (*brahmapadartha*) of the images.

The consecration procedure commences simultaneously with the carving of the images, and is first of all conducted by Brahmins. Since the images are still being made, the Brahmins devote their efforts to consecrating a separate piece of *daru* wood, which, divided into four pieces, will become the 'lids' over the cavities in the finished images containing their 'life-substance'. This piece of wood is protected with offerings to evil spirits, then elaborately bathed and purified, then placed to rest on a ritual bed. After this, the spirit of the god Narasimha (of which Jagganath is a form, as well as being a form of Krishna) is induced into the wood by the recitation of mantras on each of its parts (equated with the parts of a body) over a number of days. This invocation procedure is called *nyasadaru*. After this, the ritually treated *daru* wood—and by metonymy, the larger sections of *daru* wood which are at this moment reaching completion as images in the Daitas workshop—is spiritually speaking endowed with life, flesh, blood, sense organs, etc. It can then be cut into four lid-pieces to fit into the four images.

The crucial ceremony however, is not conducted by the Brahmins but by the Daitas. These take the 'old' images from the temple, and strip from them the many layers of resin-impregnated cloth with which they are bound. They can then reach the compartments inside the old images in which their 'life-substance' is secreted.

The Daita entrusted with the job opens the belly of the old image in dead of night with his eyes blindfolded and the hands wrapped up to the elbows so that he may neither see nor feel the *brahmapadārtha* of the image. The casket containing the Brahmapadārtha is then taken out of the old murti [image] and placed in the new one. The cavity of the new image is then covered with one of the four pieces of the Nyasdaru [sacred wood] which has been consecrated for about two weeks by the Brahmins. (Tripathi in Eschmann 1978: 260)

Nobody really knows, except the Daitas, exactly of what object or substance the *brahmapadartha* is composed. It may be a relic, a portion of a wooden Jagganath supposedly incinerated (but not completely) by the Muslim icono- clasts under Kala Pahada in 1568. In the opinion of the Brahmins, it is a *salagrama*, a type of sacred stone, usually an oval river-pebble from the Him- alayas containing fossilized ammonites, and/or cavities (see Fig. 7.12/1 from Mookerjee and Khanna 1977).

The Daitas now perform burial rites over the deceased images which have lost their life-substance. They weep and mourn, observing mortuary pollution restrictions for ten days. However, they derive benefit from this, in that they

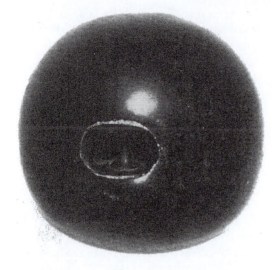

FIG. 7.12/1. 'World-seed':
salagrama. Source: Mookerjee
and Khanna 1977

are allowed to keep the cloth wrappings of the old images, which they cut into strips and sell to pilgrims. These pieces of cloth confer protection and good fortune on the purchasers.[5]

The final phase of consecration now occurs. Another caste of temple servants, said to be Kayasthas (a low form of Brahmins) undertake the wrapping of the images—who, in wooden form are just 'skeletons'—with their 'flesh', that is, with cloth and paint. The wooden 'bones' are first of all 'washed' by being impregnated with camphor oil. This gives the bones 'marrow'. Then, apparently, long red threads are wound around them, representing 'blood vessels'. After this, many strips of red cloth (for flesh) impregnated with resin (blood) and starch (fat, semen) are added, till the image begins to assume its final form. The outer wrappings are the image's skin.

Finally, the images are painted by craftsmen skilled in this art (*chitakara*). The very last act, which finalizes the consecration of the new images, is the painting in of the pupils of the immense eyes of the images, which is done by the Brahmin priests themselves, reciting Vedic mantras the while. After giving the last stroke of paint to the eyes of the images, the Brahmins give each a bath, to remove the pollution from the previous contact the images have had with low-caste carpenters, painters, etc. This is done not by bathing the image directly, but bathing the images' images, cast in large bronze mirrors kept for

[5] This prerogative recalls the 'feather exchange' following the decortication of the Tahitian *to'o* (7.6 above). The *mana* of Jagganath is disseminated via his exuviae, his body-parts, *jutha* (leavings) etc. Incidentally, the same is true in the Egyptian example discussed in 7.10 above. Every time the idols' clothes were renewed, the discarded garments were distributed to important persons, to use to wrap their own corpses in as mummy-cloths. Whereas in Polynesia and India, the cloth/feather exuviae of the god went to benefit the living, in Egypt they benefited the dead in the afterlife.

this purpose. After this, the new images are paraded and installed in their place in the temple with great pomp and ceremony (Tripathi, ibid. 262–4).

Two aspects of these interesting ceremonies are of particular concern to us. The consecration of the images evidently proceeds according to two parallel strategies simultaneously; first of all, the strategy of the Daitas, which focuses particularly on the placing of the life-substance *inside* the image, in the cavity, and secondly, the strategy of the Brahmins, which proceeds in the inverse direction, through the apostrophization of the representative billet of wood with life-endowing mantras (the phase of *nyasadaru*) and the application of the final stroke of paint to the pupils of the images' eyes. In other words, the Daitas' procedure could be called the inside-out procedure, while the Brahmins' procedure is the outside-in procedure. Both are necessary and mutually complementary.

The Daitas' procedure, is, perhaps, the more primitive, in that it seeks to render a physical analogy between the possession of a 'soul' and the possession of an interior cavity inhabited by a homunculus. Moreover, it is 'genealogical' because it establishes a kinship link between the old images and the new ones through the transmission of substance between 'generations' of images. The Brahmin strategy, for the most part, is more abstract than this; rather than fashion the image, they address it with mantras, animating it externally through 'the magical power of words' (Tambiah 1985). We can easily see that these two strategies correspond exactly to the two strands previously identified in the philosophy of mind and agency. The Daitas' strategy is the 'internalist' one, the Brahmins' the 'externalist' one. But it would be false to suppose that these two strategies are independent. In the end, the Brahmins concede to the internalist strategy to the extent that their final act is one of physical modification of the image, not mere apostrophization. Their culminating act of painting in the pupils of the eyes of the image is mimetic and iconic. Though the eyes of these images are not actually transparent, the pupils of any eyes are never 'things' but always *holes*, orifices, giving access to the hidden interior within which 'mind' resides. The surface of an idol is not an impermeable barrier, but a means of access to this essential interior.

In fact, the images of Jagganath and his companions are a series of 'skins' just like Peer Gynt's onion, with the same implication that the *ultimate centre can never be reached*. The outermost (relevant) skin of the idols consists of the temple of Puri itself (which is, of course, a microcosmos) which is filled with sacred words and odours—verbal and olfactory skins (cf. Anzieu 1989: 59). The idols reside in the centre of, and animate, this reverberating microcosmos, and are animated by the incessant flow of sacred words. Proceeding towards the centre we approach the idols through a 'social skin', the throng of pilgrims and attendant temple servants and priests, who, by their attentions and devotions, animate the idols occupying the cynosure of a great assembly of souls. The idols themselves are enshrined at the centre, framed on their altars, adorned with masses of flowers and jewellery, presiding over their material wealth of heaped-up offerings, their external skins in the form of *possessions*. We cannot approach or touch the idols, so we can proceed further on our journey towards the centre in imagination only. What we see are their visible skins, but these are only outer wrappings. These wrappings consist of numerous layers, their inner skins of flesh, fat, semen, blood, bone, marrow. These we may penetrate, one by one, or gazing into the enormous eyes of the idols, we can enter their bodies directly. But what is there, concealed beneath, behind, the inky pools? Inside, there is a primordial cavity, an internal skin. And inside the cavity, an animating presence of some kind. Conceptually, we know that, in fact, this cavity contains a casket, another inner-inner skin. And what is in the casket? Even the man who placed it there does not know perhaps; he has certainly never seen its contents. We believe that there is a *salagrama* there, a sacred stone or world-seed. If so, what is in the *salagrama*? The *salagrama* itself has an interior, and, holes leading into this interior (cf. Fig. 7.12/1). We must enter these holes. And then what would we find? Who can say—and does it matter?—for by now it is apparent that the animation of the image is not a matter of finding the 'sacred centre' at all. What matters is only the reduplication of skins, outwards towards the macrocosm and inwards towards the microcosm, and the fact that all these skins are structurally homologous; there is no definitive 'surface', there is no definitive 'inside', but only a ceaseless passage in and out, and that it is here, in this traffic to and fro, that the mystery of animation is solved.

The consecration of an image of the Buddha in Sri Lanka, described by Gombrich (1966; cf. the discussion in Freedberg 1989: 84–7, 95) follows a similar pattern, though reduced. Buddhists, especially monks, are not supposed to worship idols, but showing respect to images of the Buddha, by making offerings and gestures of submission, is one way to acquire merit and secure a good rebirth, if not a very significant one. Once again, it proves to be the case that images of the Buddha are, if they are to have any religious importance, also reliquaries. Minute portions of the Buddha's bodily remains are placed inside images to render them efficacious. However, this does not consecrate them, according to Gombrich; consecration is accomplished by the craftsman, who paints in the eyes of the image in the course of a special ceremony called *netra pinkama* the 'eye ceremony' (1966: 25).

The ceremony presents some interesting contrasts to the consecration of the Jagganath images, as well as many points of continuity. The Brahmin/Daita relationship is partially inverted in the ritual division of labour in the Sinhalese Buddhist consecration ceremonies. In Puri, it is the Daita who animates the image by putting 'life-substance' into it, and the Brahmin priest who paints in the eyes; in Sri Lanka, on the other hand, it is the monk (abbot) who places the relic into the Buddha statue, and the lay craftsman who paints in its eyes. This is a precise reflection of the difference between the Buddha (a dead human being with morally supernatural characteristics) and the Hindu gods, who are non-human immortals. A Buddha statue celebrates the possibility of 'a good death' and monks are semi-dead individuals who aspire to the ultimate good-death condition. Consequently it is only appropriate that the handling of Buddha relics, which are pieces of a dead body, should be assigned to monks, who are semi-dead themselves, and who of course always preside over funerals (but not births and marriages) in Buddhist countries like Sri Lanka (or Thailand; cf. Tambiah 1985). In a sense, then, what the relic does is make the Buddha statue like the Buddha, by making it 'dead' through the insertion of a 'death-substance'—in the rather paradoxical sense that Buddha-hood implies death-in-life. However, one can see that this ritual procedure hardly amounts to the 'animation' of the image. Gombrich understands this as the means of 'legitimating' the statue as a Buddha image, so that from the monkish perspective no taint of idolatry arises. For the laity things are otherwise. Buddha is really a god, and approaching the statue of the Buddha, the lay worshipper, immersed in life and sin, seeks personal reassurance through communion with the Buddha's living presence, conveyed through the eyes (see above on the Hindu equivalent of this form of worship, *darshan*). Because only lay people are 'superstitious' enough to engage in such theologically decried acts of worship, it is the lay craftsman who is charged with the task of animating the Buddha image.

The ceremony is regarded by its performers as very dangerous and is surrounded with tabus. It is performed by the craftsman who made the statue, after several hours of ceremonies to ensure that no evil will come to him. This evil, which is the object of all Sinhalese healing rituals, is imprecisely conceptualised, but results from making mistakes in ritual, violating tabus, or otherwise arousing the malevolent attention of a supernatural being, who usually conveys the evil by a gaze (*bälma*). The craftsman paints in the eyes at an auspicious moment and is left alone in the closed temple with only his colleagues, while everyone else stands clear even of the outer door. Moreover, the craftsman does not dare to look the statue in the face, but keeps his back to it and paints sideways or over his shoulder while looking into a mirror, which catches the gaze of the image he is bringing to life. As soon as the painting is done the craftsman himself has a dangerous gaze. He is led out blindfolded and the covering is only removed from his eyes when they will first fall upon something which he then symbolically destroys with a sword stroke. (Gombrich 1966: 24–5) [This could be an animal, such as a bull, but a pot, or a tree which exudes sap can be substituted.]

The detail of the mirror recalls the use of bronze mirrors by the Brahmin priests of Puri to 'bathe' the images by splashing water over their reflections. But the Puri Brahmins are unafraid to look at the images directly while painting in their eyes. Unlike the eyes of Jagganath, the eyes of the Buddha, when first opened, inflict death on the very person who performs the opening (a case of Artist-A ⟶ Artist-P; see above, Sect. 3.11). The craftsman must thereupon slay some creature in order not to die himself. This is very far from theologically Buddhist, and in olden times, the craftsman was dressed as a 'king' while performing the ceremony, that is to say, as the negation of a monk, a violent, worldly figure, who by sacrificing religious merit himself, allows others (monks, devotees) to achieve it.

Freedberg (1989: 95), commenting on Richard Gombrich in his magnificent treatise on the reception of religious and other types of images, raises a very basic question. Are images such as these powerful and efficacious (religiously) because of the ceremonies of consecration which have endowed them with significant, occult, characteristics, or is it because they are, first and foremost, images, linked by the power of *mimesis* to the deities they represent? Citing the support of Gadamer, he opts to assign primacy to representation. He argues that images work because they have intrinsic signifying-functions, which can be separated from the kind of efficacy possessed by religious objects (such as relics) which have not been shaped and formed by art into the semblance of persons, deities, etc. Such a point of view is necessary, and no doubt proper, for the art historian, who has to distinguish the 'power of images' from the power of mere unformed things, however sacred and sacrifying their origins. The anthropologist is in a slightly different position, however. The 'objects which resemble human beings' with which the anthropologist deals, prim-arily, are not portraits, effigies, idols, and so forth, but simply human beings themselves. Freedberg's emphasis on the centrality of artistic mimesis has, anthropologically, to be set in the context in which the 'representation' of a human being, or indeed a deity, is most commonly undertaken, not by any kind of effigy, but by a human actor playing a role. Churches may be stuffed with images of Christ, but the primary enactment of Christ in Christian worship is undertaken by the priest, who plays Christ and serves as Christ's image in performing the mass and uttering Christ's words. This is not to dismiss Freedberg's question, to which I will return in the next section, but before leaving the subject of consecration, it is interesting to compare the two con-secration sequences we have examined, with a third, in which the 'index' of the divinity is not a carved image at all, but a human being.

Kumaripuja, the worship of the goddess (primarily a form of Durga) in the form of a young virgin girl, is widely disseminated in India, and is a particular feature of the religious system of the Newars of the Kathmandu valley, where the cult has been the subject of a detailed study by Michael Allen (1976). There are some nine or ten living goddesses in the Newar region, of whom the most important is the one traditionally associated with the royal household. The virgin girl is a form of the fierce royal deity, Taleju, who herself is a form of Durga, the violent and erotic goddess in the Hindu pantheon, the slayer of the buffalo-demon who rides on a lion and brandishes a sword. Allen's analysis concentrates on the paradox whereby a virgin, premenstrual girl comes to represent so fear-some a divinity, but what concerns us is only the mechanics of her divinization.

Virgin-worship can, meanwhile, be distinguished from the more common type of divine (or demonic) possession which is found in India. Possession by the deity, in this form, is temporary and generally ecstatic; the medium goes into trance and becomes a 'horse' for the deity, making utterances in the person of the deity, and 'playing' for a while (dancing, swinging on a swing, etc.; cf. Gell 1978). There is no suggestion of ecstatic trance in the case of the *kumari*. This position is semi-permanent; once consecrated (at the age of 2 or 3), a *kumari* is and remains the goddess in person until the moment of deconsecration which transpires when certain 'negative signs' arrive—loss of milk teeth in theory, in practice, menstruation. The *kumari* comes from a particular caste, who are Buddhists, traditionally attached to the monasteries of Kathmandu which were disbanded by the present royal dynasty. She is, in caste terms, non-polluting but somewhat outside the Hindu hierarchical system. A candidate for *kumari*-hood must be old enough to walk and talk, of unblemished appearance, having lost no milk teeth, etc. Her horoscope must be auspicious, especially with regard to the king. Here is Allen's account of the circumstances of her installation, which occur at the end of Dasain (Dassara) the festival of Durga:

At nightfall eight buffaloes representing the demon are killed by having their throats slit so that the blood jets high towards the shrine that contains the Taleju icon. A few hours later at about midnight a further 54 buffaloes and 54 goats are killed in a similar manner. As may well be imagined, the small courtyard [of the Taleju temple] is by then awash with blood . . . At this point, usually about 1.00 A.M. the small Kumari-elect is brought to the entrance. She is supposed to walk by herself, in a clockwise direction around the raised edge until she reaches the bloody Taleju shrine. She must enter it, still maintaining a perfectly calm demeanour, and if all is well she is then taken upstairs to a small room for the installation ceremony . . . after the usual purificatory and other preliminary rites, the chief priest performs the main ceremony in which he removes from the girl's body all of her previous life's experience so that the spirit of Taleju may enter a perfectly pure being. The girl sits naked in front of the priest while he purifies each of her sensitive body areas in turn by reciting a mantra and by touching each area with a small bundle of such pure things as grass, tree bark and leaves. The six sensitive parts are her eyes, throat, breasts, navel, vagina and vulva. As he removes the impurities the girl is said to steadily become redder and redder as the spirit of the goddess enters into her.

At this stage the girl is dressed and made up with Kumari hairstyle, red *tika*, third eye, jewellery, etc., and then sits on her beautifully carved wooden throne on the seat of which the priest has painted the powerful *sri yantra mandala* of Taleju. She also holds the sword of Taleju and it is at this point that the final and complete transformation takes place. It is worth noting that though from now until her disqualification some years later she will be continuously regarded as Kumari, it is also believed that it is only when fully made up and sitting on her throne that identification is complete. At other times, especially when casually playing with friends, she is partly herself and partly Kumari.   (Allen 1976: 306–7)

To what extent can one detect a parallelism between the installation of the *kumari* as a 'living icon' of Taleju, and the installation rites of more conventional

FIG. 7.12/2. *Kumari* with painted
third eye. *Source*: Allen 1976

idols? As with each of our previous examples, the consecration of the *kumari*
proceeds in two phases, one focusing on her interior and the other focusing
on her exterior. The first phase consist of the 'emptying' of the *kumari*-elect
of her past life (i.e. her personhood, agency, as a mere human being), which
is objectified as the impurities removed from her orifices, eyes, throat, vulva,
etc. She becomes a 'hollow vessel' into which, through the extraction of all
previous contents, new contents may be drawn; that is, the spirit of the goddess Taleju. This phase, it seems to me, is the equivalent of the phase in the
consecration of the Jagganath images in which the Daitas hollow out a cavity
in the image and place therein a (foreign) life-substance. But after this has been
effected, the transformation, as Allen makes clear, is still not complete.

The second phase of consecration consists of 'wrapping' the *kumari* in the
dress of Taleju, and painting her, as well as providing her with the goddess's
primary attribute, her sword. Allen does not make much of the fact, but the
most striking visual symbol of *kumari*-hood, is actually the extra 'eye', the third
eye, which is painted on the middle of her forehead. Of course, the priests do
not have to paint in her pupils, as they would if she were a wooden idol—she
has very pretty eyes of her own. But they outline her existing eyes with exag-
gerated make-up, besides adding an enormous painted eye above them (see
Fig. 7.12/2). The parallel between the making-up of the *kumari* with an extra
eye and the painting-in of the eyes of conventional idols is surely rather striking. In more general terms it is clear that the dressing, painting, enthronement,
and provision of weapons correspond to the 'external' strategy of animation
which I discussed earlier. Besides which, the *kumari* is externally animated in
the usual way by the recitation of sacred words, and the metonymic effect of
being seated on a magical design of great power, the *sri yantra mandala*.

In short, there is little to differentiate the consecration of the *kumari* from
the consecration of any other idol, except that the *kumari* can walk, and talk,

and is in fact incarnate as a human being rather than a manufactured artefact. From the point of view of the anthropology of art, as outlined in this work, there is an insensible transition between 'works of art' in artefact form and human beings: in terms of the positions they may occupy in the networks of human social agency, they may be regarded as almost entirely equivalent.

7.13. *Conclusion: From the Individual to the Collective*

Thus I conclude this extended discussion of idolatry. I recognize, however, that the particular line I have taken has consistently resulted in the emphasis being placed on sociological, religious, and psychological agency at the expense of aesthetic and artistic agency. And I am left with Freedberg's pertinent objection: to travel too far down this road is to lose sight of art's specificity. While I hold that where each individual work of art (index) is concerned, anthropological analysis is always going to emphasize the relational context at the expense of artistic or aesthetic form, the network of agent/patient relations 'in the vicinity' of the work of art—the same does not apply when we come to consider artworks, not 'individually' but as *collectivities* of artworks. So far, each index that I have subjected to analysis has been regarded as a singular entity, embedded in a particular social context. However, artworks are never just singular entities; they are members of categories of artworks, and their significance is crucially affected by the relations which exist between them, as individuals, and other members of the same category of artworks, and the relationships that exist between this category and other categories of artworks within a stylistic whole—a culturally or historically specific art-production system.

Artworks, in other words, come in families, lineages, tribes, whole populations, just like people. They have relations with one another as well as with the people who create and circulate them as individual objects. They marry, so to speak, and beget offspring which bear the stamp of their antecedents. Artworks are manifestations of 'culture' as a collective phenomenon, they are, like people, enculturated beings. So far, none of the collective issues surrounding the work of art have been considered. In order to broach these issues, it is necessary to adopt a new register. Here, I can make amends for having written so many pages which may have seemed tangential to the study of works of art as normally understood. I shall, for a while, desist from the terminology of 'indexes' and abductions of agency, and suchlike, reverting to a more conventional vocabulary. Because there is one 'conventional' art-theoretical concept which even the most radical anthropologist of art cannot put to one side—the concept of style. Style, which is the harmonic principle which unites works of art into groups, into collectivities, corresponds to the anthropological theme of 'culture'. Culture is style, really, just as Fernandez suggested in a deservedly influential discussion (1973).

Each individual work of art is the projection of certain stylistic principles which form larger unities, just as each individual, in a kin-based society, is regarded as a projection, into the here and now, of principles of descent and alliance and exchange. The concept of style allows us, for the first time, to concentrate exclusively on works of art as such, and to discuss what may appear, indeed, to be their 'aesthetic' properties. So let me reassure those of my readers who are aesthetes and art-lovers (if I have any left after all the abuse I have showered on their heads)—you have reached the one chapter in this book you might possibly enjoy reading.

8

Style and Culture

8.1. *On the Concept of Style*

In this chapter, my aim is to formulate a concept of 'style' adapted to the requirements of the anthropology of visual art. In the anthropology-of-art context the concept of style is distinguishable from the concepts of style applicable in Western art history and aesthetics in that the 'units' of style are not (usually) individual artists, or schools of artists, or movements, but 'cultures' or 'societies'. Actually, the units of style are conventional ethnographic isolates as represented for study purposes by museum collections and published sources on material culture. Such ethnographic isolates are historically bounded as well as geographically bounded; usually the collections and documents belong to a particular period. Where studies of ethnographic art in museums are concerned, the period in question coincides mostly with the colonial era. The focus is primarily on 'traditional' art forms, though it hardly needs to be said that during the colonial period there were startling historical developments in the so-called 'traditional' societies of the colonial frontier, which affected their art production in diverse ways. The problem of tradition and innovation in ethnographic arts would constitute too much of a diversion to discuss at this stage; besides which the subject has already received detailed attention from numerous other researchers, most notably by N. Thomas. For the purposes of this chapter, it will be assumed that the units of style are 'cultures' and that we are dealing with 'traditional' art as conventionally understood, setting to one side the acknowledged problems which these assumptions admittedly raise.

The problems of historical contextualization do not materially affect what I have to say about style, since the description of a style may be as broad or as narrow in scope as necessary to accommodate any given historical perspective. The question that I want to address is not historical but conceptual: what does the concept of 'style' contribute to the understanding of material culture? 'Style' is a vague word of uncertain definition and many, rather disparate, uses. Finding a use for it in the context of the anthropology of material culture might be considered a waste of effort, were it not, in fact, so pervasive, at least as a mode of classification. As it is, we are routinely accustomed to classifying objects as sharing, or not sharing, stylistic attributes with one another. But exactly what is shared (or not shared) in such instances is much harder to assess. Moreover, we are inclined to believe that what objects with shared stylistic attributes have in common, is not just some formal, external, property, but something integral to their standing as expressions of 'the culture' in the wider sense; common stylistic attributes shared by artefacts are associated, via a basic scheme transfer, with shared 'cultural values' in a community.

I believe that the intuition that there is a linkage between the concept of style (as a configuration of stylistic attributes) and the concept of culture (as a configuration of intersubjective understandings) is well founded. But to convert this intuition into a series of explicit and defensible arguments is a distant goal, which can only be approached by incremental steps. One of the first of these steps is to clarify the notion of 'style' and to distinguish, from among the many possible interpretations that can be placed on this concept, the one we specifically need in the anthropological context. No anthropologist, to my knowledge, has attempted a critical analysis of the concept of 'style', and as yet, there is no distinctively anthropological style-concept as such. In this situation, the only possible procedure is to turn to the aesthetic and art-historical literature on 'style' so as to canvass the various possibilities.

A concept of style that we probably cannot make anthropological use of in its original form is the one advanced by Wollheim in his deservedly well-known discussion of style in pictorial art (1987). I mean no disrespect to Wollheim in saying so; it is merely my conviction that aesthetics and anthropology are very different enterprises. Even so, Wollheim's discussion is very useful because in excluding certain questions from the purview of stylistic analysis—because they do not coincide with his own interest in art—he succinctly adumbrates perspectives collateral to his own. He distinguishes, first of all, between 'general' (collective) and 'individual' style. He is interested in 'individual' style (as he suggests all aestheticians ought to be). On the other hand, art historians (and anthropologists) have more reason to take general or collective style as their theme. Within the category 'general' style he further distinguishes 'universal' style categories, such as the one which opposes 'representational' (realistic) style to 'geometric' style (non-realistic, abstract, etc.). Opposed to 'universal' style categories are the general or collective styles of periods, schools, and so on—these he calls 'historical' styles. The contrast between 'universal' styles and 'historical' (or cultural) styles is relevant to the anthropology of art. Certain anthropological/stylistic categories are 'universal' in this sense, that is, not confined to particular cultures or traditions, but manifesting themselves in disparate cultural contexts: and an instance of such a 'universal' stylistic trait is 'split representation' (Boas 1927; Lévi-Strauss 1963), which will be discussed at a later stage. Other anthropological/stylistic categories are historically specific, or culturally specific.

Wollheim contrasts his own view of 'individual' (painting) style, which he calls 'generative', to the view of style taken by art history which he calls 'taxonomic'. According to him, nothing is explained merely by constructing compendia of the stylistic attributes manifested in the work of a particular artist; this is mere classification or pigeon-holing. To be explanatory, a stylistic analysis must bring out those aspects of a painter's work which are especially *psychologically salient*. 'Style' is equated with psychological saliency, the capacity, possessed only by painters with a developed personal style, to so engage the spectator's attention that the aesthetically significant aspects of the work of art are the ones which actually do attract our notice. Picasso's style, so to speak, is Picasso's ability to cause us to notice his Picasso-ish artistic intentions. Style is personhood in aesthetic form, a 'precondition for aesthetic interest' (Wollheim 1987: 188). It is to be distinguished from mere 'signature'—those 'characteristics of an artist's work by reference to which we assign works to him' (ibid. 197). He argues that the traits which define a 'formed style' may be very abstract ones, of which we may not be immediately aware. And he adds the interesting observation that commonly we start to notice these subtle characteristics only once we know that a particular painting actually is by a certain named painter, and not by another artist who happened to paint rather similar works.

The 'generative' notion of style culminates in what Wollheim terms 'style-descriptions', which are descriptions of the stylistic features of the work (I think he means by this, 'all the mature work') of an artist, at a high level of abstraction, so that one can appreciate the basis upon which this work is psychologically salient. He contrasts such a style-description to a 'stylistic description' which is an account of the stylistic features of any given work of art, rather than of an artist.

Obviously, there is very little in Wollheim's programme for the production of style-descriptions of individually identifiable painters with 'formed' (distinctive) styles, that can be made use of in the anthropology of art. Of course, anthropologists can study particular artists and their output, but if they do so, they are essentially recapitulating the programme of Western aesthetic art criticism in some (relatively) exotic setting; they are not solving the stylistic problems posed by the existence of collections of 'ethnological' art and the associated cultural material, documents, etc. Here, I am assuming that what the art anthropologists deal with is unattributable, except to a particular culture, and that sorting out authorship is not the issue (but cf. Price 1989). On the other hand, there is something obviously exciting about Wollheim's argument that stylistic analysis should be 'explanatory' and 'at a high level of abstraction' rather than tamely 'taxonomic'. The trouble is that on Wollheim's argument, it would seem that unless one is dealing with artworks which manifest an individual style, the really interesting (i.e. non-taxonomic) questions cannot really be posed, let alone answered.

Is it feasible to rearrange Wollheim's programme so that 'generative' style analysis can be made applicable to 'general' or 'historical' (i.e. cultural) style, and not exclusively to individual style, as it seems to me he intends? I think this rather depends on the kind of material with which one is dealing. Wollheim is no doubt perfectly correct to believe that the important stylistic questions relating to Picasso, have to do with Picasso, not to his period, or to any of the 'group styles' with which he was (closely or distantly) affiliated at different phases of his career. And the same would apply to Michelangelo, or Ingres, or any of the masters of the Western art tradition who possessed highly individual styles and who were, and are, esteemed particularly on that basis. But this paradigm depends particularly on the social processes through which an artistic identity is achieved in the Western post-Renaissance art tradition, and cannot be applied to the kind of art I intend to discuss in this chapter.

Not only is the kind of art I am about to discuss defined with reference to collectivities and their histories, not individuals, but it is also 'traditional' in the sense that innovation was constrained within strict parameters of stylistic coherence. This is not to say that in these art-producing traditions innovation did not occur; it did so, continuously. But it was not associated with artistic identity, only with virtuosity. It is known that, for instance, individual tattoo artists among the Maori achieved great personal fame (and charged higher fees accordingly). They did so because their work instantiated, better than their competitors', what Maori collectively regarded as excellence in the matter of tattooing—not because their tattoos were appreciated as distinctive productions expressive of their artistic individuality. We may go to a dentist whom we consider to be a supreme and indeed original exponent of fillings, crownings, and bridgework. All the same, we do not prize his work because it expresses his individuality, but simply because it is the best of its kind available. It was the same with Maori tattoo artists, and artists in traditional art-production systems generally. Since in these systems there was no culturally recognized linkage between artistic excellence and the expression of artistic individuality, and since genres and motifs were subject to such stringent canons of stylistic coherence, it is much more appropriate to treat 'collectivities' rather than individuals as units of style, when dealing with this kind of material, than it would be in discussions of Western art. Besides which, there is little alternative, given the nature of the artworks and documentation at our disposal.

Even so, is it really possible to provide 'generative' (abstract, high-level) style descriptions for 'ethnological' art, or must we remain forever in the shallows of taxonomy, detecting the signatures of this or that local style? Can one achieve a style-description applicable to the art of a 'culture' which has the same kind of explanatory power that Wollheim claims for style-descriptions applicable to individual artists? One solution which immediately suggests itself is to treat cultures as analogous to individuals or persons, but on a different scale, so to speak. But this poses an immediate logical dilemma. 'Individuals' are defined contrastively with 'collectivities'. Picasso was a supreme individualist who expressed his individuality in his art. He stands out against the background of lesser artists lacking what Wollheim would recognize as 'formed' (personal) styles, whose artistic efforts lack this individualizing salience and are conse-quently of lesser art-historical importance. One cannot treat 'cultural' art styles as magnified versions of individual art styles because, being 'collective' styles, they correspond to the 'background' against which 'style' (individual style, that is) creates its individuating effect. The notion of 'individual style' impli-citly depends on the existence of collective, undifferentiated, period styles against which individuality emerges as 'figure' against 'ground'. One cannot treat collective styles as 'figural' in this sense, since there is no 'ground' to set them against. Nor can one compare a 'cultural' style against another style as if cultures were individuals, in the way that one compares, say, Picasso and Braque. Picasso and Braque stand out as possessors of distinctive styles against the same (twentieth-century Western) background, whereas there is no com-mon background against which one might compare, say, the art of the Fang and the Yolngu.

At the same time, it is hard to give up the idea that collective art styles have a kind of psychological saliency which is comparable to, though obviously not the same as, the psychological saliency of individual styles. In so far as cultural anthropologists operate with a concept of style, this is a psychological (cognit-ive) concept, rather than a taxonomic one, or at least they would like it to be. Some anthropologists are content to consider stylistic questions entirely within the taxonomic framework (i.e. identifying the provenance of museum speci-mens etc.) but most anthropologists associate 'style' with 'meaning' (Forge 1973). Anthropologists think of 'style' as the attributes of artworks which asso-ciate those artworks with other cultural parameters, such as religious belief, kinship values, political competition, etc. Since often the associations in ques-tion are communicated via the iconography of images (e.g. a carving is a carv-ing 'of' a totemic animal), anthropological notions of style are fatally entangled with semiotic questions, to the detriment of conceptual clarity. I will return to the misalliance between the anthropology of art and semiotics later. For the moment, let us assume that iconography is not the relevant issue, but style, that is, formal attributes of artworks. Can 'formal attributes of artworks' be associ-ated with other cultural parameters? If so, an 'anthropological' notion of style would focus on the psychological salience of artworks in directing attention towards cultural parameters. A 'cultural' style-description would be an abstract account of the attributes of artworks in the light of their capacity to thematize and make cognitively salient essential cultural parameters.

8.2. *Hanson on Style and Culture*

This kind of programme has been carried out by various anthropologists, though not necessarily under the heading of 'style' analysis ('style' in anthropological writing is often simply called 'aesthetics'). Very much a case in point is the article by Hanson (1983) in which he seeks 'homologous relations between artistic forms and other structures or patterns of culture' (Hanson 1983: 79). Hanson's article is devoted to Maori (traditional) art. First of all, he correctly makes the distinction alluded to above between iconography and style; though he speaks of 'aesthetic form' (following Archey 1965) rather than using the word 'style' itself. Most Maori art was not heavily invested with iconographic symbolism, he says (but cf. Neich 1996 and below, Sect. 9.6). On the other hand, this art was not 'meaningless' decoration because the formal characteristics of Maori art were such as to 'instantiate' underlying cultural patterns detectable elsewhere in other Maori institutions. His main substantive point with regard to the art is the presence therein of many types of symmetry, alternations, rotations, etc. (Hanson's article was published in the volume in which Washburn published her initial paper on symmetry analysis as a method in archaeological taxonomy, cf. Sects. 6.4–5, above.) Hanson associates the preoccupation with symmetry in Maori art with the Maori cultural emphasis on sequences of escalating reciprocal competitive exchange and/or warfare and revenge. The idea is that from the Maori point of view, the presence of complex and cognitively inaccessible types of symmetry in, say, rafter-patterns, resonated with the global, extra-artistic, pattern of Maori social life in which sequences of reciprocal action, at various levels and degrees of intensity, were pervasive. Moreover, just as reciprocity in social life was never 'perfect' but was always marginally unbalanced, giving rise to the onward momentum of competitive striving, so Maori bilateral symmetry is always marginally disturbed by contradictory elements of wilful asymmetry. This trickiness in the juxtaposition of symmetry-confirming and symmetry-disrupting elements coincided with the Maori cultural presupposition that 'nothing is what it seems' (Hanson 1983: 84).

Hanson's discussion is of great interest and is one of the most distinguished contributions to the literature of the anthropology of art. But there are certain obvious objections that can be raised to his argument. For instance, both 'bilateral symmetry' and 'slightly disturbed symmetry' are features, if you like, of a 'universal' style as much as of 'the Maori style'—that is to say, *any pattern whatsoever* manifests symmetry because that is what a 'pattern' is. 'Decorative art', by and large, consists of the application of patterns to the surfaces of things, and unless these patterns were in various ways symmetrical, they would not be recognizable as patterns. As it is, there exists what amounts to a 'universal aesthetic' of patterned surfaces; the same symmetry configurations, if not the same motifs, turn up all over the world, as Washburn has amply demonstrated in her more recent work (Washburn and Crowe 1992). So also does the technique of disrupting the symmetry of patterned surfaces with asymmetric elements. Besides which, asymmetries often arise semi-inadvertently because pattern-makers are concerned only to make their patterns 'roughly' symmetrical, not mathematically so. One cannot be sure therefore that Maori disrupted symmetry is an intentional disruption of symmetry or merely an unconcern with *exact* symmetry.

So it could be objected that Hanson's argument about the pervasiveness of bilateral symmetry in Maori art is just a tautologous consequence of his decision to look at 'formal' rather than iconographic aspects of the art. 'Formal' reduces to 'ornamental', 'ornamental' to 'patterned', and 'patterned' to 'symmetrical'. Meanwhile, is one to assume that each and every culture that produces ornamental (symmetrical, patterned) art has the same 'cultural pattern' of escalating and disrupted reciprocity, and so forth? The Taj Mahal is eminently bilaterally symmetrical, and slightly disrupted (by the inscriptions)—but nobody has seen fit to compare Maori meeting houses with the Taj Mahal, or to make inferences about reciprocity in Mughal India on the basis of this architectural preoccupation with symmetry (which extends to much other Mughal ornamental art).

I conclude from this rather fundamental difficulty that Hanson's project is somewhat premature. The formal properties Hanson identifies in Maori art are far too commonly observable in ornamental art of all kinds to serve the kind of culturally diacritic role he proposes for them. He says Maori art provides a kind of 'map' of Maori culture; but how could this be demonstrated satisfactorily if the distinctive features of this 'map' are arbitrary in relation to Maori culture specifically, as they must be, if they are also found in totally different cultures, such as Mughal India? The implication would seem to be that what connects Maori art to the rest of Maori culture is not 'formal' aesthetic or stylistic attributes such as symmetry, but the presence in the art of iconographic reference to Maori ancestors, divinities, etc.—precisely the position which Hanson set out to question in the first place.

All is not lost perhaps. Hanson concludes his essay by suggesting that the relationship between Maori artworks and the rest of Maori culture is one of 'synecdoche'; artworks are parts of culture which recapitulate the whole. It must be admitted that in the light of the objections just raised, Hanson has failed to demonstrate the existence of this synecdochic relationship between artworks as parts and cultures as wholes. Perhaps this is the result of excessive theoretical ambition; the attributes which (say) a rafter-pattern can possess, which can also be possessed by an entire culture, would inevitably be highly abstract ones. And for just this reason, it would be most unlikely that these very abstract properties, such as 'symmetry', would be *exclusively* found in the artworks of that culture, and that culture alone. The search for shared attributes between particular artworks and entire cultural systems is so grandiose that whatever is discovered is likely to prove factitious. The idea of 'synecdoche' is none the less intriguing, and seems to chime with our intuition that art styles and cultures are in some obscure way connected. Let us modify the proposed synecdochic relation so as to make the whole enterprise less ambitious. Is any given artwork, in a given style (personal or collective), related by synecdoche to *all* the artworks in that style? The answer to this is surely 'yes'—because we have unearthed one of the basic implications of the word 'style', namely, that style attributes enable individual artworks to be subsumed into the class of artworks which share these particular attributes. Consequently, any given artwork 'exemplifies' the stylistic canons of the tradition of material culture from which it originates; it 'stands for' this style. This does not immediately solve the problem of style and culture, but it suggests a solution which will be outlined later.

8.3. *Style and Cognitive Saliency*

The same considerations apply to Wollheim-type individual style-descriptions. An artwork which is being considered as exemplifying the individual style of an artist, for instance, Picasso, thematizes and makes salient Picasso's artistic intentions because it enables connections to be drawn, on the basis of style, between this particular Picasso and other Picasso artworks. Even if there were, in fact, only one Picasso in existence (*Guernica*), the same would be true, only in this case stylistic analysis would be confined to generalizing about the stylistic properties manifested in the different *parts* of this unique artwork—the horse, the bull, the various figures, and so on. Unless it were possible to find consistency in these part-to-part relationships in *Guernica*, the *whole* painting would be in no particular style, and would be 'indecipherable' (as Wollheim put it) as a result. Such is manifestly not the case. *Guernica* is stylistically decipherable and psychologically salient because part-to-part relationships within the painting cohere with the whole, and *Guernica* is an instance of 'Picasso's style' (rather than '*Guernica*'s style') because this painting is coherently related to other Picasso paintings, which are related to others still—so that ultimately all Picassos are intelligibly related to each. This is one of the reasons that we esteem Picasso so much; however much his manner transforms itself, he maintains a consistent stylistic identity, difficult though this is to pin down.

I hope it will be accepted, therefore, that the function of 'style' in associating individual artworks with the totality of artworks 'in the same style' is not confined to the 'taxonomic' domain, but is equally pertinent with respect to the use of 'style' as an explanatory concept with cognitive, as well as classificatory implications. It is unfortunately true that most discussions of 'style' focus on style in individual artworks (e.g. 'What do we mean by the "style" of *Guernica*, as opposed to the "content" or "significance"?', or, 'Is *Guernica* in the "cubist" style or not?'). I prefer to think of 'style' with reference not to individual artworks but in relation to the 'wholes' constituted by *all the works* in any given style. 'Style' is what enables any artwork to be referred to the whole(s), or 'larger unities' to which it belongs. However, this is not to capitulate to mere taxonomy, because, according to my argument, *the psychological saliency of artworks is a function of the stylistic relationship between any given artwork and other artworks in the same style.* Artworks do not do their cognitive work in isolation; they function because they co-operate synergically with one another, and the basis of their synergic action is style. This is the basis of the intuition we have that in some way stylistic affinity among works of art echoes the unity of thought which binds members of social groups together; style is to artworks what group-identification is to social agents. But this is at best a cloudy notion until we have arrived at a much clearer understanding as to exactly what 'stylistic affinity' means, particularly with reference to collective styles, such as the one observed by traditional Maori artists.

As we noted before, Hanson, in his over-ambitious attempt to find unifying patterns in Maori art and Maori socio-cultural practices, only looked for abstract properties such as 'pervasive bilateral symmetry' in the art. He does not consider the art in very much detail because such symmetries can be found in almost every artefact the Maori ever made, so it does not matter much which specific examples he chooses. Unfortunately, this unsystematic approach cannot exclude the possibility that the abstract stylistic features singled out are such as can be just as easily detected in *non*-Maori art, as is the case. How can this problem be overcome? Clearly, in order to provide a style-description for Maori art which would be applicable to no other art style, the art must be subjected to a much more detailed analysis than the mere detection of a variety of types of symmetry and/or asymmetry. Attention has to be paid to the stylistic attributes which actually tell us that a particular artwork is a Maori artwork; for example, the typical way in which the human hand is represented, the omnipresent 'fern-shoot' motif, and so on. In other words, a formal analysis of the art has to be undertaken, quite without reference to 'cultural patterns'. Once formal analysis produces a style-description which captures axes of coherence in the Maori artefacts which distinguish just those artefacts from any other culture's artefacts, then it might be feasible to attempt to align this specific style-description with the specifics of Maori culture. This Hanson cannot do, because he lacks the methodology to undertake such a formal analysis or to identify the source of the coherence of the Maori style in all its manifestations.

8.4. *Formal Analysis and the Linguistic Chimera*

'Formal analysis', alas, is not a fashionable procedure in the anthropology of art. The formal approach is doubly overshadowed in the age of interpretative anthropology, in that it is either associated with old-fashioned ethnology or with the excesses of 'ethnoscience'. The failure of 'structuralist' semiotic anthro-

pology in the 1970s has had a particularly pernicious impact on the status of
formal analysis in the anthropology of art. At that period, it was customary
to discuss systems of all kinds as 'languages'. Kinship was language-like, so was
cookery (Lévi-Strauss 1970), so was respect-behaviour (Goodenough 1956), and
so, necessarily, was art. Art was the (cultural) 'language of visual forms'. The
dominant position of the 'linguistic model' in cultural analysis in the ethnoscience period resulted in the application, to visual 'language' of the linguistic
method of decomposition into 'constituents' and the writing of constituent
'phrase-structure grammars', that is, sets of rules about how constituents could
be combined into 'well-formed strings', or acceptable 'utterances'. Each culture
was imagined to possess, not just a verbal language, but various non-verbal
languages, one of which was the language of (artistic) form, or 'visual-ese'.
The 'constituents' of visual-ese were forms, typically geometric forms such
as ovals, circles, lines, zigzags, and so on. The phrase-structure rules would,
for instance, tell one how to combine lines and zigzags so as to generate a
well-formed utterance of 'poisonous snake' in, for instance, Nuba visual-ese
(Faris 1971: 103). A great deal of effort was lavished on visual grammars of
this kind (Korn 1978) but it is fair to say that the results were not commen-
surate with the labour expended. As E. Gombrich remarked, in a review
of Faris's 'visual grammar' of Nuba body-painting, the end-product of this
type of analysis was only equivalent to a knitting-pattern, and no more productive of insight. Whatever formal analysis might be good for, providing
instructions as to how to re-synthesize 'well-formed utterances' in putative
'visual languages' is not one of them. Who wants to know how to do Nuba
body-painting by being given step-by-step instructions? Nobody but a Nuba—
besides which, the instructions provided in pseudo-linguistic form are inordinately complicated given the simplicity of the actual designs themselves; which
can be easily copied by the most untalented draughtsman by a simple process
of inspection and imitation.

   The linguistic model founders because there is no hierarchy of 'levels' in the
visual world corresponding to the multiplicity of levels in natural languages,
extending upwards from 'minimal constituents' (phonemes) to morphemes
(words) to syntactic structures (words in phrases and sentences, expressing
propositions). Lines, circles, ovals, zigzags, etc. are not 'visual phonemes' (vis-
emes). The notion of visual phonemes gained currency partly as a result of certain well-known statements made by artists, notably Cézanne (who was only
repeating the received wisdom of the art schools) that visual forms could all be
reduced to cubes, cones, cylinders, etc. The idea that forms can be assembled
from 'basic building blocks' definable in terms of plane or solid geometry is not
only ancient, but also practical, to the extent that this is often how artists actually do approach the task of drawing, and indeed, 'basic building blocks' of a
geometric kind may actually be implicated in the process of seeing, if Marr's
theory of vision is correct (Marr 1982). But none of this bears any relation to

the phoneme. Cubes, cylinders, cones, etc. stand for, or represent, *physical parts* of objects, reduced to their geometrical bare bones, whereas phonemes do not represent parts of what morphemes—combinations of phonemes—represent. Morphemes represent *concepts* within the linguistic code, but phonemes do not represent parts of these concepts.

Where geometric forms occur as graphic signs, they are meaningful in themselves (a circle can represent an eye) and where they occur as parts (components) of other graphic signs (a circle representing the iris of an eye, enclosed within an oval) they stand for parts of whatever the graphic sign as a whole represents (the iris as part of the eye). By contrast, the letter 'd' in dog, does not stand for part of a dog, and 'og' for the remainder of the dog. Any line which is included in a drawing of a dog, however, represents some *part* of a dog. The part–whole relationships between the lines entering into the composition of a graphic representation, and the representation as a whole are logically quite distinct from the part–whole relationship between the phonemes and morphemes. Consequently, the whole strategy of decomposing visual presentations into 'elements' or 'constituents' in the hope of writing 'visual grammars' is misconceived.

8.5. *Synecdoche: Axes of Coherence in Stylistic Unities*

The stylistic analysis of forms has to concern itself with visual forms as wholes, rather than with their geometrical constituents.[1] The aim of formal analysis, as I see it, is to provide a basis for the discussion of style. Style is a meaningless idea until it has been decided what the scope of the unit of style is, that is to say, the works of an individual artist, a culture/period, etc. as discussed previously.

In the present chapter, the 'larger unity' which will be analysed is the *corpus* of Marquesan artefacts, in particular the corpus available to Karl von den Steinen, who published a lavishly illustrated three-volume treatise on Marquesan material culture in 1925–8, having visited the islands himself in 1898 in order to make his own collections, document them ethnographically, and record the tattoo designs which will be discussed below. The aim of formal stylistic analysis is to show how each particular item in the corpus is connected to the corpus as a whole. In order to do this, there is no need to make any use at all of any linguistic analogy.

---

[1] To the extent that there is any mileage at all in the idea of 'visual syntax' it concerns principles of arrangement or composition, such as those which are manifested in the layout of Yolngu bark-painting, as described and analysed by Morphy (1991, 1992). This particular approach will not be pursued here, however.

However, there is a sense in which formal analysis is intrinsically semiotic, if not linguistic. This is the sense in which any part 'stands for' the whole of which it is a part (synecdoche; cf. above). Any example of Marquesan art is, to a greater or lesser extent, representative of the corpus to which it can be referred, and does indeed represent it. 'Representing' in this sense is clearly a semiotic relation, in which the object is a sign, and the corpus of stylistically related objects from which it is drawn, is what is signified thereby. This kind of 'synecdoche' is not very semantically informative, since every work in the corpus signifies almost exactly the same thing, namely all the other ones except itself.

However, synecdoche does suggest another useful metaphor for thinking about style. There is a kind of image known as a hologram (made by photographing the interference fringes reflected off objects illuminated by a coherent laser light-source) which has the curious property that any part of a holographic image contains an attenuated version of the information contained in the hologram as a totality. From, say, the bottom left-hand corner of a hologram, it is possible to reconstitute (by shining laser light onto the etched holographic plate) the image of the original object, though rather blurred. Style in art is like this in the sense that from one item in the corpus (or a selection of them) it is possible to reconstruct the others to at least some degree. Of course, one does not know which features of a given object are the stylistically significant or informative ones except with reference to the corpus as a whole, so the analogy is inexact. Each object, seen in the light of all the others in its corpus, appears as a microcosm of the corpus because our perception of it is informed by our knowledge of the macrocosm of which it is a fragment.

The position is akin to that of the palaeontologist, who has to reconstruct an extinct species on the basis of a single bone, as Baron Cuvier was famously able to do. Cuvier could reconstruct an entire animal on the basis of say, a single femur, because he was familiar, not just with the relationship between the femur and adjacent bones in the skeleton, but with the 'relations between relations' in the skeletal architecture of the vertebrate genus under consideration. He could, so to speak, see a femur as a transformed version of the femur of animals whose morphology was known, and by applying the same consistent series of transformations seen in the isolated femur to all the other bones of the extinct animal's skeleton, he could reconstruct its form. He could, in other words, infer the 'style' of the femur by comparison with the femurs of related species, and he could apply this 'style transformation' to the missing bones of the rest of the skeleton. The relation between the single bone and the skeleton is 'holographic' not because the isolated bone outwardly resembles in form the other, missing ones, but because the comparison of related forms suggests a transformational rule for 'generating' missing bones from known ones.

Rather than think of formal analysis as an adjunct to semiotics, it is more helpful to imagine it as 'morphology' applied to visual objects. The aim is to derive, by the comparison of related forms, a series of transformations through which given artworks or artefacts can be converted into other ones. The aim is not, of course, to apply these transformations so as to 'produce' new (hypothetical) artworks in the way a maker of forgeries does. The making of forgeries requires no intellectual elaboration of stylistic theory, being a quite intuitive process. The purpose of formal analysis is to identify *axes of coherence* within the corpus of works brought together for the purpose of stylistic analysis. Once these axes of stylistic coherence have been identified, it then becomes possible to understand the cognitive significance of a 'cultural' style in rendering features of the culture cognitively salient.

In a sense, cognitive sensitivity to 'axes of coherence' and the application of transformational rules is built into the process of seeing itself. Any familiar object, such as a pair of scissors, is intrinsically capable of casting infinitely many highly dissimilar images on the retina, which the brain has to interpret. Looked at end-on, from the handle end, a pair of scissors may appear as a flat bar of metal, curiously shaded in the middle, resembling the 'canonical' picture we have of scissors in no obvious respect (i.e. the picture of scissors we might insert in an illustrated dictionary). But our visual system, according to Gibson (1986: 73–5), is tuned to detecting solid objects because they map onto other available views of the same object that can be obtained by shifting the point of observation. An object of complicated contours is seen as 'structurally invariant under transformation'. In the same way, style analysis looks for the 'structural invariants under transformation' which define objects of a higher hierarchical order than the isolated object, such as a pair of scissors. Thus, 'all the works of Rembrandt' could be considered, not a collection of separate objects, but just *one* object with many parts distributed in many different places. A single object which is a set of subordinate objects is not hard to imagine; a twelve-piece dinner set is one such object, a chess-set another. If we take Rembrandt's 'complete works' as such a multiple, or 'distributed' object, then it will be seen that the process of determining Rembrandt's 'style' is precisely the same as the process of determining the 'invariants under transformation' of a Gibsonian object, such as a pair of scissors. What is 'invariant under transformation' is what links any one Rembrandt work to all the others, but unless we can see what these invariants of structure are, we are not seeing this, particular Rembrandt, 'as a Rembrandt', that is, as a component of an *œuvre*. 'Educated perception' of a Rembrandt amounts to nothing else. Stylistic perception, I argue, is the perceptual mode with which we deal with multiple or distributed objects of this kind. As such, stylistic theory is just an extension of the theory of perception itself. However, it is a very specialized task to conceptualize what the 'invariants under transformation' in Rembrandt's works are, and I do not propose to undertake it—though I believe that this would amount to a Wollheim-type 'style-description'. It is much easier to operationalize this notion of stylistic coherence with respect to Marquesan art, because, as I will shortly demonstrate, Marquesan art is particularly susceptible to analysis in terms of visually salient morphological transformations. Rembrandt's style is hidden in the subtleties of his handling, whereas Marquesan style—or such of it as we now have access to—can be disinterred with paper and pencil.

8.6. *The Marquesan Corpus*

The artefacts in the Marquesan corpus assembled by Steinen (1925) are particularly suited to morphological study, because they form a very coherent set. The corpus consists of a number of categories of artefacts, of which the most important are (i) tattooing motifs, (ii) similar decoration on artefacts such as flutes, (iii) incised work on the flat, that is, carving in very low relief, and (iv) three-dimensional carving, some of it monumental but much of it on a small, and even miniature scale. Of these categories, tattooing motifs are certainly the most important and best documented, though during the early period of European contact (from the late eighteenth to the middle of the nineteenth century) the Marquesans were prolific producers and consumers of artefacts of all kinds. Marquesan society was orientated towards magnificence and display to a greater extent than any other Polynesian society, with the possible exception of the Maori of New Zealand (see Gell 1993; Thomas 1990). I will say more about the social, political, and ideological characteristics of Marquesan society at a later stage. For the present I am concerned only with strictly formal aspects of Marquesan art, and it is sufficient to note only that almost all Marquesan art was attached to the human body (e.g. tattooing, adornment). Moreover, the art that was not intrinsically part of the human body (e.g. weapons, canoes, furnishings of houses, etc.) was conceptually treated as if it were. Thus, a chief's canoe was part of his body, had a personal name which was one of his own set of names, if injury was done to it, injury was done to him, and so on. Consequently, it is reasonable to commence the study of Marquesan art, as Steinen did, by considering tattoo art, in that this art really sets the pattern for all the others.[2]

The following analysis owes much more to Steinen than the data it uses. Steinen does not cite the art-historical literature of motif-analysis of his period, the work of Riegel, Goodyear, and Wickhoff, which has been excavated for us by Gombrich (1984: 180–200), but he probably knew of it, since these works were well known to art experts of Steinen's generation. Steinen's theoretical

---

[2] Of course, treating body-art as primary, and such arts as carving and engraving as secondary, is an eccentric procedure from the standpoint of Western art theory, which concerns itself primarily with paintings and sculptures viewed as independent aesthetic entities rather than as the mere appurtenances of living beings and social agents. Tattooing in the West is a very second-rate form of art, but in the Marquesan context this was not so.

framework (like Riegel's) is evolutionary; he is concerned to chart the history of motifs from relatively 'realistic' versions documented in the earliest images of Marquesan tattooing (especially from Langsdorff's publication of 1804 (1813–14)) to the very much more abstract versions he himself documented in the 1890s. But evolutionary and comparative speculation hardly predominates; he also devotes a great deal of attention to synchronic variation in motifs, and particularly what one can only describe as derivational or transformational relationships between motifs and forms. These he elucidates in a series of analytical figures which are frequently both ingenious and revelatory. Steinen, who made all his own illustrations, was a graphic artist of remarkable ability, and his three-volume work on the Marquesas is arguably the most aesthetically accomplished work ever to have been published in the discipline of anthropology (the design and layout of the edition is a bibliophile's dream). I hope that the following pages, which, I emphasize, rely very extensively on Steinen's original work, will encourage wider appreciation of his contribution. He was, I think, a forerunner of structuralism in the domain of material culture, like his compatriot Goethe in the domain of plant morphology. The comparison is apt, in the sense that just as Goethe imagined that all plants could be seen as modified versions of an '*Ur*-plant' (anticipating an important element in evolutionary thought) so Steinen sees Marquesan motifs and artefacts as transformations of a series of *Ur*-motifs, the *etua* (godling), the 'face' motif, the 'chiroid' (half-oval), the 'woven' motif, and so on. Each of these can be transformed into the others, as he demonstrates. Steinen's preoccupation with the 'derivation' or 'etymology' of motifs is embedded in his nineteenth-century evolutionary (devolutionary) mind-set, and to this extent I shall not follow him. On the contrary, I would argue that the motivic transformations and derivations he demonstrates cannot be placed in an evolutionary framework, since the data lack sufficient time-depth; all the reliable visual documentation of tattooing comes from the twenty years spanning the turn of the present century, while early representations of Marquesan tattooing, including Langsdorff's, are of questionable accuracy. Even the carved artefacts Steinen discusses are almost entirely of (probable) nineteenth-century date. I hope to show that the stylistic features of Marquesan art are best explained in terms of synchronic ideological and cultural forces that Steinen tended to overlook, because of his evolutionary preoccupations.

In whatever way the transformational or derivational relationships in Marquesan art are to be explained, the first necessity is to demonstrate their existence, and here I follow in Steinen's footsteps.

The Marquesan art style is an assemblage of artistic practices demonstrating a coherence which is visually immediately apparent, but which only careful motif-analysis can fully reveal. For the purposes of this analysis 'relationships' between motifs are expressed by procedures which permit one to turn any given motif (or form) into another motif (or form) found in the corpus. By contrast to the motif-analyses of 1970s ethnoscience or 'visual language' analyses, the aim is not to 'generate' motifs from their elements, but to proceed, via specified steps, from one motif to another; that is, the analysis presupposes only one level, that of the motif (or form). Motifs are recognizable both because they recur in identical form repeatedly in the corpus (as well as modified forms) and because they have documented motif-names, some of which are culturally revealing, though by no means all of them. I will not discuss the implications of motif-names at this stage, but I will use the Marquesan names to identify motifs as a matter of convenience.

The types of procedures for transforming one motif in the Marquesan corpus into another motif can be briefly enumerated at this stage. They are:

   (i)   rigid motions in the plane (plane transformations: translation, rotation, reflection, glide reflection; cf. Washburn and Crowe 1988);
   (ii) coordinate transformations (modelled on those of D'Arcy Thompson (1961: ch. 9 (1917)), i.e. changes in the proportions of motifs;
   (iii) hierarchization/decomposition (one motif becomes a component of another motif, or a component of a motif becomes a motif);
   (iv) transformations of dimensionality, i.e. a two-dimensional motif is transformed into a three-dimensional motif and vice versa.

These procedures can be applied both to motifs as a whole, or to parts of motifs. Thus, in order to transform a motif into another motif it can be split apart, and just part of it may be subjected to a motion in the plane, or a change in relative proportions etc.

The outcome of the analysis of forms along these lines is the creation of a network of transformational relationships among motifs. This network of relations has no centre in that there is no one motif which can be regarded as the apical ancestor from which all the rest are derivative. Theoretically, all the relations described in this network are symmetrical; if motif A can be derived from motif B, then motif B can be derived from A, there being no imputation of evolutionary priority either way. However, the analysis has to begin somewhere, and it is certainly convenient to commence with a motif which has as much visual saliency as possible. Steinen's discussion of tattoo motifs is divided into three sections; I. 'Plectogene Muster'—patterns which relate to plaiting, matting, basketry, etc.; II. 'Tikigene Muster'—patterns which contain images of the human body; and III. 'Gesichtsmotiv'—motifs which show or are derived from the face. I will leave 'Plectogene Muster' aside for the moment and will concentrate on II and III, which comprise the most complicated and visually interesting motifs. Of these two, it is von den Steinen's 'Tikigene Muster' which provide the most natural point of departure. As I noted earlier, Marquesan art was either placed directly on the human person, or on artefacts which were treated as persons. The 'Tikigene Muster' are motifs which essentially reduplicate the person by appending additional, subsidiary 'persons' to it in graphic form (cf. above on fractal personhood, 7.10–11).

The motif with which to commence therefore is *etua*, the generic word for any kind of godling.

8.7. *The Table of* Etua *Motifs*

FIG. 8.7/1. *Etua*: the classificatory scheme of the dominant Marquesan motif *etua* developed by Karl von den Steinen

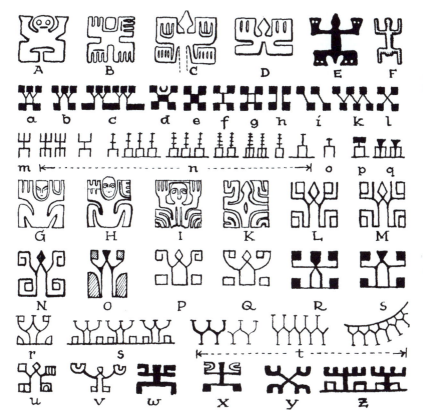

For stylistic relations between *etua* motifs in this table and other Marquesan motifs see Fig. 8.7/2 for the transformation of *etua* A to *etua* G; Fig. 8.7/3 for *etuas* L, M, and N; Fig. 8.8/1 for *etua* O and *hope vehine* motifs; Fig. 8.9/5 for *etua* N and *kea* motifs; Fig. 8.10/1 for *etua* r and the *mata hoata* motif; Fig. 8.12/3 for *etua* t and the *aniatiu* pattern. *Source*: Von den Steinen, i. 153, illus. 100

Steinen's method of motif analysis is displayed in his table of *etua* motifs which I reproduce in Fig. 8.7/1. I shall use this table as a point of departure for exploring the entire range of Marquesan motifs. In this table Steinen distinguishes seven types of *etua* motifs (in rows) which he groups into two main classes; 'standing' *etua* and 'sitting' *etua*. No iconographic significance should be attached to this distinction, which is entirely conventional. A 'standing' *etua* is one whose lower limbs form a convex curve relative to the body vertical, a 'sitting' *etua* is one whose lower limbs form a concave curve relative to the body vertical: see Fig. 8.7/2. This fig. contrasts A and G on the table of *etua*.

FIG. 8.7/2. Plane rotation in the formation of Steinen's two classes of *etua*

As will be seen from Fig. 8.7/2, the 'standing/sitting' contrast in *etua* motifs can be produced by a rigid motion in the plane affecting each of the lower limbs of the *etua*, namely, a rotation through 90 degrees. This is a typical instance of the 'visual logic' of Marquesan art, and is the first of many examples of a similar kind that I will discuss.

As inspection of the table of *etua* shows, types of standing or sitting *etua* show a high degree of variability. The uppermost row are examples taken from relief carving (on stone, bone, or in the case of E an *etua* silhouette in tortoise-shell). The next two rows of standing *etua* are very reduced forms, found in tattooing or in engraving on bamboo (whose motif repertoire is identical to tattooing). I will deal with these reduced forms later, since, as will be seen, they merge into Steinen's other major category of Plectogene Muster, 'plaited or woven' motifs. It is on the 'sitting *etua*' in the fourth and fifth rows that initially I shall concentrate, especially L, M, N, and O. L is a linear version of G, used as a tattoo motif, and M is its counterpart, produced by subjecting the 'hands' to reflection in the vertical plane (or alternately, exchanging the left for the right hand and vice versa). To produce the 'squared-off spiral' arm form of N, another reflection (in the horizontal plane) is all that is necessary (Fig. 8.7/3). The 'legs' of N are produced by subjecting the 'arms' so produced, to a reflection in the horizontal plane and a rotation of 90 degrees anticlock-wise—this leg-form can also be seen as a reflected, modified version of the basic 'sitting' leg-form seen in G, the starting-point.

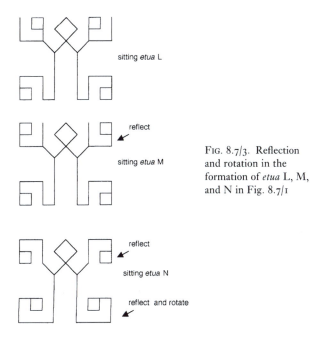

sitting *etua* L

reflect

sitting *etua* M

reflect

sitting *etua* N

reflect and rotate

Fig. 8.7/3. Reflection and rotation in the formation of *etua* L, M, and N in Fig. 8.7/1

A slightly different leg-form is seen in O, which is otherwise a close relative of N. This leg-form is the same as G but minus the nick at the base indicating the boundary between the thigh and calf of the leg in the squatting position. This line, duplicated, produces the concertina-like leg-forms of I and K, which lead towards other motifs I will mention later. But the leg-form of O (which is 1/4 of an ellipse) eliminates this line and can be treated as the origin of a very large class of semicircular and paraboloidal motifs.

Motif O, in male tattooing, is anthropomorphic, since, like L, M, and N it is a form of *Kena*, a mythological hero connected with tattooing, who is shown as a sitting *etua*. But according to Steinen's information, the identical *etua* form in female tattooing is named *Kea*, which he identifies as referring to the tortoise. These details of nomenclature would be beside the point in a formal analysis such as this but for one thing. All members of the tortoise/turtle family were considered sacred and divine by the Marquesans, so there is nothing surprising about species of *testudo* appearing as sacred *etua* in tattoo motifs. The point to note though, is that the canonical view of a tortoise is in the horizontal plane, parallel with the earth, whereas the canonical view of a sitting *etua* is vertical relative to the plane of the earth. So there is another kind of 'geometric' transformation here dependent on whether the image is viewed as a section or a plan: a sitting *etua* becomes, when the implied orientation of the observer and the *etua* are shifted from the vertical to the horizontal, a

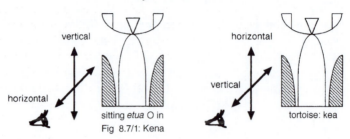

FIG. 8.7/4. Geometric orientation affecting the change of motifs: from *etua* to the female tattooing tortoise motif *kea*

tortoise-divinity viewed from above, without any actual change in the morphology of the motif whatsoever (Fig. 8.7/4). The horizontal (tortoise) form of the sitting *etua* is highly productive of further motifs (other forms of *kea* and *kake* which I will discuss in due course).

8.8. *From* Hope Vehine *to* Vai O Kena

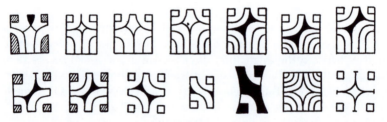

FIG. 8.8/1. *Etua* O in Fig. 8.7/1 sliding by degrees to become the *hope vehine* class of motifs. *Source*: Von den Steinen, i. 163, illus. 111

Taking O as the starting-point, I shall next consider a very prominent motif which goes under the name of *hope vehine* (literally 'buttocks-women', which I believe refers to back-to-back siamese-twin female divinities; cf. Gell 1993: 193). This motif can be derived in a number of ways, but most readily from a form of *etua* such as O or 'r' in the next row in Fig. 8.7/1. In a separate figure, Steinen shows the derivation of *hope vehine* very perspicuously by the comparison of a series of related forms, taken from tattooing (Fig. 8.8/1). This figure shows the sitting *etua* sliding, by degrees, into the form of diametrically opposed quarter-ovals which is distinctive of *hope vehine* via a reduction of one 'leg' of the *etua*, and a compensating transformation of the 'arm' on the opposite side into a quarter-oval form (cf. row 1, ii, iv, v, and row 2, ii, iii, which are standard *hope vehine* motifs). These smooth transitions indicate an evolutionary pathway, but, as I noted earlier, I am not so interested in evolutionary relationships as in transformations which can be carried out on one figure so as to convert it directly into another, without intermediary steps. Consequently, from my point of view, it is more useful to think of the relation between the sitting *etua* and *hope vehine* as shown on Fig. 8.8/2. In this figure, it is shown that the *etua* can be transformed into *hope vehine* by splitting an *etua* of the form seen in Fig. 8.8/1 vertically, and rotating one half of it through 180 degrees before rejoining the two halves. This produces a *hope vehine*-like Fig. 8.8/1, row 2, ii.[3]

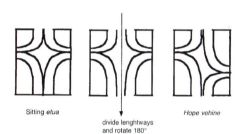

Sitting *etua*

divide lenghtways
and rotate 180°
before rejoining

Hope vehine

FIG. 8.8/2. From sitting *etua* (Fig. 8.8/1, row 1, no. iii) to *hope vehine* (row 2, ii)

Hope vehine, in turn, can be subjected to transformation so as to produce further motifs. The first of these I shall consider is the one known as *vai o Kena*, the bath of Kena, the tattooing hero mentioned earlier, whose mythology I have discussed at length elsewhere (Gell 1993: 186–8). There are three documented forms of this motif, each of which is derived from *hope vehine* in a slightly different way. The most elementary form of *vai o Kena* consists of no more than a *hope vehine* and its reflection. A different, more complex, form of *vai o Kena* is produced as shown in Fig. 8.8/3. In this figure, a *hope vehine* is subjected to reflection and translation so as to form a reflected duplicate adjacent to the original, to which it is joined. The next step is to 'stretch' each of these *hope vehine* motifs horizontally so that they overlap in the middle and partially occlude each other. This produces a form of standing *etua* motif, in which the opposed quarter-ovals of the double *hope vehine* become 'arms' and the conjoined quarter-ovals become 'legs'. The merging between this and the *etua* motif is completed by the addition of vestigial 'head' and body elements.

---

[3] Readers of this who happen to be familiar with the type of cutting, inverting, and pasting operations to which Lévi-Strauss subjects myths in order to demonstrate the affinities between myths which do not, on the surface, appear to be at all similar, will appreciate the significance of this type of procedure.

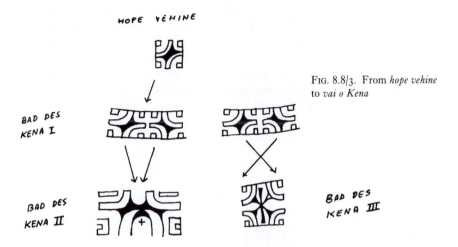

HOPE VEHINE

BAD DES KENA I

BAD DES KENA II

BAD DES KENA III

FIG. 8.8/3. From *hope vehine* to *vai o Kena*

The most complex version of *vai o Kena* is also based on *hope vehine* (Fig. 8.8/3, III). To produce this *vai o Kena* the *hope vehine* motif is first of all duplicated and rotated 90 degrees. The resulting superimposed *hope vehine* motifs are then drawn apart so as to produce a square motif four times larger, in which each quarter-oval occupies one corner. Between these quarter-ovals, the original black concave lens shape seen in *hope vehine* (now duplicated) appears as a black X joining them diagonally. Finally, the small square forms on the top and the bottom of *hope vehine*, not included within the quarter-ovals, are extended down to become the central axis of the motif, representing Kena in his bath.

8.9. *From* Hope Vehine *to* Kake/Kea

FIG. 8.9/1. Coordinate transformation of a *hope vehine* motif resulting in *kake* (type I) from Willowdean Handy. *Source*: Willowdean Handy, plate XXVI

Next, I shall turn to the second category of motifs which can be derived from *hope vehine*, the *kake* ('climbing') motifs, which merge into *kea*, and are sometimes known by that name. The *kake* motif is a stretched and twisted *hope vehine* (Fig. 8.9/1), an instance of 'coordinate transformation' in the manner of D'Arcy Thompson, rather than symmetry transformations à la Washburn of the type we have been considering hitherto—though some 'stretching' was involved in the *hope vehine* ⟶ *vai o Kena* example I discussed a moment ago.

In the case of *kake* motifs, the coordinates are much more distorted though. The *kake* shown in Fig. 8.9/2 (from Willowdean Handy, plate XXVI) consists of duplicated *hope vehine*, one of which is translated and joined to the first. However, the symmetry of the two *hope vehine* is disguised by changes in relative proportions; the top left and bottom right isolated quarter-ovals are reduced, while the two quarter-ovals which join up are expanded (Fig. 8.9/2).

FIG. 8.9/2. *Kake* from *hope vehine*: duplication, rotation, and reflection. After Willowdean Handy, plate XXVI

Then the entire figure so formed is stretched and bent so that the smaller quarter-ovals become the head/tail of a 'podoid' or 'footed creature' in Steinen's terminology. Steinen also has a different form of *kake*, which is derived directly from a sitting *etua*, rather than from *hope vehine* (Fig. 8.9/3). To produce a Steinen type II *kake*, a sitting *etua* like O in the table of *etua* is duplicated, and the duplicate is joined to the original after 180 degrees rotation, producing a different kind of 'podoid'. This is then stretched and twisted, as with the type I *kake*, Fig. 8.9/1, to produce the characteristically bent *kake* motif. There is a subtle difference in symmetry between type I and type II *kake* motifs, even when they appear to be double-headed *hope vehine* motifs, depending on whether the duplicate has been rotated (as in type II) or not, type I (Steinen, iii. 162, illus. 110, vs. Handy, pl. XXVI). *Kake* can be, and commonly are, drawn in pairs, one rotated 180 degrees relative to the other, so as to fill a rectangular space.

FIG. 8.9/3. Coordinate transformation with rotation: from sitting *etua* to *kake* (type II) from Steinen. *Source*: Von den Steinen, i. 162, illus. 110 (above); i. 164, illus. 114 (below)

Finally, before leaving *kake*, I may mention a unique design recorded by Handy (Fig. 8.9/4; Handy, pl. xv) which is the 'girdle' tattooed above the buttocks and over the sacral area of a female chief. Steinen recorded nothing like it but that may be because as a male ethnographer, he was not in a position to persuade this particular female chief to reveal her tattoo. The large motifs to the left and right are (single-headed) *kake* (Handy herself writes 'ka'ake', which I think is mistaken). Such large 'loin arches' were a feature of many Polynesian tattooing traditions (e.g. the Society Islands; see Gell 1993). What is stylistically interesting though is that here we have an instance of hierarchization, which I have hitherto not had any occasion to mention. All the designs I have discussed so far are quite small, but here we see a double pair of (mirror-image) *kake* (four in all) as major compositional elements, subsuming many subsidiary 'reduced' *etua* figures (*Pohu* and *fanaua* to be precise). Furthermore, the whole assemblage may be read as a 'face' motif on a very large scale, though I shall return to this possibility later, when I have dealt with the *etua* ⟶ 'face/eye' motif transition. Further instances of the inclusion of motifs within other motifs will crop up again, but this is a striking example.

FIG. 8.9/4. The chiefess's girdle with type III *kake*. See Section 8.11 below for face motifs. *Source*: Willowdean Handy, plate xv

It will have been noted that the heads of the 'podoids' in Fig. 8.9/4, resemble neither our type I or type II *kake* very closely. They resemble, in fact are identical to, the small *etua* immediately adjacent to them, which are instances of the *etua* motif *Pohu* (a mythological hero) here depicted with particularly large hands (or forefeet) which these *kake* also have. They are similar in this respect to another category of elongated, but not twisted 'podoids' categorized,

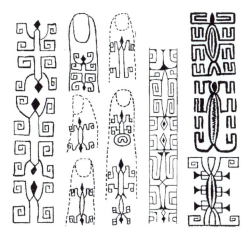

FIG. 8.9/5. *Kea* (tortoise) female tattoo motifs recorded by Steinen. *Source*: Von den Steinen, ii. 205, illus. 206

once again, as *kea* (testudinates). These are podoids which are produced by setting *etua* motifs end to end in opposed pairs (i.e. one rotated 90 degrees; see Fig. 8.9/5). Such *kea* are especially common in hand tattoos from which these examples are drawn (Steinen, i. 166, illus. 119). A large selection are found as decoration applied to a soup-bowl (terrine) which is itself the shape of a tortoise, where they are arrayed like the plates on a tortoise's shell—a tortoise of tortoises: Fig. 8.9/6. In these *kea*, the eight legs may be turned into squared-off meanders, rather than the spirals seen in the original *etua* motifs (i.e. N on row 5 of the table of *etua*, Fig. 8.7/1).[4] In so far as these 'tortoise' motifs cre-

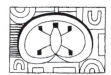

FIG. 8.9/6, *above*. A tortoise of tortoises: *kea* motifs on tortoise-shaped terrine. *Source*: Von den Steinen, ii. 205, illus. 206

FIG. 8.9/7, *left*. 'Realistic' *kea* tortoise tattoo recorded by Langsdorff in 1804. *Source*: Von den Steinen, i. 191, illus. 148b

[4] An interesting question is raised by the fact that these double-*etua* 'tortoise' motifs are alternatively known as *moko*, i.e. 'lizards' which they do indeed much more resemble by virtue of their crooked limbs and elongated body shape. One of the unsolved mysteries of the literature on Polynesian tattooing is

ated from *etua* set end to end have 'shells', these are represented by the second
and third sets of 'legs' of the resulting eight-legged creature.

In 1804 Langsdorff published an engraving of a youth with a relatively 'realistic' tortoise tattooed on his elbow; in this version of the tortoise motif, the
carapace is drawn as an oval, and the tortoise itself as an *etua* contained within
this oval (Fig. 8.9/7). If we compare this with the form *kea* (tortoise) as
recorded by Steinen in the 1890s the carapace has disappeared, and we have
only a row of *etua* motifs. But perhaps not entirely, because the way in which
the legs of *kea* are drawn (large quarter-ovals) suggests that the 'carapace' of
the original tortoise motif has been divided into quarters and redistributed as
'legs' for the *etua*—in fact, adjacent *etua* share a half-shell between them.

8.10. *From the* Etua *to the Face Motif (*Mata Hoata*)*

The next transformation of the *etua* motif to be considered is perhaps the most
fundamental one of all to the integrity of the Marquesan style. This is the
transformation of the sitting *etua* into the 'eye' or 'face' motif, *mata hoata*. The
face motif is produced by hierarchization or hypostasization of the *etua* motif,
with which it is morphologically speaking more or less identical. The derivation
is most perspicuously seen in a version of *mata hoata* ('shining eyes') featuring
on the leg tattoo of 'Frau Badora' (Fig. 8.10/1). Badora's *mata hoata* features
a particularly explicit *etua* (identical to *pohu* = 'r' on Fig. 8.7/1) forming the
'nose' element above which are to be seen the large half-ovals forming the
prominent eyes of this face design. Placed thus in conjunction, it becomes particularly apparent that the *mata hoata* design is identical to the *etua* (*pohu*)
design, of which it is a scaled-up version. The outstretched arms of the *etua* motif
become transformed into the deep curve under the eyes, the 'hands' of the *etua*
become the irises, and the head of the *etua* becomes the bridge of the nose. More
usually, the 'nose' of *mata hoata* is a transformed version of *pohu* which is not
so legible. Fig. 8.10/2 shows some more standard forms of *mata hoata* from
male tattoos recorded by Steinen. To produce this type of nose, the 'arms' of
small *etua* are reflected horizontally so that they form opposed half-ovals, and
the head is eliminated. Thus a shape more reminiscent of nostrils is produced.
However, *mata hoata* as a whole remains a legible derivative of the basic *etua*
motif. Further reflected half-ovals may be added to the curved eye margins to
add extra potency to the design. When *mata hoata* are inscribed in restricted
spaces, the motif becomes increasingly synonymous with *etua* (Fig. 8.10/3).

why the famous tattoo art of the New Zealand Maori should have been known as *moko*. The presence
of *moko* as an alternative designation for *kea* (*kake*) in Marquesan tattoo is certainly suggestive. Lizards
were, like tortoises, sacred beings, and they make numerous appearances in Marquesan art. The way in
which such dissimilar reptiles as tortoises and lizards have become visually synonymous in Marquesan
art partly reflects their similar symbolic associations.

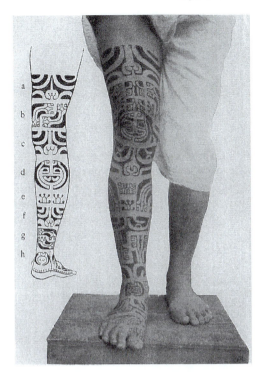

FIG. 8.10/1. Sitting *etua* hypostasized to *mata hoata*. Badora's leg tattoos: (a) *mata hoata*; (b) double *kake*; (c) *mata hoata*; (d) *kautupa*; (e) *Etua*; (f) *mata hoata*; (g) double *kake*; (h) *poriri*. *Source*: Von den Steinen, i. 132, illus. 77

FIG. 8.10/2. *Mata hoata* in male tattoos recorded by Steinen. *Source*: Von den Steinen, i, ii. (various)

ia vau

FIG. 8.10/4. From *mata hoata* to the *Vau* rock motif by the addition of spirals. *Source*: Von den Steinen, i. 169, illus. 125

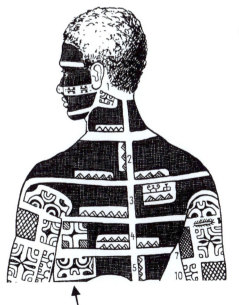

FIG. 8.10/3. The *mata hoata* tattoo indicated tends evidently towards the *etua* motif. *Source*: Von den Steinen, i. 104, illus. 54

Adding spirals to the ends of the *etua*'s 'arms' and on each side of the head produces a further motif, similar in its proportions to *mata hoata*, called *vau* (rocks). This motif recalls the ocean swells breaking over coastal rocks and was particularly placed over the buttocks. *Vau* is thus an additional derivative of *etua/mata hoata*, though to lend the motif greater verisimilitude, it was common to disrupt the symmetry of these spirals in various ways, producing the family of alternative forms shown in Fig. 8.10/4.

8.11. *From* Mata Hoata *to* Ipu: *Additional Face Motifs*

Doubling-up the 'eye' half-ovals of *mata hoata* produces the next important motif, *ipu*. *Ipu* means 'bowl' or calabash, and it was usual to place rows of these along the underside of the arm, where they would be ranged in pairs. The *mata*

FIG. 8.11/1, *far left.* From double *mata hoata* to *ipu. Source*: Von den Steinen, i. 129, illus. 74

FIG. 8.11/2, *left.* Tapa mask with *ipu* 'eyes'. *Source*: Von den Steinen, i. 173, illus. 131

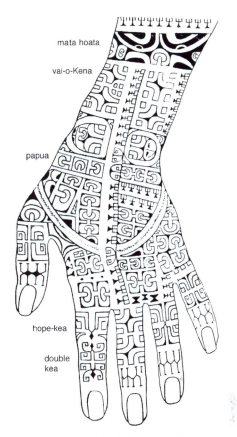

FIG. 8.11/3. 'Hand face' design 1.
Source: Von den Steinen, i. 177,
illus. 136/5

FIG. 8.11/4. 'Hand face' design 2: each eye can
also be read as a face, one single *etua*, or as one
etua containing another. *Source*: Von den
Steinen, i. 177, illus. 136/6

hoata/ipu transformation is shown in Fig. 8.11/1. This *ipu* motif, bisected horizontally, immediately transforms into *mata hoata*. Usually, *ipu* are surrounded by a motif, *papua*, which is a reduplicated derivative of the 'nose' element in *mata hoata* (cf. Fig. 8.10/2). Although the motif-name *ipu* does not refer to eyes, *ipu* are frequently placed so as to make this identity palpable (e.g. the unique tapa mask shown in Fig. 8.11/2).

Next, I turn to the family of 'face' designs other than *mata hoata* which feature circular eyes. A common site for the placement of this category of designs was on the hands, the backs of which were protected by 'faces' composed of a variety of elements. Fig. 8.11/3 shows such a 'hand face'. It will be seen that here the eyes are composed of two opposed half-*etua* figures, placed over a 'nose' element identical in form to that seen in *mata hoata*. The 'mouth' of the hand-face is composed of a transformed version of the deep 'eye' curves of *mata hoata*. An alternative 'D'-shaped rather than circular eye form is seen in the illustration in Fig. 8.11/4. Here, the eye is formed by a single *etua*, though the right-hand one of these has a small additional *etua*-figure encapsulated within it, and both verge towards becoming miniature versions of *mata hoata*. In other words, this single motif can be read simultaneously in three quite distinct ways: (i) as a single eye of the hand-face; (ii) as a face by itself *mata hoata*; and (iii) as an *etua*, or indeed, as two *etua*, one containing the other. This overflow of possible readings attaching to a single motif—surrounded by dozens of others, equally perplexing—perfectly instantiates the cerebral wit of the Marquesan style. What was the point of such displays of graphic inventiveness? That question must be set aside until the entire range of stylistic characteristics of Marquesan art has been explored in more detail.

A common face motif, seen especially on the knees in female tattoo, is called *kautupa* or *poriri* (= 'coiled shellfish' according to Willowdean Handy). Steinen himself designates this face motif as '*kake*-type' since as Fig. 8.11/5 shows, it can be regarded as a *kake* (podoid) in circular form, though the basic

Fig. 8.11/5. 'Coiled shellfish' *poriri* as a face motif. *Source*: Von den Steinen, i. 179, illus. 137

kake shape has been considerably modified to make the 'mouth' and 'eyes' of *poriri*. None the less, Steinen's suggested derivation seems well warranted.

Lastly, we may note that face motifs can be hierarchically subsumed into larger motifs, and may also subsume smaller ones. Thus the 'eyes' of Fig. 8.11/4 are also faces. The same idea is exploited on a larger scale in Fig. 8.11/6, an engraving from Langsdorff showing the (unfinished) back-design of a young warrior. Here the two large circular designs over the scapular area are 'eyes' (the eye design is similar to the one seen on the tapa mask, Fig. 8.11/2). The 'nose/mouth' of this back-face is composed of the smaller face in the small of the back immediately below. This recalls the point made earlier with reference to Fig. 8.9/4 showing the 'girdle' of a chiefess, where the eye elements are *kake* enclosing oval eyes made up (rather randomly) of *etua* forms. Here the nose is the *etua* in the centre of the design.

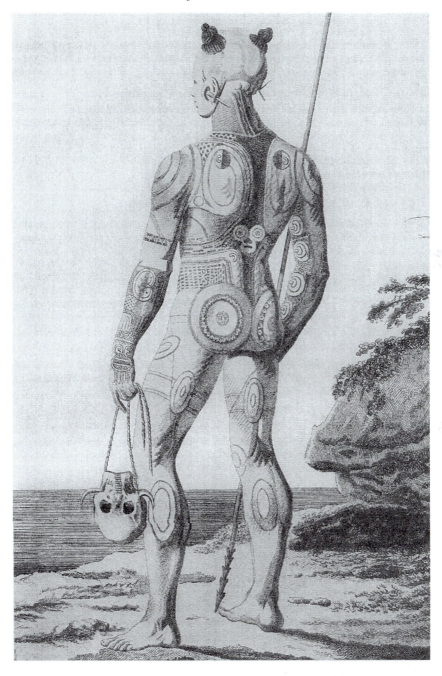

FIG. 8.11/6. Langsdorff's 1813 engraving of young warrior with eye and face designs. *Source*: Langsdorff 1813–14

8.12. *Some Additional Motif-Transformation*

The few remaining common motifs can be dealt with briefly. A very common 'filler' motif is *papua* (see Fig. 8.11/4), which features small half-ovals in a variety of configurations, and/or the 'nose' element from *mata hoata*, which, as we saw, was a small transformed *etua* motif. A motif for which I can find no satisfactory derivation is *pahito* which is also called *pokaka* (a package or bundle, which it does indeed recall). This motif is formed from opposed half-ovals in various dispositions. In practice *pahito* just delimits a space, which is usually filled with derivatives of *hope vehine* or *mata hoata*. Another common motif is the rosette (*feo'o*) which is made up of row motifs (such as forms of *pohu* or *fanaua*) arranged in a circle (Fig. 8.12/1).

Finally, I shall only mention some of the smaller motifs which Steinen discussed under the rubric of 'plaited' or woven motifs. Some of these consist of

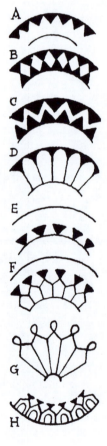

FIG. 8.12/1. Rosette motifs.
Source: Von den Steinen,
i. 148, illus. 93

FIG. 8.12/2, *left*. Hierarchization: *niho* 'teeth' motifs

FIG. 8.12/3, *below*. *Aniatiu* band containing alternating reversed *etua* motif t in Fig. 8.7/1.
Source: Von den Steinen, ii. 194, illus. 192

various arrangements of triangles, identified as 'teeth' or bonito spines (teeth can be simply transformed into spines). A common use of teeth motifs (*niho*) is to 'armour' the triangular patches of solid black tattoo on the inner thighs, in male tattoo (Fig. 8.12/2). These triangles ornamented with triangles provide a particularly transparent instance of hierarchization. Other row-motifs are the small *etua* figures, *pohu* and *fanaua*, that have already been mentioned as components of larger motifs. Their main use, however, is as fillers, arranged in single or multiple rows (they are shown on row 3 of the table of *etua* motifs (Fig. 8.7/1). An interesting variation in such small *etua* motifs is achieved by joining them up, either in the same orientation, or in alternation rotated by 90 degrees. (Fig. 8.12/3 shows this alternating band pattern in the motif *aniatiu*, from the table of *etua* 't'.) Finally, the most extreme simplification of the *etua* motif is the chequerboard pattern. Just how this pattern can be derived from the 'standing' *etua* motif is made very apparent in Steinen's table of *etua* motifs (row 2, a–l, showing variants: the symbolic and political significance of the chequerboard pattern is discussed in Gell 1993).

8.13. *Figure-Ground Reversal (Tortoiseshell Diadems)*

This is as much as I wish to say about tattoo motifs. The next category of art to be discussed is Marquesan work in tortoiseshell, which forms a bridge between the two-dimensional art of tattoo, and carving, in relief and in the round. The most delicate shell work is entirely two-dimensional, and consists of 'diadems' (Fig. 8.13/1) in which a finely incised disc of tortoiseshell is shown off against a slightly larger disc of pearl-shell, forming a most elegant ornament for the forehead. As Fig. 8.13/1 shows, there is a great deal of continuity between the style of this pierced shell work and tattooing. The disc I illustrate (Salem 1807) reminds one, at first glance, of *mata hoata*. But exactly how are the faces one sees arranged, and what are their separate components? Around the central aperture, there are four large 'eyes'—enough eyes for two faces, normally speaking. Given the circular layout of the design, however, these four eyes belong, not to two, but to four faces, each of which shares its eyes with its neighbour on either side. The large eyes, read from the centre of the disc, are composed of elements which look anthropomorphic—a figure with raised arms, or half an *etua*.

Between each pair of eyes, there is a complex form which constitutes the rest of the face. Reading each face from the rim of the disc inwards, one can make out nostrils and a mouth. However, if one reads these mouth/nostril parts from the centre of the disc outwards, a quite different set of faces emerge. What were the 'nostrils' of the big faces seen from the rim of the disc, become the eyes of smaller, skull-like faces which are seen from the centre of the disc (Fig. 8.13/1). Nor is this all, for these smaller skull-faces set between the large eyes (which one sees in white-on-black) are themselves created from standing *etua* figures (which one sees in black-on-white). This is a stunning example of figure–ground reversal, much more interesting than the hackneyed face/candlestick one cited in all the psychology textbooks. As I will show later, such virtuosity is far from the arbitrary exercise it might seem, and relates directly to certain fundamental attributes of the Marquesan cultural system—but at the same time, as I noted earlier these attributes only become thematic after one has taken the trouble to dissect the style and morphology of the material culture, not before.

FIG. 8.13/1. Figure–ground reversal and hierarchization: tortoiseshell incised disc
Source: Von den Steinen, ii. 168, illus. 156 (iv)

Diadems of this kind were made in three pieces, the central disc plus two end-plates of the kind shown in Fig. 8.13/2 (some diadems had three discs and two end-plates). The end-plates make an interesting study, in that one can see here a transition between a 'two large eyes' type (white on black) transforming itself into something apparently quite different—the image of a lizard/*etua* (in black-on-white). There is an obvious relationship between this figure–ground reversal and the one discussed in the preceding paragraph. The evident transition between 'eyes' and 'lizards' was grist to Steinen's evolutionary mill, and one can readily see why (Fig. 8.13/2). At the same time, one must recall that these end-plates were not designed to be seen grouped together for comparison, but separately and individually, so that the transitions that we can see would

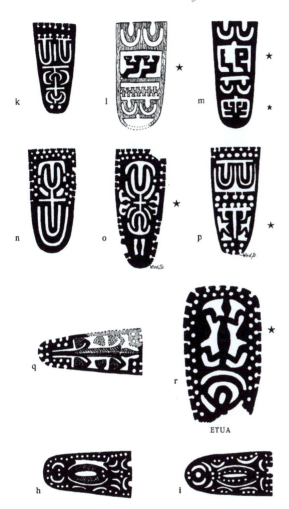

FIG. 8.13/2. From eyes to lizard: Steinen's evolutionary derivation from end-plate discs. *Source*: Von den Steinen, ii. 173, illus. 161

not necessarily have been apparent in the same way to Marquesans. Only those visual ambiguities which are co-present within a single end-piece are of unquestionable stylistic saliency. There are many such ambiguities, however (for example, 'o', 'h', where eyes and *etua*/lizards clearly coexist).

Perhaps the most significant aspect of these end-plates, in terms of Marquesan art as a whole, is the light they shed on the transformation of the frontal *etua* figure into the 'profile' *etua*, via the 'lizard'. In tattooing, 'profile' *etua* are not to be found; they only occur in 'miniature' forms of plastic art, such as these end-plates, and particularly in carved ivory earplugs, which I will describe later. The genesis of the profile-*etua* form is easily seen in end-plate 'p', in which the creature at the base could equally be a lizard-type *etua* like the one in 'r' or two *etua* with bent knees seen in profile. I shall have more to say about back-to-back divinities later, since they are the dominant motif in all forms of Marquesan plastic art in the round. In the end-plates, though, they are commonly subjected to a transformation whereby one of the back-to-back profile *etua* is reflected, so that both now face the same way (Fig. 8.13/2, 'i'; both versions of the motif occur simultaneously in 'm').

8.14. *From Two to Three Dimensions*

Now it is time to turn to Marquesan plastic art in more than two dimensions. I think it would be fair to say that no Marquesan art is fully three-dimensional in the sense of fully occupying three-dimensional space. Marquesan sculpture is conceived as a 'skin' around a core (a cylinder or cube—or a human body in the case of tattooing). The core may be three-dimensional but the carved design often seems to be conceived in the flat, in low relief, as appliqué decoration which is 'wrapped' around this core. This even applies to large free-standing figure sculpture, especially the heads. This raises an interesting point about exactly how plastic art in three dimensions is related to graphic art in two dimensions, of the kind we have been considering up to now. The Marquesans conceptualized the transition between two-dimensional and three-dimensional art in a way quite contrary to our own habitual way of thinking, as I shall now attempt to explain.

Suppose I present you with the image of a person, drawn in ink, on a sheet of paper, and I pose the question: 'what is the back view of this image?' In a sense, this is a non-question, because drawings are graphs in two dimensions (up–down and left–right) so they do not possess 'backs' or 'fronts'. We, however, naturally interpret this question as equivalent to: 'What does the back of the person you see in the drawing look like?'—or perhaps, if we choose to be literal-minded—'What does the back of the piece of paper on which this person is drawn look like?' Since the question seems a silly one in its literal interpretation, it would be natural for us to assume that the question is one about what people look like when seen from the back, and we might answer it by producing a drawing like this (Fig. 8.14/1), which is the same person in the same pose seen from the rear. We do this because we 'see' drawings as 'flat' projections of the three-dimensional objects that drawings represent, especially when these are drawings of familiar objects, such as human beings. This visual presupposition is the outcome of centuries of conditioning to naturalism in artistic representation; any drawing is a 'drawing of' something which exists separately from them (the 'subject' of the drawing) and the subject of a drawing is typically a three-dimensional object with a front and a back as well as a left and a right and a top and a bottom.

FIG. 8.14/1. From three
dimensions to two in
Western art: the back view
of the image as the back
view of the prototype

These presuppositions do not hold for Marquesan art, which was not 'representational' in our sense at all, without being 'abstract' either. Marquesan art was a ritual art whose purpose was to render the person powerful and invulnerable. I will return to this subject in the conclusion of this chapter. For the present, it is sufficient to say that the tattooing of, for example, an *etua* motif on the body was not a matter of representing an *etua* which existed (as a three-dimensional solid object) somewhere else. The tattooed *etua* was protective of the person because it *was* an *etua*, right there on the body, not because it 'looked like' an *etua* somewhere else. The graphic act was a ritual performance which brought into being a protective spirit through the utterance of a 'legitimate' (stylistically coherent) graphic gesture. One cannot speak of graphic gestures of this kind as representational in our sense; they are constitutive. This is the essence of Marquesan idolatry (and of all idolatries), which informed their entire approach to graphic and plastic art.

Let us now reconsider the question about what the back view of a drawing looks like, bearing in mind that a Marquesan graphic gesture does not represent something, but constitutes something. An *etua* motif consists, in itself, of a bundle of lines. If we stop thinking of these lines as 'representing' something (else) and just think of these lines as lines, then the answer to our initial question is plain; the 'back view' of a drawing of a person, is that drawing seen from the point of view of the paper, that is, the mirror-reversed view of the same drawing.

This proposition may be applied to the genesis of three-dimensional plastic art in the Marquesan style; whereas Western graphic art is the representation of 'flattened' three-dimensional objects in two dimensions, Marquesan three-dimensional art is the projection of two-dimensional 'flat' motifs in three dimensions via the mirror principle, that is to say, the back of a three-dimensional image is the mirror reflection of the front. Marquesan motifs, which are constitutive graphic acts rather than acts of representation, have no 'backs'; all the available views are canonical, because the principle of ritual efficacy depends on the stylistic legitimacy and 'correctness' of the gesture.

One cannot see God from the back, because if he is not watching us, he is not God. In the same way, Marquesan art cannot permit motifs to be witnessed, so to speak, at a disadvantage (just as it was sacrilege, in the Marquesas as in most Polynesian societies, to approach, or pass by, the back of a chief).

8.15. *Backlessness and Split Representation: Shell Crowns*

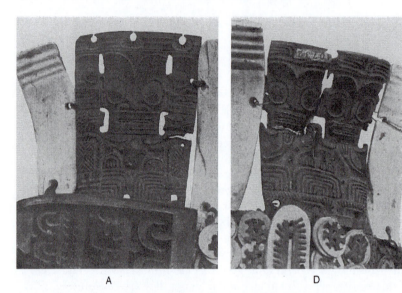

A   D

FIG. 8.15/1. From two dimensions to three in Marquesan art: providing the image with a back. *Source*: Von den Steinen, ii. 176, illus. 166 (A) and Steinen ii. 177, illus. 167 (D)

The most perspicuous instance of backlessness in Marquesan art is provided by the tortoiseshell 'crowns' made of a series of curved, rectangular plates of shell carved with *etua* images of great richness and intricacy (Fig. 8.15/1). These crowns are the 'exception which proves the rule' in the sense that they are low-relief, two-dimensional carvings rather than three-dimensional carvings. The plates are, for the most part (but see below) only decorated on one side, the side facing out. Yet in fact, they are treated, conceptually as if they were works in three dimensions, Marquesan fashion, that is, with backs mirroring their fronts. This may be seen from the plate illustrated (ii. 176, illus. 166 'A'). This is a typical example in which the main motif is an *etua*, seen from the front, full length. But the main figure is flanked by two further *etua* figures seen in profile. The other standard layout for such plates is seen in 'D'; here there are just two *etua*, each one of which is a mirror reflection of the other (see the arrangement of the arms). Meanwhile, there is not a single example of a plate consisting of just one *etua* filling the whole space. I argue that this is to be attributed to the need to ensure that these *etua* images, which are free-standing, should at least conceptually be provided with backs mirroring their fronts. These images are, as it were, folded outwards so that their backs are now in front. Thus, if we were to imagine that Fig. 8.15/1, 'A' were made of flexible material, we could turn the two outer 'profile' *etua* faces around the back of the central one, so that they met in the middle, where they would join up to make a back *etua* mirroring the front one. In other words, these 'profiles' are half-faces which can be put together again. A simpler solution to the same problem of providing a back for a free-standing *etua* is seen in the alternative layout 'D'. Here there are two mirror-reflected *etua* which, on the same basis as before, could simply be folded down the middle to make a back *etua* and a front *etua*. All the tortoiseshell crown plates are variations on one or other of these solutions to providing two-dimensional relief carvings with (protected) 'backs'. However, Marquesan concern with providing *etua* images with symmetrical backs did not end there. Some plates (ii. 182, illus. 174) have, in fact, carved backs identical to their frontal design, even though, in use, these carved backs to the plates would have been mostly, if not entirely, invisible. Laboriously adding decoration to visually inaccessible surfaces seems a perverse waste of effort; but it was necessary none the less if these crowns were to provide ritual protection from all directions, as intended.

As will be seen, *etua* faces and profiles sprout everywhere from these plates; often the bodies/limbs of the main *etua* become subsidiary *etua*, and so on. Steinen makes a detailed study of the variations in this regard (ii. 174–82). A similar analysis to the previous one of tattoo motifs might be undertaken, but I shall refrain from providing one. The last point I wish to raise with regard to these tortoiseshell plates is the Boasian/Lévi-Straussian one of 'split representation', which naturally Steinen does not discuss (he cites no non-Polynesian comparative examples). It will be apparent that both types of plates, the 1/2 + 1 + 1/2 layout and the 1 + 1 layout, are instances of 'split representation' of a kind, cognate to, though by no means the same as, the famous examples from the art of the north-west coastal tribes of America (Fig. 8.15/2). Marquesan split representation is primarily in the plane bisecting the body from left to right (as in D) rather than from back to front as in the American/ancient Chinese examples discussed by Lévi-Strauss (1963: ch. XIII). Occasionally there is back to front splitting as well (as in Fig. 8.15/1 A, though the 'halves' of the split representation face away, rather than towards, one another), and still more rarely, there are instances of split representation where the 'halves' face one another as in the Lévi-Strauss/Boas-type split representation (e.g. see ii. 179, illus. 169 a). But the precise geometry of split representation is perhaps less important than the interpretation one gives to it. Lévi-Strauss identified split representa-

tion in a rather forced way, I think, in Maori art, essentially because Maori representations of the face, carved as reliefs, tend to open the face out so that it
begins to resemble two opposed profiles rather than one single face viewed
frontally. This characteristic is equally if not more evident in Marquesan representations of the face, but the doubling of images, in the tortoiseshell plates
I have just discussed, is perhaps a more perspicuous example of the 'splitting'
principle which is really what is at issue in split representation.

Fig. 8.15/2. From
Lévi-Strauss 1963: split
representation and the
Janus-faced image in
north-west American tribal
art. *Source*: Lévi-Strauss
1963: figs. 17 and 18

Lévi-Strauss's interpretation of split representation is most thought-
provoking, however, in the Polynesian context. He maintains that split
representation occurs when social factors militate against the dissociation of
two-dimensional and three-dimensional images. 'In the end, our problem may
be formulated as follows: under what circumstances are the plastic and graphic
components [of an art system] necessarily correlated?' he asks, and responds to
his own question by asserting that the relationship between the plastic and the
graphic 'has to be functional when the plastic component consisted of the face
or human body and the graphic component of the facial or corporeal decoration (painting or tattooing) which is applied to them' (1963: 261).

A face or body in its two-dimensional aspect as the canvas for 'decoration'
(i.e. magical graphics) cannot be dissociated from the three-dimensional body
to which 'decoration' is applied. Hence, argues Lévi-Strauss, split representation is associated, not just with masking cultures, but particularly with
those masking cultures in which mask and person are indissociably linked—
as is most particularly the case with body-painting and especially tattooing,
which is quite irremovable. Recalling Mauss's discussion (1902) of the origin
of the concept of the 'person' in the social mask, persona, one might say that
where persona and person unite, representations are split because the three-
dimensional person and the two-dimensional persona cannot be dissociated.
Lévi-Strauss says that societies which are both very hierarchical and very com-

petitive are ones in which these conditions are fulfilled. Such societies typically compete over genealogical credentials linking men with gods, as was the case among the tribes of the north-west coast of America, among the hierarchical societies of South America, the archaic societies of the Far East (producers of the Shang bronzes, whose affinities with Polynesian art have been noted by E. Gombrich 1984: 262–70), among the Maori, and, equally, the Marquesans. This competitive struggle to assert genealogical status is the sociological rationale behind split representation.

I would not care to argue for the universal validity of Lévi-Strauss's sweeping generalization; evidently, competition over genealogical credentials can be engaged in without this finding expression in the particular modality of masking, split representation, or anything of the kind. However, what Lévi-Strauss says about the sociological characteristics of 'split-representation societies' is quintessentially true of the Marquesas, and there is indeed something uncanny about the precision with which he rhetorically anticipates Marquesan ethnographic data of which it is most unlikely that he had foreknowledge. Summarizing his point of view, he remarks:

split representation expresses the strict conformity of the actor to his [social] role and . . . to myths, ritual, and pedigrees. This conformity is so rigorous that, in order for the individual to be dissociated from his social role, he must be torn asunder. (1963: 264)

I say this is uncanny, because, as I have described elsewhere (1993: 213 ff.), it was actually the case in the Marquesas, that dead chiefs were 'torn asunder', and with this precise purpose in mind, that they should have removed from them the social identity conferred on them *by their tattooing*. The tattooed skin of chiefs was removed because, in Marquesan belief, deification and a pleasant afterlife were denied to the tattooed because of the association between tattooing and the mortal condition. After death, the skin reinforced by tattooing—so necessary to ward off the physical and spiritual dangers of a worldly and chiefly life—had to be left behind; social skin and immortal soul parted company and the chief rejoined the assembly of the clear-skinned gods.

I hope that the convergence between Lévi-Strauss's argument on the subject of split representation and the one advanced earlier concerning the pervasive tendency towards providing three-dimensional images with 'backs' reflecting, mirror fashion, their frontal aspect, will be appreciated. The problem of split representation and the problem of Janus-faced images—the latter being a particularly prominent characteristic of Polynesian plastic art—are of an essentially identical nature. Janus-faced images are to plastic art what split representation is to graphic art, that is, the means of securing that *no part of an image departs from the 'canonical' (ritually potent) view*. In Boas/Lévi-Strauss split representation, if an animal is seen from the front, then the whole of the animal is seen from the front, including those parts of it (the flanks) which are in fact invisible when a 'real' animal is seen from such a vantage-point. In Marquesan ('Polynesian') split representation, the strategy is slightly different; the image of the front is reduplicated and becomes the image of the back as well. Where split representation (a graphic mode) provides a canonical view of a three-dimensional object in a two-dimensional space, the making of Janus-faced images allows for the expansion of essentially two-dimensional graphic images into three dimensional plastic space without contravening the stipulation that 'only canonic images are permissible'. Hence: Janus face: split representation :: graphic art : plastic art :: three dimensions : two dimensions, etc.

8.16. *Janus-Faced Images: Scale Transformations*

However, in the course of the preceding digression into the problem of split representation, I have perhaps run a little ahead of myself, in that I have not yet introduced the full panoply of Janus-faced images with which Marquesan plastic art in three dimensions is strikingly replete. To the description of this type of image I will therefore turn without delay.

It would not be true to say that every single one of the anthropomorphic sculptural images produced by the Marquesans were in what Steinen describes as the 'doppeltiki' (double *tiki*) form, but the great majority of them are. The ones that are not include a small number of stone images, with uncarved backs, some wooden 'post figures', and a larger category of small wood and bone images which, though not true Janus-type figurines, are carved with subsidiary (protective) back-*etua* which I will describe in more detail below.

Large stone images comparable to the famous Easter Island statues were carved by the Marquesans, though they never attained the numbers, or the size, or the magnificent workmanship of Easter Island art. I would attribute their lack of back-to-front symmetry to the fact that they were probably all originally built into the stone terraces of chiefly *marae* (ceremonial platforms) rather than being free-standing (Fig. 8.16/1). The most interesting of these stone images is the one known as Makii-taua-pepe (Fig. 8.16/2), which represents a female divinity giving birth. There are other images of birth in Marquesan art (in the form of miniature carved ivory ear-ornaments) but none on this scale. I will discuss Marquesan ideas of parturition when I come to deal with these ear-ornaments. For the present, it is sufficient to note that despite its unique form, this large statue is conceptually a 'double *tiki*' as well, in that during parturition (a moment of great danger and sacredness) Marquesan mothers physically assumed the 'doubled' form, otherwise associated with divine beings, and children, produced in this way, were themselves very sacred (Gell 1993: 185). In this carving, the 'divine child' is represented, as Fig. 8.16/2 shows, by a standard *etua* motif on the underside of the distended belly.

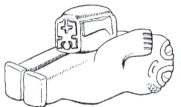

FIG. 8.16/1, *left*. Stone terrace of ceremonial platform. *Source*: Von den Steinen, ii. 74, illus. 55

FIG. 8.16/2. *Makii-taua-pepe*: female divinity giving birth. *Source*: Von den Steinen, ii. 81, illus. 61. *Source*: Von den Steinen, ii. 120, illus. 95

FIG. 8.16/3. Wooden posts carved in two-dimensional form. *Source*: Von den Steinen, ii. 100, illus. 74

From the point of view of stylistics—which is our primary concern—the point to note about all these stone images is their block-like form, and the way in which the features, especially those of the face, are not modelled in three dimensions, but are incised on the block in low relief. More or less the same considerations apply to the wooden anthropomorphic images (Fig. 8.16/3). These are not free-standing images but components of houses or other structures, such as carved posts, supporting beams, which, as with the stone images, explains their uncarved backs.

The disproportionately large eyes/mouths in all medium- to large-scale Marquesan sculpture, and the absence of noses, suggests to me that the stylistic conventions for work at this scale were derived from work at a much smaller scale. On a tiny bone carving, features of these proportions seem quite natural, the result of the need to delineate eyes and mouths visibly, which would be impossible in miniature work were the natural proportions of 'real' eyes or mouths observed. Noses, on the other hand, are redundant at this scale, since the triangular space between the enlarged eyes and mouth implies the nasal triangle with no need for more than a summary treatment of the nostrils, and the absence of a protruding nose coincides with the essentially two-dimensional nature of Marquesan carving, which is incised in low relief rather than being truly 'carved'. To my mind, all the more interesting Marquesan plastic art, from the stylistic point of view, is at the small or even miniature scale. Marquesan art, as I suggested earlier, has to be understood as a technique for enhancing the person by the addition of spiritually potent appendages or supernumeraries, all essentially in the form of *etua*. The larger art forms were appendages of structures, such as ritual platforms or houses; as such, they were enlarged equivalents of 'personal' appendages, such as fans, amulets, head ornaments, ear-ornaments, sporting gear (stilts), and weapons (clubs)—and of course, tattooing. It was in the domain of these 'person-enhancing' art forms that the basic forms of Marquesan art were generated, so it is to this area that we must devote most of our attention.

Once we enter this domain, the presence of the 'double *tiki*' form becomes overwhelming, because, as I have noted above, the requirements of magical efficacy in plastic art forms (i.e. three-dimensional ones) demands the simultaneous presentation of the canonical (efficacious) image in all spatial dimensions. A suitable point of departure is provided by the small bone *tiki* which were used as hair ornaments. These are cylindrical in form (Fig. 8.16/4). They came in two patterns, either fully symmetrical or, more commonly, with a subsidiary back-figure, which in turn was either a small *etua* motif, or a square engraved with a *hakenkreuz*. The *hakenkreuz* motif is a variant of the *etua* (Fig. 8.16/5) via *hope vehine* (see above).

FIG. 8.16/4, *left*. The double *tiki* form
in bone hair ornaments with *hakenkreuz*
motif on back, 2nd row. *Source*: Von
den Steinen, iii, βK (above) and bL
(below)

FIG. 8.16/5, *below*. The *hakenkreuz*
motif: a variant of *etua* via *hope vehine*.
Source: Von den Steinen, ii. 192,
illus. 188 and 189

Abb. 189. HAKENKREUZ-SCHEMA

Most of these small cylindrical bone ornaments are distinguished by the very
summary treatment given to the body and especially the legs, by comparison
to the head. There seems to be a relatively consistent rule of proportionality
dictating the head/body ratio which is built into the Marquesan style. If we
take it that any Marquesan plastic representation of the body is essentially a
modified cylinder, the proportional rule decrees that as the ratio between the
diameter and the height of the 'cylinder' approaches unity, the ratio between
the head and the body increases in favour of the head. The underlying constraint seems to be the need to keep the proportions of the head/face within
bounds; the distance between the brow and the chin must remain approximately equal to the ear-to-ear measurement, or in other words the face must fit,
more or less, into a square. This rule applies independently of the absolute dimensions of the 'cylinder'. As Fig. 8.16/6 shows, relatively elongated
Marquesan representations (1) of the body show ratios between the dimensions
of the head (A), the body (B), and the legs (C) which conform to the ratios
found in nature A< B < C. Reduction in overall height produced progressively

more unnatural head/body/legs ratios: (2) A = B = C, (3) A > B = C, until the ratios found in these bone *tiki* are attained, at the opposite pole from 'naturalism' (4) A > B > C.

In the plastic arts, the head as an isolated entity is very rarely found; every head must have its body; but it may be given very meagre representation, as here. I have expressed the proportionality rule by means of the D'Arcy Thompson-type system of transformed coordinates—an idiom borrowed from biological studies of morphology. It is the existence of such mathematically generalizable properties as these which lends visual coherence to the Marquesan style.

There is a second feature of these small bone hair ornaments to which we can draw attention. Because of their small dimensions, they are carved, on the whole, in very low relief. They therefore provide excellent instances of the method through which Marquesan art transforms two-dimensional *etua* images into three-dimensional free-standing objects. The procedure is simple, since it amounts to 'wrapping' a 'flat' *etua*-form around a cylindrical armature. That is to say, whereas Western art 'adds a dimension' to convert a two-dimensional flat figure (a drawing) into a three-dimensional figure (a work of sculpture), the Marquesan approach is rather to represent a two-dimensional figure in a three-dimensional 'space', while leaving its two-dimensionality essentially intact (like the two-dimensionality of a poster applied to a cylindrical telephone-pole). The bone *tiki* is a 'curved' work in the flat, rather than a three-

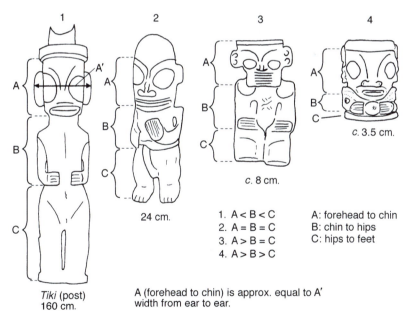

1. A < B < C
2. A = B = C
3. A > B = C
4. A > B > C

A: forehead to chin
B: chin to hips
C: hips to feet

c. 3.5 cm.
c. 8 cm.
24 cm.

Tiki (post)
160 cm.

A (forehead to chin) is approx. equal to A' width from ear to ear.

Fig. 8.16/6. The rules of body proportions in Marquesan art. *Source*: Von den Steinen, ii, illus. 74; iii, βD6; iii, βV2a (c); iii, βK19a dimensional form. This approach to three-dimensionality via the imposition of curvature onto basically flat motifs is a diagnostic feature of Marquesan plastic art, visible particularly in the rendition of the facial features of anthropomorphic figures.[5]

8.17. *Multiplication, Transposition, and Proboscis-Formation: Fan Handles*

These small bone carvings are the most 'cylindrical' of artefacts. The whale-ivory fan handles, where Marquesan artistry is particularly well displayed, are longer and flatter, and are usually divided up into a series of segments, each carved with Janus figures in various dispositions (Fig. 8.17/1) each of which broadly resembles one of the small cylindrical figurines we have just been considering. However, each of these Janus figures is treated as a unit, so they are inscribed in relatively elongated cylinders and hence have fully represented bodies and lower limbs. The fan handles present various points of interest, which they share with the stilt-steps I will consider in a moment. They show, first of all, the tendency towards sheer proliferation which is such a marked feature of Marquesan art. Although they are relatively small objects (about 20 cm.), each has a minimum of four figures represented on it, and often one or even two more on the base, besides sundry additional incised motifs, all of which can be traced back to the basic *etua* motif. The proliferation seen here is a function of the ritual importance of fan handles, which were important items of regalia owned by the most powerful chiefs and chiefesses. A chief's power was a function of how many 'supporters' he had: chiefs engaged in deadly struggles with one another to increase their numerical followings. These multitudinous fan handles refer symbolically to the salience of 'numbers' in Marquesan political life (see Gell 1993).

A second feature of these fan handles is the tendency for figures to switch their orientation; that is, be subjected to rotation horizontally or vertically. This kind of switching can mean that both of a pair of Janus figures may face the same way and that consequently the back of one of them is exposed as in the second figure in Fig. 8.17/1, but this is always offset by the upper pair of Janus figures which will face in opposite directions, protecting that side.

---

[5] Though this chapter is primarily concerned with morphology and style, it might be as well to point out, especially in connection with these ornaments of carved bone, that Marquesan works of art are almost always created from materials which were significant (i.e. ritually potent) in their own right. These hair ornaments, for instance, were made of human bone; their protective powers stemmed from their *substance* as much as their form. Although they are independent objects, they are parts of bodies, both because they were attached to the body of the wearer, and because they were extracted from the bodies of others, as bones which were subsequently carved and made into ornaments. They are thus much more like tattoo motifs than might be readily apparent. Tattoo motifs are artworks made of living flesh; these are artworks made of bones, but the implications, in either case, are very much the same.

FIG. 8.17/1. Marquesan artistic proliferation: fan handles divided into
multiple segments in different orientations. Each fan handle measures
approximately 20 cms. *Source*: Von den Steinen, iii, βM and BN 4

1   2   3   4

Alternatively, bodies may face inwards but the faces outwards, as in Fig. 8.17/1
(3). Another kind of switching affects the orientation of figures in the vertical
axis (see Fig. 8.17/2), some of which may be upside-down relative to the others.
Finally, these fan handles demonstrate a variety of 'distortions' of the head/
face. If represented spanning the broad side of the handle (as in Fig. 8.17/1 (4))
the face flattens out to a shape similar to *mata hoata*. But if the need is to
represent the face projecting out of the top or bottom of the handle, making a
kind of 'pommel', a completely new morphology is generated, which has no
tattooing analogue (Fig. 8.17/2). Steinen places these fan handles in a distinct
class, describing them as 'anchor' or 'double-anchor' handles. The new morphology of the head which is generated in these 'pommel' positions resembles
(from the side) the beak of a bird or perhaps the pointed nose and jaw of a rep-
tile. From the front, however, the resemblance disappears, and one sees only a
formulaic nose and mouth attached to a kind of flattened proboscis which has
no obvious counterpart in any family of creatures whatsoever.

FIG. 8.17/2, *far left*. Double-anchor fan handles with morphologically adapted head. *Source:* Von den Steinen, ii. 160, illus. 148

FIG. 8.17/3, *left*. Fly-whisk handle from the Austral Islands with similar proboscis face. *Source*: British Museum MM8458

Representing the face as a proboscis of this kind is a feature of Polynesian art from other islands besides the Marquesas; parallels with the fly-whisk handles imported into Tahiti from the Austral Islands immediately spring to mind (Fig. 8.17/3). This device occurs elsewhere in Marquesan art, in ear borers and in stilt-steps (see below). How is it generated? In effect, the bridge of the nose (which is hardly even suggested in the typically flat-faced images of the kind we have been looking at up till now) is sharply seized and drawn forwards and downwards, as if it were made of plasticine. The lips remain attached to the outer surface of the proboscis, at the tip, but all resemblance to a normal human face is lost. None the less, I do not think the Marquesan artists actually intended that these proboscis-faced creatures should be seen as birds or animals, despite their radical contravention of the normal human 'face' schema. They are simply geometrically reconfigured faces which fill space in the required way (e.g. accommodate the need to provide fan handles with rounded pommels).

8.18. *The Same Continued: Stilt-Steps*

The process of proboscis-formation, and various other geometric transformations, can be perspicuously studied in the carving on stilt-steps, a very characteristic form of Marquesan art (Steinen, ii, illus. 104–9; iii, β F, G, H, I). The game of fighting on stilts was a major sporting activity in the Marquesas, and much care was devoted to the carving and ornamentation of the hardwood foot-supports which were lashed to the main shafts of the stilts. All carved figures on stilt-feet essentially function as caryatids, supporting the projecting foot rest. The caryatid figure rejoins the shaft of the stilt at an acute angle, creating a triangular prism which can be subjected to ornamental treatment. Because outward-facing caryatid figures are joined at the back to the shaft of the stilt, they are not carved in Janus form, like the figures on fan handles. Stilt-steps in their simplest form are supported by a single outward-facing caryatid, as in Fig. 8.18/1. However, given that these figures were adjuncts to

FIG. 8.18/1. A simple form of stilt-step with rudimentary face at base. *Source*: Von den Steinen, iii, βH

a dangerous sport in which supernatural assistance was most necessary, the tendency towards proliferation rapidly asserts itself. Even in the simple and relatively early (1804) example I have just cited, a secondary face makes its appearance at the base, below the feet of the main caryatid figure. Very commonly, though, a second complete figure is inserted beneath the main, upper one (Fig. 8.18/2). Very many further complications of the basic caryatid figure are possible, which I will describe in a moment. Before doing so, let me return to the subject of the 'proboscis face' which commonly occurs on stilt-steps.

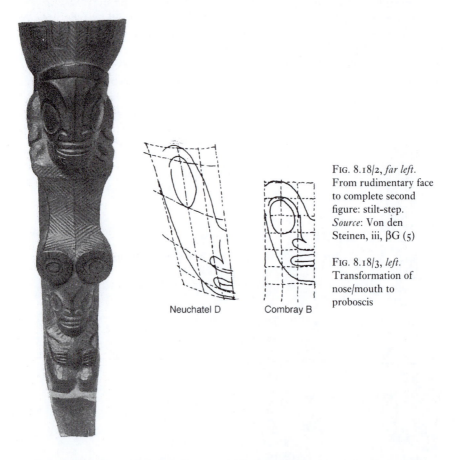

Neuchatel D   Combray B

Fig. 8.18/2, *far left*. From rudimentary face to complete second figure: stilt-step. *Source*: Von den Steinen, iii, βG (5)

Fig. 8.18/3, *left*. Transformation of nose/mouth to proboscis

Fig. 8.18/3 shows the coordinate transformations involved in the transformation of nose/mouth into proboscis from a series of stilts. It should be noted that these are not diachronic or evolutionary transitions. Marquesan artists were free to produce facial proportions as they pleased; proboscis faces neatly fill the small triangular prism left beneath the 'feet' of the main Caryatid above; 'mechanical' rather than evolutionary reasons explain this distortion, since it is a means of making maximum use of the available surface for the delineations of magically potent facial features (large outward-facing eyes, especially) in a space (an acute-angled prism) whose geometry is totally unlike that of a real head. The reigning anti-naturalism of Marquesan art has no trouble meeting such demands, indeed, ingenious solutions to spatial problems seem to have been pursued for their own sake. This spatial 'wit' is even more apparent in the contortions introduced into the basic caryatid pose seen in our simplest example. Fig. 8.18/4 summarizes the variety of these poses of single and multiple caryatid figures on stilt-steps. The first transformation (of a single caryatid) consists of rotating the body 180 degrees while leaving the face in its original orientation, facing outwards. This device gives prominence to the buttocks of the reversed caryatid, which poke out, as if it were 'mooning', to use the current expression. This buttock-poking gesture was certainly used by the Maori to insult their enemies and it seems probable to me that Marquesans had the same idea, in which case this device can be interpreted as an insult offered to the stilt-fighter's sporting opponent. It is certainly more common on stilt-steps than anywhere else, though it is also seen on fan handles. The next possible transformation is from one figure to two figures. This can be achieved in two ways. First, by converting the single caryatid into a Janus-form caryatid by duplicating it and rotating by 90 degrees, so that the two caryatids now face forwards and backwards (Fig. 8.18/5). Or the caryatids can be doubled by placing one on top of the other (Fig. 8.18/6).

Fig. 8.18/4, *left*. Stilt-step with multiple figures and 'mooning' buttocks. *Source*: Von den Steinen, βG (7 and 8)

Fig. 8.18/5, *above*. Stilt-step with rotated duplicate figure. *Source*: Von den Steinen, ii. 253, illus. 249

Finally, the design can be elaborated by introducing further subsidiary figures in various orientations. I made the point earlier, with respect to fan handles, that the theme of 'numbers of supporters' was of great significance in the symbolism of Marquesan chiefly regalia, hence the proliferation of subsidiary figures. This applies also to stilt-steps, though even more literally, since the figures carved on these artefacts do indeed 'support' their owner's elevated position in the world. Hence it is not surprising to find subsidiary 'supporters' sprouting from the basic caryatid form. One way of doing this is by converting the 'limbs' of the main caryatid into little *etua* figures, that is, the device of hierarchization mentioned earlier. The most striking example of this is analysed in Fig. 8.18/6. In this stilt-step, the main caryatid is doubled with a subsidiary 'supporting' one, below (with a proboscis face). The head of the upper caryatid is secondarily doubled twice more (these would be raised 'arms' were this figure not equipped with ordinary arms as well). The lower portion of the body of this caryatid is represented by two *etua* figures as (horizontal, inwards-pointing) 'legs' and its 'mooning' buttocks have become two more *etua* 'faces'. So in total, this stilt-step contains eight distinct *etua* figures to increase its owner's chances of victory; or sixteen, since this is only one of a pair.

Fig. 8.18/6.
Maximally
proliferated
stilt-step with
eight figures.
Source: Von den
Steinen, ii. 133,
illus. 109

8.19. U'u: *The Ultimate Double-Double-Double* Tiki

Conflicts among the Marquesans were not confined to sports like stilt-fighting, they were also very prone to more serious battles. Their main weapons of war were, as usually among Polynesians, heavy wooden clubs. The design of Marquesan clubs was derived from the paddles they used to propel their canoes, and indeed the non-chiefly combatants' weapon would be one of these paddles, or a heavy version of one for fighting use. Richer and more important warriors had clubs of a special and rather standardized kind, with carved decoration, called *u'u*.

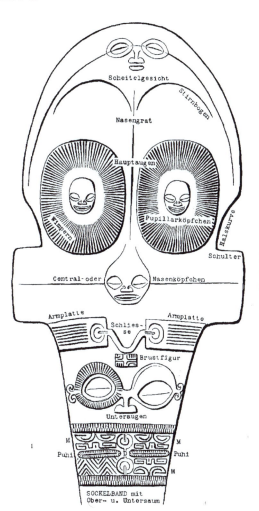

FIG. 8.19/1. *U'u* warrior's club with protective face proliferation

   Steinen devoted an enormous amount of attention to these carved clubs, which are among the most impressive and commonest Marquesan artefacts in collections. The Marquesan club is a Janiform *etua* image rendered as a lethal weapon. As might be anticipated in the light of the previous discussion of back-to-front symmetry and the Marquesan form of split representation, the club has no back or front, hence no 'unguarded' rear, and always shows its apotropaic 'face' to the viewer. The club manifests many of the stylistic characteristics of Marquesan art we have already described. In effect, the problem posed by the club from the Marquesan point of view, is to incorporate references to the *etua* schema into an artefact whose overall form remains modelled on the smooth, ovoid, and featureless canoe-paddle from which it is derived. Steinen shows how this is done in an analytical figure which I reproduce in Fig. 8.19/1 (Steinen, iii, g β 1). Descending, we see, first of all, a small protective *etua* face on the crown, then the upper part of a very large 'face' with two staring eyes, whose pupils are themselves subsidiary faces. Below this, there is a heavy horizontal bar. This is set off from the 'face' above it by a notch above and another indentation below. This bar constitutes the 'shoulder' line of the club as an anthropomorphic figure. In the middle of the bar there is a further protruding *etua* head/face. Descending further, we see a symmetrical comb-like pattern on either side connected by a 'V' shape, and below this, a protective device of the *hakenkreuz* type. I shall shortly give Steinen's ingenious explanations for these. Then there come two more 'eyes' and finally a decorative band containing *etua* and 'woven' motifs. Steinen's other drawing of a club shows the depression of 'saddle' between the faces on either side; there can be no doubt that clubs are classic Janiform or 'double *tiki*' images as well as perfectly practical weapons. However, Steinen's interpretation of the parts of the club goes further than this, since he is able to argue, correctly I believe, that each club is a composite of four, rather than two, main figures.
   Steinen's argument starts out from a very different-looking artefact on a very different scale, a small bone *etua* figure which has a splayed subsidiary figure protecting its back, above which is a further *hakenkreuz etua* protecting the head. As with the 'mooning' figures on the stilt-steps we have just looked at, the body of the little 'piggy-back' figure is orientated forwards, showing the buttocks, and only the head is rotated backwards (Fig. 8.19/2). Steinen's ingenious suggestion is that this is the basic layout seen in the club. The head which protrudes in the centre of the 'shoulder-bar' is the backwards-pointing head of a piggy-back rider. The comb-like patterns to the left and right below the bar are the splayed hands of the rider, and the 'V' shape between its shoulders, beneath which is placed the protective *hakenkreuz* motif. The legs of the piggy-back rider are not seen, but its mooning buttocks are—they have been transmogrified into the second set of eyes above the decorative band, at the bottom.

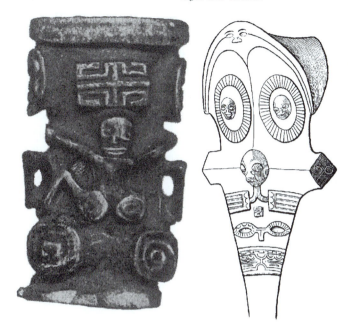

FIG. 8.19/2, *far left*. The figurative model for *U'u* displaying subsidiary figure on the back. *Source*: Von den Steinen, ii. 163, illus. 151

FIG. 8.19/3, *left*. *U'u* exemplifying Steinen's model with subsidiary head protecting 'the back of the back' of the club. *Source*: Von den Steinen, ii. 163, illus. 151

In other words, the subsidiary figure whose head we notice between the outstretched arms of the large figure facing us, is a piggy-back rider, protecting the back of the large figure on the other side of the club. Not only is the back of the club 'protected'—by being symmetrical with the front—the *back of the back* of the club is protected by a subsidiary figure on the *front* (Fig. 8.19/3). At this point it must seem that Marquesan spatial thinking is simply running out of dimensions in which to anticipate, and ward off, spiritual dangers. Especially when we remember that the back of the piggy-back rider is itself protected by a 'third-order' protective figure in the form of the 'hakenkreuz' *etua*. At the same time, the interpretation which would see the subsidiary head and the buttocks/eyes below as simple reduplications of the *etua* motif on the front of the club is not by any means ruled out; one could say that the main 'face' of the club is duplicated in the vertical axis (top to bottom) as well as the proximal–distal axis (back to front). However, it seems to me that the basic schema is exactly as Steinen claims, and this geometric play with dimensions is absolutely in tune with the basic stylistic tendency of Marquesan plastic art.

8.20. *Fusion: The Narrative Art of Ear-Ornaments*

Finally, to round off this analysis of the Marquesan style, I shall briefly discuss a less ferocious art form, indeed the most playful of the traditional Marquesan arts if one excludes string-figures. These are the carved ivory ear-ornaments (inserted into large holes in the earlobes) worn by both sexes and discussed by Steinen under the appropriate heading of 'miniaturplastik' (Steinen, ii. 136–48). As one might expect, many of these ear-ornaments feature sundry *etua*-type figures, reduplicated in various configurations. But much more interesting than these are two types of ear-ornaments which depart radically from the rest of the art we have been considering in that they involve explicit references to details of mythic narratives. The only other comparable instance is the tattoo motif discussed earlier, *vai o kena*, which refers to a particular episode in the tattooing myth of the hero Kena (for discussion, see Gell 1993: 186–8).

The fact that these ear-ornaments embody 'narrative' is, I think, connected to the fact that they are specifically *ear*-ornaments, and it is through the ear that myths enter the body. The ear is, needless to say, an orifice of the body, and, as such, vulnerable and in need of being protected. But the main way of protecting the ear was by tattooing a special category of *etua* designs on the cheek, near the margin of the ear orifice. Since the ear orifice was protected in this way, the ear-ornaments could function, for once, as purely 'secular' adornment. In fact, they might be seen as the plastic-art equivalents of Sony Walkman headphones, continually relaying mythic information into the ears to which they were attached.

FIG. 8.20/1. Narrative art: 'Pahuatiti's daughters on their swing' depicted on ear-plugs. *Source*: Von den Steinen, iii, β R

The mythic episodes referred to in the two types of 'narrative' ear-ornaments which have survived both relate to feminine themes and I think that these ornaments were specifically items of female attire. The first of these types is the 'Pahuatiti's daughters on their swing' motif (Fig. 8.20/1). Pahuatiti's two daughters were persuaded by the chief Toaetini to humiliate the mythic hero Akaui, by pissing into his *kava*. They did so by swinging above him on their swing, and just at the critical moment, directing their urine into his cup, as he was raising it to his lips. For this affront, the branch from which their swing was suspended was broken off, and they were cast into the abyss. (For a new analysis of swings and swing-myths in Polynesia, see Lavondés, *Journal of the Polynesian Society*.) The unfortunate conclusion of the story is not referred to in the ear-ornaments, only the delicious episode of the swing, which is held up by two 'slaves' rather than the branch of a tree. From a stylistic point of view, what is interesting about this set of ear-ornaments is the virtuosity with which Marquesan carvers manage to cram four figures (2 slaves + 2 girls) into such a tiny compass, often by inverting the girls, who 'swing' upside down (nos. 17 and 18). However, the design often transforms itself into a purely formal exercise in rows of miniature heads/limbs, as in no. 25. Alternatively, the design succumbs to the gravitational pull of the *etua* motif (perhaps because of its intrinsic symmetry). Number 33 is well on the way to this destination, while Fig. 8.20/2 retains only the faintest reference to the 'narrative' design, and has become an *etua/mata hoata* design.

FIG. 8.20/2. Ear-plug with swing narrative moving towards the *etua/mata hoata* motif. *Source*: Von den Steinen, ii. 148, illus. 128

Finally, let me turn to the second set of 'narrative' ear-ornaments, which relate to an episode in the myth of Kae (discussed in Gell 1993: 184–6). Kae marries Hina, a woman who rejuvenates herself by periodically being smashed in the sea, like a crab, before being washed up on the beach with a new, soft skin, which hardens so that she can become a young girl again. However Hina and her companions do not know how to give birth. The midwives on their island are two female divinities of evil omen, Fanaua, who deliver babies by cutting the mother open, so that she dies. Kae teaches Hina and her women how to deliver babies properly and the Fanaua depart in anger (complications of childbirth were attributed to their malign efforts). Fanaua really means 'fused together double'—thus, a banana which grows (as they sometimes do) as two bananas fused together on one stem is a 'fanaua' banana (Dordillon, 'fanaua'). This obstetrical myth is a very suitable one for narration in the form of ear-ornaments, if we are correct in believing that women were the ones who wore this type. And it must be said that nowhere does Marquesan artistry seem more inspired than in these microscopic tableaux of entangled bodies. There are five protagonists, whom it is impossible to identify with the characters in the myth, though Steinen gives a detailed analysis (see Fig. 8.20/3). The bird-headed individual at the bottom right seems to be the child being born, though this may not be right because in fact Marquesan mothers gave birth supported by their husbands and lying on a platform composed of the bodies of their affinal/maternal kin. So this could be one of them. The iconographic interpretation is anyway less important than the technical exploitation of the idea of ambiguously fused bodies, which is what the Fanaua myth is really about. This playful and I think essentially non-apotropaic image is the antithesis of the separation and insulation of body from body which Marquesan ritual rules about *tapu* (contagious sacredness) upheld with such stringency; instead, it shows bodies merging into one another in an indistinguishable tangle. Rather than being a ritual image in itself, it is an ironic commentary on a world suffused with the magical danger of contagion and unboundedness. But this raises issues which need to be discussed in a more general cultural framework. The time has come to leave aside these minute analyses of specific Marquesan artworks and their transformations, and to raise once more the problem of the relationship between culture and style alluded to earlier. It is possible to do this because, by now, the formal and morphological aspects of the Marquesan style, in both the graphic and plastic modes, have been more thoroughly elucidated.

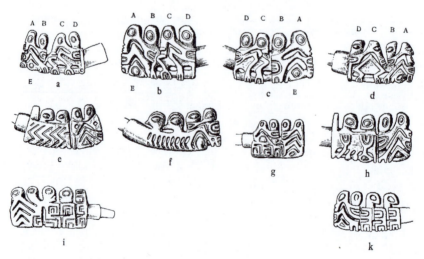

FIG. 8.20/3. Ear-plugs depicting the obstetric myth displaying a fusion of bodies. *Source*: Von den Steinen, ii. 142, illus. 120

8.21. *Conclusion: Coherence in Marquesan Art and Social Relations*

It is time to review the problem of style in the light of the ground just traversed. Style, I argue, is 'relations between relations' of forms. The aim of the preceding analyses of Marquesan art forms was to show how individual motifs (particularly in tattooing, but also in plastic art forms) could be transformed into one another by various modifications. The Marquesan style, from a formal point of view, is the complex formed by the relationships which hold between all these transformations or modifications. That is to say, the constraints governing the production (innovation within culturally prescribed parameters of style) of Marquesan artworks were constraints governing the possibility of transforming a motif or form into related forms; only if such a transformation is possible can a motif or form be said to 'belong' to the Marquesan style. In this sense, the Marquesan style is both unitary and dynamic; it is a field of possible or legitimate motivic transformations, rather than the totality of existing instantiations of such transformations.

The question that now arises is the relationship between style in Marquesan visual art and Marquesan 'culture' in the wider sense. There are really two questions here which need to be distinguished; first, the relationship between 'culture' in the form of artefacts and 'culture' in other guises—kinship, economy, politics, and religion. Secondly, there is the problem of the relationship between culture and visual-art style, which is a much narrower question. The relationship between culture and the material artefact production is at least relatively independent of stylistic considerations, in that artefacts in a variety of styles might subserve the cultural role assigned to artefacts in any given culture. Let me give an example. In the Marquesan context, there is a demonstrable relationship between the general form of the kinship system (Dravidian, with preferential matrilateral cross-cousin marriage) and tattooing/body arts. Tattooing is a form of 'wrapping' (*pahu tiki*, 'wrapping in images') and *pahu* is also a kinship category meaning 'matrikin + affines' (Gell 1993: 176 ff.). In other words, the characteristic involution of the Dravidian kinship universe, where political succour and brides come from an enclosing circle of matrilateral relatives, is connected, via a scheme transfer, to body arts which enclose the individual in a protective wrapping of tattooing. Let us suppose, however, that Marquesan tattooing did not have the visual appearance it actually does have, and that it looked instead like Samoan tattooing. Samoan tattoo motifs are generated in a quite different way from Marquesan tattoo motifs, and represent a different stylistic system altogether. But if, as our gedankexperiment supposes, the Marquesans had had 'Samoan' tattooing in place of their own, it would still have been perfectly possible to advance exactly the same argument concerning the connection between Dravidian kinship and tattooing.

For this reason, one has to beware of making inferences about the relationship between 'style' and culture if these inferences are really based on the role of artefacts in culture, quite independently of their style. Similarly, one has not demonstrated a link between art style and culture if the arguments used rely on iconography. This applies, for instance, to images of religious or cult significance. An image which represents or embodies a certain divinity might take on a wide variety of different visual forms; there is no saying, a priori, that the stylistically standardized form actually assumed by a representation of a divinity is *necessarily* connected to any other cultural aspect of this divinity. The standard representation of the divinity might be different, yet every other cultural parameter connected with the divinity remain the same.

In fact, it is an error to imagine that 'culture' in some general sense, is responsible for the visual style of artefacts. Culture may dictate the practical and/or symbolic significance of artefacts, and their iconographic interpretation; but the only factor which governs the visual appearance of artefacts is their relationship to other artefacts in the same style. Visual style is an autonomous domain in the sense that it is only definable in terms of the relationships between artefacts and other artefacts; it is a mistake to think of 'culture' as a kind of 'head office' which decrees, on the one hand, what form political competition will assume, and on the other, what artefacts will look like. Artefacts are shaped in the 'inter-artefactual domain', obeying the immanent injunctions governing formal stylistic relationships among artefacts, not in response to external injunctions from some imaginary 'head office'.

If it is true, as I have just argued, that the relative autonomy of visual style implies that the factors governing the appearance of artefacts belong primarily to the artefactual domain, then does that imply a complete disjunction between style and culture? Not quite, I think, but in order to formulate a theory of this relationship which does not fall into the same pitfalls as Hanson's (1983: discussed above) it is necessary to proceed with care. We certainly cannot argue, as he does, directly from stylistic properties of artworks (such as bifold symmetry) to properties of socio-cultural systems. On the other hand, it may be possible to construct arguments connecting the 'axes of coherence' within styles as systems, and other systematic properties of culture.

This is admittedly rather a mouthful, so I must try to explain myself more clearly. What are these 'axes of coherence'? In the preceding discussion of Marquesan art, I showed that relationships among artefacts could be produced by applying transformations; among these were:

- plane geometric transformations of whole or part-motifs (translation, rotation, reflection, etc.)
- cutting-and-pasting operations (such as those described in the analysis of *hope vehine*)
- coordinate transformations (reconfiguring motifs in different coordinates cf. the analysis of *Kea* or the analysis of 'proboscis formation')

- hierarchization (one motif being subordinated to another, e.g. a subordinate *etua* protecting the 'back' of a superior *etua* as in the 'club' design)
- motif-transformation (one motif becomes another, e.g. *etua → mata hoata*)
- transformation by figure-ground reversal (as in the analysis of shell diadems)
- transformation from two to three dimensions by front-to-back reduplication (Janus figures)
- transformation from two to three dimensions by 'curvature' (small bone *tiki*)
- rule-governed transformations of proportions, as in the head-to-body ratio
- solid-geometry transformations (e.g. switching the orientation of the body with respect to the head as in 'mooning' stilt-figures)
- formalization (as with the *etua → hakenkreuz* transformation)
- fusion (as in the analysis of *fanaua* ear-ornaments).

This is quite a long list. My claim is that it more or less covers the types of motivic or shape transformations which define the relationships between Marquesan artworks. This is the nearest one can get to an explicit description of 'the Marquesan style'. It is reasonable to assume that no other art style, anywhere, would produce exactly the same list if analysed from the same point of view. Some items on the list might be included, but not all, and other transformational modes might be detected, which are not to be found in Marquesan art.

The next step is to formulate the Marquesan style in terms of 'relations between relations'—given that the primary inter-artefactual 'relations' are the ones identified in the preceding listing.

Here, it is important to bear in mind that the 'list' has been arrived at via induction from Marquesan artefacts; it is by no means a theory about the intrinsic possibilities of inter-artefactual relationships. The approach I suggest is totally permissive in this respect. All I assert is that 'style' is founded on connections between artefacts. This would apply to 'the complete works of Rembrandt' just as much as to 'all Marquesan artefacts'. Relationships between Rembrandt's works certainly exist, but they are nothing like the ones which exist between Marquesan tattoo-motifs or carvings. Inter-Rembrandt relationships derive from handling, lighting, pose, physiognomy, etc.—considerations which are completely foreign to the Marquesan collective style. 'Relations between relations' (between Rembrandt paintings) would involve different factors from the ones I am about to advance with respect to Marquesan artefacts, and would, accordingly, orient the discussion in an entirely different direction (emotional psychology, drama, etc.).

As it is, there is no difficulty in sensing a certain homogeneity in this listing, a certain basic trend. This homogeneity derives, I think, from a structural principle which one could call 'the principle of *least difference*', that is to say the forms taken by motifs and figures are the ones *involving the least modification of neighbouring motifs consistent with the establishment of a distinction between them.* Thus, there is no intrinsic reason why a 'face' (*mata hoata*) should look like a 'seated *etua*'; but the Marquesan style decrees that they should look as much like one another as possible, given that they are, in fact, to be distinguished. Similarly, there is no intrinsic reason why a three-dimensional 'face' (on a carved image) should be a 'curved' version of a two-dimensional face rather than a face carved in three fully realized dimensions. But the Marquesan style demands that carved faces be represented as 'curved' two-dimensional faces; that is, the least possible concession to three-dimensionality. Similarly, two-dimensional images become three-dimensional Janus figures by back-to-front reduplication, minimizing the conceptual distance between two and three dimensions. A seated *etua*, to give a further example, can be transformed into a tortoise, by a purely 'virtual' shift in the canonic orientation of the motif (from vertical to horizontal) without any change in the form of the motif what-soever. The same considerations apply to coordinate transformations, figure-ground reversals, and so on.

The principle of least difference also applies in the context of *hierarchization*. Marquesan art shares with other eastern Polynesian art styles a propensity for producing what might be termed 'fractal' figures, images such as the famed Rurutan 'A'a' in which a figure is composed of lesser figures (discussed above, 7.11). Marquesan examples are provided by stilt-steps (Fig. 8.18/4) and the 'club' design (Fig. 8.19/1). 'Fractal' artworks exemplify the least difference principle in that (subsidiary) 'parts' of (superordinate) figures are forms which are themselves figures, and hence are as similar as possible (in fact, identical) to neighbouring figures (or motifs) leading independent existences. Where, as is commonly the case (cf. Figs. 8.18/4, 8.19/1, and 8.20/3), the subordinate motif is actually a transformed version of the superordinate one, parts are related to wholes by the 'least difference' principle as well.

The 'least difference principle' (except possibly in the last instance) is not detectable in any specific Marquesan artefact, taken in isolation, but only in the *ensemble* of relations constituted by *all* Marquesan artefacts. 'Relations between relations' (between Marquesan artefacts) are characterized by convergence towards the 'least difference' principle: this is the 'axis of coherence' of the Marquesan style, overall. Since we are now considering a totally abstract prin-ciple which is not concretely instantiated in any given Marquesan artefact, but only in the ensemble of their relations with one another, it may be reasonable to suggest that at this point we have arrived at a level of abstraction at which it may be possible to provide a cultural interpretation of the Marquesan style. That is to say, although it would be mistaken, as I argued earlier, to believe that 'Marquesan culture' dictates the visual form taken by Marquesan artefacts dir-ectly, it is not so unreasonable to infer that the abstract principles governing 'relations between relations' belong to 'culture' in the wider sense, rather than the inter-artefactual domain.

Let us consider the 'least difference principle' from a cultural standpoint. Marquesan society, as I have described elsewhere (1993 drawing particularly on the work of Thomas 1990) was characterized by an acute preoccupation with 'social difference' in a political context of 'devolved' or fractured hierarchy in which 'difference' was exceptionally difficult to sustain, practically. Because of the prevailing political instability and turmoil, and the vehemence of status-competition, Marquesans had continually to seek to reinforce and protect their social identities against external threats to their wealth, power, and social support. This struggle to maintain integrity against the threat of dispersal and de-differentiation was expressed ritually in an acute preoccupation with rules of inter-individual contact and commensality. Stringent rules were observed in social interaction so that an individual's *tapu* (contagious sacredness) should not harm others, or, by being infringed, harm its possessor. I have shown in detail elsewhere how Marquesan tattoo and other body arts are consistent with this picture of continually threatened personal and spiritual integrity. But identity was only under threat *because* it was so labile, so relative and situational. Marquesans could switch social identities at will (by name-exchange, adoption, and other practices) so we have the (apparently) paradoxical situation that a culture whose central preoccupation seems to have been the assertion and protection of social/spiritual identity is also the culture in which identity is exceptionally tenuous. This was a society, to recall our earlier discussion of Lévi-Strauss, in which social status was, theoretically speaking, wholly a matter of pedigree—and in which it was, simultaneously, accepted that pedigrees could be arbitrary political fictions.

It seems at least plausible to argue that there is a connection between the 'principle of least difference' in Marquesan stylistic, and the prevailing preoccupation with differentiation in the context of dissolution which is the hallmark of Marquesan socio-cultural attitudes generally.

How did this consonance arise? Here one must recall that the Marquesan style is only the sedimented product of an infinite number of tiny social initiatives taken by Marquesan artists over a long period of historical development. Each new artefact, however standardized, cannot come into being without the need for stylistic decisions, be they ever so apparently trivial and inconsequential. These stylistic decisions, from which the coherence, stability, and long-term transformation of the Marquesan style ensued, were taken without deliberate reflection, but never without cognizance of a prevailing social context of social forms, pervaded by a dread of spiritual/political transgression. That is to say, there was an elective affinity between a *modus operandi* in the artefactual domain, which generated motifs from other motifs by interpolating minuscule variations, and a *modus operandi* in the social realm which created 'differences' arbitrarily against a background of fusional sameness. The limitless fertility of the Marquesan style in generating variant forms, each subtly distinct, coupled with its striking formal homogeneity simultaneously suggest an overwhelming need to establish difference and a recognition of the merely *relative* character of all differences.

In this sense, it is true to say that the relationships among motifs and figures in the Marquesan art style are akin to the relations which existed, on the social plane, between the Marquesans themselves. Artworks are like social agents, in that they are the outcome of social initiatives which reflect a specific, socially inculcated sensibility. This judgement coincides in essential respects with the view taken by the Marquesans themselves of their art. The motifs and figures I have discussed are all categorized, in their language, as *tiki*: 'images'. There are two other contexts in which this word has meaning. 'Tiki' (as the name of a mythological hero) is the Marquesan Adam. Humankind were originally created through the impregnation of a woman made of sand by the original ancestor (Tiki), who produced a human daughter, who was in turn incestuously impregnated by her father, who disguised himself by blackening his face in order to conceal his appearance. From this union humankind are supposed to spring (Steinen 1988). This maker and un-maker of appearances is Tiki, the first man. Here we observe the fundamental scheme-transfer between image-making and the making of persons.

The other meaning of *tiki* is 'portions' or 'shares' of some distributed object (Dordillon). If I cut a cake into twelve slices, each slice is a *tiki* of the cake. Human persons are *tiki* because their identities are defined in terms of the collectivities they participate in and divide from. At the same time, this usage adumbrates an idea which has been thematic throughout this chapter, namely that artworks are holographic fragments of the 'larger unities' to which they are united by stylistic linkages. The *tiki* (images/portions) which represent (or more precisely, constitute) *etua*, are holographic fragments, or refractions, of the imaginary totality of all *etua*. Artworks are shares or portions of a *distributed object* corresponding to all of the artworks in the Marquesan system, distributed in time and space. This idea will be explored in more detail in the next chapter.

9

Conclusion: The Extended Mind

9.1. *Distributed Objects*

The discussion of Marquesan graphic/plastic stylistics, just concluded, has been founded on the notion of a 'corpus' of artworks as a kind of spatio-temporally dispersed 'population'. Marquesan art, considered as a whole, can be conceptualized, macroscopically, as a 'distributed object' in time and space. Like the 216 separate items in a 24-place luxury set of china tea and dinner-ware, all Marquesan artworks belong to a kind of 'set', though, of course, a more loosely integrated set than the sets of china which are presented to young couples as wedding presents by rich relatives. A china dinner-set is bound together, as a distributed object (an object having many spatially separated parts with different micro-histories) by prior design, that is, by the intentional actions of the design and manufacturing staff of Spode, or Wedgwood, or who-ever. The corpus of Marquesan art, on the other hand, emanates from no such central executive organization, and has come into being only by historical accretion (and deletion) via a network of social relations, among Marquesans (artists and patrons) and outsiders (collectors, scholars, etc.) over the course of more than two centuries. Except, perhaps, from a stylistic point of view, Marquesan art has only a tenuous unity as a distributed object. It consists of no more than the detritus or exuviae of the once flourishing art-production and circulation system of the Marquesas now sundered and scattered, like the bones of the Marquesans whose living bodies bore the tattoos which so impressed visitors to the islands in the nineteenth century. All that remain are museum specimens, curiosities in private hands, sketches and drawings, and scholarly texts, such as Steinen's (and this one). None the less, despite this geo-graphical scattering and contextual transformation Marquesan art retains an inner integrity of its own, as a macroscopic whole rather than as an aggregate of fragments. Each piece, each motif, each line or groove, speaks to every other one. It is as if they bore kinship to one another, and could be positioned within a common genealogy, just as their makers could be. Above all, each fragment of Marquesan art resonates with every other, because each has passed, uniquely, through a Marquesan mind, and each was directed towards a Marquesan mind.

Marquesan minds are and always were, of course, minds belonging to indi-vidual agents, different and distinct. I do not want to suggest that Marquesan art is the product of a 'group mind' or collective consciousness. But in the ensuing sections I do want to approach, with due caution, the problem of the relationship between the macroscopic characteristics of distributed objects (such as 'the corpus of Marquesan art') and 'the mind' in both the individual and collective sense. The pith of my argument is that there is *isomorphy of structure* between the cognitive processes we know (from inside) as 'consciousness' and the spatio-temporal structures of distributed objects in the artefactual realm—such as the *œuvre* of one particular artist (Duchamp provides my example) or the historical corpus of types of artworks (e.g. Maori meeting houses, see below). In other words, the structures of art history demonstrate an externalized and collectivized cognitive process.

I must prepare my argument with care, for I recognize that I am traversing dangerous ground. Let me return to some of the ideas I introduced in earlier chapters, so that these may provide something by way of a stable platform from which to launch the ideas I want to develop now. These ideas, to reiterate, concern the structural isomorphy between something 'internal' (mind or consciousness) and something 'external'—aggregates of artworks as 'distributed objects' combining multiplicity and spatio-temporal dispersion with immanent coherence.

The contrast between 'internal' and 'external' will be familiar from preceding sections of this work—in particular sections 7.9–11, dealing with the externalist and internalist strategies for animating idols. One major upshot of that discussion, I hope, was that the contrast between 'inner' and 'outer' is always only a relative rather than absolute difference. The contrast between 'mind' (the internal person) and the external person, though real, is only relative. If we seek to delve inside the person all we seem to find are other persons—the homunculi of Dennett—and if, as sociologists rather than as cognitive psychologists, we try to give an account of the external aspect of persons, we find that any one social individual is the sum of their relations (distributed over biographical time and space) with other persons (M. Strathern 1988; Gell 'Strathernograms' 1998). Our inner personhood seems to consist of replications of what we are externally, as suggested in the parable of Peer Gynt and his famous onion. So, bearing this in mind, it may not be so aberrant to suggest that what persons are externally (and collectively) is a kind of enlarged replication of what they are internally. Especially if, as I shall be doing, we consider 'persons' not as bounded biological organisms, but use this label to apply to all the objects and/or events in the milieu from which agency or personhood can be abducted.

Seen in this light, a person and a person's mind are not confined to particular spatio-temporal coordinates, but consist of a spread of biographical events and memories of events, and a dispersed category of material objects, traces, and leavings, which can be attributed to a person and which, in aggregate, testify to agency and patienthood during a biographical career which may, indeed, prolong itself long after biological death. The person is thus understood as the sum total of the indexes which testify, in life and subsequently, to the biographical existence of this or that individual. Personal agency, as intervention in the causal milieu, generates one of these 'distributed objects', that is, all the material differences in 'the way things are' from which some particular agency can be abducted.

I recognize that this conception of personhood is both vague and abstruse. Fortunately it is not my task to describe personhood as such, but only to abstract certain themes which can be brought to bear on much more clearly demarcated 'distributed objects' than the notional 'object' which corresponds to the aggregate biographical effect wrought by the existence (rather than non-existence) of a particular agent or person. The relatively well-defined distributed objects testifying to agency that I have in mind, are, of course, categories of art objects.

The idea of personhood being spread around in time and space is a component of innumerable cultural institutions and practices. Ancestral shrines, tombs, memorials, ossuaries, sacred sites, etc. all have to do with the extension of personhood beyond the confines of biological life via indexes distributed in the milieu. The first example to which I shall devote detailed consideration belongs to this category, namely, the type of memorial carvings produced in northern New Ireland, and some adjoining islands, known as Malangan (Fig. 9.1/1), whose characteristics and significance have been analysed by Suzanne Küchler in a series of articles (Küchler 1985, 1988, 1992). I have a particular reason for highlighting these memorial carvings, because they instantiate, particularly clearly, not just the idea of 'distribution' (the object and/or person being distributed in time and space) but also the extraordinary, yet essential, notion that *images* of something (a prototype) are *parts* of that thing (as a distributed object). This is Yrjö Hirn's idea (see above, Sect. 7.4), traceable, as we saw, to Epicurus and Lucretius—the idea that sensible, perceptible objects, give off *parts* of themselves—rinds or skins or vapours—which diffuse out into the ambience and are incorporated by the onlooker in the process of perception. The purpose of Malangan, as we will see, is the transmission of ancestral social efficacy (social prestige, ritual privileges, land-rights, etc.) through the display of memorial sculptures which are incorporated into successors as *memories* (internalized visual images).

9.2. *Malangan*

There are some 5,000 carvings of the type known as Malangan in collections, which makes them among the commonest 'collectible' ethnographic art objects from any art-producing region of the globe. Yet Küchler tells us that, even though they are still produced in various forms, and are to the highest degree salient in contemporary political and ritual life in New Ireland, hardly a single one is actually to be seen *in situ* there—they are all in the hands of foreigners, and, as physical objects, of no concern to their erstwhile makers. Being sold off

FIG. 9.2/1. Malangan carving. *Source*: British Museum. New Ireland registration no. 1884, 7-28.1

for cash is the final 'death' of objects of this type, and has been since the latter decades of the nineteenth century. Conceptually, from the New Ireland point of view, a Malangan carving which has fulfilled its ritual role has rotted away and is no more, and its future as a museum piece is irrelevant. Malangan only 'exist' as socially salient objects, for a very short period, during the mortuary ceremonies for important persons, during which they are gradually imbued with life by being carved and painted, brought to perfection and displayed for a few hours at the culminating point of the mortuary ritual—only to be 'killed' with gifts of shell-money. Once they have been 'killed' they no longer exist as ritual objects (which is why they may subsequently be sold to collectors). The gift of money which 'kills' the Malangan entitles the donor to *remember* the image on display, and it is this internalized memory of the image, parcelled out among the contributors to the ceremony, which constitutes the ceremonial asset—entitling the possessor to social privileges—which is transacted at the mortuary ceremony and transmitted from the senior to the junior generations.

The Malangan, as an object whose physical existence can thus be measured only in days, or even hours, is an index of agency of an explicitly temporary nature. During the brief duration of the ceremony, the carving objectifies a dense and enduring network of past and future relationships between members of the land-occupying matrilineal units which constitute northern New Ireland society. Social relationships between land-occupying units are legitimized on the basis of members' *previously purchased rights to remember Malangan carvings and motifs*, and thus to act as agents in perpetuating these motifs (in different combinations) in subsequent Malangan ceremonies, where these memories will again be briefly objectified in carvings (in varied combinations) and again transacted and parcelled out among participants, against ceremonial payments.

But let us consider the Malangan carving more closely. There are various kinds, but I shall discuss only the familiar painted wooden variety seen in Fig. 9.1/1, which take the form of ancestral figures accompanied by a variety of subsidiary motifs. Which particular forms and motifs occur on any given Malangan carving depends on the identities of the land-occupying units mounting the ceremony and the particular strategies of political alliance these units anticipate for the future, once these alliances have been ceremonially legitimized by parcelling out Malangan memories.

The purpose of a Malangan is to provide a 'body', or more precisely, a 'skin' for a recently deceased person of importance. On death, the agency of such a person is in a dispersed state. In our terms, indexes of their agency abound, but are not concentrated anywhere in particular. The gardens and plantations of the deceased, scattered here and there, are still in production, their wealth is held by various exchange-partners, their houses are still standing, their wives or husbands are still married to them, and so on. The process of making the carving coincides with the process of reorganization and adjustment through which local society adjusts to the subtraction of the deceased from active participation in political and productive life. The gardens are harvested, the houses decay and become, in turn, particularly productive fields, and so on. That is to say, all the dispersed 'social effectiveness' of the deceased, the difference they made to how things were, gradually becomes an objectifiable quantity, something to which a single material index may be attached, and from which this accumulated effectiveness may be abducted. This is what the Malangan is; a kind of body which accumulates, like a charged battery, the potential energy of the deceased dispersed in the life-world. Küchler (1992) speaks of the carving as a temporary repository for the 'life-force' of the deceased, but we should perhaps observe that there is no difference between 'life' itself and this life-force; the life-force which accumulates in the Malangan carving is the net result or product of a lifetime's activity in the social world, not a species of mystical energy distinguishable categorically from ordinary life and activity.

The mechanism for the accumulation of dispersed life into the physical index of the Malangan carving is via the mechanism of fire. The process of making the image is conceptualized as the building up of a fire from ashes, to glowing embers, to the final blaze (1992: 104). The raw wood is charged with efficacy by a technique of heating and burning (this is connected to the technical use of fire to create the very numerous and complicated holes and cavities in the finished carving, especially in the epoch before metal tools were available). As the forms emerge (the carver, a hired specialist, is guided by dreams sent by the ancestors), the carving grows (conceptually) hotter and hotter. The culminating process is painting, at which time the carving is ready to redistribute its accumulated charge or 'heat' at the climactic ceremony during which it will be publicly displayed and remembered by those privileged to do so, and during which it will, itself, 'die' and become cold and rotten.

The carving, as I mentioned, is understood to be a 'skin' for the deceased. The concept of a skin is of the utmost importance here, for a number of reasons. In northern New Ireland, 'skin' stands for affinal relations. Political relationships (primarily, control over land) are founded on strategic affinal relationships created by ties of 'skin'—skin stands for the *transactable person*, the person divided up, recombined, and reconstituted. (For more on 'skin' cf. Gell 1993: 23 ff.) The carving, as Küchler implies, is both a three-dimensional, solid wooden 'container' for ancestral life-force, but at the same time, as an external surface (a two-dimensional field) it is a parchment on which participants in the Malangan ceremony inscribe their *anticipated* affinal alliances, in the form of specific painted decorations in red, white, and black. It is the transacted memory of the external, painted form of the carving which will legitimize future relationships between land-occupying units. As a carving/container, the Malangan is a repository of *past* 'social effectiveness' accumulated and contained, while as a spectacle, an exterior, the Malangan projects the future that these past relationships will produce, as a result of the legitimization of certain anticipated relationships (between affines) that the Malangan ceremony enables. The Malangan, in other words, mediates and transmits agency between past and future. Though the carving itself exists only within certain (restricted) time–space coordinates, conceptually, it is a *temporally dispersed object*, an object *at* no specific time or place, but moving through time and place, like a thunderstorm.

But the notion of 'skin' has an additional significance, which may not have escaped the reader. Let us proceed to the climactic moment, at which the participants in the ceremony witness the carving in its final form and register its memory. At this moment, the privileged ones (the ones who have made the appropriate ritual payments) receive 'the knowledge of Malangan'—that is, the right to reproduce not just the visible form of Malangan but the social relations, including land-rights, which this visible form indexes. The word which is used to refer to this empowering knowledge is *wune*, which, among other things, means 'smoke'. Since the carving has, at this stage, a surface charged to bursting with fire and heat, it is in no way puzzling to find that the idiom used to describe the transmission of potency from the carving (index) to the recipient (spectator) is a fiery one. But we also find, irresistibly recalled to mind, the words of Lucretius cited earlier (Sect. 7.4) in which he associates the 'flying simulacra' of things, the 'idols' which are emitted from things and which enable us to perceive them, with '[little bodies] in a state of loose diffusion, like smoke which logs of oak, heat and fires emit'. The Epicurean model implies that images of things are diffusible parts of things, just as smoke is a diffusible part of burning logs. Lucretius' association between the emission of heat and smoke—formless, quasi-material diffusion from the object—and the more familiar 'idols' which have visible form is recapitulated, almost magically, in New Ireland thought. For *wune* (as powerful knowledge) is not just the 'smoke' which emanates from the fiery surface of the carving; equally it is 'likeness' (the simulacra) in visible form, the 'skin' of the carving which is internalized as a memory image.

The Malangan carving is a skin-idol, which like the 'gossamer coats of cicadas' is distributed in quasi-material form in the memories of the onlookers, who internalize the ancestral 'skin' as a new 'skin' of their own, a new skin which anticipates new 'skin' relationships with affinal partners. Memorizing the image is a way of growing a new skin *internally* and thus projecting a new identity into the future. Poor Peer Gynt (above, Sect. 7.11) could only acquire *his* new skins by undergoing all the manifold vicissitudes related in Ibsen's play, resulting in the biographical accumulation of memory-skins which he disassembles along with his onion. New Irelanders proceed differently, for they have elaborated the art of transacting 'memories' as a conscious, public, strategy; the accumulation of memories is institutionalized rather than being the product of happenstance, like Peer Gynt's. Their accumulated, interlocking memories consist of internal skins, mediated via the Malangan, which can be taken apart and reconfigured at will.

This happens at the climactic moment of transmission, as the surface of the Malangan, animated by fire, is dissipated in the form of Lucretian simulacra which are internalized, more or less as internal body parts, by the privileged onlookers, who, in this way, receive the substance—not just of the ancestral body, but the entire *agentive capacity* of the deceased—for future redeployment. This is, as it were, the supreme abduction of agency from the index, in that the other's agency is not just *suffered* via the index; it is also thereby perpetuated and reproduced. Thus memory becomes a socially engineered medium for the transmission of the power to change the world and shape the course of events, rather than a mere passive registration of the past. Once the index has been witnessed in its 'charged' state, it is a mere corpse, drained of its power, because whatever memory images others may form of it (by witnessing it in its inert condition in a museum or a shop) they will not be *those* memories, the ones uniquely stipulated as potent and efficacious.

The example of Malangan art is useful in that it can start to undermine the distinction we commonly make between the material and the mental (or cognitive) with respect to material culture. The Malangan are indisputably material objects, but the *socially relevant* Malangan are internalized images which New Irelanders carry about inside their heads. Being a material object is merely a transitional phase in the biography of a Malangan, most of whose existence is as a memory trace, or, more idiomatically, as an internal 'skin'. The Malangans of northern New Ireland itself—rather than the Malangans in collections—are walking about, making gardens and political speeches, engaging in exchange transactions, marrying and having children, yet, paradoxically, they are not accessible to external ethnographic observation at all. Only an extended survey of past, present, and prospective Malangan ceremonies, and the associated kinship and land transactions—which Küchler is completing as I write—will reveal the ideal form of Malangan as a regional system of socially distributed memory images.

We, meanwhile, cannot pursue this fascinating prospect, but we can continue the general theme by turning our attention to similar systems of regionally distributed artworks (this time, consisting of enduring objects, rather than memory images) forming a dynamic whole, by referring to certain well-known studies by Nancy Munn (1977, 1986).

9.3. *Gawan Kula*

Nancy Munn's work is particularly salient in the context of this discussion, in that she has devoted particular attention in a series of studies, to the relationship between material indexes—Gawan canoes and Kula valuables—and (social) space-time. The argument on which I am embarking turns on this issue. My thesis is that 'cognition', or more precisely, consciousness, is a mental process through which subjective temporality is constituted via a process of *transformation* of conscious experience over time. In the next section I shall briefly present Husserl's model of the mind as a series of 'modifications' of perceptual/memory images. Concurrently, I am arguing that the 'indexes of agency' which exist and circulate in the external social world create, so to speak, an inter-indexical space-time field which bears an analogous structure, that is to say that it, too, consists of a series of transformations of contents (images) over time. This thesis will be instantiated later, with regard to the works of Marcel Duchamp and Maori meeting houses. But before we are in a position to embark on this argument, it would be helpful to consider further the question of the relation between artworks (or other indexes of agency) and space-time. In this area Munn has made certain very important contributions.

Nancy Munn's article 'The Spatiotemporal Transformation of Gawa Canoes' (1977) traces the biography of Gawa canoes, which start life as trees growing on the land held by a particular clan and are fashioned into canoes by members of other clans (moving through exchange pathways internal to Gawa in the process). Once made into canoes, they enter further exchange pathways within Gawa. Here they are transacted against the yams which are transmitted from wife-giving matrilines to wife-receiving ones. So in a sense, the canoes are converted into yams on Gawa, while outside Gawa they are converted into shell valuables—which are exchanged for them by their eventual users, men from other islands in the so-called 'Kula Ring' who use them for carrying on overseas (inter-island) exchanges.

From the point of view of the Gawa matriline which has exchanged a seagoing canoe for certain shell valuables (valuables that will themselves be circulated in overseas exchanges) the canoe is still 'owned'; but it is owned in another form, as shell valuables rather than as a wooden canoe. Munn detects a consistent process of de-materialization here. The canoe that was, heretofore, a heavy, rooted, earthy thing, a massive tree, becomes, by degrees, something totally immaterial, or rather, material but unconfined. That is, the canoe is converted into a 'field of influence'. This field is generated by the magnetism exerted by the Kula-exchange valuables into which the canoe has been converted. By virtue of being the unencumbered property of the owning clan (a type of property designated as *kitoum*) these valuables have the power to move other valuables (of different origin and type) in the direction of Gawa, and reciprocally, as they travel outwards, carrying the name and fame of Gawa far and wide. Munn argues that they are converted ultimately into what she calls 'sociotemporal space-time'. This space-time is not so much a dimensional manifold as a field of forces (like an electromagnetic field) exerted by objects of value (indexes of agency) ultimately attached to powerful persons but circulating in the milieu. This field constitutes transactional space polarized by the multiple forces generated by objects in continuous motion and undergoing successive metamorphoses. Each of these *kitoum* (unencumbered valuables) is traceable to a member of the owning matriline, who constitutes its social point of attachment, where it ceases to be a liberated object and becomes a partible component of a person, its original hole, so to speak.

A Kula operator, one who participates in the inter-island and internal exchanges in Kula valuables (arm-shells and necklaces) is a spatio-temporally extended person. The actual mechanics of the Kula system have been discussed so often since Malinowski's original description (1922) that it is hardly necessary to provide a detailed account here. Suffice it to say that men who participate in the system do so because they can lay claim to ownership of *kitoum*, that is, Kula valuables which are their own unencumbered ritual property, not valuables which they may be holding as intermediaries between one *kitoum*-holder and another. The relationship between *kitoum*-owner and the valuable which is held is indissociable, as if the *kitoum* were a body-part, but at the same time the *kitoum* is an object that can be transmitted abroad as an exchange item, that can circulate freely in space and time, and that can be converted into another object. The attachment to the original owner persists, however, because important *kitoum* are individually named, recognized, objects, and wherever the *kitoum* travels from island to island, the name of its owner will travel with it as well. The *kitoum*-holder inserts his *kitoum* into one of the exchange 'pathways' (*keda*) to which he has access, in exchange for return gifts which do not match the *kitoum* itself, but which are a sort of rent, paid by the recipient, for the privilege of being the one to serve as intermediary in the forwarding of this prestigious *kitoum* to its ultimate destination. Thus a flow of wealth is generated in the opposite direction to the passage of the *kitoum*. Eventually, though, after passing through many hands, in different Kula communities, the *kitoum* will encounter another valuable in the system which matches it, being equal in renown. This will be another *kitoum*, the unencumbered property of an equally important man on some distant island. When this happens, the original *kitoum* (an arm-shell, let us say) will 'marry' its opposite-number *kitoum* (which would be a necklace, because an arm-shell can only be exchanged for a necklace and vice versa) and the necklace, will begin to travel back towards the original *kitoum*-holder, again passing through many intermediaries along the way and setting up further countervailing flows of wealth. The aim of Kula operators is to gain control of numerous *kitoum*, manipulating the pathways of exchange so as to contrive that their 'names'—attached to prestigious valuables—travel far and wide. A man whose name is known in distant communities as one who controls the pathways along which renowned valuables are transferred, can influence the calculations of Kula operators in faraway places. He is, so to speak, more than a merely incarnate man. He is an expanded and disseminated being, present here, there, and everywhere because his name is attached to circulating objects, and still more because the movements of these objects are influenced, at long range, by his intentional agency, his calculativeness, and (magically assisted) persuasion (Munn 1986).

The Kula valuables which are associated with a Kula operator's name are conceptualized as indexes of his bodily presence as a person of commanding powers; from them, distant recipients abduct not just his power but his bodily beauty, for these Kula valuables are, after all, body-decorations as well as body-parts, and they are regarded as beautiful as well as ancient and prestigious. As a distributed person, the Kula operator attracts wealth as a young man attracts lovers; other's minds are swayed by his long-range allure and tokens of this love, in the form of valuables, speed towards him. Munn (1983) tells us that the ranking system of Kula valuables corresponds to the ranking system of Kula operators. The ranking scheme applied to valuables opposes new-ish, non-prestigious, items with little of the golden patina that comes from years of polishing and handling, and which have yet to be associated with the names of many famous men, to ancient, treasured items, which powerfully evoke the identities of men who, through Kula, have transcended time and space, who are timelessly potent, attractive, and influential. An important arm-shell or necklace does not 'stand for' someone important, in a symbolic way; to all intents and purposes it *is* an important person in that age, influence, and something like 'wisdom' inheres in its physical substance, in its smooth and patinated surfaces, just as they do in the mind and body of the man of renown to whom it was attached, and from whom it has flown away as an idol of distributed personhood. (Once again, we can draw an analogy between the Kula valuable as a migratory bodily index and the flying simulacra of Lucretius.)

But we cannot place the whole weight of the discussion on the 'distributedness' of distributed personhood, at the expense of the core of agency which lies at its heart. How does one, in practice, become a great Kula operator, a man able to 'move minds' at great distances and dominate an expended region of social space and time? How does one become so enchantingly attractive, so irresistibly persuasive, that the paths of inter-island exchange converge ineluctably in the desired direction? Only through knowledge, intelligence, and calculation. For success to accrue, the Kula operator must possess a superior capacity to engage in strategic action, which necessitates a comprehensive *internal model* of the external field within which Kula valuables move about (cf. Gell 1992*a*: 280–5). The operator must be able to comprehend the manifold and inordinately complex field of exchanges, must be able to remember innumerable past histories of exchanges, and evaluate their outcomes. He must construct 'what if' scenarios that anticipate the future with precision, guiding strategic intervention. His mind, in other words, must work as a simulation device—and this indeed is what all minds do, more or less—presenting a synoptic view of the totality of Kula transactions, past, present, and to come.

In his own person, the operator must reconstruct a working simulacrum—a dynamic space-time map of the maze of Kula transactions, so that, with somnambulistic dexterity, he knows which delicate strings to pull. Everything depends on the coherence of inner strategic intentions grounded in accumulated experience and memory, and the historically produced world 'out there'—the real world in which minds, objectified in exchange objects, expand, meet, and contend. The successful Kula operator controls the world of Kula because his mind has become coextensive with that world. He has internalized its causal texture as part of his being as a person and as an independent agent. 'Internal' (mental processes) and 'outside' (transactions in objectified personhood) have fused together; mind and reality are one, and—not to put too fine a point on it—something like godhead is achievable. This (relative) divinization through the fusing together of an expanded, objectified agency, and the myriad causal texture of the real world seems to me to be the ultimate objective of Kula. It suggests, to me at any rate, pathways towards transcendence which are as accessible to us, secular souls and die-hard materialists, as to the inhabitants of the Melanesian islands which participate in Kula transactions, but that is only by the by. The point that I wish to extract from all this is more limited. It is simply that when we come to consider the expanded, transactable, 'persons' and personhood on which the Kula system is founded, we are brought to recognize that 'mind' can exist objectively as well as subjectively; that is, as a pattern of transactable objects—indexes of personhood, in this instance, arm-shells, and necklaces—as well as a fleeting succession of 'thoughts', 'intentions', 'mental states', etc. The Kula system as a whole is a *form of cognition*, which takes place outside the body, which is diffused in space and time, and which is carried on through the medium of physical indexes and transactions involving them.

9.4. *The Artist's Œuvre as a Distributed Object*

Let us turn from the consideration of Oceanic instances of 'distributed objects' and 'distributed personhood' to an example closer to home. We, in the West, are familiar with one form of 'distributed object' (indexing a distributed person) above all—the *œuvre* or 'complete works' of famous artists. Any artist of renown is represented by numerous works, disseminated in various collections, and also capable of being reassembled for retrospective exhibitions, or published in a de luxe edition with a complete *catalogue raisonné*.

Let us consider the characteristic make-up of an artist's *œuvre*, an artist of the kind with which we are most familiar, a post-Renaissance professional artist with a distinctive personal style and a personal critical following. The artist's *œuvre* consists primarily of a series of finished works, produced, it may be, at different places, and subsequently distributed in numerous collections. These finished works are usually dated or datable, and can be assigned to a chronological sequence, early works, middle-period works, late works, and so on. So the artist's *œuvre* is both spatially dispersed and temporally dispersed. After the artist's death, once the *œuvre* is complete, it constitutes, as it were, an independent chunk of space-time, which can be accessed via each work individually, each standing, indexically, for all of them and the historical-biographical context of their production.

But the artist's *œuvre* does not consist exclusively of finished works each one of which stands as an independent entity. If we study the output of many famous artists (e.g. Leonardo, Michelangelo, Constable) we find that numerically speaking the greater part consists of 'preparatory studies' for finished works, rather than finished works themselves. Moreover, the *historical value* placed on these ostensibly 'provisional' technical studies, not produced for the art public but for private use in the studio, is as great, or even greater, than the value placed on the finished works (saleroom prices are another matter). From an historical point of view, these preparatory sketches are invaluable, because they inform us about the cognitive processes of generation of the finished works produced for public exhibition. Moreover, they are often crucial pointers to the underlying trend of development of the artist's style, and indeed the development of wider historical trends in art (e.g. the relationship between Constable's sketches and later nineteenth-century art, including Impressionism, etc.). The availability of sketches and provisional versions of works allows us insight into artistic activity as a process unfolding over (cognitive and biographical) time.

Meanwhile, the distinction I have just drawn between 'preparatory studies' and 'finished works' is not absolute. Because we know the dates of finished works, we are also able to see these finished works as being, simultaneously, 'preparatory studies' for later works. Thus, Cézanne's earlier 'bathers', and certain of his landscapes, while conceived independently, actually serve as preparatory studies for *Les Grandes Baigneuses*—a work in which Cézanne tries to epitomize, and further develop, a long series of previous experiments over twenty or thirty years.

Many artists produce works in recognizable series, consciously evolving a distinctive treatment of a particular motif over the course of their career. Braque, for instance, started painting pictures on the theme 'the artist's studio' (featuring a canvas on an easel) from the 1930s onwards; this series culminates in the 1950s and 1960s in a number of unforgettable masterpieces which synthesize Braque's mature style. We also have famous 'series' from Picasso, Bacon, Monet, Matisse, etc. In other words, it is frequently the case that works of art form 'moments' of temporal series, not just because they are datable objects (originating at certain space-time coordinates) but because they form *lineages*; they are ancestral to, and descended from, other works in the *œuvre*. Taken together, they form a macro-object, or temporal object, which evolves over time.

Finally, we may notice that the constituents of an artist's *œuvre* do not just point 'forwards' in time, as the 'preparatory sketch' points upstream towards the finished work, or Bacon's first 'Pope' points towards his later 'Popes'. Artists also 'remember' previous works in making new ones, 'quote' themselves, and even produce downright copies and replicas of previous work. We do not know which of the two versions of *The Virgin of the Rocks* by Leonardo (the one in London or the one in Paris) is the original and which is the copy; all that can be said for sure is that both display the same degree of technical excellence, and both equally are 'Leonardos'. Artists are nowadays reprimanded by critics for 'repeating themselves' since this is considered short-changing the public who demand continuous innovation. But actually all artistic practice is inevitably dependent on wholesale repetition, otherwise the concept of 'style' (which depends on some degree of resemblance between all the works in an *œuvre*) would be impossible to apply. Without repetition, art would lose its memory. Indeed, the concept of a 'preparatory study' implies, in itself, that the artist will subsequently 'copy' his own previous work (in private, 'study' format) so as to produce the subsequent 'public' work. So the mesh of temporal connections between the works in an artist's *œuvre* points in both directions. Any given work of art, in gross terms, considered in the context of its maker's *œuvre*, is likely to be both a 'preparation' for later works, and a 'recapitulation' of previous works.

However, where both artistic projection and artistic retrospection are at issue, we are able to render this thought a little more precise. There is a distinction to be drawn between, say, a 'preparatory study' which is produced in the process of designing a subsequent work which is envisaged in concrete terms, and the rather weaker relationship between a 'precursory' work which, undertaken as an end in itself, subsequently turns out to be ancestral to some later work, which was not *specifically* envisaged at the time of its production. While, in practice, there may be a shading-off between the 'preparatory sketch' and the 'precursor' of a subsequent work, they may, none the less, be opposed as ideal types. Similarly, we may oppose the 'artist's replica' (like the later version of the *Virgin of the Rocks*) which is produced with the idea of specifically replicating a previous work, with the unintentional replication of previous works which is a necessary feature of the origination of new works; that is, the painter, intending to produce new work, reproduces his previous work because stylistic coherence and painterly praxis (deeply ingrained artistic habits) demand it. Once again, in reality, there is a shading-off between intentional replication and unintentional recapitulation, but the ideal-typical distinction may be allowed to stand.

Thus, we may distinguish two relatively 'strong' temporal relationships between works and two relatively 'weak' ones. The 'strong' relationship subsists, in the future, or prospective, orientation, between the 'preparatory sketch' and the finished work, while, in this orientation, the 'weak' relation is between the 'precursory' work (the first in a series which was not *planned in advance* as a series) and subsequent works in the same series. Conversely, in the past, or retrospective orientation, the 'strong' relationship subsists between the (past) original and the subsequent copy, which is intended to *replicate* this past work, while the 'weak' relationship subsists between the 'original' work which —through a process of stylistic evolution in which not everything changes all at once—is *partially recapitulated* in subsequent work which returns to it, modifies it, and develops it further.

We now have the technical concepts in place to essay a general model of the artist's *œuvre* as a distributed object—in particular, as a distributed object in *time*, since the distribution of the artist's *œuvre* in space, though an interesting historical question, is beside the point here. The elements of our model are the separate components of the artist's total *œuvre*, that is, the 'complete works' as individual items, which are mutually related via the four relations just described.

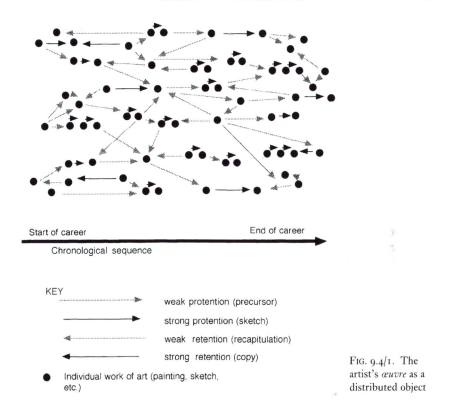

Start of career   End of career

Chronological sequence

KEY

....▶ weak protention (precursor)

————————————▶ strong protention (sketch)

◀....................................... weak retention (recapitulation)

◀———————————— strong retention (copy)

● Individual work of art (painting, sketch, etc.)

FIG. 9.4/1. The artist's *œuvre* as a distributed object

These relations, from now on, will be called strong and weak *protentions* for 'prospective' or future-orientated relations, and strong and weak *retentions* for 'retrospective' or past-orientated relations. The reason for using these particular terms will become clear once I introduce Husserl's model of time-consciousness, which I intend to do in a moment.

Before I do that, though, let me present an ideal model, in summary form, of the artist's *œuvre* (as a distributed object) as a temporal-relational diagram or map (Fig. 9.4/1). What we have are a spread of individual, dated, works which form the nodal points in a network of temporal relationships of protention and retention. Since all these relationships are temporal ones, we could have displayed the individual works in Fig. 9.4/1 simply as a linear sequence:

. . . .

with the protention/retention arrows looping over and under the row of chronologically arranged works (dots), but that would have resulted in rather an illegible diagram. The point of this diagram is simply to communicate the idea that we can imagine the artist's *œuvre*, at the macro-scale, as one indivisible work, consisting of many physical indexes (works) but amounting to a single temporal entity, like a persistent thunderstorm which is made up of many, quasi-instantaneous, flashes of lightning. The artist's *œuvre* is an object which, so to speak, is *made out of time*; not the tenuous, dimensional time of physics (which I have discussed, and indeed defended, elsewhere; cf. Gell 1992*a*) but the kind of substantialized time which Bergson named *durée*. Bergsonian *durée*, a model for which is provided by biological evolution regarded as a teleonomic process rather than as a random accumulation of chance mutations, has no significance for the physicist, but that is not to say that *durée* has no psychological or cognitive validity as a concept. Indeed, there is every reason to think that personhood, understood cognitively, is coextensive with subjective temporal experience. To refer to a person as a possessor of 'consciousness' is to refer to a series of cognitions arranged temporally along an axis of *durée*. But here we reach the crux of the matter. The chronologically arranged set of works which comprise an artist's *œuvre* are a set of material objects; they are not a person or a set of subjective experiences (cognitive states). They comprise a set of indexes from which the artist's personhood and agency can be abducted, as was described earlier (Sect. 9.2). But at the same time we can easily conceive that 'remembering' something which happened in the past is *very like* 'copying' a picture that one has painted in the past, or that 'making a preliminary sketch for a picture' is *very like* mentally anticipating some future happening or course of action.

In other words, the arrangement of individual works in an artist's *œuvre*, each of which is partly a recapitulation of previous works and partly an anticipation of works as yet uncommenced, seems to generate the same kind of relationships between *indexes* (which are objects in the external world) as exist between *mental states* in the cognitive process we recognize as consciousness. In other words, the temporal structure of index-to-index relations in the artist's *œuvre* externalizes or objectifies the same type of relations as exist between the artist's internal states of mind as a being endowed with consciousness. The artist's *œuvre* is artistic consciousness (personhood in the cognitive, temporal sense) writ large and rendered public and accessible.

But where does 'cognition' take place?—in the artist's head, or on his canvases? Mostly, of course, the cognitive processes of any mind, especially over a whole biographical career, are inaccessible private experiences which leave only the most indecipherable traces. And we could hardly aggregate an artist's *œuvre* as an unified 'temporal object' unless each of the individual works had, at one stage, originated as an *intention* in the artist's mind to produce such and such an index (i.e. a state of mind giving rise to artistic agency). But the generate-and-test model of creative agency, which we briefly examined earlier on, reveals most clearly that 'thinking' takes place outside us as well as inside us. The poet writes down his lines, and then scratches them out, altering and improving his verses in ways that crucially depend on the existence of physical traces of his previous (mental) activity. And this is still truer of the graphic artist, who continually uses his own past production as a spur to his future production, altering and modifying freely as he goes along. And in more general terms, the artist lives surrounded by his own works, completed or half-completed, which litter the studio and provide him with an ever-present record of his activity over many years (maybe *all* his activity in the case of artists whose works find no buyers).

The artist's *œuvre* can be understood like this; each separate work is a modification, a recension, of previous ones, the leftovers of a particular cycle in a career-long generate-and-test sequence. To be sure, this model is somewhat idealized, and much of art consists of routine output rather than the results of strivings after perfection. But the more inventive and historically important artists do develop in this way, and their work can be read as a cumulative process of discovery rather than the mere exploitation of technical procedures learnt early, never forgotten, and never surpassed.

The concept that I want to draw out further from the 'generate-and-test' model of creativity is that of *modification*. For one versed in the philosophical literature of cognition this word rings bells, because it is a word used (in English translations) by Husserl, who assigns the concept of 'modification' (of images, perceptions, i.e. the objects of thought) a central role in his model of consciousness as a temporal process. I have provided an account of Husserl's model of 'internal time-consciousness' in a previous work, and I propose to recapitulate some of my comments on Husserl's model here. My reason for doing so is that Husserl's model can help us to clarify certain features of the model of the artist's *œuvre* as a temporal object (or perhaps one should say, as a 'trans-temporal object') that has been presented in the preceding pages. In particular, it will help us to escape from a serious contradiction that I have not yet brought to light.

Suppose we have two works, X and Y, such that X is a 'weak protention' towards Y, that is that X can be seen as a precursor of Y but not as a definite 'study for' Y. Now, while X is in the process of being painted, Y is unimagined by the painter or by anybody else, in concrete terms. All that one can say is that the painter, while engaged on X, 'hopes' to paint future paintings, which will probably be related, technically and thematically, to X, but he only has a vague intuition as to what his 'next' picture will be. Y is still (and only) a 'future' painting, nothing in the world corresponds to it. Eventually, the painter will get round to painting his next picture (let us say, the next in a series) and it turns out to be Y. Now we have both X and Y whereas before we only had X. On inspecting Y we (and the painter) are able to see that Y was prefigured in X in very many respects, and, on this basis, we are inclined to say that Y recapitulates X, that Y is a 'weak retention' of X in that X is retained in Y as a 'preliminary version' of Y. But wait, there is a problem here, because we have already supposed that (in vague, if not specific, terms) Y has been *protended from* X, that is, Y is visibly what X *protends* in terms of the artist's development.

How can it be simultaneously the case that Y is protended from X (as a not-yet-realized 'future' painting) and simultaneously that Y 'retains' X as a kind of memory-trace now that Y has actually come into existence. How can we identify the 'Y' which was a *protention from* X and the Y which *is a retention of* X, when it would appear that these two Ys have contradictory properties; that is, can Y be a protention from X *and* a retention of X, at one and the same moment? This seems to involve some kind of logical conflict, yet, when we think about the relations between works of art in an artist's *œuvre*, we want to have it both ways; we want to see later pictures 'prefigured' in earlier ones, and we want to see 'traces' or memories of earlier pictures in later ones. These two types of relation between temporally separated pictures are clearly not the same, yet when we place them together they seem to collapse into one another in a most confusing way.

This, if you like, is the art-historical version of a familiar dilemma in the philosophy of time—the problem of events and tenses. Let me explain this by means of an example. Tomorrow I have a doctor's appointment. I protend this event, today, as a future event which will (probably) transpire, but I do not know, for instance, what the doctor will say or what treatment he will recommend. By the day after tomorrow, tomorrow's doctor's appointment will be a past event (of which I will have a memory, or retention) having transiently been a 'present' event (tomorrow). Obviously, this event (the appointment) is the 'same event' whether today is 'today' (15 October 1996), or yesterday, or last week, or tomorrow, or the day after tomorrow, or whatever day you please. Yet this unique event, on these various days, has the contradictory properties of presentness, pastness, or futurity; and how can 'one event' be past and present and future, without contradiction arising?

The answer to this puzzle is obviously that events like doctors' appointments, which are anticipated in advance, become present, and fall away into the past, do not possess attributes of pastness, presentness, and futurity in a once-and-for-all way, but only transiently, depending on the 'point of view' we have on the event in question from a certain 'now' moment, which continually shifts. The 'future' quality of a future event certainly colours our attitude to it (it has an *irrealis* shading, to use the grammarians' term), but even so we have no difficulty in identifying a future event which was only 'anticipated' with the event corresponding to our anticipations (more or less) which actually does happen, and the memory of that event which becomes *irrealis* in a rather different way as it slips back into the past and becomes a 'mere memory'. The same event, as a possible future event, as a present event which is being experienced, and as a past event which can be recalled, remains one event, but as our temporal perspective on this event shifts, the event undergoes a series of *modifications* from the standpoint of the cognitive subject. It is seen through various thicknesses of future and past time, which alter its appearance, its temporal patination, so to speak.

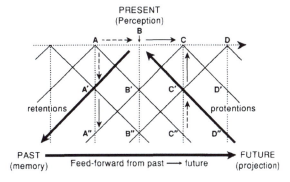

FIG. 9.4/2. A version
of Husserl's diagram of
time-consciousness from
Gell, *The Anthropology of
Time. Source*: A. Gell 1992*a*

Husserl, working on this problem towards the beginning of his career, when he was interested in describing cognitive processes in general so as to be able (eventually) to separate 'psychological' facts about cognition from transcendental philosophical certainties, put forward a most useful model of 'time-consciousness'. This is designed to depict the systematic modification of the 'noemata' (the objects of cognition) as a function of the passage of successive 'now' moments, that is, shifts in the subject's time-perspective.

In order to expound his ideas, Husserl makes use of a diagram, of which Fig. 9.4/2 (from Gell 1992*a*) is a version. The horizontal line A ⟶ B ⟶ C ⟶ D corresponds to the succession of events or 'states of affairs' occurring at 'now' moments strung out between the past and the future. Suppose we are at B: our perceptions up to date at B. The temporal landscape at B consists of the now-present perceptual experience of the state of affairs at B plus retentions of A, as A′, shading away into pastness. A′ (A seen from B) is a *modification* of the original A—what A 'looks like' from B, that is, attenuated or diminished, but still connected to the present. Perhaps one can think of the 'modification' of A as it sinks (diagonally to the left on Fig. 9.4/2) down into the past (A ⟶ A′ ⟶ A″ ⟶ A‴ ...) as a gradual *loss of verisimilitude* affecting the perceptions entertained at A as these are superseded by the perceptions entertained at B, C, D, etc. Our perceptions of the state of affairs as it is at any one 'now' moment do not become inapplicable immediately, but only gradually, because the world does not change all at once and in all respects. We can no longer, at B, say that the state of affairs at A is 'now' the case, because of the change of temporal perspective; but many of the features of A have counterparts at B, and features of B have counterparts at C, and so on.

Retentions can thus be construed as the background of out-of-date perceptions against which more up-to-date perceptions are projected, and significant trends and changes are calibrated. As perceptions become more seriously out of date, they diminish in salience and are lost to view. We thus perceive the present not as a knife-edge 'now' but as a temporally extended field within

which trends emerge out of the patterns we discern in the successive updat-
ings of perceptions relating to the proximate past, the next more proximate
past, and the next, and so on. This trend is projected into the future in the
form of protentions, that is, anticipations of the pattern of updating of current
perceptions which will be necessitated in the proximate future, the next most
proximate future, and the next, in a manner symmetric with the past, but in
inverse temporal order.

Let us continue with Husserl's own explanation of his model. At B, A is
retained as A' (A seen through a certain thickness of time) and C is protended
as C', the favoured candidate as successor to B. Time passes, and C' comes
about as C (presumably not quite as anticipated, but approximately so). B is
now retained in consciousness as B', related to (current) C as A' was to B when
B was current. But how is A related to C? From the standpoint of C, A is no
longer retained as A', because this is to put A' and B' on a par with one another,
and fails to reflect the fact that when B (currently B') was current, A was *even
then* only a retention (A'). Consequently, from the standpoint of C, A has to be
retained *as a retention* of A', which is itself a retention of A: that is, as A''.

Husserl says that as A sinks to A' at B, A'' at C, A''' at D, and so on, a perception becomes a retention, then a retention of a retention, then a retention of
a retention of a retention, and so on, until reaching the stage of final attenua-
tion and sinking beneath the temporal horizon. The effect of this argument
is to abolish the hard-and-fast distinction between the dynamic present and the
fixed and unchanging past. Past, present, and future are all of a piece, and all
equally dynamic in the Husserl model (embodying an important cognitive
truth) because any modification, anywhere in the system, sets up correlative
modifications everywhere else in the system. Thus the modification in the present which converts C into C' automatically entrains corresponding modifica-
tions everywhere (B' $\longrightarrow$ B'', A'' $\longrightarrow$ A''', D' $\longrightarrow$ D, etc.). 'The whole past sinks
in a mass, taking all its arranged contents with it' (Findlay 1975: 11). But the
past does not just 'sink' as the present progresses; it changes its significance,
is evaluated in different ways, and sets up different patterns of protentions,
according to the way in which the present evolves. This dynamic past, and
the future which continually alters in complexion, cannot be accommodated
in 'physical' time, but only in cognitive time. In providing his model of retentions, protentions, modifications, etc., Husserl is not describing an arcane
physical process which occurs to events as they loom out of the future, actu-
alize themselves in the present, and sink into the past, but is describing the
changing spectrum of intentionalities linking the experiencing subject and the
present-focused world which he experiences. 'Modification' is not a change in
A itself, but a change in our view of A as the result of subsequent accretions of
experience.

Husserl summarizes his view of internal time-consciousness in the following
passage:

Every actual Now of consciousness is subject to the law of modification. It changes into the retention of a retention and does so continuously. There accordingly arises a regular continuum of retention such that every later point is the retention of every earlier one. Each retention is already a continuum. A tone begins and goes on steadily: its now-phase changes into a was-phase, and our impressional consciousness constantly flows over into an ever new retentional consciousness. Going down the stream, we encounter a continuous series of retentions harking back to the starting point. To each of such retentions a continuum of retentional modifications is added, and this continuum is itself a point in the actuality that is being retentionally projected . . . Each retention is intrinsically a continuous modification, which so to say carries the heritage of its past in itself. It is not merely the case, that, going downstream, each earlier retention is continuously replaced by a new one. Each later retention is not merely a continuous modification stemming from an original impression: it is also a continuous modification of all previous continuous modifications of the same starting point.   (1928: 390, cited in Findlay 1975: 10)

Similarly, future events, do not really 'change' as a result of the fact that, from our point of view, they are becoming less indefinite, more imminent, and can be anticipated with increasing degrees of precision as they approach. But we have a strong compulsion to view them in such a light. Husserl's model treats this via a continuum of continua of protentional modifications. Protentions are continuations of the present in the light of the kind of temporal whole the present seems to belong to: 'To be aware of a developing whole incompletely, and as it develops, is yet always to be aware of it as a whole: what is not yet written in, is written in as yet to be written in' (Findlay 1975: 9).

The As and Bs and Cs in Husserl's model correspond to 'events' or states of affairs. What I want to suggest is that they can be replaced by individual works of art as constituents of an artist's *œuvre*. These are physical objects rather than 'events', but, all the same, they are *traces* or indexes of events, that is, the events or performances which brought them physically into being. What I am arguing is that if one seeks to construct the artist's *œuvre* as a unified temporal object, the same basic 'law of modifications' applies. What this means is that we cannot see the artist's *œuvre* as a temporal object except on condition that we select one particular work as corresponding to a 'now' moment, and see all the other works in the *œuvre* as either 'past' or 'future' works in relation to the 'now' defined by the particular work that we have selected as our temporal vantage-point.

Thus, to return to our previous discussion, we can only see an earlier painting, X, as a 'precursor' of Y (protention of Y from X) by situating ourselves at a vantage-point in time *at which Y does not yet exist*, and conversely, we can only see Y as a recapitulation of X (a retention of X) by shifting our point of vantage to a later 'now' at which Y has come into existence, and X is a 'past' work. We cannot occupy both of these vantage-points at the same time. This is the same as saying that we cannot totalize an artist's *œuvre* as a temporal object which can be regarded *sub specie aeternitatis*. All we can do is compile a 'file' of different temporal perspectives on the *œuvre* as a whole.

Suppose an artist creates, in the course of his career, 500 works which we can number Op. 1 through to Op. 500. We can construct the artist's *œuvre* 'from the standpoint of Op. 1' (i.e. as a very vague set of protentions from Op. 1), or from mid-career (protentions and retentions from Op. 250), or from 'last works' (retentions from Op. 500 and protentions towards works which we can only imagine, which the artist might have completed had he lived longer). Depending on which opus number we take as our point of vantage, I would argue, we obtain a different, unique, patterning of protentional and retentional relationships between works, and thus a different interpretation of the artist's *œuvre*. There is no absolute sense in which any given work can be seen, either as a recapitulation of a previous work, or as a precursor of a future one; the ensemble of an artist's works, strung out in time, constitutes a dynamic, unstable, entity; not a mere accumulation of datable artefacts. We can only appreciate it by participating in its unfolding life.

The reader may object at this point; 'this is all very well, but try as I may I find it hard to connect what you are saying to the actual *œuvre* of any artist whose works I know—Canaletto for instance'. And I would be obliged to admit that Canaletto's cityscapes, admirable though they are, hardly seem amenable to interpretation as psychological documents, as opposed to topographical ones. The model I have been advancing best applies to artists whose *œuvre* embodies a high degree of conscious self-reference and coherent development. I am far from claiming that the model just advanced would be particularly useful in all art-historical contexts. However, the model can easily be made to apply in at least some historical contexts, and it is to one of these I shall now turn.

9.5. *The Œuvre of Marcel Duchamp*

In a sense, I am going to cheat. Husserl's model of time-consciousness dates from a period in which problems of space-time, continuity, and the relation between physical reality and mental states were very much 'in the air'. His treatment of the subject shows, markedly, the influence of William James, while another contemporary philosopher who tackled these problems—and who may have exercised some direct influence on the course of art history —was Henri Bergson. The birth of analytical Cubism, the appearance of Husserl's *Psychology of Internal Time Consciousness*, and the publication of Bergson's most widely read work *Creative Evolution* were almost simultaneous events (between 1906 and 1907). The artist whose work I am going to use to illustrate my thesis, Marcel Duchamp, underwent his formative intellectual experiences during precisely this period. Though Duchamp never studied philosophy or mathematics systematically, he readily picked up the ideas that were doing the rounds in intellectual circles in his youth. Moreover, he read and mastered a number of texts (notably by Poincaré and Jouffret; see Adcock

1984) which popularized advanced mathematical and scientific thinking. Consequently, although the actual diffusion of ideas might never be documentable —and I certainly do not intend to document it—the fact is that Duchamp was probably to some extent aware, even if only indirectly, via the Cubists (and their in-house philosopher, Princet) of the James–Bergson–Husserl conception of temporal flux or the 'stream of consciousness'. So there might be an element of tautology involved in using Duchamp to illustrate a 'Husserlian' model of art history, when, in fact, Duchamp may actually have *set out* to illustrate it.

However that may be, Duchamp certainly provides by far the most perspicuous instance of an important artist whose total *œuvre* repays study as a network of protentions and retentions fanning out from particular works (particularly from his masterpiece *La Mariée mise à nu par les célibataires, même*—otherwise known as *The Large Glass* (1913–25)). I cannot, obviously, do more than hint at the richness of Duchamp's *œuvre* here—that would require a monograph to add to the many that already exist on this artist, certain of which copiously document the basic idea I am exploring here (see, especially, the work of C. E. Adcock 1984).

Duchamp's work is, essentially, *about* the notion of the continuum, in that it is based on the exploitation of the idea of the 'fourth dimension'. This dimension, I should immediately say, is not 'time' in the ordinary sense, especially not time as a mere measure of duration, or physicists' time. The 'fourth dimension' for Duchamp—as for certain of his contemporaries—was essentially the 'real' but strictly *unrepresentable* domain beyond, or encompassing, the 'ordinary' world we live in and perceive in the normal way. Duchamp's work originates in a mathematician's parable. A two-dimensional object (in the plane, e.g. in Abbot's famous *Flatland*) casts a one-dimensional shadow. A three-dimensional object (the kind of object we are familiar with in our 3-d world) casts a two-dimensional shadow. So what kind of object would cast a three-dimensional shadow?—obviously, that would have to be a 'fourth-dimensional object'; which is thus something which one can conceive of, but not represent, because to do so requires more dimensions than we have at our disposal, here in three-dimensional land. Duchamp's art, to simplify radically, consists of a series of essentially comic attempts to produce 'shadows' of fourth-dimensional entities, or at least to suggest procedures for obtaining these shadows of fourth-dimensional objects by extrapolating the shadows of three-dimensional ones.

To begin with, Duchamp merely identified the fourth dimension vaguely with a Symbolist never-never land. In 1910–11 he produced 'Symbolist' works which culminate in the *Young Man and Girl in Spring* (1911), which we will encounter in a different guise later. From mid-1911 onwards, he fell under the influence of the Cubists. The Cubists were interested in the fourth dimension, not as a symbolic myth but as a fact of subjective experience, and under Cubist influence Duchamp's notion of the fourth dimension became aligned, more and more, with Bergsonian *durée*. The underlying intention behind the 'classic' phase of Cubism was to create images which were 'realistic' in showing the spectator what the object *really was like*, rather than merely what the object 'looked' like. The earlier nineteenth-century artists admired by the Cubists were the 'realists', notably Courbet and Corot. The philistine public was bemused by Cubist claims to the effect that superior 'realism' was their goal, but the Cubists could cite copious philosophical precedents for their project. It is not philosophically unprecedented to suggest that there could be more to guitars and bottles than their visible appearance, viewed instantaneously and from a fixed point of view. Translating this insight into artistic practice was more difficult. Cézanne had shown the way, for example in some of his late depictions of Mont Sainte-Victoire, which—as later photographic researches at the spots at which Cézanne set up his easel were to prove—showed more of Mont Sainte-Victoire than could ever actually be seen from any *one* of these vantage-points. These landscapes depict, not any fixed appearance of Mont Sainte-Victoire, but Cézanne's interaction with this object over time, as he moved about in its vicinity and absorbed each of its varied aspects. Or, in other words, Mont Sainte-Victoire is revealed as a *process*, a movement of *durée*, rather than as a 'thing'. The weak point of Cubist 'multiple perspective' was that it could easily degenerate into a kind of painted cinema, in which successive 'frames' of a moving object, or an object seen by a moving camera, were simply pasted one on top of another. Cubist theoreticians, such as Gleizes and Metzinger, sedulously sought to emphasize the idealistic element in Cubism, its search for the pictorial equivalent of 'the absolute' rather than the facile evocation of dynamic motion and change. The Italian Futurists, on the other hand, embraced 'cinematism' heartily, since, unlike their Parisian Cubist colleagues, they were specifically interested in movement and dynamic phenomena (e.g. Boccioni).

Duchamp became a Cubist rather late in the day, just as 'classical' Cubist aspirations were beginning to unravel, and, being of a saturnine disposition, he joined the movement in order to indulge his increasing predilection for mockery, rather than because he was a true believer. (There were personal reasons for Duchamp's misanthropy, which have been extensively disinterred by his biographers.) Luckily for him, one of his 'satirical' Cubist works, the famous *Nude Descending a Staircase* of 1912, established his name as a leading avant-garde artist in the United States, where he subsequently secured lifelong patronage, though it resulted in his expulsion from the 'official' Cubist movement (for 'Futurist' deviationism). The *Nude* transparently employed 'cinematic' methods and was, in fact, based directly on stop-motion photographs by E. Marey and others. Duchamp's intentionally comic picture was designed to demonstrate the fact that while 'realism' remained the ultimate objective, the 'fourth dimension' could only, in the end, be physical time, and 'realistic' images (Cubist realist images, that is to say) would always reduce to chopped-up partial images of the object pasted onto one another or strewn over the canvas, as in the notorious *Nude*.

Duchamp was more ambitious; he still wanted to represent the unrepresentable flux of 'being' (to employ the Heideggerian term) but without simply reducing the multiplicity and fullness of experience to a series of partial snapshots. He

FIG. 9.5/1. *The Large Glass* or
*The Bride stripped bare by her
Bachelors even* by Marcel
Duchamp. Philadelphia Museum
of Art

consequently embarked, from 1913, on a long series of preparatory studies of a work which could, truly, adumbrate the fourth dimension. Because almost all of Duchamp's work, from 1913, is part of a single, coherent project, which subsequently, after the (semi-)completion of the *Large Glass* in 1925, extended itself until the close of his career, his *œuvre* is particularly interesting from our point of view. It is literally the case that Duchamp's *œuvre* consists of a single distributed object, in that each of Duchamp's separate works is a preparation for, or a development of, other works of his, and all may be traced, by direct or circuitous pathways, to all the others. This was intentional and explicit, since Duchamp's basic objective was to create a fourth-dimensional entity, and an *œuvre* such as his is perhaps as close as we will ever get to possessing such an entity.

Considerations of space—and the patience of my readers—oblige me to confine the demonstration of the characteristics of Duchamp's *œuvre* as a temporal object to a discussion of just one work, or rather, the *œuvre* 'seen from' just one work. The work I have chosen is one of the numerous studies for the *Large Glass* (see Fig. 9.5/1). In fact, it is a study for the 'Capillary Tubes' which draw

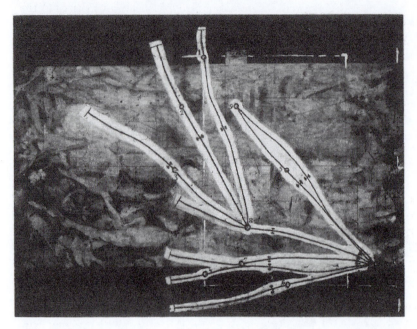

FIG. 9.5/2. *The Network of Stoppages* by Marcel Duchamp. © Succession Marcel Duchamp, ADAGP, Paris and DACS, London 1998.

off 'Love Gasoline' from the 'Cemetery of Uniforms and Liveries' on the left-hand side of the lower half of the *Large Glass* and feed it into the conical 'Sieves' in the centre. These tubes are no more than a minor detail of the *Large Glass* itself, yet Duchamp devotes an important study to them, indeed, more than one.

The work I shall discuss is known as *The Network of Stoppages* (no. 214 in Schwarz's complete catalogue; Fig. 9.5/2). It is both an independent work and a preparatory study for the *Large Glass*. At first glance, it looks rather like a map of some railway-system, the main depot (at the lower right, or south-east) serving a number of branch-lines fanning out to the west and branching again to the north. One sees little numbered symbols on the lines (which may be stations) and other symbols which might, possibly, be bridges or tunnels. Each 'branch' seems to come to an end in a 'terminus' of some kind. If one looks at this 'transport system' sideways on, from the lower right, one can perceive its relation to the Capillary Tubes in the *Large Glass*, for here the system is reproduced in 'perspective' projection (from this point of view), rather than 'map' projection. In the *Large Glass* the two-dimensional map shown in the *Network* has become a three-dimensional perspective view of the Capillary Tubes (hinting at the transition from a 3-d to a 4-d world by providing an instance of the transition from a 2-d world to a 3-d one).

The *Network of Stoppages* is therefore a protention towards (part of) the *Large Glass*, even though the *Network* only appears there in transformed perspective. At the same time the *Network* is a retention of certain earlier works. In particular it recapitulates directly a piece called *The Three Standard Stoppages* which consists of three curved wooden templates which were used to draw the curved 'tracks' shown in the *Network*.

One idea Duchamp was working on was that in the 'fourth dimension' events which seem to us like 'pure chance' would correspond to *necessity*. An 'arbitrary' length, or a 'random' curve would, in the fourth dimension, be something really basic like 'one metre' or 'a perfectly straight line'. Accordingly, Duchamp took three one-metre lengths of string, allowed these to drop freely onto sticky varnished boards, and from these arbitrary curves he cut templates, called the *Three Standard Stoppages*, which would be the basic geometrical forms and units of measurement for 'fourth dimensional' use. The network is obviously a 'strong retention' of these templates, just as it is a 'strong protention' towards the Capillary Tubes.

But there is much more to it than this. If we inspect the *Network* more carefully, we observe that it is painted over something else. Duchamp has not used a fresh, pristine canvas, but has done his design-work for the Capillary Tubes on a reused canvas on which more than one image has already been inscribed. In fact, the canvas has already been used twice, for apparently different purposes. Counting from the 'top' layer downwards, the *Network of Stoppages* consists of:

1. The 'map' of the *Network*;
2. A (quite faint) preliminary line-sketch for the *entire layout* of the *Large Glass*, as Duchamp conceived it in 1913, before many details had been worked out;
3. A version of *Young Man and Girl in Spring*—Duchamp's 'Symbolist' canvas of 1911, his first major painting, dealing with the theme of 'initiation' and (possibly) incestuous longing (for his sister, Suzanne, to whom he gave it as a wedding present); cf. Fig. 9.5/3.

Now obviously, Duchamp could perfectly well have afforded to use a fresh canvas (or simply a large sheet of paper) for both 1 and 2, if all he required was something drawable-upon to do his design-work; especially if he intended to sell his sketches to patrons once they had served their purpose, as most artists do and as he himself subsequently did. Instead, he produced what amounts to a *series* of works while using only *one* canvas; self-defeating parsimony one would have thought—which he made up for later by producing, or having others produce for him, many identical replicas of his earlier works.

Clearly, there must be more to this than mere economy. By creating a palimpsest of three works to serve as a preparatory study for a fourth (and indeed many more) Duchamp is approaching the fourth dimension in yet

FIG. 9.5/3. *The Young Man and Girl in Spring* by Marcel Duchamp (1911)

another way—and a very perspicuous way from an anthropological perspective. Just recall the title of this work again: *The Network of Stoppages*. For us anthropologists, those words ring certain bells, because we have Durkheim's *Elementary Forms of the Religious Life*, engraved on our memories. And if not, then at least we have all read Lévi-Strauss's *Totemism* (1964) where Durkheim's words are quoted. The original source is a Dakota Indian, discussing metaphysics:

Everything as it moves, now and then, here and there, makes stops. The bird as it flies stops in one place to make its nest, and in another to rest in its flight. A man when he goes forth stops when he wills. So the god has stopped. The sun, which is so bright and beautiful, is one place where he has stopped. The moon, the stars, the winds, he has been with. The trees, the animals, are all where he has stopped, and the Indian thinks of these places and sends his prayers there to reach the place where the god has stopped and win help and a blessing. (Durkheim, quoted in Lévi-Strauss, *Totemism*: 98)

Lévi-Strauss quotes this passage in the course of a discussion of Bergson, who, he says, propounded remarkably similar views in *Creative Evolution*, and who was undoubtedly familiar with the passage in Durkheim in which they are quoted. Lévi-Strauss goes on to remark:

The better to underline the comparison, let us quote without break from the paragraph in *Les Deux Sources* [*The Two Sources of Morality and Religion*] where Bergson sums up his metaphysics:

A great current of creative energy gushes forth through matter, to obtain from it what it can. At most points it is stopped; these stops are transmuted, in our eyes, into the appearances of so many living species, i.e., of organisms in which our perception, being essentially analytical and synthetic, distinguishes a multitude of elements combining to fulfil a multitude of functions; but the process of organisation was only the stop itself, a simple act analogous to the impress of a foot which instantaneously causes thousands of grains of sand to contrive to form a pattern.

The two accounts agree so exactly that it may seem less risky, after reading them, to claim that Bergson was able to understand what lay behind totemism because his own thought, unbeknownst to him, was in sympathy with that of totemic peoples. What is it, then, that they have in common? It seems that the relationship results from one and the same desire to apprehend in a total fashion the two aspects of reality which the philosopher terms *continuous* and *discontinuous*; from the same refusal to choose between the two; and from the same effort to see them as complementary perspectives giving on to the same truth. (Lévi-Strauss 1964: 98; for refs. see original)

It is surely not difficult to grasp the connection, now, between the subject-matter of Duchamp's *Network of Stoppages*, and the peculiar manner in which it has been presented, as a layer-cake of artworks placed one over the other. The 'Net-work', both shows us a Network of Stoppages, *and also is a network of stoppages*, i.e. a series of 'perchings' at which Duchamp, in his 'flight' becomes visible in the form of an index of his agency, a particular work of art. *The Network* looks like a 'map' because it is part of a 'map' of *time*. But this can only be a four-dimensional map. Like Bergson, Duchamp downplays the 'merely' visible, or its illusionistic representation. Like Bergson, he distrusts our perception 'which is merely analytic and synthetic', and seeks instead the 'current of creative energy' (i.e. *durée*, or Heideggerian 'being') which 'gushes forth through matter'. This is the fourth dimension.

In Husserlian terms, there is a most startling analogy between the transparent layering of *The Network of Stoppages*, and the concept of *durée* constituted out of retentions, retentions of retentions, and so on. *The Network* is a protention towards the *Large Glass*, which is a retention, first, of the original abstract layout for that work (before its content was finalized) and secondly a retention, from this retention, of Duchamp's Symbolist beginnings, the thirst for transcendence and release from incestuous longing ('initiation') which set him on the path he subsequently followed. Duchamp allows us to see his 'sinking' past as a transformable component of his present, retained as something already superseded in the course of his intervening life. And indeed, there are ample art-historical reasons for interpreting *The Large Glass* as a transformed version, a distant memory, of *The Young Man and Girl in Spring* (see e.g. Golding 1973: ch. 3).

What I am proposing, therefore, may be called a 'Dakota' model of the artist's *œuvre*; each artwork, as Duchamp's picture so strikingly reveals to us, is a place where agency 'stops' and assumes visible form. *The Large Glass* itself was subtitled, by its creator, as a 'delay in glass' (*retard en verre*), suggesting precisely this idea (the glass, like a photographic plate) delays the passage of the shadows of the fourth dimension, and captures their visible traces. In later works the procedure is repeated more explicitly: for instance, in *Tu m'* (1918), which features *trompe-l'œil* 'shadows' of Duchamp's previous 'ready-made' works (the *Bicycle-Wheel* (1913), the *Hat-rack* (1914), etc.).

Each Duchamp work, in other words, invites us to adopt a particular perspective on all Duchamp's works, often by providing explicit quotations or references to past and future works, though also adumbrating retentions and protentions in a more elliptical fashion. The sum total of the infinitely transformable network of internal references (protentions and retentions) uniting the *œuvre* from *all* of these temporal 'perches'—which we can only, in fact, adopt serially, is the unrepresentable but very *conceptualizable* and by no means 'mystic' fourth dimension. In this way Duchamp triumphantly vindicates himself as a comic, secularist, psychopomp.

At this point, without having done more than scratch the surface, I curtail further discussion of Duchamp's *œuvre*, though I hope that I have said enough to encourage any interested readers to pursue the subject further, since the literature and documentation available is unusually extensive and revealing. My purpose is only to establish the point that Duchamp's subjectivity, his inner *durée* is concretely instantiated, as a series of moments, or 'delays' or 'perchings', in the objective traces of his agency, that is, his artworks and the texts he produced to go with them. Here we have, in public, accessible, form, the 'continuum of continua of protentional and retentional modifications' described by Husserl for the purposes of elucidating the purely *subjective* process of cognition, or consciousness. In other words, as a distributed object, Duchamp's consciousness, the very flux of his being as an agent, is not just 'accessible to us' but has assumed this form. Duchamp has simply *turned into* this object, and now rattles around the world, in innumerable forms, as these detached person-parts, or idols, or skins, or cherished valuables. So we return to our starting-point. But there is one more step to be taken. Duchamp is (or was) an individual mind, one particular person exercising one particular agency. What about the art produced, not by individuals over a lifetime, but by collectivities over longer periods of time; what, in other words, can we say about collective 'traditions'. Can we, so to speak, expand the model that we have just constructed of 'the artist's *œuvre*' to encompass something wider, something corresponding to a 'cultural tradition' so that we can see that, too, as a distributed object structurally isomorphous to consciousness as a temporal process, or *durée?*

This is the final problem to which I will turn, in concluding the present work.

9.6. *The Maori Meeting House*

Copious data relevant to the question just raised have recently been provided by Roger Neich (1996). He has completed a detailed study of all the extant or photographically documented meeting houses constructed by the Maori of North Island between *c.*1850 and 1930, which were, in turn, a development of chiefly houses (large structures erected with magnificence in mind) of the earlier nineteenth century and the pre-European period (Fig 9.6./1 from Neich, fig. 68). The present-day Maori 'meeting house' came into its own during the latter half of the nineteenth century, especially from 1870 onwards, a period during which the Maori found themselves unable to compete with one another (or Europeans) via the traditional warlike means. Their competitive spirit focused more and more on the construction of large, elaborately carved and painted meeting houses, each Maori community trying, so far as lay within its power, to outdo its neighbours and rivals in this respect. The totality of Maori meeting houses, therefore, constitutes a particular genre of art production, over a particular historical phase in the course of Maori history (in many ways, a glorious period, which contemporary Maoris rightly recall with pride), which can be considered 'coherent' in the sense we require. All Maori meeting houses, that is to say, followed a common 'ground plan', all were designed with a common purpose, namely, to serve as an objectification of the wealth, sophistication, technical skill, and ancestral endowment of the community responsible for the construction, and as a means to ensure that persons not of this community, who might be entertained there, would be consumed with jealousy and thoroughly intimidated. As Nick Thomas has written, apropos of Maori art:

houses . . . were *not* 'symbols' . . . but vehicles of a collectivity's power. They simultaneously indexed a group's own vitality and ideally or effectively disempowered others. Distinctions between function and meaning, use and expression, instrumentality and symbolism obscure what was integrated and processual in these collective presentations of tribal efficacy . . . (Thomas 1995: 103)[1]

---

[1] The reader would not be mistaken in thinking that these comments by Thomas played an important part in shaping the views expressed in Ch.1 of the present work.

FIG. 9.6/1. The Maori meeting house as a collective index of communal power. *Source*: Nga Tau-e-Waru, te Ore Ore Marae, Masterton. Auckland Public Library.

Maori meeting houses may have been the collective production of many separate artists and builders, working in separate communities at different times, each striving to produce something distinctive, yet all are expressions of a common historical trajectory, a common cultural system, a common ideological and political purpose. We are entitled, therefore, to group them together, as Neich does, since they constituted the 'final common pathway' for the physical expression of 'Maoridom' as a collective experience, during the relevant period.

Because these collective 'indexes of agency' were *houses*—artefacts with very special characteristics all their own (cf. Hugh-Jones and Carsten 1995)—they possess features which render them especially suited to the projection of collective agency. First of all, houses are 'collective' in the simplest sense of all, that people collect in them, and are joined together by them; this applies to any house and is the reason why so many social groups are referred to as 'houses' (Lévi-Strauss; cf. Hugh-Jones and Carstens, op. cit.). Secondly, houses are complex artefacts consisting of many separate, standard, parts; they are thus organized, or 'organic' entities, unlike, say, a bowl or a spear, however wonderfully wrought. Their organic plan and capacity for disassembly and reassembly, remodelling and redecoration allows them to objectify the organic connectedness of historical processes. And finally—and above all—they are bodies. The house is a body *for* the body. Houses are bodies because they are containers which, like the body, have entrances and exits. Houses are cavities filled with living contents. Houses are bodies because they have strong bones and armoured shells, because they have gaudy, mesmerizing skins which beguile and terrify; and because they have organs of sense and expression—eyes which peer out through windows and spyholes, voices which reverberate through the night. To enter a house is to enter a mind, a sensibility; especially if it is such a house as the Maori were accustomed to make. Like many traditional psychologists, the Maori located mind and intention in the viscera. To enter a house is to enter the belly of the ancestor and to be overwhelmed by the encompassing ancestral presence; overhead are the ribs of the ancestor, in the form of the superbly decorated rafters which converge towards the ancestral backbone, the ridge-pole—the fountainhead of ancestral continuity. On all sides, idols of ancestral beings gaze down hypnotically, entrapping the onlooker in their thought-processes (cf. above, Ch. 7 on idols). The flying simulacra of the ancestors criss-cross this interior space with unbelievable rapidity and profusion; all merely private, independent, thought is overwhelmed and only those cognitions which actually emanate from the house, those cognitions which are part of the house's very structure, are attainable.

Neich provides a very comprehensive discussion of the cosmological 'symbolism' of Maori meeting houses. He shows in great detail how each such house was explicitly conceptualized as the body of the eponymous ancestor of the community, who was not so much 'memorialized' in the house which bore his name, as reinstated in this form. The house was not a surviving trace of the ancestor's existence and agency at some other, distant, coordinates, but was the body which he possessed in the here and now, and through which his agency was exercised in the immediate present (to describe this as 'symbolic' is obviously a misnomer). At the same time the house was a multiplicity of connected bodies, a bodily 'fractal' in Wagner's sense (1991; cf. Sect. 7.11), since it consisted of the bodies of the ancestor's descendants, by genealogical succession, both living and deceased. The ridge-pole objectifies the genealogical continuity of the chiefly line (notionally by male primogeniture) while the descending rafters indicate the proliferation of cadet lines on either side. These were decorated with captivating patterns of the type called *kowhaiwhai* (Fig. 9.6/2 from Neich, fig. 17), which evoked the tendrils and runners of the ever-productive, ever proliferating *kumara*, the sweet potato plant which provided the Maori with their staple diet. Body, genealogy, gardens, were all copresent and synergically active. The living members of the community, gathered in the house, were, so to speak, only 'furnishings'. They were mobile appurtenances of its solid, enduring structure, into which they would eventually be absorbed as 'fixtures'.

But the point of this section is not to discuss the cultural significance of the Maori meeting house, which would be redundant given the excellent work that has already been published on this subject by Neich and his colleagues. The preceding remarks only reiterate the thesis, argued in earlier parts of this work, that artefacts like Maori meeting houses are not 'symbols' but indexes of agency. In this instance, the agency is collective, ancestral, and essentially political in tone.

FIG. 9.6/2. Kowhaiwhai patterns: part of the verandah or porch of the large house of the Ngati-Porou at Wai-o-Matatini, East Cape. *Source*: Plate XIII from Augustus Hamilton, *Maori Art* (1896).

My aim in introducing this material is to explore the theme of 'traditions'. To what extent can we study the whole gamut of Maori meeting houses, distributed in space and time, as a single, coherent, object, distributed in space and time, which, in a certain sense, recapitulates, on the historical and collective scale, the processes of cognition or consciousness? Fortunately, through the very meticulous studies undertaken by Neich, we can indeed make progress in this direction. In order to show this, I need do little more than reproduce a table, devised by Neich himself, which appears on page 220 of his book (Fig. 9.6/3). Neich's table 'The Transmission of Selected Figurative Painting Traditions' is organized in the following way. The left-to-right axis of the table corresponds to the axis of historical time (between 1870 and 1930) while the top-to-bottom axis, which is unlabelled, corresponds, implicitly, to geographical space; that is, meeting houses (the large black spots with numbers and letters in them) which lie on a horizontal axis are or were spatially contiguous. The numbers denote particular meeting houses in Neich's comprehensive catalogue of the same, and the letters correspond to 'traditions' of Maori figurative painting, which began to develop and proliferate from 1870 onwards—before which time only Maori carving was 'figurative' and painting (on meeting houses) was in the *kowhaiwhai* style and developments therefrom. We do not actually need to discuss Neich's material in any depth, since it is very detailed and contextual. All that I primarily wish to do is to underline and explore an observation that must have inevitably occurred to the reader already, that there is a great deal of similarity between Neich's diagram and the

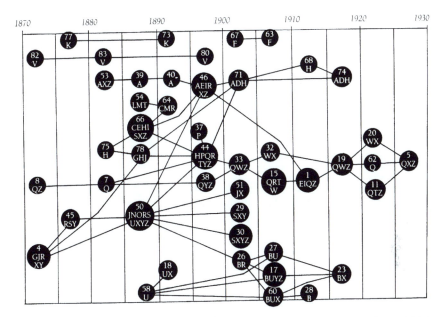

Fig. 9.6/3. The Maori meeting house as an object distributed in space and time. *Source*: Neich 1996: table titled 'The Transmission of Selected Figurative Painting Traditions'. Reproduced courtesy of Roger Neich and Auckland University Press.

diagram I presented as Fig. 9.4./1—the spot-and-arrow diagram in which I sought to provide an abstract model of the 'artist's *œuvre*'.

Instead of arrows, Neich joins the nodal points in his historico-geographical network by simple lines; he is not thinking in terms of protentions and retentions which, from any given 'now' moment, or from the temporal standpoint of any given work of art at the moment of its completion, always have a definite directionality, towards the past (memory, recapitulation) or towards the future (project, preliminary sketch). Meanwhile, Neich is thinking, as most art historians do, in terms of 'progress'; from the past and towards the future, because his whole book is premised, not unjustifiably, on the idea of the 'development' of a distinctive Maori art. So I guess that had he used arrows instead of lines on his table, his arrows would all have been rightwards-pointing ones. But this is not really logical, in that the concept of 'the transmission of traditions' really involves, primarily, the artist, commissioned to decorate a house at time 'T-zero' 'remembering' an exemplar that he witnessed, somewhere else, on some previous building, at 'T-minus-one'. The transmission of a 'tradition', the recapitulation of a model, is the objectification of memory, and thus inherently retrospective. So the arrows ought, most logically, point not from left to right, but from right to left. But this will not do either, because whatever the artists who made the Maori meeting houses had in mind, it certainly was not to reproduce, tamely, the houses that had been constructed, by other communities, sometime in the immediate or more distant past. The whole point of these houses, as was emphasized earlier, was to bring about the crushing of the (architectural) self-esteem of members of rival communities, to exalt the ancestors of the house-building community over everybody else's ancestors, by objectifying them with superior magnificence and sophistication (which meant, *inter alia*, incorporating references to *pakeha*—'white'—art into the décor, alongside 'traditional' art forms). It is not just that Maori meeting houses incorporated 'innovations' (i.e. non-traditional elements which, later, being imitated, became 'traditions' in themselves), each house was totally an 'innovation' (cf. Wagner 1977) in that the house was orientated towards the future, the political triumph which would be the *anticipated* outcome of the effort invested in its construction. The building of the house was a collective, intentional, action, and 'action' is intrinsically future-orientated. The 'agency of the ancestor' of which the house is an index, is equally future-orientated; the ancestor's body/house is not a corpse or a memorial to the departed. So once again, it seems that we should make our arrows point from left to right, towards the future. After all this, it may seem that Neich has done well to refrain from using arrows at all, in that doing so results in paradoxes; as 'traditional' artefacts, Maori meeting houses are undeniably retrospective, as political gestures they are prospective. Yet how can meeting houses be both prospective and retrospective at the same time?

But we have encountered, and (I hope) surmounted this difficulty already. An artefact or event is never either traditional or innovatory in any absolute sense, or, as time-philosophers are inclined to put it, *sub specie aeternitatis*. A 'traditional' artefact (or event) is only 'traditional' when viewed from a latter-day perspective, and as a screen, or transparency, through which its precursors are adumbrated. The traditional object is grasped as a retention, a retention of retentions, and so on. Conversely, an 'innovatory' object (or event) is innovatory only on condition that we situate ourselves anterior to it in time (i.e. at a moment in time at which it has not yet, or is just about to, come into existence)—so that we can likewise see it as a screen through which still later objects may be protended, as a protention, protention of protentions, etc. The temporal object constituted by the totality of the meeting houses displayed on Neich's diagram consists therefore, not of a network of temporal relations which can be totalized in a single synoptic mapping; but only as a 'file' consisting of a whole series of such mappings corresponding to different temporal (and spatial) points of vantage; each one of which generates a distinctive distribution of retentional and protentional relations between any given meeting house and its spatio-temporal neighbours. The logically mandatory nature of such a continuously shifting perspective on tradition and innovation in an historical assemblage of artefacts means that the process of understanding art history is essentially akin to the processes of consciousness itself, which is marked, likewise, by a continuous perspectival flux.

To express this more concretely, we can interpret any given meeting house, viewed from the latter-day perspective, as a 'memory' in objectified form, of meeting houses anterior to this one. Indeed, in terms of the cognitive processes of the Maori builders, 'memory' is the faculty responsible for the transmission of the lore, the skills—the 'tradition' in other words—which the house embodies. But this would not be 'tradition' unless the memory-antecedents of the house constructed 'from memory' were remembered as having antecedents of their own, of which they, in turn, were memories, back into the past. Each house embodies not just the memory of its immediate exemplar, but a cumulative series of memories, memories of memories, and so on. That is to say, it carries with it the whole thickness of *durée*, and belongs not just to a 'now'—the temporal coordinates of its dates of construction—but to an extended temporal field which reaches back into the past and which is drawn up into the present again.

Conversely, each meeting house is a project for future houses, a 'sketch' towards a series of as yet unbuilt houses. We are inclined to see artefacts, especially rather splendid artefacts like these, as if they embodied the final intentions of their makers. But anyone who has ever had anything to do with building anything (even an extension to a suburban home) will instantly recognize that this is hardly the case. What gets built is whatever seems the best possible compromise in the light of all the practical difficulties and constraints entering into the situation; given that the decision to build 'something or other' has already been taken. We may think that our house-extension is vastly superior to our neighbours', but that does not mean that we would not like to tear the whole thing down and start again, were that a practicable option. We are certainly entitled to suppose that the same disparity between aspiration and actuality entered into the process of building Maori meeting houses. These, it will be recalled, were erected in an overt spirit of competition, in order to indexicalize the superiority of one community, and its legions of ancestors, over other, neighbouring, communities. No meeting house could, in this context, be too large, too sophisticated, too expensive and magnificent. But the nineteenth-century Maori were, as a matter of fact, impoverished, oppressed, and diminishing in numbers, while the assistance afforded them by their ancestors was, in the end, finite. The houses that were built were far, probably, from being the houses the Maori would have liked to build; they were, perhaps, superior to the houses which preceded them, they might, arguably, be superior to the meeting houses of rival communities (though this would probably not be conceded in public)—but they could hardly be superior, or even equal, to what they were *intended* to be. There were only 'sketches' or 'protentions towards' the ultimate meeting house, which, for practical reasons, would always remain unrealizable. The meeting house as a 'sketch' embodied, the promise, some time in the future, to build the meeting house to beat all meeting houses; and it was this 'threat' to build, once circumstances became *really* favourable, the 'ultimate' meeting house, which was aimed at the neighbours, as much as the 'realized' house itself.

Thus we are enabled to see the totality of Maori meeting houses as a cognitive process writ large, a movement of inner *durée* as well as a collection of existing objects, and documents appertaining to objects which time has obliterated. The Maori meeting house (in its totalized form) is an object which we are able to trace as a movement of thought, a movement of memory reaching down into the past and a movement of aspiration, probing towards an unrealized, and perhaps unrealizable futurity. Through the study of these artefacts, we are able to grasp 'mind' as an external (and eternal) disposition of public acts of objectification, and simultaneously as the evolving consciousness of a collectivity, transcending the individual *cogito* and the coordinates of any particular here and now.

BIBLIOGRAPHY

ACKERMAN, J. S. (1970), The Architecture of Michelangelo (Harmondsworth: Penguin Books).

ADCOCK, C. E. (1983), *The Large Glass* (Epping: Bowker Publishing House).

ALLEN, M. (1976), 'Kumari or Virgin Worship in Kathmandu Valley', *Contributions to Indian Sociology*, 10/2: 293–316.

ANZIEU, D. (1989), *The Skin Ego* (New Haven: Yale University Press).

ARCHEY, G. (1965), *The Art Forms of Polynesia* (Auckland Institute & Museum Bulletin, no. 4).

ARNHEIM, R. (1974), *Art and Visual Perception* (Berkeley: University of California Press).

BABADZAN, A. (1993), *Les Dépouilles des dieux: Essai sur la religion tahitienne à l'époque de la découverte* (Paris: Maison des Sciences de l'Homme).

BABB, L. (1987), *Redemptive Encounters: Three Modern Styles in the Hindu Tradition* (Berkeley: University of California Press).

BARTHES, R. (1981), *Camera Lucida: Reflections on Photography*, trans. R. Howard (London: Cape, 1982).

BATESON, G. (1936), *Naven* (Stanford, Calif.: Stanford University Press).

—— (1973), 'Style, Grace and Information in Primitive Art', in A. Forge (ed.), *Primitive Art and Society* (London: Oxford University Press), 235–55.

BAXENDALL, L. (1972) (ed.), *Radical Perspectives in the Arts* (Harmondsworth: Pelican).

BEATTIE, J. (1966), 'Ritual and Social Change', *Man*, 1/9: 60–74.

BENJAMIN, W. (1979), 'On the Mimetic Faculty', *Reflections*, ed. P. Demetz, trans. E. Jephcott (New York: Harcourt Brace Jovanovich), 333.

BERGER, J. (1972), *Ways of Seeing* (London: BBC/Penguin).

BEST, E. (1909), 'Maori Forest Lore', *Transactions of the New Zealand Institute*, 52: 433–81.

BEVAN, E. (1940), *Holy Images* (London: George Allen & Unwin).

BLAIKIE, J. (1914), 'Images and Idols (Egyptian)', in J. Hastings (ed.), *Encyclopaedia of Religion and Ethics* (Edinburgh: T. & T. Clark), vol. 7, 131–3.

BLOCH, M. (1991), *Prey into Hunter* (Cambridge: Cambridge University Press).

BOAS, F. (1927), *Primitive Art* (repr. 1955, New York: Dover Books).

BOURDIEU, P. (1968), 'Outline of a Sociological Theory of Art Perception', *International Social Science Journal*, 20/4: 589–612.

—— (1977), *Outline of a Theory of Practice* (Cambridge: Cambridge University Press).

—— (1984), *Distinction: A Social Critique of Judgements of Taste*, trans. Richard Nice (London: Routledge & Kegan Paul).

BOYER, P. (1994), *The Naturalness of Religious Ideas: A Cognitive Theory of Religion* (Berkeley: University of California Press).

—— (1996), 'What Makes Anthropomorphism Natural: Intuitive Ontology and Cultural Representations', *Journal of the Royal Anthropological Institute*, 2/1: 83–97.

CAMILLE, M. (1989), *The Gothic Idol* (Cambridge: Cambridge University Press).

CAREY, S. (1985), *Conceptual Change in Childhood* (Cambridge, Mass.: MIT Press).

CARPENTER, E., and SCHUSTER, C. (1986), *Materials for the Study of Social Symbolism in Ancient and Tribal Art: A Record of Tradition and Continuity*, based on the researches and writings of Carl Schuster, ed. and written by Edmund Carpenter assisted by Lorraine Spiess (New York: Rock Foundation).

COOTE, J. (1992), 'Marvels of Everyday Vision: The Anthropology of Aesthetics and the Cattle Keeping Nilotes', in J. Coote and A. Shelton (eds.), *Anthropology, Art and Aesthetics* (Oxford: Clarendon Press), 245–75.

—— (1996), 'Aesthetics is a Cross-Cultural Category: For the Motion', in T. Ingold (ed.), *Key Debates in Anthropology* (London and New York: Routledge), 266–75.

DALLAPICCOLA, A. L. (1989) (ed.), *Shastric Traditions in Indian Arts* (Stuttgart: Steiner).

DANTO, A. C. (1964), 'The Artworld', *Journal of Philosophy*, 61: 571–84.

—— (1981), *The Transfiguration of the Commonplace: A Philosophy of Art* (Cambridge, Mass: Harvard University Press).

D'AZEVEDO, W. L. (1973), 'Mask Makers and Myth in Western Liberia', in A. Forge (ed.), *Primitive Art and Society* (London: Oxford University Press), 126–68.

—— (1973) (ed.), *The Traditional Artist in African Societies* (Bloomington and London: International Affairs Center).

DEACON, A. B. (1934), 'Geometrical Drawings from Malekula and Other Islands of the New Hebrides', *Journal of the Royal Anthropological Institute*, 64: 129–75.

DENNETT, D. (1979), *Brainstorms* (London: Harvester).

DENNETT, R. E. (1906), *At the back of the black man's mind; or notes on the Kingly Office in West Africa* (reprinted 1968, London: Haarlem).

DORDILLON, R. I. (1931) *Grammaire et dictionnaire de la langue des îles Marquises* (Paris: Institut d'Ethnologie).

DOUGLAS, M. (1966), *Purity and Danger* (London: Routledge & Kegan Paul).

DUMÉZIL, G. (1980), *Camillus: A Study of Indo-European Religion as Roman History*, trans. A. Aronowicz and J. Bryson (Berkeley: University of California Press).

ECK, D. (1985), *Darsan: Seeing the Divine Image in India* (Chambersburg, Pa.: Anima Books).

ECO, UMBERTO (1976), *A Theory of Semantics* (Bloomington: Indiana University Press).

—— (1984), *Semiotics and the Philosophy of Language* (London: Macmillan).

ELLIS, W. (1831), *Polynesian Researches*, 4 vols. (2nd edn.; London: Fisher, Son & Jackson).

ESCHMANN, A., et al. (1978), *Cult of Jagannath and the Regional Tradition of Orissa* (Delhi: Manohar Press).

FARIS, J. (1971), *Nuba Personal Art* (London: Duckworth).

FERNANDEZ, J. (1973), 'The Exposition and Imposition of Order: Artistic Expression in Fang Culture', in W. L. d'Azevedo (ed.), *The Traditional Artist in African Societies* (Bloomington and London: Indiana University Press), 194–220.

FINDLAY, J. (1975), 'Husserl's Analysis of the Time Inner Consciousness', *Monist* 59/1: 3–20.

FODOR, JERRY, A. (1994), 'Fodor, Jerry A.', in S. Guttenplan (ed.), *A Companion to the Philosophy of Mind* (Oxford: Blackwell), 292–300.

FORGE, A. (1966), 'Art and Environment in the Sepik', *Proceedings of the Royal Anthropological Institute of Great Britain and Ireland for 1965*, 23–31.

—— (1973) (ed.), *Primitive Art and Society* (London: Oxford University Press).

FRAZER, J. (1980), *The Golden Bough: A Study in Magic and Religion* (London: Macmillan).

FREEDBERG, D. (1989), *The Power of Images* (Chicago: University of Chicago Press).

GADAMER, H. G. (1979), *Truth and Method*, trans. and ed. G. Barden and J. Cumming (London: Sheed & Ward).

GELL, A. (1978), 'The Gods at Play: Vertigo and Possession in Muria Religion', *Man*, NS 15: 219–48.

——(1992a), *The Anthropology of Time* (Oxford: Berg).

——(1992b), 'The Technology of Enchantment and the Enchantment of Technology', in J. Coote and A. Shelton (eds.), *Anthropology, Art and Aesthetics* (Oxford: Clarendon Press), 40–67.

——(1993), *Wrapping in Images: Tattooing in Polynesia* (Oxford: Clarendon Press).

——(1994) n.d., Tattooing in India. Paper presented to the World Archaeological Congress, Delhi, 1994.

——(1995), 'On Coote's "Marvels of Everyday Vision"', in J. F. Weiner (ed.), *Too Many Meanings: A Critique of the Anthropology of Aesthetics*, special issue, Social Analysis, no. 38, pp. 18–31.

——(1996), 'Vogel's Net: Traps as Artworks and Artworks as Traps', *Journal of Material Culture*, 1/1: 15–38.

—— (forthcoming), *The Art of Anthropology: Essays and Diagrams by Alfred Gell* (London: Athlone).

GELL, S. (1992), *The Ghotul in Muria Society* (Reading: Harwood Academic Publishers).

GIBSON, J. J. (1986), *The Ecological Approach to Visual Perception* (Boston: Houghton Mifflin).

GOLDING, J. (1973), *Marcel Duchamp: The Bride Stripped Bare by her Bachelors even* (London: Allen Lane).

GOMBRICH, E. (1984), *The Sense of Order* (London: Phaidon).

GOMBRICH, R. (1966), 'The Consecration of a Buddhist Image', *Journal of Asian Studies*, 26/1: 23–36.

GOODENOUGH, W. H. (1956), 'Componential Analysis and the Study of Meaning', *Language*, 32: 195–216.

GOODMAN, N. (1976), *Languages of Art* (Indianapolis: Hackett).

GUTHRIE, S. (1993), *Faces in the Clouds* (New York: Oxford University Press).

HANDY, W. (1922), 'Tattooing in the Marquesas', *Bishop Museum Bulletin*, 1 (Honolulu).

HANSON, F. A. (1983), 'When the Map is the Territory: Art in Maori Culture', in D. K. Washburn (ed.), *Structure and Cognition in Art* (Cambridge: Cambridge University Press), 74–89.

HARRISON, S. (1985), 'Concepts of the Person in Avatip Religious Thought', *Man*, 20/1: 115–30.

HENRY, T. (1928), 'Ancient Tahiti', *Bishop Museum Bulletin*, 48 (Honolulu).

HIRN, YRJÖ (1900), *The Origins of Art* (repr. 1971, New York: Benjamin Bloom).

HOFSTADTER, D., and DENNETT, D. (1982), *The Mind's I: Fantasies and Reflections on Self and Soul* (Harmondsworth: Penguin).

HOLLIS, M. (1970), 'Reason and Ritual', in B. R. Wilson (ed.), *Rationality* (London: Basil Blackwell), 221–39.

HOLT, E. G. (1957), *A Documentary History of Art*, 3 vols. (Princeton: Princeton University Press).

HUGH-JONES S., and CARSTEN, J. (1995), *About the House* (Cambridge: Cambridge University Press).

IBSEN, H. (1966), *Peer Gynt*, trans. P. Watts (Harmondsworth: Penguin).

KAEPPLER, A. L. (1978), *Artificial Curiosities: Being an Exposition of Native Manufactures Collected on the Three Pacific Journeys of Captain James Cook at the Bernice Puahi Bishop Museum* (Honolulu: Bishop Museum Press).

KORN, S. M. (1978), 'The Formal Analysis of Visual Systems as Exemplified by a Study of Abelam (Papua New Guinea) Painting', in M. Greenhalgh and V. Megaw (eds.), *Art in Society: Studies in Style, Culture and Aesthetics* (London: Duckworth), 161–73.

KRAMRISCH, S. (1946), *The Hindu Temple*, 2 vols. (repr. 1976, Delhi: Motilal Banarsidass).

KRIS, E., and KURTZ, O. (1979), *Legend, Myth and Magic in the Image of the Artist: A Historical Experiment* (New Haven and London: Yale University Press).

KÜCHLER, S. (1985), 'Malangan: Art and Memory in a Melanesian Society', *Man*, 22/2: 238–55.

—— (1988), 'Malangan: Objects, Sacrifice and the Production of Memory', *American Ethnologist*, 15/4: 625–37.

—— (1992), 'Making Skins: Malangan and the Idiom of Kinship in Northern New Ireland', in J. Coote and A. Shelton (eds.), *Anthropology, Art and Aesthetics* (Oxford: Clarendon Press), 94–112.

LANGSDORFF, G. H. VON (1813–14), *Voyages and Travels in Various Parts of the World 1803–1807*, 2 vols. (London: Colburn).

LAVONDÉS, H. (1996) 'A Polynesian Game of Swings', *Journal of the Polynesian Society*, 105(2), 201–16.

LAYARD, J. (1936), 'Maze-Dances and the Ritual of the Labyrinth in Malekula', *Folklore*, 47: 123–70.

—— (1937), 'Labyrinth Ritual in South India', *Folklore*, 48: 115–82.

LEACH, J., and LEACH, E. (1983) (eds.), *The Kula: New Perspectives on Massim Exchange* (Cambridge: Cambridge University Press).

LÉVI-STRAUSS, C. (1962), *La Pensée sauvage* (Paris: Plon).

—— (1963), *Structural Anthropology*, trans. C. Jacobson and B. G. Schoepf (New York and London: Basic Books).

—— (1964), *Totemism*, trans. R. Needham (London: Merlin Press).

—— (1969), *The Elementary Structures of Kinship*, trans. J. H. Belle, J. R. von Sturmer, and Rodney Needham (Boston: Beacon Press).

—— (1970), *The Raw and the Cooked* (London: Cape).

—— (1972), *The Savage Mind* (London: Weidenfeld & Nicolson).

LUCRETIUS (1952 edn.), *De Rerum Natura*, trans. H. A. J. Munro (Great Books of the Western World; Chicago: Encyclopaedia Britannica Inc.).

MALINOWSKI, BRONISLAW (1922), *Argonauts of the Western Pacific: An Account of Native Enterprise and Adventure in the Archipelagos of Melanesian New Guinea* (London: Routledge).

—— (1935), *Coral Gardens and their Magic: A Study of the Methods of Tilling the Soil and of Agricultural Rites in the Trobriand Islands*, 2 vols. (London: Allen & Unwin).

MARR, D. (1982), *Vision: A Computational Investigation into the Human Representation and Processing of Visual Information* (San Francisco: Freeman).

MAUSS, M. (1902), *A General Theory of Magic*, trans. R. Brain (repr. 1972, New York: Norton).

——(1954), *The Gift* (London: Cohen & West).

MILLER, D. (1987), *Material Culture and Mass Consumption* (Oxford: Basil Blackwell).

MOOKERJEE, A., and KHANNA, M. (1977), *The Tantric Way* (London: Thames & Hudson).

MORPHY, H. (1991), *Ancestral Connections: Art and an Aboriginal System of Knowledge* (Chicago: Chicago University Press).

——(1994), 'The Anthropology of Art', in T. Ingold (ed.), *Companion Encyclopedia of Anthropology* (London and New York: Routledge), 648–85.

——(1996), 'Aesthetics is a Cross-Cultural Category', in T. Ingold (ed.), *Key Debates in Anthropology* (London and New York: Routledge), 255–60.

——(1992), 'From Dull to Brilliant: The Aesthetics of Spiritual Power amongst the Yolngu', in J. Coote and A. Shelton (eds.), *Anthropology, Art and Aesthetics* (Oxford: Clarendon Press).

MUNN, N. (1973), *Walbiri Iconography, Graphic Representation and Cultural Symbolism in a Central Australian Society* (Ithaca, NY: Cornell University Press).

——(1977), 'The Spatiotemporal Transformation of Gawa Canoes', *Journal de Société des Océanistes*, 39–51.

——(1983), 'Gawan Kula: Spatiotemporal control and the symbolism of influence', in J. Leach and E. Leach (eds.), *The Kula: New Perspectives on Massim Exchange* (Cambridge: Cambridge University Press).

——(1986), *The Fame of Gawa: A Symbolic Study of Value Transformation in a Massim (P.N.G.) Society* (Cambridge: Cambridge University Press).

NEICH, R. (1996), *Painted Histories* (Auckland: Auckland University Press).

PARRY, J. (1985), 'Tradition and the Technology of the Intellect', in J. Overing (ed.), *Reason and Morality* (ASA Monographs, 24; London and New York: Tavistock), 200–25.

PRICE, S. (1989), *Primitive Art in Civilized Places* (Chicago: Chicago University Press).

—— and PRICE, R. (1980), *Afro-American Arts of the Surinam Rain Forest* (Berkeley: University of California Press).

SAHLINS, M. (1974), *Stone Age Economics* (London: Tavistock).

SCHIER, F. (1986), *Deeper into Pictures* (Cambridge: Cambridge University Press).

SINHA, J. (1934), *Indian Psychology of Perception* (London: Routledge & Kegan Paul).

SPERBER, D. (1985), 'Anthropology and Psychology: Towards an Epidemiology of Representations', *Man*, 20: 73–98.

STEINEN, Karl von den (1925), *Die Marquesaner und ihre Kunst*, 3 vols. (Berlin: Dietrich Reimer (Ernst Vohsem)).

——(1988), *Von den Steinen's Marquesan Myths*, ed. M. Langridge and trans. J. Terrell (Canberra: Target Oceania/Journal of Pacific Studies).

STEINER, C. B. (1994), *African Art in Transit* (Cambridge and New York: Cambridge University Press).

STEINMANN, R. (1989), 'Kolam: Form, Technique and Application of a Changing Ritual Folk Art of Tamil Nadu', in A. L. Dallapiccola (ed.), *Shastric Traditions in Indian Arts* (Stuttgart: Steiner), 475–91.

STRATHERN, A. (1971), *The Rope of Moka* (Cambridge: Cambridge University Press).

STRATHERN, M. (1988), *The Gender of the Gift* (Berkeley: University of California Press).

TAMBIAH, S. J. (1985), *Culture, Thought and Social Action* (Cambridge, Mass.: Harvard University Press).

TAUSSIG, M. (1993), *Mimesis and Alterity* (London & New York: Routledge).

THOMAS, N. (1990), *Marquesan Societies: Inequality and Political Transformation in Eastern Polynesia* (Oxford: Clarendon University Press).

THOMAS, N. (1995), 'Kiss the Baby Goodbye: *Kowhaiwhai* and Aesthetics in Aotearoa New Zealand', *Critical Inquiry* 22 (Autumn): 90–121.

—— (1991), *Entangled Objects* (Cambridge, Mass.: Harvard University Press).

THOMPSON, D'ARCY (1961), *On Growth and Form* (Cambridge: Cambridge University Press).

THOMPSON, R. F. (1973), 'Yoruba Artistic Criticism', in W. L. d'Azevedo (ed.), *The Traditional Artist in African Societies* (Bloomington: Indiana University Press), 19–61.

TREGEAR, E. (1891), *The Maori–Polynesian Comparative Dictionary* (Wellington: Lyon & Blair).

TURNER, V. (1968), *Drums of Affliction* (Oxford: Oxford University Press).

TYLOR, J. (1875), *Primitive Culture* (London: Murray).

WAGNER, R. (1977), *The Invention of Culture* (Englewood Cliffs, NJ: Prentice Hall).

—— (1991), 'The Fractal Person', in M. Strathern and M. Godelier (eds.), *Big Men and Great Men: Personifications of Power in Melanesia* (Cambridge: Cambridge University Press), 159–73.

WASHBURN, D. K. (1983) (ed.), *Structure and Cognition in Art* (Cambridge: Cambridge University Press).

—— and CROWE, D. W. (1992), *Symmetries of Culture* (2nd edn.; Seattle and London: University of Washington Press).

WINCH, P. G. (1958), *The Idea of a Social Science and its Relation to Philosophy: Studies in Philosophical Psychology* (London and Henley: Routledge & Kegan Paul).

WITTKOWER, R. (1978), *Idea and Image: Studies in the Italian Renaissance* (London: Thames & Hudson).

WOLLHEIM, R. (1987), 'Pictorial Style: Two Views', in Berel Lang (ed.), *The Concept of Style* (Ithaca, NY: Cornell University Press), 183–202.

INDEX

Printed and bound by CPI Group (UK) Ltd, Croydon, CR0 4YY